Grief Diaries

SHATTERED

True accounts of crimes caused by driving under the influence

LYNDA CHELDELIN FELL
WITH
BILL & JULIE DOWNS
Founders, AVIDD
Advocates for Victims of Impaired/Distracted Driving

A portion of proceeds from the sale of this book is donated to AVIDD–Advocates for Victims of Impaired/Distracted Driving, a nonprofit organization serving families affected by drunk, drugged, and distracted driving. For information visit Advocatesforvicitimsofimpaireddriving.org.

Grief Diaries
Shattered – 1st ed.
True stories of being hit by a drunk, drugged or impaired driver.
Lynda Cheldelin Fell/Bill Downs/Julie Downs/
Grief Diaries www.GriefDiaries.com

Cover Design by AlyBlue Media, LLC
Interior Design by AlyBlue Media LLC
Published by AlyBlue Media, LLC

ISBN: 978-1-944328-37-5
Library of Congress Control Number: 2016911244

AlyBlue Media, LLC
Ferndale, WA 98248
www.AlyBlueMedia.com

PRINTED IN THE UNITED STATES OF AMERICA

GRIEF DIARIES

TESTIMONIALS

"CRITICALLY IMPORTANT... *I want to say to Lynda that what you are doing is so critically important.*" –DR. BERNICE A. KING, Daughter of Dr. Martin Luther King

"INSPIRATIONAL.... *Grief Diaries is the result of heartfelt testimonials from a dedicated and loving group of people. By sharing their stories, the reader will find inspiration and a renewed sense of comfort as they move through their own journey.*" -CANDACE LIGHTNER, Founder of Mothers Against Drunk Driving

"BRAVE... *The brave individuals who share their truth in this book do it for the benefit of all who are seeking to know the inner world of this devastating and difficult to treat illness.*" CAROLYN COSTIN - Founder, Monte Nido Treatment Centers

"DEEPLY INTIMATE... *Grief Diaries is a deeply intimate, authentic collection of narratives that speak to the powerful, often ambiguous, and wide spectrum of emotions that arise from loss. I so appreciate the vulnerability and truth embedded in these stories, which honor and bear witness to the many forms of bereavement that arise in the aftermath of death.*" -DR. ERICA GOLDBLATT HYATT, Chair of Psychology, Bryn Athyn College

"VITAL... *Grief Diaries: Surviving Loss of a Pregnancy gives voice to the thousands of women who face this painful journey every day. Often alone in their time of need, these stories will play a vital role in surrounding each reader with warmth and comfort as they seek understanding and healing in the aftermath of their own loss.*" -JENNIFER CLARKE, obstetrical R.N., Perinatal Bereavement Committee at AMITA Health Adventist Medical Center

"HEALING... *Grief Diaries gives voice to a grief so private, most women bear it alone. These diaries can heal hearts and begin to build community and acceptance to speak the unspeakable.*" -DIANNA VAGIANOS ARMENTROUT, Poetry Therapist & Author of Walking the Labyrinth of My Heart: A Journey of Pregnancy, Grief and Infant Death

"WONDERFUL....*Grief Diaries is a wonderful computation of stories written by the best of experts, the bereaved themselves. Thank you for building awareness about a topic so near and dear to my heart.*" -DR. HEIDI HORSLEY, Adjunct Professor, School of Social Work, Columbia University, Author, Co-Founder of Open to Hope Organization

"A FORCE...*The writers of this project, the Grief Diaries anthology series, are a force to be reckoned with. I'm betting we will be agents of great change.*" -MARY LEE ROBINSON, Author and Founder of Set an Extra Plate initiative

"MOVING... *In Grief Diaries, the stories are not only moving but often provide a rich background for any mourner to find a gem of insight that can be used in coping with loss. Reread each story* with pen in hand and you will find many that are just right for you." -DR. LOUIS LAGRAND, Author of Healing Grief, Finding Peace

"INCREDIBLE...*Thank you so much for doing this project, it's absolutely incredible!*"-JULIE MJELVE, Founder, Grieving Together

"STUNNING... *Grief Diaries treats the reader to a rare combination of candor and fragility through the eyes of the bereaved. Delving into the deepest recesses of the heartbroken, the reader easily identifies with the diverse collection of stories and richly colored threads of profound love that create a stunning read full of comfort and hope.*" -DR. GLORIA HORSLEY, President, Open to Hope Foundation

"HOPE AND HEALING... *You are a pioneer in this field and you are breaking the trail for others to find hope and healing.*" -KRISTI SMITH, Bestselling Author & International Speaker

"GLOBAL...*One of The Five Facets of Healing mantras is together we can heal a world of hurt. This anthology series is testimony to the power we have as global neighbors to do just that.*" -ANNAH ELIZABETH, Founder of The Five Facets of Healing

DEDICATION

This book is lovingly dedicated to:
Ashlyn Nicole Barnes
Tammy Bluth
Anna Noel Bronson
Diane Kay Bronson
Leroy "Buddy" Bronson
Rafael Heredia Cardenas
Tiffany Lyn Clawson
Kale Daren Clay
Kimberly Copelan
Chris Dafoe
Brad Downs
Samantha Downs
Faithlynn Lawson
Kirk Mahaffey Jr.
Mayson Mahaffey
Travis D. McNamara
Mackenzie McWhorter
Nicholas Adam Poindexter
Donnie (Donald) W.E. Pratt
Ethan Cody Bleu Saltar
Janakae Toinette Sargent
Brandon Stanley Walter Thomas
Matthew Thompson
Monica Renee Rachford Trammell
Christopher Webb
Shane Webb
Randy Jordan Williams
Jennifer-Leigh Edwards Zartman

For support, visit
www.advocatesforvicitimsofimpaireddriving.org
avid4duivictims@cableone.net

For victims who have lost a love one:
Facebook.com/groups/AVID4DUIvictims

For victims who have been injured
or have an injured loved one and survived:
Facebook.com/groups/AVID4DUIsurvivors

For victims who have been impacted
by a distracted driving crash:
Facebook.com/groups/AVID.Distracted

For victims who have been impacted by a BUI
(boating under the influence) crash:
Facebook.com/groups/AVIDDimpairedboatingvictims

CONTENTS

PREFACE

One night in 2007, I had one of *those* dreams, the vivid kind you can't shake. In the dream, I was the front passenger in a car and my daughter Aly was sitting behind the driver. Suddenly, the car missed a curve in the road and sailed into a lake. The driver and I escaped the sinking car, but Aly did not. Desperately flailing through the deep murky water to find my daughter, I failed. She was gone. Aly was gone, leaving behind an open book floating in the water where she disappeared.

Two years later that nightmare became reality when my daughter died as a back seat passenger in a car accident on August 5, 2009. She was just fifteen years old.

I now understand that the dream two years before Aly's death was a glimpse into a divine plan that would eventually touch many lives. The book left floating in the water was symbolic of my future. But the devastation I felt in my heart would blind me to the meaning of that dream for a long time to come.

In the aftermath of losing Aly, I eventually discovered that helping others was a powerful way to heal my own heart. The Grief Diaries series was born and built on this belief. By writing books narrating our journeys through hardship and losses, our written words become a portable support group for others. When we swap stories, we feel less alone. It is comforting to know someone else understands the shoes we walk in, and the challenges we face along the way. Which brings us to this book, *Grief Diaries: Shattered.* The devastation left in the aftermath of being hit by a drunk or drugged driver can steal your breath, and leave you with more questions than answers. Further, you might encounter people who don't understand your emotions or, worse, lack compassion for your journey. This is where the Grief Diaries series can help.

Helen Keller once said, "Walking with a friend in the dark is better than walking alone in the light." This is especially true in the aftermath of tragedy. If you've been impacted by a drunk or drugged driver, the following stories are written by courageous people who know exactly how you feel, for they've been in your shoes and have walked the same path. Perhaps the shoes are a different size and style, but may you find comfort in these stories and the understanding that you aren't truly alone on the journey. For we walk ahead, behind, and right beside you.

Wishing you healing, and hope from the Grief Diaries village.

Warm regards,

Lynda Cheldelin Fell

Creator, Grief Diaries
www.LyndaFell.com

CHAPTER ONE

FROM PAIN TO PEACE

BY PAT BLUTH

Healing follows forgiveness.
PAT BLUTH

Tammy, the oldest of three children, was a senior in high school and looked forward to graduating in May 1986. She was a beautiful brunette, full of life and fun. She was involved in many things at school. Tammy played piano, the clarinet in band, sang in the church choir, was on the girls' basketball team, student council, National Honor Society, and was in the top ten percent of her graduating class of 532. She had a positive outlook on life with a great sense of humor. Her dream was to become an airline pilot or a doctor.

On Friday, September 13, our family had planned to attend the high school football game. After the game, Gary and I found Tammy and her friend Mike, and we spent a few minutes talking to them. We had just met Mike that evening. As we left, I said, "See you later." Following the game, Tammy, Mike (Tammy's date) and Chris (a friend of Tammy) had been on their way to pick up Chris' boyfriend, who was getting off work. Then they would attend a high school dance.

Mike was driving a Ford Mustang, and Tammy was sitting in the middle of the front seat without a seat belt. Their car was stopped on the highway with its left signal light blinking, waiting for an oncoming car to pass so they could turn. As they waited to turn left, a speeding car came up behind them and smashed into the rear of the Mustang. Because Tammy was sitting in the middle of bucket seats, the impact of the crash threw her into the back seat. The gas tank exploded and the back seat of the car as well as Tammy were engulfed in flames. Tammy died at the scene of fourth-degree burns.

On Friday, September 13, 1985, all of Tammy's dreams were taken from her. No one could have prepared me for the knock on the door, giving me the devastating news about the death of my daughter. The doorbell rang a short while after 10:30 p.m. and the North Ambulance personnel came to tell us he had bad news about our daughter. Tammy had died in a car crash. Only an hour earlier my husband and I had talked with her. Little did I know that the last words I would ever utter to my daughter were, "See you later."

How could she be dead? When I heard the news that my daughter had died, I became hysterical, emitting a gut-wrenching scream. My first thought was to go to her, but I did not know where she was. I fell sobbing into my husband's arms. I could not believe what I had just been told. I did not want to believe that my daughter was dead.

Death was not supposed to happen to my family. I could not conceive of Tammy dying in a car crash. In the past, of course, a tragedy like this had always happened to some other family. But not this time. The rest of what happened after those first moments is a blur. The tears and pain were too much. Many jumbled thoughts crowded my mind. I need to go to Tammy. Where was she? How did this happen? What should I do for my other children? There were too many questions and no answers. We simply clung to each other in tears.

Tammy's friends' world had been shattered, as had mine. Seventeen-year-olds are not supposed to die. They are to be with you forever. Nothing is to interfere with their plans and dreams,

2

especially not a tragic, unexpected death like the one that had just happened to Tammy. It wasn't fair.

Now our family had to quickly learn how to deal with the tragedy of losing Tammy, but lacked a blueprint for how to do that. We had been getting ready to plan her high school graduation; instead we were faced with having to plan her funeral. Going to the funeral home the first time and then seeing the casket for the first time was a terrible experience; I collapsed in a chair and just sobbed. It had finally sunk in that we had to have a closed casket because Tammy's body had been burned beyond recognition. At the funeral home I wanted one last glimpse of my daughter before having to say the final goodbye. Knowing she was there—right there in the casket—and I couldn't see her was very painful. I wanted to hold her and tell her I loved her. I could only do that to the closed casket. It seems so cold and unreal to be talking to a wooden box surrounded with flowers.

Walking out of church behind the casket is something that I, as a mother, will never forget. It is not anything that I would wish on anyone. It was difficult to conceive that the time had come to place my daughter in her final resting place. Arriving at the cemetery and seeing the big mound of dirt and the dark, cold hole to put my daughter in was too much. I lost control of my emotions. Even though the service at the cemetery takes only minutes, it seemed to take years off my life. I leaned over the casket, gave my daughter one final kiss, said "I love you," and turned to leave. I could not stay one more second. I turned my back on the casket and went to the car. I did not look back. That was the final goodbye. Following the funeral, on the surface it appeared that the grief was over and behind us, but it had only just begun.

We began to hear speculation that the person who hit the car our daughter was in had been driving drunk. I didn't want to hear anything about that at that time—it was way too much to deal with just then. Apparently one person's fun became our family's tragedy. A few days following the funeral, a Minnesota State Patrol officer came to our house to talk to us regarding Tammy's car crash. He confirmed that the person responsible for Tammy's death had been driving drunk. I didn't want to hear that there was a drunk driver involved; it would add too much to the grieving process. My immediate reaction was anger.

Sadness, depression, crying, withdrawal from friends, and other symptoms of grief overtook my life. There were hours, and days, with no peace. The grief turned to anger, rage, and turmoil inside. I felt like I was going crazy.

I put my faith in the justice system. I thought the courts would put the drunk driver in jail for a very long time. How naive I was. Since a drunk driver killed our daughter, our family had now earned the label of "victim." We were a drunk driving statistic at the local, state, and national level. Opening the courtroom door and walking inside was traumatic.

Our family was uninformed as to what to expect in the court procedure. We did not know of any rights that we might have had. In contrast, the defense side was well prepared. There was a character witness who talked about the good qualities the defendant had. There was a letter written and read by the defendant's wife about his family needing him at home to be with their children. The defense attorney asked that the defendant be given ninety days for the death of my daughter. I gasped loudly after hearing that. Another attorney in the courtroom came over and asked if I wanted to say something. You bet I did, but what? I stood up and said some words, but I wish I had been informed and prepared.

After attending the court hearing and expecting justice, I learned quickly that the criminal justice system is not a fair procedure for victims. It was all about the defendant. The defendant had been given one year in the county jail with the Huber privilege, so he could be released for work each day. He'd gotten no fine except for having to pay court costs of three hundred and fifty dollars. After being released from jail, he would be on probation for five years. He'd have a chemical dependency evaluation. He was assigned five hundred hours of community service.

I couldn't believe that this killer would have to serve only one year in jail and could go to his job every day. What kind of a punishment was that for someone who had killed my daughter? I felt so helpless and defeated. There was nothing I could do. The sentence had been given. It was now over. My faith in the justice system had just been destroyed. There was no peace after that day in court. No peace, but a lot of anger, rage, and turmoil inside. You can read a detailed account of the court system process in my book *From Pain to Peace – A Journey from Rage to Forgiveness*.

Following the court process, I was so blazing-red angry that I could barely breathe. And now there were some tough choices for me to make: I could do something with my anger or I could run from it. It was too late to make any changes in what happened to us in the courtroom, but I could make a difference for others. After learning about Mothers Against Drunk Driving, Bonnie Alexander and I took the steps required by MADD to begin a chapter in our community. Six months after beginning the interviews, gathering information, and discovering all we could regarding drunk driving, we became chartered as a chapter in August 1986. MADD National had approved our paperwork and the requirements to begin a chapter.

Several things I did helped me with my grief, but none brought me total peace. After beginning a Mothers Against Drunk Driving chapter in my community, I helped other victims. Helping them was rewarding for me and was the whole impetus for beginning the MADD chapter. Helping other victims did reduce the anger I felt inside, but it never took the anger away completely. I joined The Compassionate Friends, a support group for parents whose children have died. During the times I felt I was going crazy with grief, The Compassionate Friends validated that what I was feeling was normal. That validation was important. The people there just listened and accepted. After attending this support group for a period of time, I became a facilitator. I wanted to find ways to help others with their grief.

As with everything that is painful, recovery is a slow process. I expected to feel much better than I was. My expectations of grief were that I would share it, the pain would be reduced over time, and I could get on with my life. There were many days when I didn't want to face another day of my body aching. I could get no relief from the intense physical and emotional pain I experienced each day. Support from others began to taper off. My counselor suggested I begin a journal to record my feelings. That was easier said than done. But I found that journaling my feelings became an effective way to release the many emotions I experienced. Writing down what I was feeling helped me clarify whatever I was struggling with at the time. Journaling my feelings was a tool I found to be very effective.

Counseling became a regular part of my weekly routine. All of these methods helped me redefine my new normal of life. When something traumatic happens, such as your child being killed, the rational thinking process is affected. I didn't like the fact that I had become capable of such violent thoughts and having such intense feelings of hatred and violence inside me. Normally I was not a violent person with feelings of hatred. What was normal to me before Tammy died now had to be redefined. What was normal before was never again to be a part of my life. Normal now had no meaning.

My grief was always unpredictable, and many times it surfaced when I least expected it. Grief has a way of coming along and tapping you on the shoulder when you least expect it. The first year after a loved one dies, there are too many first events that must be faced. The first birthday, holiday, wedding, funeral, or family gathering are tough to bear. Half of my grief work was anticipating how I would act when the holiday or event arrived. What would I do? How would I be affected by my grief? Could I get through this event without falling apart? What would have been Tammy's graduation day was so very difficult. I was so angry and felt so cheated at not being able to be part of Tammy's graduation.

Grief was a great deal of work. So much of my time and energy was being wasted because of the crash that took the life of my precious daughter. If she hadn't been killed, I wouldn't be going through all this. Feeling sorry for myself was a new concept for me, but one with which I began to become all too familiar. Just when I'd have a few days in succession when I was gaining some strength and getting control over my grief, those feelings erupted and began all over again. Tears consumed many hours of my day. I relived over and over all that had happened from the time of being notified of my daughter's death.

I didn't like my life and all that grief brought with it. There were very few happy moments, and not much laughter. Gary, Jennifer, and Jeff wanted me to feel better, to be involved, to get on with life, but I couldn't find a strategy to do that. I did a lot of pretending to others that I was doing better than I was. What was going on inside me emotionally wasn't what I wanted to show to others; what others saw and what I felt were not the same. I tried to be what others wanted me to be. I tried to present myself in the way that I thought others expected me to be. I spent many hours each day home alone, just staring into space. My purpose in life was lost. Most days had no meaning for me. I began to think I could not go on like this any more.

Whenever I thought about our legal system and what they call justice, anger overpowered me. Because my daughter's death was so traumatic, the intensity of my anger was frightening. Even the word "rage" doesn't describe the fury I harbored. Hateful thoughts ate at me all day long. It began to affect almost everything I did. I was short and snappy with comments to my family. I had wild bursts of anger inappropriate to what was going on at the time. I would fly off the handle at a sales clerk for no reason. My voice had a harsh and edgy tone to it. I went berserk whenever I heard of

7

someone getting killed by a drunk driver. I had a steady, pounding anger inside me constantly. There seemed to be no way to release this anger so it wouldn't return. Anger began to control me, to consume me, and to overshadow my whole being.

One morning in January 1989 I was in total despair. I was sick and tired of being in the pits. I wanted my pain to end. I didn't want any more of this grieving stuff. I was crying that day as if it were the beginning of my grieving, not almost four years later. I was depressed and feeling sorry for myself. After grieving for three years and three months, I couldn't take one more day of feeling this intense sadness, depression, and hopelessness. I thought about committing suicide. I was frightened by that. I had no suicide plan, and I don't think I would have ever carried one out, but the fact that I had such a heavy black cloud of despair over my head more than three years after Tammy's death was disheartening. I couldn't understand why I wasn't getting over it. Why wasn't I able to get my act together? I was beginning to withdraw from others and isolate myself. I wouldn't reach out to others. I felt as if I had nothing for which to live. I was in such intense pain.

I called out to the Lord. "Lord, you had better give me the name of a person I can talk to before I do something crazy." Immediately the name of Father Con came to mind. My first reaction was to say, "No way am I going to call Father Con." He was new to our parish and had arrived at church after the death of Tammy. I was sinking in my grief. I knew I had to do something.

Finally I called Father Con. He answered the phone. How often does a priest himself answer the phone? I told him I was in a lot of pain and needed someone to listen to me. He said he had time to listen, and I could come right over to the church. He listened attentively as I told my story of how Tammy had died, the mourning I was still suffering through, and how desperate I was feeling that day. He let me pour my heart out and babble my words through the tears. After I finished telling my story, Father Con asked me if I would consider going on a retreat — an eight-day silent retreat at a place called Dunrovin. I would be assigned a director I could meet with one hour a day. The rest of the day would be spent in silence with God. This was a retreat for people working in the ministry, but lay people were allowed to attend. I didn't understand how a retreat could be an answer for me, but I was so desperate I would have agreed to most anything that day.

My depression wasn't so intense during the six months from January through June 1989. It never disappeared, but I was able to cope better, knowing I had a plan to do something. In June I drove to the retreat center. At this point I knew two things: one, my director was Brother Bill, and two, everyone was to gather at 7 p.m. upstairs in the chapel. I looked over the place, found where I needed to be, and surveyed the grounds. The surroundings could not have been more perfect. The St. Croix River flowed along the east side of the property. A peaceful-looking pond featured birds chirping everywhere. There was even an outdoor swimming pool. If I had not had to think about my pain and anxiety, Dunrovin would have been a perfect setting for rest and relaxation—nothing too fancy, just quiet and serene.

We were welcomed by the retreat personnel and given an opportunity to introduce ourselves and to say if we had any prayer requests. When it came to my turn, I said, "I am Pat Bluth. I attend St. Andrew's Church in Brainerd." Tears abruptly streamed down my face as I added, "And I need a lot of prayer." I didn't think I was going to be able to say any more, but I took a deep breath and said, "I am here for healing, grieving, and dealing with how angry I am." I couldn't say anything else, because if I did I would have completely fallen apart.

Before going to my room that evening I met with Brother Bill, my director. Before excusing me the first evening, he suggested I try to use imagery. I was to imagine sitting on a bleacher in the person's lap behind me, or sitting on the lawn having fallen into someone's lap. Now I was to imagine that it was God's lap in which I was sitting. At this point in the retreat, I could not allow myself to do that. My reaction surprised me; I would have thought that I could have leaned into God's lap and relaxed there.

Every day at the retreat I did something to get rid of anger, such as sharing my story with my director. Writing out my story again, as I had written much over the past three-plus years. I taught my director how intense the grief of a grieving parent can be. Brother Bill told me he went to a library to research parent's grief, as he didn't understand the intensity of the grief. One day my assignment was to find a new image of God.

What did forgiveness mean to me? I had to define this, and I found out that I had some preconceived ideas about forgiveness that proved to be wrong. One afternoon I was sitting outside on a bench overlooking the pond. I started to think about meeting with Richard, the drunk driver, and instantly grew angry. I stood up from the bench and started walking around the pond. My pace began to pick up. All my angry thoughts were pushed forward. I began to march around the pond. I began to verbalize my anger toward the drunk driver. The anger turned to rage. My words got louder and my walking was more like stomping. I don't know how many times I marched around that pond. With each step I took, I'd scream out loud my thoughts about the drunk driver and God. When I finished, I was completely exhausted. I had just sat down on the bench again when the voice inside me said, "Now go inside and write out all these angry thoughts and feelings you have harbored for so long." I wrote a thirteen-page letter to the drunk driver and expressed my rage, anger, resentment and hatred.

The next day I spent time with my director. I read him my angry letter to Richard. Brother Bill listened intently. He did not judge me for what I had written and read to him. We sat in silence for a while. I knew he was searching for what to do next. He then gave me the task of asking Jesus to help me rewrite the letter and to see what happened. I left with a plan, but I didn't know how to go about it. I turned to the Lord and asked Him if He would help me rewrite the letter. I heard nothing for the rest of the day. I walked. I swam. I listened. I read Scripture. I waited. Nothing came.

Oh me of little faith. I woke up thinking about Richard at 5 a.m. the next morning. I didn't like what I was hearing. I knew I should get up and begin writing out my thoughts, but I fought it. "Lord, I cannot do what You are asking of me. I cannot put these words I am hearing on a piece of paper." I had to have a talk with myself. I said, "This is the answer you have been seeking. You asked the Lord to help you, and now you have been given the answer. Trust the process and do not let your head rule over your heart."

Forgiveness was the main theme. I was fighting putting the words down. Concern about the drunk driver and his family came to me. I didn't care about them. I decided I wasn't going to do this. God wasn't going to accept that decision. I got up and wrote.

I wrote a one-and-a-half-page letter of forgiveness. You can read in detail my letters of anger and forgiveness in my book, *From Pain to Peace – A Journey from Rage to Forgiveness*. After writing out that letter, I was completely overwhelmed and sat down to weep. The crying was different this time. The tears were not triggered by pain but from the realization of how much the Lord loved me. He did want complete peace for me. I was able to forgive because I let Jesus work within me. I had to forgive, or I would have lost myself. After forgiving, I felt free. A heavy burden was lifted from my shoulders. The negativity, anger, bitterness, and rage within me were released. Gone. They were no more.

Later I sat on the bench overlooking the pond and connected with all the anger and pain I was feeling inside. Returning to the same bench today and experiencing joy and energy was a great gift from the Lord. I now feel as if I have come full circle. Being able to lean into the Lord's lap on the bench shows me how far I have come this week. After releasing all the feelings of anger, rage, resentment, and bitterness I then had room for God's love.

I went to the retreat filled with anger, bitterness, rage, and an unforgiving heart. My seventeen-year-old daughter had been killed on September 13, 1985, by a drunk driver. The pain of her death had consumed my every moment for the past three and a half years. I left the retreat with my anger, resentment, bitterness, and rage stomped into the ground around the pond. I left with a heart filled with love, joy, and peace. I have been able to forgive the drunk driver. I have experienced one of God's miracles. After thirty years, I have never had the anger, bitterness, resentment or hatred return.

There are miracles waiting for you, as there were for me. Don't let them pass by. I hope you will experience the gift of peace through God's miracles. If there are people you need to forgive, turn to God in prayer. Ask for His help. Forgiveness is possible. Forgiveness was my answer to peace in my life. It may also be the answer you are searching for. If you like this condensed version of my story, then you may want to read in great detail all the events I experienced in finding peace. You can find my book, *From Pain to Peace – A Journey from Rage to Forgiveness* on Amazon.com, or it can be ordered from any bookstore.

PAT BLUTH
NISSWA, MINNESOTA
Co-Founder of MADD – Crow Wing
Speaker & Author, *From Pain to Peace—A Journey from Rage to Forgiveness*

JEFF, TAMMY & JENNIFER BLUTH

BLUTH FAMILY

Remember Me In Your Heart
UNKNOWN

To the living, I am gone,
To the sorrowful, I will never return,
To the angry, I was cheated,
But to the happy, I am at peace,
And to the faithful, I have never left.
I cannot speak, but I can listen.
I cannot be seen, but I can be heard.
So as you stand upon a shore gazing at a beautiful sea...
As you look upon a flower and admire its simplicity....
Remember me.
Remember me in your heart:
Your thoughts, and your memories,
Of the times we loved,
The times we cried,
The times we fought,
The times we laughed.
For if you always think of me,
I will never have gone.

*

TAMMY BLUTH

CHAPTER TWO

MY NEW NORMAL

BY AMY CARTER

All things grow with time, except grief.
PROVERB

For as long as I can remember, my Aunt Diane was always a very important part of my life. I had a special bond with her that is impossible to put into words. I was the only child in the family for five years, so of course I was spoiled rotten, but loved so entirely and immensely by all those around me. This story has affected all who knew Aunt Diane, Uncle Buddy, and my cousin Anna.

Aunt Diane was my grandparents' middle child. My immediate family consists of my mother Annette, her husband Jim, and my siblings Jordan and Cole. My grandparents also had a third child, my aunt Diane's younger brother, David. He and his wife Samantha have three children, Amanda, Zac, and Logan. The wreck also affected my great-aunt Lola from Kansas, and two great-aunts from Iowa, Marilyn and Carla. My Aunt Diane, Uncle Buddy, and cousins Cody, Tyler, and Anna lived in Belton, Missouri. The rest of my family lived in Independence, Missouri, about thirty minutes north.

When my cousin Cody came along, I was thrilled to have someone to play with, even though I wasn't ready to share all the attention quite yet. Therefore I was Aunt Diane's "almost daughter." She always used to tell me that I should have been her own. My aunt would do anything for me. I think the most priceless thing I can remember is when she gave me her own Cabbage Patch kid from when she was a kid. His name is Simon. I still have him, too. It's a positive reminder of her whenever I come across him.

Two years later, Aunt Diane started dating Buddy after getting out of an abusive marriage. Buddy lived in Belton, Missouri. After they began dating, she found out she was pregnant with Tyler from her previous marriage. It was a lot for Buddy to take on, two kids and woman with a broken heart, but he stepped up to the plate better than I think anyone could have. Diane was filled with joy again. She had happiness in her life all around. Her smile was absolutely beautiful. It was a smile that will forever be engraved on my heart.

When Tyler was about nine months old, my aunt got a phone call from Children's Mercy Hospital in Kansas City explaining that Cody had leukemia. Cody was only two when Aunt Diane received this dreadful news. It was a trying time for our family. Cody was at Children's Mercy Hospital, and I remember Tyler staying with my mom and me a lot. We all took turns visiting Cody in the hospital. He looked so hopeless in his hospital bed. It was heartbreaking. Some of the best times he had in the hospital were when my mom and I came to visit him. We would bring Disney movies and snacks. One time we went to Toys R Us and bought five cans of silly string. We took them to the hospital and sprayed Cody until the cans were empty and tears were streaming down our faces with laughter. I can still hear his little belly laugh when I remember that day.

Cody eventually healed and our entire family could breathe again, and life went back to normal. It was during this time, I believe, when my aunt realized that she had a passion for helping others. Once Cody overcame cancer and kicked its butt, Aunt Diane at the age of thirty, decided to become a nurse. I remember how proud my grandparents were of their daughter at her graduation in 1996.

Uncle Buddy grew up around motorcycles for the first part of his life. Buddy introduced my aunt to the love of his life, Harley-Davidsons and old school cars. He even taught the boys about the sounds of the bikes. The low grumble was a Harley, and the high-pitched grumble was his bike made in Japan. My uncle had a name for those bikes too. He called them "Jap junk." When Cody and Tyler would hear the high-pitched grumble they would run out and start yelling "Jap junk, Jap junk."

A few years passed. Diane and Buddy married and were expecting their first child together, a little girl named Anna. They were over the moon elated. Aunt Diane had always wanted a little girl, and since technically I wasn't hers, her wish had finally come true.

Because of their love for motorcycles, Aunt Diane and Uncle Buddy always went on vacation to Sturgis, South Dakota, for the big motorcycle rally. In August 1999, when Aunt Diane was pregnant with Anna, they had returned to Sturgis for another rally. Diane's due date was in November, but she really wanted to go and felt well enough to do so. Uncle Buddy was driving his truck with a motorcycle in the bed of the truck. When they had gotten up there and were just about to enter Sturgis, there was a wreck involving them and a large Department of Transportation vehicle. They were hit with such force that the motorcycle in the back actually sliced the front cab of the truck my uncle was driving. The steering wheel pinned my uncle into his seat, and my aunt was unable to get out of the truck. The paramedics had to cut my pregnant aunt out of the truck.

My uncle thought that he had lost the love of his life and his unborn child. My aunt was air lifted to a hospital in Kansas City. She suffered extensive injuries that caused memory loss and dizzy spells. She would have panic attacks when she heard any kind of siren. After a long and tiring six weeks, Diane was back in the hospital giving birth to my cousin Anna. After the wreck in Sturgis, my aunt was on disability for some time.

Never once did Aunt Diane and Uncle Buddy have a problem with her. Uncle Buddy had said in a news interview that "she was a peach." He also said, "I tried to make her a daddy's girl, but Anna would not have it, and she was a momma's girl all the way!" Anna always had a smile on. I think that I only saw her mad once or twice. I know once she was so upset that she had to get braces. She did not want braces. Anna was also in gymnastics and softball.

All holidays and other family events were spent with my grandparents, and Aunt Diane would always be there. She would call to see if I was going to be there too. If Diane was there, you knew that Anna would be there too. My aunt would always go to my grandparents every Wednesday, and spend most of the day there. When I found that out, I would be there too, spending time with my aunt. During school Anna would not be there, but summer was the always time to spend with Grandma. My grandmother loves to spend time with her grandchildren. What grandmother doesn't, right?

It had been years since Aunt Diane had worked. Now that she was feeling normal again she wanted to get back to work. She already knew what she wanted to do. She wanted to be a hospice nurse. Since she already had her R.N. degree, she did not have to go to school. She ended up getting a job at Heartland Hospice Home as a hospice case manager.

It was Saturday night, June 25, 2011, and all my family was at Aunt Samantha and Uncle David's house for their kid's birthdays; my cousins have back-to-back birthdays, so we would normally celebrate the birthdays together. This was the last time I ever saw my aunt alive, along with my cousin. I always enjoyed the time with Aunt Diane and Anna even though they were always the last people to show up and the last ones to leave.

As the night ended at the birthday parties, my husband Shaun and I were getting ready to go home and I turned to wave at everyone. I have a pretty big family and didn't really want to take the time to make my rounds on hugs, but my aunt insisted on me giving her a hug. She had said, "AJ, what do you think you're doing?" I turn to give Diane a hug. Then I walked into the kitchen to give Anna a hug. I said to her, "Anna, get your butt over here and hug me." She turned from what she was doing, rolled her eyes, shined her brace grin, threw back her head and came to give me a hug. I never dreamed that would be the last time when I or anyone in my family would get to see them. The following Wednesday, I got to talk to my aunt for the last time. She and I would always be on the phone for hours, as she would always want to know how my week was. She and I never lacked for things to talk about.

July 4, 2011, was the day to celebrate our country's birthday; my family did so by going to have breakfast at an all-you-can eat restaurant, and then to the parade in Sugar Creek, Missouri. As my family proceeded to arrive at the all-you-can eat buffet at 8 a.m., my grandma paid for my family; my grandfather, my mom, my stepdad, my little brother, my sister; myself and my husband; and Uncle David and Aunt Samantha and their three kids. Diane and Anna were always late, so we thought that they had just gotten a late start to their day. We gathered our food and sat down to eat. Aunt Diane and Anna still had not arrived yet; it was 8:30 a.m. My whole family started calling Diane's and Anna's phones, trying to find out if they were still coming. We even tried calling my aunt's older sons and husband; no one had heard from them. Uncle Buddy said they had already left. I will never forget the time: 9:16 a.m. It was the last time I called Aunt Diane.

My family and I went our separate ways. We left the restaurant at about 9:30. My family went to the parade, but I had to be at work at 11 a.m. When we got home, I checked my Facebook account to see what I had missed that morning. I saw a news post about a deadly wreck but overlooked it as I scrolled through Facebook before going to work.

At about 1:30 p.m. the lobby of McDonald's was packed due to the Sugar Creek parade just letting out. I looked up to see my mom coming straight toward me with my husband close behind. I was at the counter taking orders when my mom approached the counter. She pulled me by my left wrist, saying she had something important that she needed to tell me, and continued pulling my wrist. Since we were busy, I could not leave without telling someone where I was going. I rushed around the corner to tell Kim, one of the managers making food in the grill area, that my mom was there and needed to talk to me.

I circled around to the front to join my mom and my husband. My mom started pulling me toward the door. My little brother was five at the time and I thought that something had happened to him. My mom pulled me out the door and then said something that I will never forget: "Diane and Anna have been in a wreck and were killed. We need to go to Grandma's and then go out to Belton to be with Uncle Buddy."

I dropped to the ground in disbelief that they had actually been killed. My husband Shaun picked me up, put me back on my feet and helped me walk to my car. I needed to let my store know what had happened. The phone calls started; I was calling anyone and everyone who would listen. I couldn't think. My mind went blank. I could not believe this was really happening. I started to have questions. My first instinct was to call Aunt Diane to talk about the wreck. I don't remember not knowing about the drunk driver.

As we reached my grandparents' house, I saw family cars in the driveway. Even my great-aunt Lola from Kansas was there. As we piled into my grandma's van to drive to Belton, all I could think about was did this just happen? Why did this happen? Who did this to my family? My family has been broken, big time!

The drive to Uncle Buddy's in Belton seemed really long, but was only thirty minutes. My family got to the house and everyone was there, including Uncle Buddy's friends and family. My family and I stood outside just looking at the house. I could not just stand and look at the house, I had to go in and see if my cousins were okay, and then my Uncle Buddy. I knew the answer already would be no, but I still had to see.

My family and I found out a little more about the man who killed Aunt Diane and cousin Anna. He had two licenses, each had a different name and birth date. My family and I were so confused at the time. We had no clue who had broken our family. We also found out that he blew a breath alcohol content of .185 percent, over two times the legal limit, two hours after the wreck.

When I entered their house, I expected to see Aunt Diane and Anna come out and hug me like nothing had happened. When they didn't, I began to touch everything: the furniture, the countertops, Aunt Diane's pie pans that she had bake me apple pies in so many times before. Time had escaped me, and not knowing what time it was, Shaun and I had to leave. Shaun wanted me to eat (hadn't eaten since the morning). I told him that I was not hungry, but he made me eat anyway. I had a small sandwich from Burger King. I don't think I ate at all the rest of the day. Shaun had asked me if I wanted to do anything at all that day and I just kept telling him no.

It started to get dark, and people were starting up on their fireworks. I just wanted to be inside and sulk. My mom had invited us to the Blue Springs High School fireworks display. We went. I didn't really want to, but I pulled myself together and went. After that we returned home.

Shaun and I had the 10 o'clock news on and there they were, Diane and Anna's faces plastered all over the news. Diane had tried so hard to keep her family out of the limelight, especially Anna. The news showed Aunt Diane's smashed black Impala and the drunk driver's smashed white SUV. The news said that the drunk driver was an illegal alien who had been driving the wrong way on I-70 and I-435. Instead of going west in the westbound lane he was going west in the eastbound lane and then exited south onto the northbound lane. The illegal alien had driven fourteen miles the wrong way. Missing everyone he encountered, when he had ended with the wreck at 8:30 in the morning, he was two times the legal limit two hours after the wreck. I didn't want to watch this; I had to go outside.

I sat on the side of the road in my lawn chair and watched the neighbor kids shoot off fireworks. As the night ended, I got ready for bed. I could not sleep very well that night, but I had to sleep. I had to be at work at 11 the next morning.

With all this going on with my family, we met a nice lady with MADD named Avis. She had been through the same thing that we were going though.

After not sleeping well the night before, in the morning I updated my Facebook status to "Need not to think about what happened yesterday...Going to work at 11, let's hope I don't get sent home early." I was as ready for work as I would ever be. I pulled myself up, got dressed and headed to work. Everyone at work was sympathetic with me and I didn't even want to think about what had happened the day before, but everyone was making it very hard not to think about what had happened. Everyone I worked with kept asking me if I was okay, if there was anything they could do. I told them no and no. I could not make it through the full day.

I ended up going home at 5 p.m. I just wanted to go home and sulk some more and sleep. Sleep became my friend because when I slept, I didn't think about Aunt Dane and Anna. On Wednesday, Avis set up a candlelight vigil for my aunt and cousin for Thursday. About two hundred people showed up including all of my family, minus two, plus all of Anna's friends. Kids from Anna's school were there too. I remember some of what my Uncle Buddy told the group of people. He said it was the hardest day of his life, signing cremation papers for his wife and only daughter.

I had awakened on Wednesday and went to my best friend's house. As soon as I walked up to the front door, she opened the door and gave me a hug. She had told me that she does not do well with situations like this and tried to make jokes, but I was thankful for her just being there. I went to work that day too. I remember not taking much time off. I did not want to sit and think about what had happened. If I had sat and thought, I would have gone in to a deeper depression. I remember sitting on the couch crying, staring though my tears at the wall, not knowing what I needed to do.

Wednesday night I had very little sleep again. I remember waking on Thursday morning with tears streaming down my face. Shaun was at work and had called to make sure that I was okay on my day off. I had told him that I was as good as I was going to be for the time being. Friday came and went. Saturday, the day of the funeral, I remember getting up showering and getting ready to leave from our home to the funeral home in Belton. As we took the dreaded thirty-minute drive, Shaun turned in to the funeral home parking lot. We could not find a close parking spot. We had to park on the grass in the next lot. At the funeral there were about fourteen hundred people who came including Diane's friends and Anna's classmates.

The funeral home was busting at the seams. The visitation was scheduled from 1 to 3 p.m. There were so many people who came to say goodbye that the funeral didn't start to close until 4 p.m. As the visitation went on, I could not hold still and be in the family room for very long. I started weaving in and out of the crowd just to see who was there. I ran across my dad, my stepmom and her husband, and my friends from elementary school.

I didn't want to say goodbye to someone I had known all my life. Aunt Diane was like a second mother to me. I just didn't want to say goodbye yet. The next couple of weeks were very trying for everyone in my family. I just wanted to call Aunt Diane and talk about the wreck but couldn't, and it was killing me.

The first trial date was July 25, 2011. I don't remember much of the trials but I do remember that the drunk driver wrote an apology letter telling us how sorry that he had been driving drunk. There wasn't anything that the driver could say or do to make me forgive him. There was another trial date, August 15, 2011.

September 21 was Anna's birthday. She would have been twelve that year. Uncle Buddy had everyone over for a big blowout for Anna. Anna's friends made Uncle Buddy a shirt with Anna's favorite colors on it, pink, green, and blue. We released balloons for Anna in the hope that she would get them.

On Anna's birthday, Avis had set up a sobriety check. I remember going, but I'm not sure how many people police pulled over for their drunkenness. Avis had Aunt Diane and Anna's picture put on a 24x32" poster board, with the death date on it to make the point that my aunt and cousin had been killed by a drunk driver and to make sure that the drunk drivers knew why they were getting pulled over.

The final trial date, March 19, 2012, the driver got fifteen years for killing Aunt Diane and cousin Anna. My family and I didn't think that was nearly enough time for killing an eleven-year-old girl who was excited to be starting the next grade with all her classmates.

Over the next year and nine months I occasionally went out to see my Uncle Buddy and my other cousins, Cody and Tyler, just to see how Uncle Buddy was doing. Cody and Tyler were both dating people whom Aunt Diane and Anna had met. Both of their girlfriends had attended the funeral. Cody was with Jamiee and Tyler was with Sarah. Tyler and Sarah went on vacation in October 2011. Tyler proposed on that vacation and Sarah said yes. Almost a year later Cody and Jamiee announced that they were expecting their first child.

While Cody and Jamiee were getting ready for their first child, Tyler and Sarah were getting ready to have their wedding. On March 4, 2013, two days after Cody's birthday, my Uncle Buddy became a grandfather. It was one of the happiest days he had had in the longest time. He helped Cody and Jamiee welcome their daughter into the world that day and spent every chance he got with his granddaughter, and the next month flew by.

On Sunday, April 7, 2013, I received a phone call from Tyler that I was not ready to hear. Ever! Again! Tyler said Uncle Buddy had been riding his motorcycle the night before and was killed by a drunk driver. The only thing I could think of was who had done this again? Why had our family been broken again? Shaun and I had made plans the night before to go see a movie that day. I could not handle going out to the house again. Shaun and I stuck to our plans and saw the movie, instead of going to be with family again. After the movie, I decided to go to the house. There were a ton of people at my Uncle Buddy's house again, people I had not seen since Aunt Diane and Anna's wreck.

We did not know how drunk the man was who killed my Uncle Buddy. The wreck was a hit-and-run. The driver turned himself in the next day so the police were not able to get a blood alcohol reading. But he had turned himself in and that's all he needed to do, and he fessed up to what he had done.

Uncle Buddy's funeral was not nearly as big as Aunt Diane and Anna's. My family showed up for the funeral. Almost all of my Uncle Buddy's biker friends were there along with his family. My family and I went to court again to deal with this driver. This time the case lasted almost a year, and it seemed like it just dragged on. The driver received only one hundred and twenty days for the murder of my Uncle Buddy. He then could go on living his life. I attended all the court dates I could.

My mom kept telling me that this is our new normal, that I would not see Aunt Diane's car in my grandparents' driveway ever again. I was not ready to face our new normal. Somehow, some way, I have struggled with my new normal. Every single day it is a constant reminder that I am unable to call my aunt and talk like I want to.

People keep telling me that time heals all wounds. Let me tell you, it has been almost four years since Aunt Diane and cousin Anna were taken from my family, and I am still grieving. It has been a little over two years for my Uncle Buddy. I still cannot get over the fact that it seems like just yesterday when I was at my cousin's birthday parties and hugging my aunt goodbye, yet so long since I talked on the phone with any of them. I have promised myself never to tell anyone that time heals all wounds, because it does not heal.

AMY CARTER
INDEPENDENCE, MISSOURI

UNCLE BUDDY, AUNT DIANE & COUSIN ANNA

CHAPTER THREE

THE KNOCK AT THE DOOR

BY NANCY CLAY

*If love could have saved you,
you would live forever.* -ANONYMOUS

A knock at the door can mean so many things. It could be friends coming to visit, the postman delivering a package, a pesky salesperson whom you can't wait to shut the door on. But this one was the one that every military parent dreaded—the one that changes your life forever.

It is so amazing to me, the contrast of our life prior to 9 p.m. on Saturday, February 13, 2010. Life was good, hard, challenging and full of daily joys and trials in the busy, crazy household that was ours. We have eight children, a bit of "yours mine and ours" that we are so blessed with. I would refer to our family as "the Brady Bunch on steroids."

My husband, Mark, and I had married over twenty-eight years earlier. He took on an instant family with my three children, ranging in ages from two to five: Tiffany, Brian, and Kale, and adopted them a year after we married. Mark had one small daughter, Kassy, and together we had four more children, Jessica, Rebecca, Jordan and Megan. In our first year of marriage he had gone from zero children to five children! When Mark and I went out while I was pregnant with our first child, people would often ask, "Is this your first child?" We would say, "Yes, it is. Our first, his second, my fourth, and *our* fifth!" It was so much fun to blow their minds as they tried to figure that one out.

We moved many times during our marriage. I usually just explained the moves by saying we were part of "witness protection!" The reality was that it was the life of being a salesman as well as our family lineage of gypsies and sea captains. That blood ran through our veins; we loved to see new places. The kids had to learn to adapt and grow in whatever new circumstances they were in. What they also learned from this was that friends come and go, but your family is your rock. They were all close in age and grew up as good friends.

One by one, it came time for them to leave and move out on their own. We were now down to four living at home. Two of our grown children lived out of state; Tiffany was in Washington state, and Kassy lived in Virginia. Our oldest son, Brian, lived near us in Gilbert, Arizona. We had four more teenagers at home.

Kale was our third child and second son; he had begun to drift in his life after high school. He had a lot of dead-end jobs, and had gained over one hundred pounds. As a teenager he struggled with depression. There was a period in his life as a teenager when I just did not think he would survive this time. His depression would just sink him into a black hole. He would sleep for hours. He had been in ROTC in high school briefly, and I think this planted a seed. At the age of twenty, he decided he wanted to serve in the Army. He knew he wanted more from his life, and believed this would help him reach the goals he wanted to reach. He had to lose weight, though. During this time he had been living in Arizona, and we had moved on to Boise, Idaho, for a new job.

The day Kale called to tell me he was ready to enlist, my heart sank. I didn't realize how much progress he had made toward this goal, and that he was actually serious. He had quit so many other things when they began to resemble work. I was afraid of being a military parent because of the risk he faced for his safety. I had just finished with his phone call when I went to start my shift at the airlines reservation call center I worked at. One of my first calls of the evening was a woman whose son had just been killed in Iraq, and they needed to bring back his body. I finished helping her and then went into the bathroom and cried. I did not know how I would handle this kind of worry and stress over my son, knowing this was the possible outcome. I went home and prayed that night about it, knowing I could not carry this huge weight alone. I felt a very strong assurance that my son was in the care of Jesus. I didn't know the outcome of it all, but knew that he could be in no better care.

During basic training at Fort Jackson, Kale had written home and stated that even though it was so hard, he would not quit. He said that for the first time in his life he was truly happy. He could do hard things and push himself in ways he had never imagined. He barely graduated because of his timing on *the run*. He was never a fast runner, and this was something that was holding him back. On the very last run to qualify, the other soldiers in his unit fell back and ran in with him, encouraging him every step of the way. He made it!!

Our family trip to Fort Jackson to be at his graduation was one of the choicest and precious days we've had with Kale. We surprised him by bringing Dad and a few of his siblings, Rebecca, Megan and Jordan. He showed us all around the post, telling us the great adventures he had while he was there. Climbing Victory Hill, getting gassed in the gas chamber, and a tour of his barracks. He was so proud and wore his dress uniform, his Class A's. I remember standing next to him, feeling his strong arms around me. I was surprised that those shiny gold buttons did not pop off as his proud chest puffed out his uniform. This memory is seared into my brain. The next time I would see him in this uniform was when his body arrived at the funeral home.

Kale had a brief break before his next training, due to the Christmas holiday. He and Dad cooked up his surprise visit home. What a sweet memory of seeing him walk into the house just before dinner! He loved all the attention and soaked it up. For advanced training Kale was sent to Fort Sill in Texas, and then he was stationed at Fort Carson, Colorado. He was trained for infantry and was a weapons specialist. Six months later he was sent to Iraq where he was part of a security detail for his commander. The whole year he was gone, I tried so hard to put all my faith in his care with God. I was reminded that Kale was His child before he was mine. I knew he was in good hands. I did not realize the weight that had been on my heart, though, until a year later when he returned to the U.S. *safe*! He had made it through a *war zone*!

Kale had been home from Iraq for about six months, arriving in September 2009. We were now living back in Arizona and looked forward to seeing our son after his return. Our last visit was so very precious to us. I remember just watching him sleep on the couch and savoring his presence. He had surprised his siblings at their school, having them pulled out of class for a tearful and joyful reunion with them. The whole office was in tears at the sight. He *loved* wearing his uniform. He was so proud of what he represented in the Army and the work it took for him to earn that.

On the evening of February 13, 2010, it was a rare night when our kids all had plans, leaving Mark and I with a quiet date night in front of the television. I just remember so clearly feeling like all the kids were in a good place. I wasn't worried about any of them, especially Kale. We had been talking about his next deployment coming up, to Afghanistan. I was even more worried about him going there. He had just reenlisted and soon would be transferred to Fort Drum in New York. I had this sweet window of time when I was not worried about his safety.

My last conversation with Kale was just the day before when we talked about his plans for the future. He was so happy to finally enroll in college, something he had wanted to pursue for a long time. He was working hard at achieving his next rank, sergeant, and had just gotten a tattoo on his right bicep commemorating the security detail he served on with his battle buddy, as they would soon be split up with Kale's upcoming transfer to a new station. I said, "I love you, son." He said, "Love you, Mom." So even though I had just spoken to him, he was on my mind that morning. I called his cell phone, but it just went to voicemail. I didn't realize it then, but my son was already dead.

About 9 p.m. there was a knock at the door. We were not expecting anyone, but our children's friends often came by to visit. This knock just heightened my senses for some reason. I heard men's voices trying to confirm with Mark who he was, and then *that* moment, when time stopped. In slow motion, it seemed, two soldiers dressed in uniforms entered our living room. Their faces were solemn. Oh, God, *no*! I know what their presence means. Please, *no*! The instant I saw them, I knew that my son Kale was dead. I knew that this visit was one that every serviceman's family dreads.

The man closest to me said, "How are you doing this evening, ma'am?"

I looked him straight in the eye, my voice shaking, scared for the answer, and said, "I don't know. You tell me how I'm doing."

He then began his message, "We regret to inform you that your son, Specialist Kale Daren Clay, has died."

I cried out, "Oh, no, not my Kale! Not my son, not my baby…!"

It was all I could say, crying, moaning over and over. I ran for Kale's bear in my bedroom, a bear I had bought before he left for basic training. Calling it Kale Bear, it was a surrogate son I could hug if I needed it. I knew that he would be gone long periods of time, and this bear represented him. I held it, as well as a small silver frame containing a photo of Kale, my smiling little blond boy. Even though he was now a man, he was and always will be my little boy. I also held a white linen handkerchief that would soon hold a million tears. Those three items never left my side for days afterward.

The soldiers told us that Kale was killed in a car crash, and that alcohol was involved, but they couldn't tell us much else. Kale was killed in the early morning hours, around 5:20 a.m. on February 13, 2010. My husband finished getting the information from the soldiers, and then we were alone with this horrible, ugly news dropped into our life. A nuclear bomb just blew up my heart.

We had little time to try to absorb this, and knew we would have to somehow tell all our children that their brother was gone. We called each of the four kids to come home *now*, and a call to Brian that he needed to come over *now*. While we waited for the kids to arrive, we called our two daughters, Tiffany and Kassy. We worried so much over how they would take this news. Tiffany has struggled with lifelong depression and has made suicide attempts, and has other mental health problems. The year Kale was deployed, she was at her lowest. I never knew if the knock I would get at the door would be over him or her. I was so worried over how she would deal with this, with no family close by to be with her. I made sure her landlord was there. To hear her screams and cries before she dropped the phone just tore at our already aching hearts.

We called our next daughter, Kassy, in Virginia and got the same reaction. Luckily, she had family and friends close by to help. Jordan, our youngest son, walked into the house just as he heard Dad tell Kassy her brother was dead, and he hit the floor, a big burly cowboy brought to his knees. He idolized his brother; they had plans to serve together in the Army as soon as Jordan graduated, and Kale would reenlist. The girls, Jessica, Rebecca, and Megan, came in mostly at the same time, and we had to say those horrible words again and again, and watch it crush their world. Brian arrived soon after, and his reactions were just anger, swinging wildly around him. These two were closest in age, but far apart in the heart. There was too much competition and differences between the two of them, and they hadn't yet found a good place to relate to each other. It was just unbearable to see the pain we were going through and not be able to spare them this agony and hell we all found ourselves in.

That night we all just clung to each other, saying the words again, and again trying to believe them. I could not sleep; my husband gave up on trying to get me to come lie down and get some rest. I combed the internet for any news of the crash. I found a memorial website, and I set up one for Kale at kale-clay.memory-of.com. I wanted there to be a place where all who knew him could go. I wanted every memory from anyone to be recorded there and not lost. Each memory felt like a precious drop that I had to collect and keep from escaping. It was now all I had.

The days that followed were just a blur, crying, going through the motions to begin a funeral. We had a casualty officer assigned to our family, through the military. His assistance was truly heaven sent because I cannot imagine making all the decisions that we did without his help. Sargent Dan spoke quietly, telling us just enough in each step of what had to be decided or signed next.

Kale's body was being flown from the Denver airport, and it needed to arrive at a funeral home. You never imagine having to decide these things for your child. We were advised we should not view his body, due to his injuries. We decided Dad would make the decision if he thought we could handle this. He went in to see Kale first, and after seeing him he felt we could take it, knowing how badly some of the siblings wanted to see their brother one last time. I could not believe this body in the casket was my sweet boy. His face was badly distorted from the injuries sustained in the crash that killed him instantly. He was wearing his Class A's, his dress uniform. his white-gloved hands crossing his chest. As I stood over the casket, this once warm chest was now cold and hard. Before I closed that lid, I read to him one last time, from a book I read to them often, "I'll love you forever, I'll like you for always, as long as I'm living my baby you'll be." I said goodbye to my son's body.

Next came decisions about his funeral, and I decided that I would speak about my son. It would be one of the hardest things I had done, but I was his mother and wanted to honor my son in this way. Brian also spoke, giving his brother a most beautiful eulogy. I think most of Brian's heartache was losing a brother with whom he had not gotten a chance to find that good place.

We had to decide where to bury him. The military cemetery was over an hour and a half away. My grandfather was buried there. I did not want him that far away. As a family, we wanted to have him closer to us. We drove from cemetery to cemetery, trying to find a place that felt right. There is no right place, but we finally found one that felt best. We had put a temporary marker as his headstone, made of marble, to give us time to think what his permanent headstone should say. It took over seven months to decide what those words should be, and the funeral home was calling back repeatedly, as they had to order it from the military. I could not find those words; nothing seemed right. How do you sum up what a person, your child, his life means? We finally decided on what it would say: "Kale Daren Clay, Specialist U.S. Army, March 3, 1986 – Feb. 13, 2010. Too Loved to Be Forgotten, Until We Meet Again." I filled up every space on it that I could. I just could not order it. It was one of two things I could not do for my son. My husband finally took over for me, because I just could not do it. Because then, somehow, it would be more real than it already was.

The details of the crash that we came to learn were that Kale had gone out with two friends from his unit. One was new to the unit, but the driver was his good friend who had served in Iraq with Kale. His friend's wife had left him, and they were going out to cheer up their buddy. They had been drinking and were headed back to the base early that morning. The driver missed the turnoff to the post and headed up a hill that had a curve, driving too fast, and drove into the oncoming lane. An older man on his way to work in a Ford 350 utility truck hit their car, with my son's side receiving the full impact. Kale was killed instantly. The back seat passenger also died instantly. He was not belted in, and his body was responsible for one of the three instant death injuries my son suffered. The driver survived with injuries to his spleen, a broken femur, and dislocated hip. His blood alcohol content was .162 percent. The driver of the truck did not have serious injuries. Kale died at the age of twenty-three, just seventeen days before his twenty-fourth birthday.

From the very first that we were given this news, I felt blessed that my heart was not filled with hate for the driver who took my son's life. All it could contain was overwhelming grief and heartbreaking sorrow. I somehow tracked down his mother's cell phone as she was traveling from Florida to Colorado to be with her son. I asked her to please kiss her son's forehead for me since I could not do that for my son. Part of me was so angry at Kale for getting into that car. He paid for a very tragic decision with his life.

With the funeral behind us, the next hurdle was getting through his birthday. All I can remember about it was that our family gathered at the cemetery and released balloons. My brain was in a complete fog; I felt as if I had been damaged and could not focus, concentrate or remember anything. I was just completely numb, going through the emotions, feeling nothing and everything. Everything just felt so raw. It was like my heart and mind could take only so much. It amazes me that the body can continue functioning and go on autopilot. All my brain could think of or focus on was Kale. It was like I was afraid that I would forget him, or a memory would fade. I couldn't lose what I had left of him. It's like trying to hold water in your hands.

Shortly after Kale's birthday came our next ordeal, to travel fourteen hours to Fort Carson in Colorado and attend the military memorial held for our son and three other soldiers who had recently died. We met with the prosecutor in Denver to discuss how their case would be handled. The Army wanted to take over the case since it was three of their soldiers involved, even though it occurred outside the post.

We met with the family of the young man who died with our son there. His mother spoke little English, as they had emigrated from Poland a few years earlier. I had tried to learn a phrase or two to communicate with her, but my brain was mush. Instead, I purchased a bear similar to mine and gave it to her. My bear now contained a voice chip so I could hear Kale's voice in it. I have five precious recordings that I was so glad I had kept from when he was deployed. She was very grateful to have a bear that represented her son. It conveyed what my words could not.

After we had met with the prosecution team, we traveled to see the car our sons died in. I saw the seatbelt, cut by the emergency responders. This was where my son took his last breath. On so many nights I was haunted by the thoughts of what his last moments were like. Did he hurt? Did he have any moment of recognition of what had just happened? My son's body was so injured that it could not sustain life. Next, we drove to where the crash had occurred. The last place my son was alive. Kale's buddy, Paul Blohm, had a cross made up for them, and posted it in memory of these two friends.

Lastly, we attended the memorial. We saw other families hurting like ours were. If you have not attended a military service, I can tell you it is more painful than anything I have ever gone through. It was hard enough to be surrounded by men and women in uniform. For the longest time after, I would just cry when seeing a military member. The chapel on the post was filled with them. His good friend and battle buddy, Michael Blanton, gave a beautiful eulogy of his dear friend. He and Kale had matching tattoos done a few days before the crash. Just after it, he had the same artist put a photo of Kale on his other bicep. While in town on this trip, our daughter Jessica had this same artist put a soldier's cross on her right side in memory of him. She cried not just with pain, but with many memories of him. They were very close.

Next in the service was roll call. The deceased soldier's name is called three times, each getting louder, to the silence of the reply.

"Specialist Clay! Specialist Kale Clay! SPECIALIST KALE DAREN CLAY!"

It rips your heart right out of your chest knowing they will never answer that call again. They are gone. Then came the bagpipes playing taps. To this day, I hate the sound of them. By this time, I was just spent. I had nothing left in my heart or soul. We then stood in a line to receive the fellow officers and soldiers who gave us a handshake or hug and words of condolences. Fort Carson was his home, and this was his family.

Returning to Carson was a very hard thing to do. The memories I have there at that base were very good ones prior to this. Jordan, Megan and I had made the trek there from Washington, where we were living then, in August 2008 to visit with Kale before he deployed to Iraq. We spent a week there, enjoying our time together. Part of me worried whether I would see my son again, going off to such a dangerous place. We explored the post with him, went to the Garden of the Gods, and I would just watch the kids together enjoying time with their big brother. The last time I saw Kale here he was alive.

That whole next year was a blur as we tried to grasp this horrible new reality. There was not an area of life that it did not affect. We now had to deal with cutting Kale's ties to this world, canceling credit cards, bank accounts, filing his taxes. His personal effects were sent to us from the Army, arriving in five black cargo containers. We sorted through them, examining all the things that made up his life. I washed some of his clothes. He had thirty-one pairs of socks. I'm sure it was so he had to do laundry only once a month if he needed to. Each cut made it seem as if he was slipping farther and farther away.

Our next trip to Fort Carson would now be for the court-martial trial. The Army had officially taken the case over from the state. I was relieved, as I felt that they would best represent Kale. It would also occur sooner than the state would prosecute. It can take sometimes two to three years for the court, and I could not imagine carrying this next heavy load on us. It was scheduled for October 2010. I could not sleep for days as the trial was approaching. My brain kept trying to find the words. Trying to find the most powerful, succinct words that would portray and represent our son as well as the loss of him. How could I sum up him or all that we had lost?

Just as we were getting ready to travel to Colorado, we were called and told there would be a delay in the trial. It was now set for January 2011! I fell apart. I could barely think or speak for three days, as I shut myself in my room, crying and consumed by the pain I was in. I had only enough in me to go this far, and now I had to bear it longer still. This would go into the holidays. I dreaded going through our *firsts* of things, and how could one feel merry with so much hurt in their heart? Knowing that the driver got to be a free man longer, and enjoy his family, the holidays felt beyond unfair. I stalked his movements as best as I could via Facebook. He fell in love with some girl over the holiday trip home. My son was cold in his grave, and this man was having the time of his life.

The holidays began to arrive. How can you even manage feeling joy when your heart has been broken? You have people who count on you to be there for them. My husband now had a wife who was changed, and was not fully present. My children deserved their mom to love them and care about them. They were always jostling for their time and attention as kids in a big family, and now one of them was dead, and with it had taken their parents, as they knew them. How do you compete with that and not feel guilty for wanting time and love too?

We put up a Christmas tree, but I couldn't stand getting out our family ornaments, I put up generic red and gold bulbs. We were trying to make some new memories, since the old ones hurt too much. I put a small Christmas tree up at Kale's grave. Somehow we made it. I don't know how, but we did. The kids didn't mention his name much. It became the elephant in the room. I didn't know how much to say about him. Do I mention him too much, and will they resent that? Do I say his name at all so they too can open up if they feel like it? Sometimes people are afraid that by saying the name, it will cause hurt or make you cry. It's always with you, so knowing that others are thinking of him too really helps. In the beginning, you talk about it ALL the time, but as time passes it buries deeper, and you don't want to share it as much. It becomes your private pain. Few people understand how long-term grief is carried.

Finally, the day arrived in January to travel to Colorado Springs. It was winter and snowy, and a hard, long drive there. As we were nearing the city, a few more hours left, we got another call. A potential delay *again*! Do we turn around, keep going? We decided to continue the journey and prayed it would get resolved. Mark and I, as well as our daughters, Jessica, Rebecca and Megan were attending with us. The boys, Jordan and Brian, simply could not deal with this. For them, anger was an easier emotion than their grief. Tiffany's health would not allow her to deal with this either, and Kassy was too far away with a small baby. Thankfully, the trial would have only a short delay and would begin as scheduled. Attending with us was a MADD representative, and a dear friend we made from the company of No DUI of Colorado Springs, Nonie Rispin. These dear women walked this difficult path with us and made it more bearable.

It was here when we came face to face with the man responsible for taking our son's life. The trial was held in a small courtroom, and things were very informal, as we sat just a row behind him, and near his family. The tension in the room was a tangible force. For days we had to listen to the defense make up lies, excuses, and try to fabricate possible scenarios trying to cast doubt on their client's actions, blaming everyone and everything other than him. It is such a test of will to sit there poker-faced and show no reaction whatsoever to anything said, due to the risk of being thrown out or barred from the courtroom.

Each night we would return to our hotel room completely worn, exhausted, and numb. When it was time for the coroner to read his report, I walked out. It was the second thing that I could not do. I had spent so much time already torn up inside, wondering how mangled my son's body was and what he had gone through. We sat next to the other family, and they showed a photo of her son with his head smashed into the windshield. That was something that no parent should have to see. The images I saw are forever seared into the flesh of my heart. In the end, the driver was sentenced to ten years for taking two lives, Kale Daren Clay and the other young man. He would serve this at Fort Leavenworth. With this major hurdle over, I thought, "Now, the healing can begin." Every year since then, it has never been completely over. We have had to deal with a clemency request for the last four years, a parole request, and an appeal request regard the sentence. These requests often came around Mother's Day, or right before Christmas, adding more stress and pain to already hard times, and adding further torment to our family and me. Each time, I would write the board with my letters asking for his sentence to be upheld. Then wait. It would take months to hear back on the ruling.

About two years into our grief journey, Mark hit a very deep dark place. He could not function very well at all. Going to work was extremely hard. My husband was going through a depression that we did not realize was going on. Men grieve so differently than women. They hold it in, knowing that the family needs strength, and not knowing an outlet or way to process his feelings about losing someone. Mark was and always has been my rock. I don't know how I could have coped with this great loss without his constant love and support.

I wished that I could just sleep, the place of slumber where reality was not there. In time, I would dream about Kale, and it was bittersweet. I would try to hold him, hang on to him, and as I felt the dream ebb, my mind would be awake to a day when Kale was no longer with us. This year, 2016, marks six years since his death. It's hard to believe that somehow we have survived that long.

Earlier this year, we had a much anticipated vacation to California with our daughter, Rebecca, her husband, and our almost three-year-old granddaughter, Paisley, and ten-year-old grandson, Mason. It had taken a long time to feel joy again, to enjoy and savor all of life's riches and time with my family. We were going into Disneyland when I got the call. "His appeal was successful; his sentence has been overturned. He is being released from Leavenworth *today*." A bomb just dropped in my life. My world just crashed again.

On the outside, I tried to be Fun Mom and Nana, but inside I was just dying. I was determined to not let him steal more from me during this trip. It had taken us so much just to get to this point, and now once again he rears his ugly head in our lives. It was beyond wrong. The military process that I had once trusted to administer justice ruled that a technicality of the judge regarding a captain who had known a member of the prosecution was enough reason to bias the verdict. Aside from the fact that he was only one of several who also voted guilty, somehow this erased it all. After just four years, the driver was released. He was going to be offered a plea deal, with credit for time served.

The case cost over one hundred thousand dollars to bring to trial. The lab that processed the blood evidence of his blood alcohol content is no longer in business, and military members who served as witnesses are spread throughout the globe. The prosecution did not think, based on those factors, that we would be successful in getting the driver more prison time and ran the risk of an acquittal, in which case he would be eligible for all his back pay. He pleaded guilty to the charges, and accepted his responsibility for the crash.

The new prosecutor for the case told me that the defense team he had was required to file all those legal motions on behalf of their client, and that they could be disbarred if they did not do so. This news made me realize that all the years I thought he had been denying his responsibility and trying to get out early was not the case. The prosecutor said he had listened to all the phone calls he had made while incarcerated to evaluate where he was at, and based on what he heard he felt that he was truly remorseful. While we were there for the signing of the plea deal, we once again faced the judge and gave testimony about our son. We were his voice one last time, and shared with the court what Kale meant to us.

The driver had asked to meet with us before court, which we agreed to. I had wanted to know all along how he was in terms of his mental and emotional recognition of his actions. I knew that regardless of how much time he served, nothing would ever be enough or equal to what was taken. Justice is not found on this earth. What I wanted to know was, did he get it? Did he understand in some measure what his actions had done, taking so much from Kale and all who loved him?

He looked so scared when he approached us, so uncertain of what to say to us, unsure of what our response to him might be. He told us that he took every counseling group, therapy or program offered by the prison. He spent his years trying to better himself and he fully took upon himself the guilt of his actions. We talked for nearly an hour, and each poured our hearts out. At the end, we hugged each other. I felt so much pain lift from my heart. I could not have asked for a better outcome for what this horrible situation was, and we finally felt at peace with where we stood in relation to him. All we asked of him was that somehow, some way, he would find a way to live his life with honor, in memory of Kale, and find a way to make a difference in this world. Somehow, good must come from this preventable tragedy. It has to mean something.

This seems to be the decision you have to make when something out of your control happens. How will it affect you in the long term? I knew that I did not want this event to control my life. I didn't want to remain stuck in a place of never-ending torture, grief and bitterness. I would have to find a way to carry this burden, this loss. I had to find a way to live with purpose from this.

One night while soaking in the bathtub, my mind numb from the constant tears that came so easily, words from somewhere else penetrated my mind: "Focus on living. Focus on *the* living." I had to try to understand somehow that I was not just Kale's mom, I was Mark's wife and mother to seven other children who needed me. While at times that felt like an anchor, it was also my lifeline and I had to grab it or I would sink into an abyss so deep that I would never find my way out. I knew I had to pay attention to what I still had in my life. A husband who needed his wife, children who wanted to know that they still mattered to their mother. All this focus and energy regarding Kale's death had made them question and wonder, "Do I still matter? I'm still here, do you love me?" It's a hard thing to resent the dead for stealing their parent from them. Sibling grief is very challenging. The whole family dynamic changed. Kale was such an instigator of laughter in our family. Each of my children has my whole heart, and one does not replace the other. Each person brings such a unique personality and occupies a place no other can.

I often hear the words from someone who is trying to bring me comfort that I will see my son again. I know that with every breath in my body. What gets me through life is that knowledge. Yet, it is *every* day of my life that I miss my son. It's like a beat of your heart. Your child exists within you. It is cellular, part of your DNA. You cannot remove them. Trying to live or exist in a world in which they are not here is the worst kind of pain. I missed out on so much: seeing him continue in his career, watching him marry and have children. He would have been such a great dad. This was one of his greatest dreams, to have a family. I would not be able to watch him grow old. I miss hearing his laughter, his phone calls home, or feeling his great bear hugs. He was an awesome storyteller. He was a huge prankster and loved to play practical jokes on others. He was generous of whatever he had. Kale was someone who made a friend of anyone.

His captain told us that he often sought out Kale's company while they were deployed because "You could not leave Kale's side and not feel better." Another soldier told us that it was because of Kale that his own deployment was bearable. One of the lives Kale had touched named their son after him, Kale Clay Harrison. It meant more than words could express to have his name honored and that it is carried on in the life of another.

Kale brought many amazing people into our lives who have been a balm to our hurting hearts. It is how we hold to part of him through these relationships. He was loved by so many. He lived life as fully as he could. I have wondered whether Kale knew his time here would be short. He was worried as he was being deployed; he was convinced he wasn't going to make it back. I assured him he would live to be an old man, and give us lots of grandbabies, and that his time here was not over.

In the six years since his death, six of his siblings have married. Our daughters cried on their wedding days, sad that their brother was not with them to share their special day. As all our family gathers, we are all so painfully aware of his missing place.

Since Kale's death, I have been involved with MADD, and thousands have heard his story throughout the world. A military base I spoke at shared it at ten of their bases throughout the world. He would think that was pretty cool. He always loved attention and didn't care how he got it. The day I buried my son, I promised him that I would do hard things. I live every day without him, and share his story with anyone who will listen. This is how I honor his name; Kale Daren Clay lived, and his life mattered.

This motto really sums up Kale, how he lived. It's what I choose to do every day. *Live, laugh, love — I can do hard things!*

NANCY CLAY
MESA, AZ

KALE CLAY WITH MOM NANCY

MARK, KALE & NANCY CLAY

KALE CLAY

CLAY FAMILY

LIKE THE WAVES IN THE OCEAN
BY Nancy Edwards – JULY 30, 2015

How could it be that nine years have passed
Since the time your father and I spoke to you last.
In some ways it's a blur, and other ways, slow motion.
The ride's been up and down like the waves in the ocean.

From the surface, the ocean appears calm and serene
But just below are strong currents, often unseen.
Those currents will pull you and throw you about.
They'll catch you off guard if you don't watch out.

I draw in a deep breath but am knocked back down.
I panic as I feel I am about to drown.
Reality hits me with the force of the next wave.
You're gone, really gone. I have to be brave.

So I fight to rise to the surface for air
Desperately hoping I'll see you swimming there.
But I don't and I won't. Those days are no more.
Exhausted from the struggle, I head for the shore.

There are castles to build and new shells to be found.
The sun's rays warm me as I glance around.
In some ways it's a blur, and other ways, slow motion.
The ride's been up and down like the waves in the ocean.

CHAPTER FOUR

OUT OF THE DARKNESS

One Father's Journey from Death to Life

BY BILL DOWNS

*For He rescued us from the domain of
darkness, and transferred us to the
kingdom of His beloved Son (Colossians 1:13).*

Since the beginning of time the question has been, "Does God really exist?" We deal with issues in our lives that bring doubt and sorrow every day. How can a God of mercy and grace allow such sorrow and pain? The choices we make have a direct impact on our relationship with God. When all is going well we don't feel we need His blessings, but when all seems to be falling apart we tend to turn to Him for help. When we rely on ourselves instead of His guidance we fall into the pit of despair. The story you are about to read is "my story." My journey from the darkness brought on by my choice to turn from God because of the death of my son, Brad, his wife, Samantha, and a young man I loved as a son, Chris, at the hands of a drunk driver.

My life with my wife started on March 5, 1982. Within the next three years we had two wonderful children, Cindy and Brad. Cindy was born mentally handicapped due to a lack of oxygen to the brain. She is our miracle baby. So it was a little scary when Julie became pregnant with Brad because of our past experience. But Brad was born a healthy, bouncy boy. I was in the Air Force at the time and we were stationed at Sheppard Air Force Base in Wichita Falls, Texas. Cindy was three years old, and with Brad's birth our little family was complete. As we went about our daily life of my going to work, Cindy going to special school, Brad being a toddler and Julie a housewife staying home to raise the kids, we spent a lot of time together. We loved living in Texas. We often went to Scott Mountain in Lawton, Oklahoma, where Brad and I would climb all over the rocks and boulders like we were mountain goats. We did everything as a family: fishing, hiking, swimming, camping, and going to church. We were always together. We felt we were invincible. Nothing could touch us or take away our happiness.

We were in church every week sitting side by side, worshipping God and enjoying the friendships we made. One of our dear friends from church belonged to the North Texas Speleological Society, which gave him access to some of the wild caves in Texas. He would organize trips into these caves and take a group of church members with him, and I would always go. I loved caving. This was actually the only activity that we did not do as a family. I tried talking Julie into going, but she had no desire to crawl in the mud or be in the dark. As Brad got older, I would take him and he thoroughly enjoyed it. He was my caving buddy.

On one occasion we were sliding along a muddy, wet and dark tunnel with nothing but a headlamp mounted to a hard hat to guide us. Brad was five years old at the time, and while I was crawling on my belly struggling through the tunnel, he was able to walk right through it. I looked at him with envy and he said, "Dad, it pays to be little." He always had a way with words and knew how to make me smile.

With me being in the Air Force and us living on the base, Brad grew up around the sound of fighter jets. Planes were Brad's passion. He told me, "Dad, one day I'm going to be a fighter pilot." In return I would tell him, "You can do anything you set your mind to, son." He loved the sound of the planes and would stop and run outside every time one would fly over. He had books about planes, flashcards and models and would constantly be reading and studying about them. Most boys had a hot wheel car collection, but Brad had planes: little planes, big planes and midsize planes. He learned to recognize both military and commercial aircraft simply by listening to them, and with great accuracy he was able to tell what they were before he even saw them.

The first time he was up close to an airplane was when I got orders to Woomera, Australia. It was a remote assignment which meant my family could not go with me. At the time, saying goodbye was the hardest thing we had ever had to do. I was going to be gone for eighteen months, and to Brad, Cindy and Julie and even to myself that seemed like a lifetime. The day came for me to leave. As we stood at the airport looking at the planes, Brad clung to me, begging me not to go. It was hard explaining to him that I didn't have a choice. When it came time for me to walk to the gate to board the plane, Julie had to pry Brad from my arms. He was holding on to me for dear life.

As Julie consoled Brad, I walked away and as I got to the gate I went to turn around to blow kisses, and felt little arms encircling my legs. I looked down and it was Cindy. She had followed me and in her sweet innocent way was asking me to take her with me. I picked her up and walked her back to Julie and turned and left my family, my life, standing there. I thought leaving them was the hardest thing I would ever have to do. I knew they were halfway around the world waiting for me.

I had been gone for four months when Julie started having some health problems and needed surgery. The Red Cross put me on a plane back to the States so I could be there. As the plane touched down I felt that my life had returned to normal again. I was reunited with my family. I had been home for a couple weeks when I learned that President Clinton was downsizing the military, and I fell into the category of those who were being discharged. We felt as if our world was coming to an end. Suddenly I was a civilian.

I found a job in Wichita Falls so we stayed there and bought a house. Brad was in the second grade and Cindy was still going to a special school for the handicapped. Two years later Julie's dad passed away and we had to take an unexpected trip to Mississippi. After the funeral we decided we would sell our home in Wichita Falls and move back to our hometown. We felt the kids were missing out on having grandparents, aunts and uncles and cousins to grow up near them. So when we got back to Wichita Falls we put the house up for sale and I put in my notice at work. I made the move to Mississippi to find a job, leaving Julie and the kids behind. When the house sold I went back to move them to be with me.

I joined the Mississippi Air National Guard once we settled in, to keep from losing the thirteen and a half years toward retirement I had built up on active duty in the Air Force. The extra income each month and the monthly guard drills turned out to be a good part-time job. Julie started working as an attendant at a laundromat that her family ran, and she was able to take the kids with her to work.

One of the good things about being in the Air National Guard was the ability for Brad to see his beloved planes again. He would often make Julie take him to the local airport where the base was located so he could see the planes and helicopters take off and land. The Air National Guard shared the airport not only with the Army National Guard, but commercial airlines as well. So there were many planes for Brad to enjoy. His favorites were the C5 military cargo plane, the F15, F16, and F18. I had the pleasure of taking him on one occasion to watch a visiting Guard squadron as they practiced their war games. We were sitting on a concrete ramp facing the airstrip when the A10s began to taxi by. As one got close with the cockpit open, Brad jumped up and stood at attention and saluted the pilot. To Brad's surprise, the pilot saluted back. He looked at me and said, "Dad, did you see that?"

"Yes, son. I did." I smiled up at him, because I knew how proud this made him feel.

As Brad got older and his interests changed, we didn't spend as much time together. I was busy working and he was busy with his friends and afterschool activities. When we were together it seemed like I spent more time fussing at him instead of enjoying him. I felt it was my job to keep him on the straight and narrow so he would not get into trouble. We were so much alike that it seems like we were always clashing. We struggled through his teenage years and I watched him mature into a young man.

In his last year of high school, he befriended a young lady named Samantha. The first time I met her was on his eighteenth birthday. Brad was born on the Fourth of July, so each year we would have a big barbecue/birthday party, inviting family and friends. Samantha had been invited to his party, and once Brad's guest arrived he brought her to us to introduce us. She was a beauty. Black hair and crystal-blue eyes. Julie looked at her and said, "Wow, you have beautiful eyes!" She rolled her eyes to indicate sarcasm and said, "Whatever!" This stunned both Julie and me. I whispered to Julie as she and Brad walked away, "She's a brat." Little did I know at the time that she would become my daughter-in-law.

It was tradition that when it got dark Brad and I would put on a fireworks display. I have to admit that in that year we did get a little crazy and maybe a little dangerous, throwing fireworks at each other. But we had fun.

Several months later Brad and Samantha started dating. I wasn't really sure how I felt about that, because my first impression of her was a little shaky, but as I got to know her I realized that she was a sweet girl, but with attitude. If she had something to say she definitely didn't hold back. They were so young, and Julie and I tried our best to slow Brad down, but we could tell that Samantha had won his heart. Samantha's family was doing the same, trying to slow her down, but these two were destined to be together. Against better judgment, they moved into a three-bedroom apartment they shared with two other people. Samantha was eighteen and Brad twenty. We had several heated discussions about their living arrangements because we did not approve, but Brad and Samantha were both determined to be together no matter what anyone said. They were in love, and how could you fight that?

Brad was giving his part of the rent to one of the roommates. Three months later when they received an eviction notice, Brad found out that this roommate was not paying rent and instead was pocketing the money. Not knowing what else to do, Brad and Samantha showed up on our doorstep asking if they could stay with us until they found another place. At first I said "No!" I told him that we did not approve of their living together without being married, and that Samantha needed to go home to her family and Brad could move back in with us. He told me that they would live in his car before they did that. The more Brad talked and I listened, I told him that his mother and I would discuss it and we would let him know. Reluctantly, Julie and I agreed and told him that it would be temporary and that they would not sleep in the same room. Brad would sleep in the living room and Samantha could take the bedroom. He tried to argue with me, but I told him that we would not have it any other way. He wasn't happy about it, but he agreed.

When they showed up at the house to move in they had a young man with them named Chris. Brad asked if he could stay a couple of nights until he found a place to go, because he was the other roommate who was also being evicted. Again, we reluctantly agreed. Chris took the couch, Brad got the floor in the living room and Samantha moved into Brad's bedroom. I kept after them about finding an apartment because I did not like the living arrangements but before I knew it days had turned into eight months and all three of them were still with us. Chris became a part of our family. He called me Dad and called Julie Mom. It seemed so natural to have him around.

Brad and Samantha constantly talked about getting married, but they both were too young to be married in Mississippi without their parents' signature. They came to us and asked if we could help them. We knew they were in love and they wanted to be together so we said yes.

We started making plans and on June 22, 2007, we drove over to Bay Minette, Alabama, and witnessed them becoming husband and wife. They were married in a little chapel named New Hope. When the pastor asked if they were going to exchange rings, Samantha sadly said, "No. Our rings have to be resized, so we don't have any." I looked at Julie and she nodded her head. I said, "Wait, yes, they will exchange rings." Brad looked at me, puzzled, as I took my wedding ring off my finger and Julie removed the anniversary ring I had just given her for our twenty-fifth anniversary the past March. Brad said, "But Dad, you have never taken that ring off." I told him that I wanted him to use it but that I wanted it back as soon as the ceremony was over. He hugged me with tears in his eyes. The ceremony was beautiful. As they exchanged their vows and looked into each other's eyes every doubt I had about their getting married vanished. They were in love and it was meant to be.

When we returned home later that day, Brad and Sam walked up to me with smiles on their faces and asked if they could sleep in the same room. I laughed and said, "Yes, you're legal." They were so happy, and had great expectations for their life together.

Brad was working hard training to be an oil tech, and Samantha worked part time at Outback Burgers. Brad's credit was established and he financed his first car, a 2001 Ford Mustang. It was his dream car. He turned twenty-one on July 4, 2007, and Samantha turned nineteen on September 4 that same year. Their life together was just beginning.

October 6, 2007, started like any other Saturday morning. Julie was working for her sister at the laundromat and I was to relieve her at 3 p.m. My regular job was with the Gulfport City School District as an HVAC technician, but every once in a while I would help out at the laundromat if needed. That morning my phone rang around 9, waking me up. Thinking it was Julie, I grabbed it only to hear Chris' voice on the other end asking what highway he needed to be on to get home. He had gone to visit his girlfriend in Jackson. He was upset, but told me he would talk to me when he got home about what had happened.

Chris was not a blood relation, but he was my son in heart. He had won a place in our family. We couldn't talk him into finding an apartment of his own because he liked it there with us. So we allowed him to stay. I told him the highway he needed to be on and I dozed back off.

I got up around 9:30 a.m. Brad and Sam were working out in the yard. Brad thought that if they cleared off the back part of the property that the code office would let them put a trailer there. I didn't think it would happen, but Brad still wanted to try. I left the house around 1 p.m. and walked outside to let them know I was leaving. Brad was chopping trees and Sam was hauling them to the burn pile. I told them to look out for Chris, who should be home any time, and asked if they were going to go look at the antique cars that were down for Cruising the Coast. Brad said they weren't really sure what they were going to do, but they were meeting some friends later. I told him to watch the traffic and the drunks on the road. I then made him promise that they would be extra careful. I told him I loved him, and he said he loved me too.

When I got to the laundromat Julie ran and got us something for dinner. She and Cindy ate with me and then they left. I watched TV and talked to Julie as she drove home. Chris beeped in so we hung up. She called a little later to let me know that she had made it home and that Brad and Sam were going to hang out with Chris to try to cheer him up, because apparently things didn't go the way he had hoped in Jackson. They decide to go to the car races, so they piled into Chris' truck, but when they got there the races had been canceled because it had rained earlier and the track was wet. They went back to the house to change clothes and decide what they were going to do. They decided on the movies. This time they took Brad's Mustang. He had only had it for three weeks and he wanted

Chris to ride in it. After they left the house Chris called me; it was 8:50 p.m. He told me they were going to the movies and I told him the same thing I had told Brad. "It's Cruising the Coast weekend; just watch the traffic." He said, "No problem, Dad. We will see you when we get home. I love you." I replied "I love you too," and we hung up.

I was able to get out of the laundromat around 9:45 p.m. and headed home. I called Julie to let her know I was on my way. As I drove down Highway 49 I couldn't believe how many people were out that late. Cruising the Coast weekend is always busy with the antique cars and tourists that visit. The traffic was awful, and I was thankful when I turned onto Highway 53, because I was almost home. I noticed that there seemed to be a mist in the air and dampness on the road. I came to the intersection of Highway 53 and Canal Road and there was a roadblock. The Harrison County Sheriff's Department was detouring traffic down Canal Road. I called Julie as soon as I turned onto Canal Road to let her know I would be a little late. I noticed that the curve beyond the intersection was lit up like daylight from all the emergency vehicles there. Apparently there had been a tremendous car wreck. I had never seen so many emergency lights and vehicles in one spot. I told this to Julie as I took the detour. She said she would call the kids to check on them and let them know to avoid that area on their way home.

She called me back in a panic. "Bill, they didn't answer the phone." I immediately turned around and headed back to the roadblock. When I got there I stopped. The deputy blocking the road walked up to the car and told me I couldn't go through, that I needed to continue down the road. I turned around and headed back the way I came. I called Julie's brother and told him what was going on and asked him to get to Julie and not let her leave the house until I found something out. She wanted to go look for the kids. Julie called me again to say she still could not reach the kids. When I got to the other side of the roadblock, a highway patrolman walked up to my window and told me I needed to leave. I told him

I was not leaving until I found out who was in the crash. He then gave me two choices: go home or be arrested. Julie was still on the phone when the officer said that, and in a panic she told me to go to the movie theater and find Brad's car. I drove to the theater. In the meantime, Julie was on the phone to dispatch, highway patrol, hospitals, anyone who might know something. By this time we were pretty anxious, and our hearts were telling us that the kids were in the crash.

I searched the theater parking lot, checking every parking space. Brad's Mustang was not there. I headed back to Highway 53 and called Julie to let her know I did not find Brad's car. I pulled off the road into the parking lot of a tobacco store and just sat there, panicked, not knowing what to do. I could see the flashing lights from where I sat. I had a lump in my throat and all I kept thinking was, "It can't be them, it just can't be them." I hoped that if I sat there I would see the wrecker come by and see if it was Brad's car.

My phone rang and it was Julie. "Go to the hospital. Two of the victims in the crash have been transported there." I spun out of the parking lot, praying they were okay.

When I got to the emergency room I went immediately to the nurses' station window and told the nurse on duty why I was there. She said she would go see what she could find out. While she was checking in the back, a friend's wife, Donna, came in. Her church had just concluded a youth meeting and when she heard about the crash she came to the hospital to make sure none of the kids from the meeting were involved.

I was standing there talking to her, telling her my fears and what I knew when the phone rang. It was Julie. My face went expressionless when I heard her say, "Bill, Bill, your baby didn't make it. He's gone. All three of them are gone."

Apparently while Julie and her family were trying to find out what had happened, the coroner had gotten hold of Julie through the 911 dispatch and was questioning her about Chris. How he was dressed, what color his hair was, his eyes, etc. Julie kept asking him if her son was dead. He was persistent in trying to get her to identify Chris, and she was more persistent in finding out if Brad was dead. The coroner finally told her, "Yes ma'am, I believe he is." Julie insisted that her sister drive her to the hospital, and she was calling me en route because she felt I needed to hear it from her, not the coroner.

When I heard what Julie was saying, I dropped the phone and collapsed into the arms of Donna, falling to my knees, wailing uncontrollably. While Donna was consoling me, waiting for Julie to get there, the coroner came out and asked me to identify Chris. I walked with him into the back where they had Chris' body. When I looked at him I could not believe this was the young man I had grown to love as a son. This young man who was so full of life and had so many dreams and hopes, but there he was lying on the gurney. There was so much blood. His neck was broken. In tears, I confirmed that it was Chris.

The coroner walked me to a waiting room. He said that as soon as Julie got there he would bring her to me. Minutes passed, but it seemed like hours. The door opened and there she was. We fell into each other's arms and sobbed uncontrollably. When I was able to get myself together, I asked the coroner if he knew what had happened. He said the driver of the other vehicle had crossed over into Brad's lane, hitting them head on. He then said, "Unofficially, she was drunk."

The driver had come around the curve, which was also on a hill, traveling eighty miles per hour with no headlights. She missed the curve and crossed over into Brad's lane. She hit Brad's Mustang head-on, throwing his car into a tailspin. Her passenger was ejected from the vehicle and was found alive in the ditch. She and Chris were transported to the hospital. The driver was partially ejected through the windshield as the vehicle caught on fire, and she died.

Brad had been traveling east and she had been traveling west. Brad's car spun around several times, coming to a stop pointing south. Brad died instantly due to blunt force trauma to the head and chest. His lungs were punctured by his crushed ribs because the airbags did not deploy. Samantha was killed when the Mustang's engine exploded on impact, impelling her into her seat. Chris' neck was broken when he was thrown forward and hit the roof of the car. He died in transit to the hospital. The passenger of the other vehicle, after reaching the hospital was airlifted to Alabama University Medical Hospital. She lost her leg, a lung and her spleen.

The driver had a blood alcohol content of .112 percent and had illegal drugs in her system, and it was believed that she had been texting, due to the phone being open to a text which was lying beside her. Her vehicle was cluttered with beer bottles. The eyewitness said that in his opinion, Brad, Samantha and Chris never knew what hit them. Brad never swerved or put on his brakes. He had no time to react.

Julie and I were in shock. For the next several days we didn't know what was going on around us. We met with Samantha's family at the funeral home to make arrangements. Chris' mom had decided to have him cremated. We called the funeral home where Chris was and asked if we could see him. They said yes, so Sandy, Julie's sister, drove us there. We went in to see Chris and he looked like he was asleep. Sandy walked up to him to say her goodbyes and as she walked away she looked at Julie and asked, "Do you smell that?" Julie looked at her and asked, "What?" Sandy said, "It's like fresh pure oxygen." Julie's mouth fell open as she glared at me. For the past two weeks I had been telling her that I smelled something like fresh pure oxygen. When Sandy said that she smelled it there in the funeral home, I had to sit down in the chair before I collapsed. Could it have been a sign?

At Brad and Samantha's wake, we had the coffins open for family only. We allowed our families to view the kids before the public were allowed to pay their respects. Brad looked so peaceful lying there. His face was swollen, but other than that he looked like he was asleep. My sister Crystal took Cindy up to the coffin to see him. Julie had always called Brad "son." Standing there watching Cindy, we were not sure how much she understood. When Brad was little and had a hard time sleeping, Julie would rub his forehead until he fell asleep. Cindy stood there looking down at Brad in the coffin. She leaned down and kissed him on the cheek and began rubbing his forehead like she had seen Julie do, repeating over and over, "Sleep, son, sleep." A tear ran down her cheek. We knew then that she understood.

Before the public viewing we closed the coffins. While standing there greeting everyone who came to pay their respects, we were amazed at the number of people who showed up. There were people from both our jobs, people from our church, the military squadron I had retired from, people from Samantha's family, Chris' family, and other people the kids knew. We could not believe our kids were dead. We were in a daze as we drove out to the cemetery for the funeral. As I sat there and listened to the eulogy, it just seemed so unreal, so unfair.

On Brad's last day of school, he allowed his friends to sign his car with permanent markers. So we thought it might help his friends face this horrific emptiness if we let them write messages to Brad on his coffin. Cindy even doodled on it. I wrote, "Rest in peace, my son, Daddy loves you. I will see you again." On Sam's I wrote, "Sleep well, my daughter, I love you." Julie and I stood there and watched as they lowered the coffins into the ground. I sprinkled Chris' ashes into the grave and took the first handful of dirt and dropped it on my son's coffin. I promised Brad, Sam and Chris that I would be their voice and I would not stop until I took my last breath. We slowly walked away, feeling like we were being buried in the grave with them.

Days turned into weeks and weeks into months. Nothing anyone could say or do could comfort us. We were just going through the motions. After two weeks I had to go back to work at the school district. There were days when I would get halfway there and have to turn around and go back home. I just couldn't do it. Over a period of six months I used up seventy-two days of leave. I would try to do my work, and as long as I stayed busy I was okay. Driving to the different schools where I worked was hardest, because idle time was not my friend. I would often pull up to the school where Brad and Samantha had attended, and break down in uncontrollable sobs because of the memories. The teachers would ask me how I was doing, and I would have to fight back the tears just to answer. Some of them avoided me to keep the thoughts of Brad and Samantha out of their heads because they were in disbelief of what had happened to them. Going to work became a burden, but a necessity to survive and clothe and feed us. Julie had quit her job because she was having severe panic attacks and the pain left her lifeless. She did not return to work for three years.

For ten months I walked around in a fog. It was so hard to face each day without the kids. I finally decided I needed to keep my promise to the kids to be their voice. I searched on the internet for MADD, Mothers Against Drunk Driving. I could volunteer and be their voice that way. I made contact with the state office but was not pleased with the response, so I called the national office in Irving, Texas. I talked with victim services and they made contact with the state office on my behalf. I first went through the Court Monitoring Program. This program taught volunteers how to sit in felony DUI court proceedings and make reports on the cases. After trying this for a while, it just didn't seem to be what I wanted to do to be a voice for the kids, so again I called MADD victim services to see what else I could do. They told me about their Victim Advocacy Program and asked if I would be interested in becoming a victim advocate. Not really knowing what I would do, I said yes. I completed the program and became a victim advocate, but I wanted to do more.

I wanted to tell my story to whoever would listen, so I started helping with the local Victim Impact Panel. It's a panel of victims who tell their stories to offenders who are ordered by the court to attend the class that MADD provides, but they didn't need me to tell my story, they just needed me to help with the paperwork. So I called victim services again. I heard that they needed volunteers to answer the MADD Helpline. So I volunteered for a four-hour shift every Friday night. Victims would call the helpline seeking advice, information or just needed someone to talk to. I would get their information and pass it on to the Victim Services coordinator who would then set them up with a victim advocate in their area. But this still was not enough.

Julie and I talked about starting our own nonprofit in the kids' memory, but then I received a phone call from MADD. They were contacting me to ask if I would be interested in being the Gulf Coast chapter leader. The previous leaders had stepped down and they needed someone to take over. I eagerly said yes. In March 2009 I became the contact person for MADD in my area and started coordinating activities. MADD was giving me what I needed to be the voice for my kids and every victim on the Gulf Coast. I was now the host for the Victim Impact Panel and I was able to tell the kids' story. It was a form of therapy for me. I was also able to go into schools, churches, military bases, and even businesses, talking about what had happened to our kids and how it had affected our lives and the lives of those around us. Julie eventually joined me by helping to do paperwork, but her emotions would not allow her to tell her story. She had found comfort by starting an online support group on Facebook. We finally felt that we were making a difference.

Volunteering for MADD gave us the opportunity to attend the MADD national conference in Washington, D.C., where we were able to lobby for the Ignition Interlock Law for first-time offenders and for approval of funding toward the research for car manufactures to produce vehicles that would be able to detect a person's breath alcohol content levels when starting the car. We also had the opportunity of meeting some of the members of the online support group Julie had started. Being a part of MADD helped both Julie and me to deal with the pain of losing our kids. We felt like we had a purpose in life, even though the sadness was still in our hearts. I became so busy in what I was doing for MADD that I had stopped grieving for my son. I lost myself in other victims' grief so I would not have to face my own. The anger and bitterness escalated with each new victim I met and with each new story I heard. I hid my pain deep inside.

Julie had grieved hard for three years and she was slowly finding a new normal. She missed the kids desperately, but she was moving forward. She started working again and started going to church. I wanted nothing to do with God. I blamed Him for my kid's death. Julie just assumed I was in the same place she was in our grief, but I wasn't, and this angered me also. She would try to talk to me about forgiveness and turning everything over to God, but I didn't want to hear it. Instead, I chose not to allow God to work in my heart as He had done in hers.

It wasn't until four years after the kids' death in 2011 that I had what I call a nervous breakdown. Though I was going through the motions of everyday life, work, church, and MADD, I still had not grieved for the kids. The bottled-up anger and grief became too much for me to bear, and I turned on God and I turned on my family. It was tearing me apart from the inside out. I became emotionally dead; I was like a walking dead person. I started cutting myself, trying to feel physical pain in order to relieve the emotional pain. I just wanted to die.

Julie and I began to drift apart, despite her attempts to break down the walls I was putting up. The one time I needed her most, I rejected her. I found it hard to talk to her because of my anger, guilt and denial. I drove a wedge between us, and she did not know why and neither did I. I emotionally left our marriage and told her I didn't love her any more. She was devastated. For over a year I gave her the cold shoulder and refused to seek help. The anger had completely taken me over. Julie turned to God. She loved me so much, yet she was losing me and I would not talk to her about what I was feeling, or what was tearing our marriage apart. She prayed every night for me, and I would lie there and pretend I was asleep so I would not have to respond. I kept pushing her farther and farther away. Her prayers were never-ending. She pleaded with God to touch my heart, to free me of my anger and hate so I would open my heart to Him, which in turn would reopen my heart to her. I am ashamed as I write this, but my anger had blinded me to the truth and it was tearing my marriage apart. I put Julie through hell trying to hurt God for taking my son.

After a year and two months, Julie had taken all she humanly could handle. She was through with being walked on and verbally and emotionally abused. If God would not do something, she would. She literally told me to leave. She said she would always love me, but she respected herself too much to put up with the way I was acting. She had tried, she had prayed and the only thing I did was throw it back at her in pain and anger. I left that night with so much anger in my mind and in my heart. The pain had consumed me. I drove down Highway 53 and as I approached the curve in which the kids had been killed I took my hands off the steering wheel and accelerated, heading for the tree that stood there. I was done fighting with God, with Julie and with the world. My life was meaningless and no one cared if I lived or died, especially me. I headed into that curve, hands at my sides; I wanted to end the hell I was living.

The next thing I remember I was sitting on the side of the road where my son had taken his last breath. I don't know how I missed the tree, but I just sat there and cried. It seemed like hours passed, but it had only been minutes. I drove back home.

I stumbled into the house to find that Julie had locked herself in the bedroom. I could hear her crying. I collapsed on the couch. I was exhausted from the emotions I was feeling and I slipped into a dreamful sleep. In my dream, I was standing in an enormous room. I could see God standing there and I shielded my eyes to protect my sight. I was screaming at Him, "Where were you when my kids needed you?" I stood there in front of Him, screaming louder, shaking my fist, "Where were you when my kids were killed? Why didn't you prevent it from happening? It is *your* fault they are dead!" As I stood there glaring at God, I was so angry that I collapsed to my knees. It was then when He spoke. I could not only hear His voice, but I could feel it.

He said, "Who are you to question me? Who are you to stand before me and pass judgment? I am your Father and I was at the same place when your son died as I was when my son died."

His words rumbled the floor where I knelt. I could see a tear in His eye, yet my anger and hate would not let me back down. I yelled, "You could have stopped this from happening. You could have saved them. They were just starting their lives."

He said, "Life is about choices. I choose not to interfere with the freedom of choice I have given man. The impaired driver killed your kids. She chose to drink and do drugs that night and then to drive. If I had intervened, I would have taken her choice away. Sadly, your kids paid for that choice."

I shook my fist at Him and said, "You call that fair? You think they wanted to die? I HATE THAT YOU DIDN'T SAVE MY SON! I want nothing to do with you! Get out of my life!"

God asked. "Is that really what you want?"

Feeling defeated, I said, "Yes, it's what I want."

God then said, "So be it. You will feel the darkness of being eternally separated from me. You will feel what every sinner will feel on the Day of Judgment."

As He spoke, He began to turn His face from me. The light of His divine glory began to fade and I was left in total darkness. It was pitch black. It reminded me of the caves Brad and I had gone into years before when we turned the flashlights off and you could feel the darkness, but this was worse than that. I have never known such despair and aloneness.

I became the nothingness, the darkness. I could feel the darkness of my soul overtaking me. The pain and fear one feels when facing death. I was that death; I was that damnation. It felt like it would never end. Just when I thought I would be consumed I heard Julie praying; I could *feel* her praying. In that moment, I knew I still had a chance to make things right, to choose to live.

I cried out with a voice I could not hear. I cried out, begging God to forgive me; to save me though I deserved to die. Just as I began to think I had waited too long to beg forgiveness, I felt His love. I could see a speck of light. I do not know from where it came, but it was there and it was growing, like a door opening. I saw His grace and love reaching for me; His voice calling me to Him.

As I stood there, I heard Him say, "Well, are you coming?" As I stepped through the door into the light, a tremendous intense pain began to burn in my body. My blood began to boil as if acid was flowing through my veins. The pain was so intense, seemingly from the inside out, I cried out to God, "I can't take this; take it from me!"

God gently said, "I cannot, my son, for it is the Holy Spirit cleansing your body of sin."

At that moment, I felt Julie's gentle tug on my arm. I came out of my dream, I looked into her eyes as she sat there on the side of the couch and I begged her for forgiveness as I sobbed in her arms. I begged her to take me back to give me another chance.

She gently kissed me and told me that she forgave me, and she held me like I had never been held by her before, and I held her. I told her I realized how wrong I was. I was hurting so bad; my grief took me places I did not want to go.

I realized when I stood before God how wrong I was.

I was looking in all the wrong places, looking for relief from the pain of my grief. I looked in her eyes and told her over and over how much I loved her and how sorry I was for hurting her. I had made a mistake and instead of turning to her, the pain and grief blinded me to the truth and to her. I had failed her and I was so sorry. I looked at her and said, "We will go to a counselor and get help." That morning at 3 a.m. on December 7, 2012, I gave my life to Christ. I felt the change in my heart.

Julie and I started counseling the next week. When we went to our first session, after telling the counselor what we had been through and what was going on, she looked at me and said, "Bill, you have not grieved your son and you are walking around like a dead man." The counselor had not spoken to us for more than fifteen minutes and yet she already knew what I was feeling. She told us that she could work with us on our marriage issues but she did not feel that we would get anywhere until I faced the pain of losing my son. She said I needed to grieve. So we agreed to grief counseling first. She gave me a homework assignment that I was to finish by the next week. She wanted me to make a list of what I lost when I lost my son.

I struggled with this for several days and waited until the last minute to make my list. This was hard for me. I had lost so much because of a choice that could have been avoided. A choice that sentenced me to a life without my son and all he was.

I had it in hand as I walked into the counselor's office for our second meeting. She listened to me as I explained my list to her. She asked me if it was hard to write, and I said "Very."

She said, "Okay, next week's assignment is going to be a little tougher."

I was thinking that nothing could be as hard as that. But when she told me that she wanted me to write a letter to Brad telling him everything I needed to tell him but couldn't. I told her that I didn't think I could do it. I felt like I had failed him as a father.

As he got older there were so many times when he wanted me to do something with him that I couldn't or wouldn't make time for. It seemed like I always had an excuse. I felt so guilty. I was his father, his protector and I was not even able to protect him from death. I agreed to try to write the letter.

We had taken a break from counseling because of Christmas, so I had two weeks to complete the letter. I started it over and over again. I didn't know what to say. I would pick up the pen and couldn't even see the paper because of the tears. My time was running out. I didn't want to show up at the counselor's office without having it done. I didn't want her to think I wasn't trying. So I sat down and started writing. It turned out to be the best thing I had ever done. I wrote from my heart and was able to tell Brad what he meant to me and how sorry I was for the things I should have done but didn't. I told him how proud of him I was and that it was an honor to be his father. The letter was several pages long and many tears were shed, but at the end when I wrote, "I will always love you and I promise to be your voice until I take my last breath," I could hear him in my heart saying, "Dad, I forgive you." With that letter I was able to take a step in the grieving process. I will never be over losing my son, but I am walking forward and each day I find something new to be thankful for.

On February 9, 2013, I dedicated my life to God during the morning church service through baptism and that night Julie and I renewed our wedding vows. I fell madly in love with my wife of thirty years again and we felt like newlyweds. We continued counseling for three months when the counselor said we could come each week if we felt like we still needed to, but she felt that we were back on track and that we did not need her any longer.

Our lives had come full circle. Julie and I were closer than we ever had been. We were back in church worshiping our Savior and we were being the kids' voice. We started talking again about starting our own nonprofit. We parted ways with MADD and on June 5, 2014, AVIDD-Advocates for Victims of Impaired & Distracted Driving was founded. The online support group that Julie started has become our main focus. We have a total of four groups now. One is for those who lost a loved one in a DUI crash, one for those injured in a DUI crash, one for those who have been impacted by distracted driving, and our fourth one for those who have been affected by boating under the influence, BUI. We also have an AVIDD VOICE class that we have once a month where the court orders DUI and distracted driving offenders to attend the class to hear victims tell their stories in hopes of educating them about the dangers of impaired or distracted driving. We are the voice of the victims.

God has truly taken a horrific event in my life and turned it into something positive. He pulled me out of the darkness into the light of His love. He has been with me through the worst time of my life. I see now that He never left me. It was not Him that killed my son, but the choice of an impaired driver. I have been blessed with a beautiful wife, daughter, and twenty-one years of memories with my son. The promise I made to the kids, to my son, to be their voice until I take my last breath will be carried out through AVIDD. This chapter in our lives has only begun.

Giving my life to Christ opened a door to many blessings and promises from God. Choosing to follow God's will and allowing Him to work through us through AVIDD, we know our voices will be heard and the memory of the kids will never die.

Life is about choices. Each choice we make affects not only our lives, but the lives of those around us. Whatever choice we make, we must be willing to face the consequences of our choices. I choose to believe that God will use our voices to change the lives of those we meet who are victims of impaired and distracted driving. If I can save one life, then I have fulfilled my mission from God.

BILL DOWNS
GULFPORT, MS
President/Co-Founder
AVIDD—Advocates for Victims of Impaired/Distracted Driving
Coauthor, *Grief Diaries: Loss by Impaired Driving*

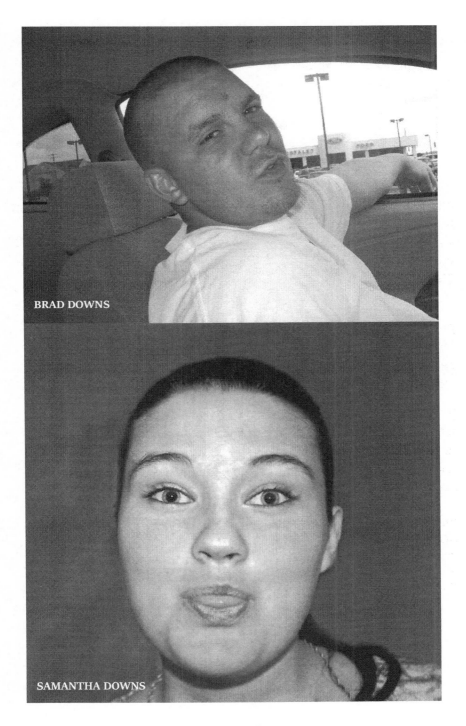

BRAD DOWNS

SAMANTHA DOWNS

BRAD DOWNS, SAMANTHA DOWNS, CHRIS DAFOE

CHRIS DAFOE

BRAD DOWNS, SAMANTHA DOWNS & CHRIS DAFOE

I HAVE A CHILD
By Julie Downs

I Have a Child.....
I have his death certificate but HE is not dead to me.
He will always live in my heart and in my memories.
As long as I have a breath, I will speak HIS name.
HE is never far from my thoughts and I love HIM the same.
For I will never allow HIS memory to fade.
As long as I have a breath I will speak HIS name: Brad.
I love and miss you, son.

*

CHRIS DAFOE, BRAD DOWNS & SAMANTHA DOWNS

CHAPTER FIVE

IS MY SON DEAD?

BY JULIE DOWNS

I loved you like there was no tomorrow –
and then one day, there wasn't.
AUTHOR UNKNOWN

I can hear myself screaming into the phone, "Is my son dead? Is my son dead? *Is my son dead?*" I hear the voice on the other end saying "Yes, ma'am, I believe he is. All three of them are dead. They didn't make it."

That voice on the phone was the beginning of the nightmare I have yet to wake up from. I still hear his words ringing in my ears.

October 6, 2007, was a Saturday, and the alarm went off at 5:30 a.m. I remember wondering what in the world I was thinking when I volunteered to work that day at the laundromat for my sister. I pulled the covers back and, being as quiet as I could so I would not disturb my sleeping husband, reluctantly crawled out of bed. The floor was cold on my feet as I walked through the quiet house. I needed coffee. I noticed as I passed the living room that the couch was empty and remembered that Chris, the young man whom my son had brought home almost a year before was in Jackson, Mississippi, visiting his girlfriend. It's strange how a person can come into your life and steal your heart. Chris was like a son to us. He was supposed to have stayed only for a couple of nights, sleeping on the couch until he found a place of his own, but those couple of nights had turned into almost a year and he was still with us and a big part of our lives. He called me Mom, and Bill, Dad. He told everyone that we were his family. He loved us as much as we had grown to love him.

As I got closer to the coffee pot I looked down the hall. Brad and Samantha's bedroom door was closed. They would be getting up soon to start their day. They had been married for three and a half months and were so in love. We loved that they lived with us but we knew that a day would be coming soon when they would move into their own place. They had so many hopes and dreams for their future. And we had hopes and dreams for them. Brad wanted to become a certified mechanic and was working hard at work to be promoted. Samantha wanted to go to college to become a teacher. They both wanted a houseful of babies, and I loved that idea because I wanted to spoil them and do the things that a grandmother gets to do.

I could hear my daughter, Cindy, moving around her bedroom. She was and is our miracle child. She had a blockage of oxygen at birth and was not expected to live. Thankfully, God had other plans for her. Although she is mentally challenged because of the brain damage and needs supervision at all times, she is truly a blessing. I had taken comfort in knowing that if anything were to happen to Bill and I that Brad and Samantha would step into our place and take care of her.

Cindy was going to work with me that morning so her daddy could sleep late. I worked with my mother and sisters running a coin laundry full-time. Bill's full-time job was with the Gulfport City Schools, but he would jump in and help at the laundromat whenever he was needed. He was scheduled to work that night to take the place of one of the girls who had taken the night off. It was an easy job for both of us and I liked the fact that I could take Cindy with me.

With coffee in hand and Cindy following me, we headed out the door. As soon as I got to the laundromat the phone rang; it was

Chris. He was fighting back tears as he told me that he was on his way home. He said that things didn't work out with his girlfriend and he had made a mistake by going to see her. I wanted to tell him "I told you so," but I held my tongue because he was so upset. He was confused on what road he needed to be on to get home, so I told him to head south and to call his dad for directions. Jackson is two and a half hours north of us.

Bill called me around 10 a.m. to let me know that he had gotten Chris on the right road and that he was up and slowly getting motivated. Brad and Sam were outside doing yardwork. Brad hoped that if he cleared the back side of the property, the building code office would allow him to put a trailer out there for him and Sam. We told him that we didn't think they would allow it but that he could try. We didn't want to discourage him too much because he was out working in the yard. Minutes and then hours ticked away on the clock, and before I knew it, Bill was pulling up at the laundromat to relieve me. He was hungry, so I ran and grabbed hamburgers and french fries for dinner. Cindy and I stayed for a while and ate with him and then went home about 5 p.m.

As I was driving down the road my phone rang. It was Chris. He wanted me to stop and get him, Brad and Sam something to eat. He said they were hungry. I told him that the refrigerator was full of food and that they were adults and could cook something to eat. He said "But Mom, pleaseeeee." I asked him who was going to pay for it, and he said "You are." My thought was, "Will they ever grow up?" Shaking my head, I gave in to him and told him okay.

I pulled into Backyard Burgers and went through the drive through. Sitting there looking at the menu, I chuckled to myself and ordered three kid meals with the toy and kiddie drink. If they couldn't cook for themselves then I would treat them like kids. Besides, I figured they would get a laugh out of it. Brad and Chris must have been really hungry because they did not even let me get all the way down the driveway before they were out of the house getting their food. The look on their faces when they saw the kid meals was priceless. Chris proclaimed, "Kid's meals? We are not children!" I just raised my eyebrow and smiled as I looked at him with a smirk on my face. Brad said, "Gosh, Mom. We're going to have to stop and get us something else when we leave. This is not going to fill us up." I smiled more while laughing inside, thinking that their acting like helpless kids was what prompted me to buy the kid meals in the first place. And since I got stuck paying for them, the kid meals were cheaper. We went inside and all three of them laughed and made jokes about what I had done as they sat at the table eating. They even opened their toys and were messing with them. Sam gathered up the toys and Brad pretended to throw a fit and we all got a laugh out of that. She gave the toys to Cindy who loved them. I didn't know at that time, nor did they, that this would be their last meal.

Brad and Sam had planned to meet some friends that night but with Chris being upset about his girlfriend, they canceled their plans and decided to hang out with him and go to the car races in hopes of cheering him up. Chris had offered to pay their way, and Brad and Sam did not want to pass that up. They jumped into Chris' truck and left the house around 6 p.m. only to return within the hour. The races had been canceled because the track was wet from rain earlier in the day. Instead of being disappointed, they just changed their plans and decided to go to the movies. As they were getting ready I sat there and listened to them laughing and teasing each other as they changed clothes, feeling blessed to have each one of them in my life. Chris suggested to Sam to leave her hair down and even helped her by tucking it behind her ears. I was surprised because Chris and Sam had a love-hate relationship and most of the time they couldn't stand each other, but this time she let him touch her without going off on him. Brad changed his shoes several times until he had just the right pair on. He and Sam dressed in the same colors, black and white.

They decided to take Brad's car instead of Chris' truck. As they were leaving, Chris gave me a hug and told me he loved me. I told him to have a good time and that I loved him also. As Brad went to walk past me, Chris nudged him and told him to hug me. Brad jumped back, teasingly throwing his arms into the air and saying, "I'm not going to hug her." We laughed, and I popped him in the stomach and told them to go and have fun. As Sam walked past, I told her that she looked pretty; she smiled and followed Chris out the door. When Brad got to the door he stopped and turned, and for the last time I heard him call me "Mom." He told me that he loved me and that he would see me when they got home. I told him that I loved him also and for them to be careful and to have fun. And they were gone; gone from my life forever. I can only speculate on what happened in the next thirty minutes, but I do know that the choice made by an individual to drink and drive changed the lives that I loved in the blink of an eye.

Bill called at 9:35 p.m. to tell me that he had to detour around a car crash on Highway 53, three miles from where we lived. He said he had never seen so many emergency vehicles in one place at the same time. He told me to say a prayer because it wasn't good. I told him to be careful and that I would call the kids to make sure they were okay, and to tell them to avoid the area on their way home. Brad didn't answer his phone. It went to voicemail. I hung up and called Samantha. She didn't answer either. I tried Brad again; same thing—voicemail. It wasn't unusual for Brad not to answer his phone when he was at the movie, but Sam always answered hers. So I called her again; no answer. And I knew. I felt it in the pit of my stomach, but my heart didn't want it to be them. It just couldn't be them.

I called Bill and told him that they didn't answer and that he needed to go back to the roadblock and make sure they were okay. I then called Chris and he didn't answer either. I knew it was them. Bill called back and said the police would not let him through the roadblock. I was furious, but I am so thankful now that they did not let him through. Seeing his son dead would have been totally devastating to him, something he probably would never have recovered from. I paced the floor with tears and fear. My mind would not acknowledge that they could be dead. "DEAD" was a concept I could not comprehend. I was trying to hold on to the hope that it wasn't them. I was panicking over not knowing when my brother Alan knocked on the door. Bill had called him and told him to get to me and not let me leave. All I had wanted to do was get into my car and find my kids.

My two sisters, Susan and Sandy, showed up and we started calling everyone we could think of as we stood outside, watching and waiting. We called the police station, the Sheriff's office, the highway patrol, Brad, Sam and Chris and even the hospitals. We kept in contact with Bill as he frantically searched for answers neither one of us wanted to know.

I finally talked with someone at the hospital who said two of the victims involved in the crash were there. I called Bill and told him to get to the hospital and make sure they were okay. I heard Alan talking on his phone and he asked me questions that the person on the other end asked him. He asked if Brad had a dealer tag on his car. I told him yes, he did. He had gotten the car only three weeks earlier and had not gotten his tag yet. It was his dream car, a Ford Mustang. He hadn't even made the first payment. Alan then asked if Brad was going into town or coming home. I told him that he was going into town. They were going to the movies.

I couldn't take it any longer, so I grabbed the phone away from Alan and said "Hello?!"

The voice on the other end said, "Mrs. Downs, this is Gary Hargrove, the Harrison County coroner. Could you please tell me what Chris looks like?" My thought was, "The coroner, oh no. The coroner means death."

I told him that Chris had blondish-red hair, and then screamed, "*Is my son dead?*" He didn't answer, and instead asked how tall Chris was. I screamed, "At least six feet. *Is my son dead? Is my son dead?*" The silence on the other end of the phone was deafening, and then the voice said, "Yes, ma'am, I believe he is. All three of them are dead. They didn't make it."

I threw the phone, and it hit Alan in the chest as I fell to my knees screaming at the top of my lungs. My cries broke the night's silence. "Nooooooooo...nooooooo, not my baby! Nooooo, not my kids!" In a panic, I jumped up and got into the passenger seat of my car begging someone, anyone, to take me to the hospital where Bill was. I had to get to him. He was fixing to hear news that would destroy him like it had just destroyed me. My sister got into the car and we left for the hospital. In shock and disbelief, I dialed Bill's number. I didn't want some stranger telling him that his son was dead. When I heard his voice I said, "Bill, Bill, your baby didn't make it. He's gone. All three of them are gone." In the twenty-five years we've been married, I've never before heard cries like those that echoed from the phone. And then I heard the phone drop and it went dead. I tried calling Bill back, but he didn't answer.

Mr. Hargrove met me at the emergency room entrance. I wanted him to tell me that my son was alive and well, but he didn't change his story. He told me that my son was indeed dead. He took me to a little room where Bill was and as soon as we saw each other we fell into each other's arms, crying like we had never cried before. Nothing made sense.

I was so afraid that somehow my son was responsible for Samantha and Chris' death. I needed to hear what had happened. The coroner said that Brad was not at fault in any way. He said the other vehicle was speeding at eighty miles per hour when she lost control going around a curve, crossed into Brad's lane, hitting them head on. Brad never knew what hit him. He and Samantha died on impact from blunt force trauma.

Mr. Hargrove said that if Brad would have been delayed by seconds, the other car would have crossed in front of his, hitting the ditch. My mind immediately went to them leaving the house earlier that night. If I had insisted on that hug from Brad, instead of telling them to go and have fun, I could have delayed their leaving and they would likely still be alive. Not only did I miss out on my last hug, but I could have saved them.

The coroner's next words are branded into my very being. He said, "Unofficially, the driver of the other vehicle was drunk." He said they would not know for sure until her blood alcohol level test came back, but she had open beer cans in her vehicle and was wearing a wristband from a local bar. The anger immediately took over. Who in their right mind would drink and drive? My kids had been murdered. It was not an accident. The crash could have been prevented if she had made a better choice. My kids did not have to die. Bill's mom and dad arrived at the hospital, and the look of pain in their eyes was too much to bear. The reality of the situation showed on each of our faces. We were devastated.

I wanted to see my son but they said that he and Sam were taken straight to the funeral home and I would have to contact them. Chris and the passenger of the other vehicle were there at the hospital. Chris had a faint heartbeat so they had to transport him. His neck was broken and he died en route. How could that be possible? They had just left the house a couple of hours before this, full of life. They were laughing and smiling. Chris was supposed to start his new job on Monday. I had washed his uniforms for him so they would be nice and fresh. Brad and Sam had just started their life together. They couldn't be dead. THEY WERE JUST ALIVE! It couldn't be true. I wanted to wake up from the nightmare that we had been thrown into. It wasn't fair.

The next several days are a blur. There were so many decisions that had to be made. We had a funeral to plan. We had to pick a cemetery, choose a plot, pick out a coffin, order flowers, and decide what clothes we wanted them to wear. We had to pick pallbearers, write an obituary, and pick out pictures and music. We had to answer phone calls and explain over and over to family and friends what had happened. We had to say our goodbyes. I didn't know how to say goodbye to someone I couldn't live without. We had to bury our son, our hopes and dreams for him, our future grandkids, our friend, our heart, and our daughter-in-law. We had to constantly remind ourselves to breathe. But the hardest thing was telling Brad's handicapped sister that three people she adored were never coming home. How do you explain something like that to someone who will not totally understand? Cindy didn't know what "dead" meant. She didn't comprehend "forever." We did the best we could to try to explain. Between the time of the crash and the day of the funeral she constantly asked where Brad, Sam and Chris were. She knew something was wrong because she tried to console me in my tears. She would just hold me in her arms and whisper, "Shhhh, shhhh."

I called the funeral home every day asking if I could see Brad. They had one excuse after another, and I was so emotionally weak that I didn't argue. We did get to see Chris before his family had him cremated. He looked like he was asleep. He had a bruise on his forehead but other than that he looked perfectly fine. His mother gave us some of his ashes so we could bury him with Brad and Sam. The day of the funeral finally came. Bill and I had a private moment with Brad and Sam before we let the family come in. I had myself convinced that when I finally saw who they were saying was Brad that I would be able to tell them that it wasn't him, but I was wrong. My son was really dead. His face was swollen but I could tell it was him; my precious baby.

Our private time was almost over and we walked across the room to see our beautiful Samantha. My heart was outside of my body. Sam's side of the car had received the brunt of the impact. She was broken. It didn't even look like her, but I stood there and ran my fingers through her beautiful black hair. We had brought from home the teddy bear that Brad had gotten her and tucked it beside her. When she and Brad were apart she would sleep with the bear wrapped in her arms.

It was time for us to say goodbye. I kissed her on the cheek and told her I loved her. We stood there as the funeral director lowered the lid on her coffin. We had chosen to have a closed coffin ceremony for friends and guests, but we did keep Brad's coffin open for family. Our family started coming in. They would get their time to say goodbye to Brad. I was standing there beside Brad, numb, in disbelief and nonfunctioning, when my sister-in-law Crystal brought Cindy up to see her brother. Crystal explained to her that Brad was with Jesus. Cindy bent and kissed Brad on the cheek and stood there rubbing his forehead saying, "Sleep…sleep." That was something we had done when he was a baby and couldn't sleep. When I saw the tear run down her cheek it was then that I knew she did understand that she was saying goodbye. We all had to say goodbye.

It has been eight and half years, and the intense pain has eased but the heartache is still there. Not a day goes by that I don't long to be with my son. That tragic night changed everything for me. It wasn't a gradual change; it happened immediately when part of me died in that crash with those kids. It took two years for me to be able to breathe. I had to quit work because the panic attacks were so severe that they left me lifeless. I feared everything and found comfort in nothing. I isolated myself inside my house and didn't leave for two years unless someone was with me. I would spend my days searching the internet for my sanity. I read everything I could find on grief and the loss of a child. I found comfort among those who understood what I was going through. I started a Facebook support group in 2008 for victims of impaired driving so that we, the victims, could have a safe place to get and give support. We had reached out to MADD and found no support there until Bill joined ten months after the kids had been killed and started volunteering. I joined MADD a year later. We found comfort in fighting the fight against drunk driving. Six years after the kids had been killed we left MADD and founded our own nonprofit, AVIDD — Advocates for Victims of Impaired/Distracted Driving. We then changed the name of our Facebook support group to reflect our nonprofit. AVIDD operates a total of four online support groups on Facebook.

For victims who have lost a love one:
Facebook.com/groups/AVID4DUIvictims

For victims who have been injured or have an injured loved one and survived: Facebook.com/groups/AVID4DUIsurvivors

For victims who have been impacted by a Distracted Driving Crash: Facebook.com/groups/AVID.Distracted

For victims who have been impacted by boating under the influence crash: Facebook.com/groups/AVIDDimpairedboatingvictims

The drunk driver who killed my kids also died in the crash that night. I was left with hate and anger toward her for the choice she made. I have never hated anyone like I have hated her. But I can honestly say today that I have forgiven her. I have released the hate and anger and given it to God, and in its place is a sense of peace. In forgiving her, I released the hold that her actions had on me. My forgiveness does not say that what she did was okay, because it is not. My forgiveness is allowing me to let go of the bitterness and hate that was eating at me and stopping me from taking a step forward in my grief. I will never be over the death of my kids, and I will miss them every day for the rest of my life. And I promise that I will keep their memory alive and I will be their voice against impaired/distracted driving until I take my last breath.

JULIE DOWNS
SAUCIER, MISSISSIPPI
Secretary/Co-Founder, AVIDD-Advocates for Victims of Impaired/Distracted Driving and coauthor of *Grief Diaries: Loss by Impaired Driving*

BRAD DOWNS WITH MOM (JULIE)

BRAD DOWNS WITH DAD (BILL) AND SISTER (CINDY)

SAMANTHA DOWNS

BRAD DOWNS

BRAD & SAMANTHA DOWNS

CHRIS DAFOE

CHAPTER SIX

A BUTTERFLY AMONG US

BY NANCY EDWARDS

Jennifer-Leigh Edwards Zartman
May 8, 1985 – August 5, 2006

The butterfly is nature's way of reminding us that there is hope in grief. When the caterpillar is no more, the butterfly exists in ultimate freedom and beauty. -TANYA LORD

Family…parenthood…motherhood…children. As far back as I can remember I wanted to be a mother. I don't think there is a harder nor more important job than to be a parent. So of course I was ecstatic to learn I was expecting! I could hardly contain my excitement as I planned how I would announce it to my husband, Randy Zartman. My pregnancy was textbook perfect! I had none of the common complaints of pregnancy such as swelling, morning sickness, heartburn, aches and pains. I gained only nine pounds. I ate healthier, walked more and felt better than I ever had. Yep, I was also happier than I'd ever been.

We planned to have another child to share our love, and Katie arrived when Jenny was almost three and a half years old. I had always wanted four children but we decided two was a better choice for us. Our family was complete! My dream had come true! I was married to my soulmate. We had two adorable healthy, well adjusted children and lived in a small but lovely home in Charlotte,

North Carolina. We had support from both of our families. Randy was a glazier foreman and I was a licensed clinical social worker. Life was incredible! So why did I have this feeling of doom hanging over my head all the time? I remember telling Randy and a few close friends long ago that my life was too perfect, almost too good to be true. I had this sick feeling for years that something was going to happen to one of my children. I was told to stop worrying! Still, I just couldn't shake it.

I was always intrigued by the complexity of Jenny's mind. I knew we were going to have our hands full trying to keep her challenged in school when at the age of four she asked me why clouds don't fall from the sky after we discussed the principle of gravity! Reading was already her passion. As early as first grade, Jenny was looking for ways to help those around her. Finishing her class work before the other students, this six-year-old, whose reading skills already far outpaced most of her classmates, began helping kindergartners learn to read. This was also the year Jenny joined the Girl Scouts, an organization that would become a key part of her life. She was hooked! She loved making others happy, and helping them made her happy! Scouting provided her the opportunities to feed her passion.

We like to tell the story of a night when Jenny was eight years old. I noticed her bedroom light on, long past her curfew. I marched in there, ready to lecture her about the importance of getting adequate sleep and following the "lights out" rule, only to find her reading the Webster's Dictionary! I couldn't scold her for reading the dictionary! Who does that? Instead, I told her not to read much longer as I stepped out of the room, shaking my head in amazement.

Typically, students are tested in the third grade for admission into the Program for Exceptional Students. Jenny was granted early admission in the second grade to keep her mind stimulated. She began mentoring a Hispanic English as Second Language student in the third grade. During fourth through sixth grades, Jenny worked in her school's program helping physically challenged students. In grades seven and eight, Jenny worked with Katie as pet therapy volunteers in a nursing home. Those same years, she and Katie also worked with Hands On Charlotte, an organization that links volunteers with a variety of social agencies throughout Charlotte. Many Saturday mornings were spent making cards for terminally ill children. Jenny raised the most money in her school for St. Jude Children's Research Hospital. In the eighth grade, she teamed with Michael Stewart to create an award-winning public service video for Substance Abuse Awareness Month that was used by the Mecklenburg County Drug Awareness Council.

As Jenny entered high school, she began three years of volunteering at Carolina's Medical Center. After completing the first year, the Neurology Department asked Jenny to assist in the selection and review of patient records to help identify those eligible to participate in a medical research project. No previous student volunteer had been given that responsibility.

From Brownie Scout to Senior Scout, for sixteen years Girl Scouting was one of the constants in Jenny's life. She also participated in Explorer Scouts, a co-ed program. Jenny loved being an assistant leader for a Daisy Scout Troop and eventually became a lifetime member of the Girl Scouts. After nine summers as a camper, she spent several summers as a counselor-in-training, then as a counselor at Girl Scout Camp Occoneechee, missing only one summer to attend Governor's School. Her family and I were so proud to see her receive Girl Scouting's two highest awards, the Silver and Gold Awards. Only five percent of all Girl Scouts nationwide earn the prestigious Gold Award. Her Silver Award project was collecting over eight hundred new and gently used children's books to donate to the children living at our women's shelter. She also volunteered to read to the younger residents several times. The project portion of her Gold Award was collecting new baby items and pretty baskets and distributing them to sixty indigent expectant women.

Jenny was the first and only Scout in the Hornet's Nest Girl Scout Council allowed to be a Troop's Cookie Manager. Previously, a parent had always held this position since it meant coordinating the ordering and distribution of the entire troop's cookie orders and managing several thousand dollars. No surprise to anyone who knew her, Jenny was selected by the Hornet's Nest Girl Scout Council to serve for two years as an ambassador promoting Camp Occoneechee. Her enthusiasm and passion for Scouting was contagious!

Jenny was seventeen when her teachers selected her to attend Governor's School in biology. The Governor's School of North Carolina is a prestigious six-week residential program for intellectually gifted rising high school seniors. As club president of HOSA, Jenny represented her school, advancing to the Regional Health Occupation Student Association competition, and bringing home medals! Always interested in obstetrics, she earned a nearly perfect score on her Senior Exit project on Unnecessary Cesarean Sections. In addition to playing on the soccer team, she was an officer in Harding High School's National Honor Society and Spanish Honor Society. In 2003, she received the Presidential Award for Educational Excellence and was selected as her high school's 2003 choice for Carolina's Outstanding Graduate. She graduated summa cum laude from Harding High School. In addition to receiving a National Merit Scholarship, Jenny was also selected as the 2003 recipient of the Hornet's Nest Girl Scout Council's Gold Scholarship for outstanding contributions to her community and for exceptional grades.

Michael and Jenny's friendship grew exponentially over the nine years since they made the PSA video. They were inseparable. She called him her lobster because lobsters mate for life. He was her soulmate and fiancé. They were opposed to slave trafficking and work conditions in the African diamond mines, so Jenny chose a moissanite stone for her engagement ring. Although they considered canceling the wedding to protest the banning of same-sex marriages, plans were under way for a beautiful June wedding at the Daniel Stowe Botanical Gardens in Belmont, North Carolina.

Off to the University of North Carolina at Chapel Hill in the fall of 2003, she was one of two hundred and sixty out of the four thousand freshmen enrolled who were selected for the UNC Honors Program. Jenny received UNC's 2003 William Richardson Davie Scholarship, given in recognition of superior academic achievement and leadership. While maintaining the dean's list every semester, Jenny volunteered as an instructor with the English as Second Language Program at UNC for 2003-2004. She taught English to Russians, Latinos, French, Italians, and Germans among others and was appointed co-director of the program for 2004-2005.

Majoring in biology for pre-med and minoring in Spanish in preparation for the accelerated program for Bachelor of Science in Nursing, she struggled with the difficult decision between becoming an obstetrician or a certified nurse midwife. Jenny eventually decided the midwifery philosophy was more congruent with her philosophy of childbirth. While maintaining her grades and volunteer work, she completed the rigorous training program to become a certified doula, a birthing coach, and served as a volunteer doula at UNC Hospital in Chapel Hill. Enthralled with the miracle of birth, she particularly enjoyed working with the indigent Spanish-speaking patients. She often spoke of her dream to open a birthing center for them. Fluent in Spanish, she was accepted to study in Xalapa, Mexico at the University of Veracruz in 2005. She touched the lives of her host family and the other residents of Xalapa.

Trying new things was exhilarating. She had fun whether it was taking a local cooking class or riding a llama bareback. While there, she financially sponsored two endangered sea turtles and released them back into the sea. Back in the States, she recruited her college friends to volunteer with her in the UNC Domestic Violence Awareness program and the UNC Breast Cancer Awareness program. Jenny never hesitated to take on controversial challenges such as LGBT rights and equal pay for women. Nor would she step away from a confrontation if she felt someone was being a bully, a racist or just being insensitive. I remember one incident where she called out a good friend during dinner when the friend was rude to their server!

Jennifer was selected to be a resident advisor in her dormitory for the 2005-2006 academic year and then was hired by the university as the office manager for the new five dormitory complex, Ram Village. She had just completed the first week training her staff of fourteen office assistants when she left to help a cousin in Wilmington, North Carolina, that fateful August night.

"Be the change you wish to see in the world." This quote by Gandhi was one of Jenny's favorites, and those who knew her also knew that those were words by which she genuinely lived. To know Jenny was to love her. Somehow, she always managed to find a way to make those around her feel better, whether it was by lending a helping hand, making people laugh, or simply by listening to them. She made others want to be better persons. Her teachers and friends refer to her as compassionate, insightful, inspirational to others and passionate about life. Acknowledging, but not focusing on her brilliance, they also describe her as having attributes such as leadership, honesty, and joyfulness. She loved music and although she couldn't carry a tune in a bucket, she would belt out songs unashamedly, especially camp songs! She played on her high school soccer team, and what she lacked in athleticism she made up for in her enthusiasm and determination to do her best for the team.

So many sides to Jenny! She could be serious and contemplative or silly and mischievous. In many ways she was an old soul. She was the life of the party, and her ability to laugh at herself and to help others not to take everything so seriously drew people to her like moths to a flame. How we miss that belly-shaking, deep laugh that made her eyes twinkle! She taught us that letting our inner child out is healthy and invigorating. Jenny loved to puddle jump, especially during a warm spring rain. She and Katie would squeal with delight as we all kicked off our shoes and ran out into the rain. Laughing until our sides hurt, we would jump in the puddles, trying to splash higher than everyone else. Then we would race to find the biggest puddle to plop down in together. There was never a dry speck on anyone. We still puddle jump, especially if it rains on her birthday!

Mommy disclaimer: A friend reading my rough draft asked why I included so many of Jenny's accomplishments. I explained that I want everyone to know that, yes, I grieve for my precious daughter but I also grieve because this incredible young woman who had so much to offer and who would have done so much to improve society was taken from all of them as well. There will be one less strong woman fighting for the underprivileged, the discriminated, and the downtrodden. This book is my opportunity to be her voice and to let everyone know just how special she was.

After moving Jenny into her dorm room to start her senior year at UNC-Chapel Hill, Randy and I flew to Naples, Florida, for a week of relaxation and we would then drive home in a car we bought for Katie. Jenny called Friday night saying she was driving to Wilmington to help her cousin Whitney. I begged her to wait until morning but she insisted she'd be fine and would call upon her arrival. I tried to watch TV and play computer games to pass the time until she called to say she had arrived safely. I couldn't concentrate. I had a nagging feeling that wouldn't go away.

Once I had allowed plenty of time for her to arrive in Wilmington, I became concerned when I didn't hear from her. As the minutes crept by, I grew more and more uneasy. My husband wrote it off as my typical worrying, rolled over and fell asleep. Finally I began calling Jenny. No answer. I called her cousin. No answer. Over and over again, hitting speed dial. First Jenny, then Whitney. No answer. By now I was panicking, overwhelmed with a foreboding sense of disaster. I woke up Randy so he could join my efforts to reach one of the girls.

Sometime later that night, Katie called, saying there was a highway patrol officer at our home asking for us. I felt nauseated as I instructed her to put him on the phone.

Initially the officer refused to tell me anything because we weren't home. Exasperated and protective of Katie and the friend staying with her, I vehemently told the officer, "You can't show up at our home at 2 a.m. and not tell us what happened. You are terrifying our other daughter, Katie. She is only seventeen!" I explained that her father and I were in Naples. "Tell me what happened or put someone on the damn phone who can!"

Now out of control and hysterical, I was screaming at him, "She's dead. She's dead, isn't she? Tell me. I know she's dead!"

Then he confirmed a parent's worst nightmare! Jenny had been killed just three miles from her cousin's apartment.

The officer said the highway patrol had received several calls about a car traveling at an excessive speed going the wrong direction on Interstate 40 in Wilmington and were on their way to stop him. By the time Derrick M. crashed head-on into Jenny, he had driven four miles westbound in an eastbound lane! His vehicle hit hers with such force that the impact sent Jenny's car airborne. It landed partially on another car. Miraculously, the family of five in that car received only minor injuries. Reportedly, my Jenny died instantly, as did the drunk driver, Derrick. His blood alcohol level was greater than three times the limit. The medical examiner did not test for drugs although Derrick had a police record for prior drug charges.

I was hysterical as I called my four siblings to tell them Jenny was dead. Arrangements were made for my brother, Bill, to go stay with Katie until we could get to Charlotte. Unable to understand what I was saying, one sister called back to clarify who had been killed, my daughter Jenny or our sister, Ginny. Hanging up from the last call, a strange calmness and numbness fell over my body. In silence, Randy and I made the bed and packed up our things.

Just going through the motions, we loaded dishes into the dish-washer and even fed the fish. Not thinking clearly, I felt we had to straighten up my sister's house before we left. Then came the difficult part of driving just a few streets away to my parents' home. How do you tell your elderly parents whom you've just awakened from a deep sleep that their twenty-one-year-old granddaughter has just been killed by a drunk driver? I will never forget the look on my father's face as he collapsed onto the sofa. It still haunts me today. In shock, my mother just kept repeating, "What do you mean she's dead?" "What do you mean she's dead?" My oldest sister, Barrett, called a friend to come stay with our parents until she could fly in from Colorado. Another sister, Darcy, flew from Virginia to Wilmington to be with our niece and to handle the cremation arrangements.

Having notified family, Randy and I started the dreadful drive from Naples to Wilmington. We were certainly in no condition to drive, but I insisted we get to Wilmington. Devastated, I had to get to my baby! It was normally a thirteen-hour drive, but I remember stopping several times because we were crying so hard that it wasn't safe to drive. Losing a child is horrendous enough, but having to drive so far after receiving the horrifying news was almost too much to bear. Poor Randy had to drive the entire way because I was in such shock, almost paralyzed! I remember at some point in the trip finally realizing we needed to get to Katie, not Jenny. There was nothing we could do for Jenny. Katie needed us more, so we pushed forward and arrived home early the next afternoon. There are so many things I can't remember, such as whether Katie was home when we arrived. I can't recall having any conversations about Jenny with her during the first month.

Jenny had wanted to be cremated when she died. As her parents, we had to authorize the cremation. Since we were in Charlotte and Jenny was still in Wilmington, we had to have the authorization notarized and faxed to the crematorium. I was too emotionally distraught to walk inside to the notary, so someone brought the authorization form to me. Having to sign the paper was still impossible until someone held my trembling hand and guided the pen. How could I sign this? What if she wasn't dead? Maybe she was just in a deep coma! I couldn't let them burn her alive. Wait! Maybe it wasn't her. It was someone from the other car. They just needed to find my Jenny. I could hardly breathe! I thought my chest was going to explode. My head was spinning as my world crashed down around me.

A few days later, my brother and sister-in-law drove us to Wilmington to bring Jenny home, another incredibly difficult, long drive. Everyone tried to talk me out of going, but nobody was keeping me from bringing my baby home! Strange as it may sound, I carried the Sunday comics with me because Jenny loved reading the comics! Looking back, I find it amazing how seemingly insignificant things suddenly become powerful! Ten years later and those comics are still on her dresser.

So many painful things had to be done. We had to endure hearing Jenny that couldn't be an organ donor, something she'd told everyone she wanted to be. So many people to notify! There were contracts for her wedding to cancel. It seemed like everyone, from the credit card companies and banks to the insurance company needed a copy of the death certificate. We received so many letters addressed to Jenny from ambulance chasers, wanting to "help" her sue Derrick! Ten years later and we still receive mail addressed to her! It really stings!

Randy and I had to go to Chapel Hill to retrieve her things from her office and dorm room. Several people from the university were on hand to help with this difficult task. Having completed enough college credits in high school to begin at UNC as a sophomore, she had earned her degree in three years and was awarded her diploma posthumously. Had she finished the fourth year, Jenny would have graduated from UNC with high honors.

I returned to work the week following Jenny's death. Unable to face the reality of our tragedy, I developed a remarkable ability to push the demon of truth back into its cave when it tries to break free. I wasn't sure I could keep it together, because working with patients in an obstetrics clinic was a constant reminder of jenny's dream of becoming a certified midwife in her own birthing center.

The first few years, I couldn't make myself counsel patients charged with driving while intoxicated. I never did, but I wanted to lash out at them, wanted to show them Jenny's picture and make them listen to how my family's lives were ruined because someone just like them drove drunk. It is still difficult, but I tighten the straps on my professional mask, make sure the demon is locked in its cave, and I objectively counsel them on the dangers of driving impaired.

Still unable to grasp that my precious Jenny was dead, I forced myself to read the medical examiner's report repeatedly. I kept challenging people to tell me how anyone could know with one hundred percent certainty that Jenny died instantly. I spent hours every night lying in bed ruminating about how terrified she had to have been in those last moments. Did she die instantly as they reported, or was she alive as her car sailed through the air? Maybe she didn't die until her car landed. I obsessed over the photos from the wreck, desperately searching for answers. I was trying to break through the robe of denial I was wearing, but I was unfazed by what I saw. I hoped seeing Derrick's lifeless body sprawled across the front seat of his car would help me accept what happened. Instead, seeing him only made me angry that he died instantly when his neck snapped like a twig. He didn't suffer and by God, I wanted him to have lived in excruciating pain, even if only briefly! Looking at the photos didn't have any effect on me. It was surreal looking at them and thinking this is the wreck they say killed my daughter, but how could that be? The mind has an incredible way of protecting us from the unbearable, doesn't it?

When I started writing this story, I finally got up the nerve to ask my niece, Whitney, about the wreck. We'd not spoken of it previously. For a while she blamed herself, although we never did. She shared her vivid memories about that night, saying Jenny had called her to let her know she was almost there. When Jenny didn't arrive ten minutes later, Whitney began to worry. After she began to receive my back-to-back calls, Whitney felt something was terribly wrong. Rather than answer my calls, she and her boyfriend went to look for Jenny, desperately hoping to find her changing a flat tire on the side of the road. When they came upon multiple flashing lights on the other side of the interstate, Whitney said she knew it was her cousin. She slowed her vehicle down but jumped out while it was still moving and began running across the highway median, screaming Jenny's name.

Several highway patrol officers stopped her just before she could reach the wreck. It was necessary to physically restrain her to keep her away from Jenny's car. Concerned for Whitney's emotional state, they insisted she wait in one of the ambulances to block her view of the wreck. Whitney recalled asking repeatedly during the ninety minutes she was there if her cousin was alive, yet knowing the answer because none of the officers would answer her. "If Jenny were alive," she thought, "they would tell me." The officers would not let her answer her cell phone. Whitney refused to leave the scene of her own volition, so the officers had her boyfriend drive her home with a police escort and the under-standing that she was not to return. The interstate remained closed for four hours while the highway patrol's Reconstruction Unit determined what had happened.

When people talk about how their lives have been forever changed by the bad decisions of others, they seldom mention guilt, yet I still struggle with the guilt that neither my husband nor I were able to be the support Katie needed desperately. We were so devastated and drowning in our own grief that we failed her. "She understands," friends tell me, but that doesn't soften the guilt. Charlotte is fortunate to have a wonderful organization, Kinder Mourn, which works with families and individuals experiencing the death of a child. All of us attending a few family sessions and also having Katie attend the teen group for several weeks helps me feel somewhat less guilty, but the truth is that we were not there for her when she needed us.

Even though Jenny was three and a half years older than Katie, they were quite close. They loved and respected each other. It wasn't easy following in Jenny's footsteps! This resulted in a little jealousy on Katie's part and led to an occasional sibling rivalry flare-up. I don't know if Jenny ever admitted it to Katie, but she was so proud of her little sister, even trying things because Katie had done them. Katie played soccer in middle school and inspired her sister to try out. They attended camp together every summer. If Katie had questions about homework, boys, or makeup, she always turned to her sister. Jenny looked to Katie for advice on fashion, music, and soccer. Inspired by her younger sister who had donated twice, Jenny donated her hair to Locks of Love, which uses the hair to make wigs for children and adults with cancer or alopecia.

When they would annoy each other, as sisters will do, it wasn't long before they were back plotting how to gang up on their parents for something they wanted. Jenny was Katie's mentor, close friend, advisor, and teacher. Katie was only seventeen when her sister was killed. Such a critical age to need one's big sister. Katie was left alone to learn the ins and outs of dating, handling the inevitable spats with her parents, and applying for college. She didn't have her sister there for senior prom or graduations from high school and college. Katie has been remarkably resilient. Without support from her parents, she had to battle her own posttraumatic stress demons. Forced to face many challenges without her older sister's guidance, support and friendship, Katie struggled. Independent and sharing many of Jenny's attributes, she has survived the unimaginable, emerging stronger and determined to make her own mark on the world. Katie has always been a daddy's girl, so it makes my heart sing to see that they have grown even closer. She and I have formed a stronger mother-daughter bond too!

Jenny's death has been particularly difficult for her father. As if caught in a quagmire of quicksand, Randy struggled to keep his head above the surface. He has tried to accept this tragedy so he can be there for Katie and me, but it has been too unbearable to grasp, too difficult to process for him as well. Like Katie and I, Randy takes things one "Jenny moment" at a time. All one of us has to say is "I'm having a Jenny moment." No further explanations are needed.

A close-knit family, we always took vacations together. We were content to go to the beach or just relax playing board games at our lake home, but our fondest memories were of our trips to California, cruising the Caribbean, and driving up the east coast to Maine. Family vacations will never be the same. We used to have professional family photos taken annually. It was several years before I could have portraits of just Randy, Katie and me. We've only done it once. Imagine how I felt when the photographer introduced herself as Jennifer! Processing that coincidence, I hoped that it was a sign from Jenny, letting us know it was okay to take the pictures. Not a day goes by without something reminding me of Jenny. Some days it's a butterfly on a delicate flower or a song playing on the radio. Other days, it's seeing Katie's car and remembering riding in it from Naples that horrible night. It is still difficult to hear that another of Jenny's close friends is getting married or having a baby.

A dear friend commented that she couldn't live if her only child was killed. Unable to grasp surviving the depth of the pain and despair, she questioned how I was able to handle it. I asked her if she'd ever seen a volcano. At first glance, it looks similar to the other mountains around it. People living near the volcano continue with their lives, oblivious to the scalding force lying below. What appears calm and normal on the surface actually holds a tempestuous and unpredictable caldron of fiery molten rocks. Experts know that the pressure continues to build until the earth can no longer contain it. At some point the volcano will explode, releasing ash and steam, then spewing boulders and boiling lava into the air. The lava flows down the sides of the volcano, destroying everything in its path. The landscape is scarred and weakened by each eruption. The scientists know that without safer, alternative outlets there is nothing they can do to ease the pressure. Truly, only time can make a difference.

The lava flow eventually slows down, though it's still dangerous to be near. Survivors cannot predict when another eruption will occur or if it will be as destructive as previous outbursts. We wonder if there will be as much lava next time. We remain hypervigilant, always waiting for those tremors hinting that another violent eruption is imminent. Those dreaded, foreboding triggers...

I explained that traumatic grief from the tragic loss of a loved one is much like a volcano. It is unpredictable, destructive, and a part of our new reality. Just as volcanoes can lie dormant for periods of time, grief can as well. I've learned that grief changes but never ends. Grief, like inactive volcanoes, will erupt if the conditions are right. It never completely stops spewing from our fractured hearts. Life goes on, so we learn to live with the eruptions. Strength to withstand them can be acquired through our faith, support of loved ones, and professional or peer counseling. Bibliotherapy, blogs, and grief websites can also pacify the volcano gods. Time teaches us that to prevent grief from turning our hearts into hardened lava, we must embrace all that it spews toward us. Avoiding it won't stop the volcanic activity. Safe in our protective gear, we can learn how to deflect the boulders and go around the molten lava as it flows. We can continue with our lives and acknowledge that even when it's been calm for a while, without warning the molten lava can flow again. This time we are a bit stronger and better prepared to handle whatever comes our way.

Paralyzed by flashbacks and panic attacks until recently, I was unable to drive at night. Since the wreck, even as a passenger, remaining calm was impossible if I heard a siren or saw flashing lights. I would break down, sobbing and trembling. Ten years later, I still have physical reactions when I hear or see any emergency vehicles. Will the flashbacks of all the fire trucks, highway patrol cars, and ambulances with blue and red lights flashing at her wreck ever stop torturing me? The vivid image is seared into my mind.

Derrick's dying has resulted in one fewer drunk driver on the road and saved the judicial system a lot of money. Although I am so glad he is dead, his death deprived me of the satisfaction of confronting him. Unfortunately, he died without knowing that he had killed an amazing young woman, destroying my family! Fortunately for my family and me, he died before I could confront him. Had I been given the chance, our tête-à-tête would have only complicated my family's healing, because I would have been arrested. As angry as I was at him, as a mother I felt compelled to reach out to his mother, offering my condolences in a sympathy card. I assumed his mother would be grieving her twenty-three-year-old son's death. I never heard from her or any of the mothers of his children. No one blames Derrick's family for his actions, but a note or phone call acknowledging the murder of our daughter at the hands of their drunk son would have been appreciated!

Derrick will never know I still must take antidepressants to function and that I have not had a full night's sleep in ten years without taking sleeping pills. Except for when I was in Europe, I have slept with Jenny's pillow since removing it from her dorm room, changing only the pillowcase I put over hers. No room for the pillow in Europe; I just took her pillowcase. The ring she was wearing at her death has never been off my finger. Someone said the task of a grieving person is to "find an enduring connection with your loved one in the mist of embarking on a new life without her." Perhaps her pillow and ring are my ways of feeling connected. A friend asked me if I had the choice of having Jenny or avoiding the pain of losing her by not having had her, which I would choose. I responded with a quote by Dr. Seuss that I modified to read, "I cry because she is gone, but I smile because she was mine for twenty-one years!" She enriched our lives more in her short life, and contributed more to make the world a better place than most adults will ever do!

For years, we could not return to Florida. We did not celebrate Christmas. Jenny's birthday is so close to Mother's Day that I still find it difficult to celebrate the day. At some point in this dark journey, I realized that I had to join the living. I had to be a mother to Katie and a wife to Randy. John Lennon said, "Everything will be okay in the end. If it's not okay, then it's not the end." Most days, my family and I are okay. Although I no longer cry every day, I haven't been able to fully enjoy anything because of the heart-piercing thoughts that Jenny would have loved to do it or remembering when we did something similar with Jenny. I wish I were stronger, but have accepted that I am as healed as I will ever be. Such a big part of me died that night, and I am resentful that Derrick's decision to drive drunk dissolved my soul.

By age twenty-one, Jenny had already donated more than one gallon of blood to the American Red Cross, so in her memory Katie arranged for a community blood drive. Thus far, my husband and I worked with the Charlotte police and have participated in each of the four annual traffic checkpoints held in her memory, dedicated to stopping drunk drivers. Other friends and family members have also arranged for traffic checkpoints in four states. We have had a team in four annual Walk Like MADD events, raising the most money in two of the four years!

Jenny's camp name was Fez, so a large group of her fellow counselors arrived at her Celebration of Life, each wearing a red fez. After singing a beautiful camp song for us, they presented me with a fez, which I cherish and display to this day. Jenny's Girl Scout family held a memorial service and planted a tree at Camp Occoneechee, Jenny's favorite place to be. After planting the tree, they presented us with a beautiful stone marker to place at the base of the tree as they softly sang reverent camp songs.

Education, Girl Scouts, and childbirth were three of her biggest passions. We could not think of a more fitting tribute to our daughter's memory than to establish two college scholarships. One is through the Doula Center at UNC-Chapel Hill and the other is through the Hornet's Nest Girl Scout Council for a Gold Award recipient. Both are awarded annually to women of Jenny's caliber.

My family has been so blessed that Jenny's fiancé, Michael, remains our bonus son and has expanded our family by sharing his wonderful wife, Emily, and our bonus grandbaby Marion!

Accepting that Michael had met someone only a year and one day after losing Jenny and had fallen in love so quickly almost pushed me to the breaking point. Trying to desensitize myself in preparation for meeting Emily, I posted pictures of the happy couple around my house, in my car and at work. I arranged to meet Emily alone, knowing it would be too hard meeting her with Michael. Even though I was genuinely happy he had met a lovely young woman, I was fighting such internal turmoil. Knowing that I was causing Michael and Emily stress only heightened my suffering. Emily was so gracious and understanding as I tried to explain it wasn't her who upset me so. It was that she was a constant reminder that she was in my life because my daughter wasn't! I also wondered how Michael could really love Emily because she is so different from Jenny. It should have been Jenny and Michael getting married. It should have been Jenny and Michael's baby.

Although my family attended Michael and Emily's wedding, I couldn't bring myself to go. I had a significant meltdown the first time I tried to meet Emily and was terrified that attending the ceremony would trigger another emotional outburst. I would not risk ruining their beautiful day. With much determination to support Michael, I had to accept that there was room in my heart for Emily too. A major breakthrough, I finally realized that caring for her didn't mean I loved Jenny any less. Although I still struggle with this, our lives are so much richer with Michael, Emily, and Marion in it.

I hope one day to be able to talk openly with Katie about what happened, to read all the letters and cards we received and to watch the video of Jenny's Celebration of Life ceremony. At the celebration, guests were asked to use fabric pens to decorate five-inch squares of white material with a special memory, drawing or comment about Jenny. These are to be sewn into a quilt, but I cannot bear to look at them yet. Until then, these precious keepsakes remain tightly locked away. We cherish each square for the love it expresses.

The girls' aunt Darcy shared, "When I think of Jenny and her brief but beautiful time on this earth, I am flooded with the sense of her many gifts and am led, by her own example, to choose for myself only to celebrate her. To be near Jenny was to see the joy that always shone from her eyes whenever she smiled or giggled. To be near her was to be challenged to think openly, differently — and to be a better person. How can anyone bring so much to our world in such a short time? Her parents received the gift of that baby girl in May many years ago and provided the love, the home, and the guidance to allow her to blossom into a truly amazing little girl and on into an even more amazing young woman. She had a giving, loving soul even as a very young girl. Most of us go through life without a fraction of the sense of purpose she had, and I am a different person today because of her. Jenny's was a consciously lived life that changed for the better countless others' lives, who now I'm sure pay it forward in their own way."

Those who knew her would agree that the following quote describes how she lived her short life. Jenny included it at the end of every email she sent. "This is what you shall do: Love the earth and sun and the animals, despise riches, give alms to everyone who asks, stand up for the stupid and crazy, devote your income and labor to others, hate tyrants, argue not concerning God, have patience and indulgence toward the people, take off your hat to nothing known or unknown or to any man or number of men, go freely with powerful uneducated persons and with the young and with the mothers of families, read these leaves in the open air every season of every year of your life, re-examine all you have been told at school or church or in any book, dismiss whatever insults your own soul, and your very flesh shall be a great poem and have the richest fluency not only in its words but in the silent lines of its lips and face and between the lashes of your eyes and in every motion and joint of your body..." — Walt Whitman.

My wise brother, Bill, wrote, "Life is fragile, and it is temporary. Many of us too often take the miracle of life for granted, choosing instead to indulge in the here and now, oblivious to the ever-ticking clock. Some are fortunate, living beyond the norm, while others pass through so quickly, trailing fond memories, bold plans and expectations in the wind, for others to retrieve. Such is the story of Jenny Zartman, who was tragically in the wrong place at the wrong time through no fault of her own. Jenny was much the butterfly, full of promise and trusting of the wind. Unfortunately, the end of her life story is far too common; its inflicted pain is both real and permanent. Nonetheless, it is a story that must be told so that others will know that life is indeed fragile, and it is temporary. We must never forget that."

Someone asked me how I would define hope now since trauma and its aftermath have a way of redefining our lives. Simplistically, I say hope is the carrot on the stick in front of the donkey. Dangling just out of his reach, he continues moving toward it, optimistic that with enough determination and hard effort, he will reach it. The thought of being so close that he can smell it, can almost taste it, keeps him motivated. The donkey won't give up hope that he will get that carrot!

Hope is the internal expectation that a desired outcome is possible. It's a belief, a conviction that something is achievable. It is one's perception that a certain thing will or at least possibly could happen. Perhaps one hopes traffic is light on the way to work. Someone else hopes for a cure. Without the hope that something is possible, there is no motivation. There is no reason to change an attitude, a belief, or to switch direction. Without hope that something better is feasible, the drive to move toward it withers. Hope allows us to hold on when we want to give up. It nourishes us. The impossible becomes the possible with the existence of hope! My hope is that someday I will be in a place where I am fully living in the present, acknowledging that all my life experiences, incredible and unfortunate, have made me the person I am today. I have to believe that eventually I can move onward, focusing on the present to shape my tomorrows so that I may live my life to its fullest. My goal is to learn to manage my stress and gain control of the symptoms rather than continuing to allow the posttraumatic stress to affect my life. There is no way to get back the ten years I have lost through my grief, but I can always hope for a happier future. One lesson I have learned on this journey is that grief never ends. It changes, it softens, and eventually becomes a part of you.

To me, life after losing a child is about finding a new reality, not a new normal. I cringe when I hear someone say it is a new normal! There is nothing normal about a child dying. Life will never be normal again. The reality is learning how to push through the searing pain and living some semblance of a life. It's about not giving up when every fiber of your heart and soul screams for you to do so. It's about slowly recognizing the little joys in life again like the smell of freshly mowed grass or a summer rain, a shooting star, or a phone call from a friend. It's reaching the point when you smile more often than you cry when you think of her.

It's a journey without shortcuts, yet full of roadblocks and detours. Hopefully, we're moving forward but recognizing that sometimes we will take sidesteps. Many times we will take steps backwards, but always with our child held tightly in our hearts. It's about rejoining life and experiencing it with gratitude. This challenge is our new reality. Mary Anne Radmacher said, "Sometimes courage is the quiet voice at the end of the day saying I will try again tomorrow." And so, I will cherish the butterfly among us again tomorrow!

Written out of love and admiration for Jennifer Zartman by her mother, Nancy Edwards.

NANCY EDWARDS
CHARLOTTE, NORTH CAROLINA

I GLANCE AT YOUR PHOTO
By Nancy Edwards - August 5, 2010

I glance at your photo throughout the day
And ask why did that drunk driver take you away.
More than three times the limit and behind the wheel
My daughter's precious life from us he did steal.

You'd just turned 21, back at school less than a week
Soon to graduate with honors, a biology degree you did seek.
A Doula, ESL Director, Equal Rights Champ and R.A.
These and other great accomplishments ended abruptly one day.

My drive is depleted; my smile's been deleted.
Between all the tears, I feel angry and cheated.
Like a festering wound from a splinter in deep,
Grief invades every moment, shattering my days and my sleep.
I glance at your photo throughout the day.
My friends stand by helplessly. There's nothing to say.
I've so many regrets of things I would change.
Things I would do, not do or rearrange.

Family trips to the Grand Canyon, Williamsburg and D.C.
To Yellowstone, New York City and back to Disney.
I'd teach more about ancestors, family traditions and such.
I'd talk less and listen more, something I didn't do too much.

I glance at your photo throughout the day
Remembering all the things I didn't get to say.
I deeply regret you not knowing just why
Your Grandma and PopPop, we didn't see eye to eye.

Trying to keep your admiration of them strong and intact,
I kept quiet through your anger, maybe deserving it in fact.
I chose to let you resent me as young teens will do
Rather than have you learn what they'd put us through.

Dreams of marriage, children, and midwifery unfilled.
Because Derrick drove drunk August 5, you were killed.
Your family, your fiancé, your friends – changed forever.
Your laughter, your brilliance, your smile forgotten never.

I glance at your photo throughout the day,
Desperately wondering if you are okay.
Are you the icicle on the eves, or a warm summer breeze?
Are you the bird chirping of spring, high up in the trees?

Maybe you're the sweet smile on a wee baby's face
Or the butterfly flitting from place to place.
We've wondered about the day that I found Bim
And if you were responsible for sending him.

Waking up each morning, to give the new day a try
Those twenty-one years passed in the blink of an eye.
I love you and miss you more than words can say
So I glance at your photo throughout the day.

*

THE EDWARDS ZARTMAN FAMILY

JENNY RECEIVING HER GOLD AWARD

JENNIFER ZARTMAN

JENNY AS A DOULA   JENNY RELEASING A TURTLE

CHAPTER SEVEN

I NEVER GOT TO SAY GOODBYE

BY ROSE HELLER

*When everything is dark, when we are
surrounded by despairing voices, when we
do not see any exits, then we can find
salvation in a remembered love, a love which
is not simply a recollection of a bygone past
but a living force which sustains us in the
present. Through memory, love transcends
the limits of time and offers hope at any
moment of our lives.* -HENRI NOUWEN

On September 21, 1989, at 2:35 p.m. my precious baby boy was born. He weighed eight pounds and six ounces, and was twenty-three inches long. I named him Kirk Mahaffey Jr. and was so excited even though I had no idea how to take care of this new bundle of joy. I was only sixteen, but I was determined to be the best mom I could. Kirk's father and I got married a month before Kirk was born. I felt it was the right thing to do. I was very thankful I had supportive parents and siblings. I was a high school student trying to tackle schoolwork and a new baby. I spent many nights dancing to "Lost in Your Eyes" to get him to sleep. I was not able to stay in school because I kept falling asleep in class. I quit school to take care of my son but then decided to get my high school equivalency. I didn't get to do all those fun things in high school, as I was a mom who was responsible for this little boy.

Kirk's father and I got our own place at the age of eighteen, but I soon realized he wasn't going to support us like he should, which only pushed me to be better. Two years after Kirk was born I had my daughter, Nicole, who was a total surprise as I was on birth control. Kirk was a toddler and loved his little sister. He always wanted to hold her. My doctor had switched my birth control, and I ended up pregnant with my son John when his sister was only eight months old. John looked so much like his brother. By the time I was twenty, I had three children to take care of and did it by myself as their father wanted a life that didn't tie him down. I tried to make our marriage work, but it was evident he didn't. I went to technical school and from there I was offered a position for the state as a clerk typist. I worked hard to ensure my children were taken care of. I eventually advanced to become a purchasing agent for the Commonwealth of Pennsylvania. I wanted my children to know that if you work hard enough you can succeed. I always told my children that you can become whatever you want in life if you work hard enough. But after seven years of marriage, I was fed up. I filed for divorce.

I was a single mom struggling to raise three children by myself, working a full-time job to keep a roof over their heads and food on the table until I met my second husband, Todd. He had four children of his own: Todd Jr., Brian, David, and Felicia. David and Felicia were the youngest two and they moved in with us. We had Todd Jr. and Brian every other weekend.

After dating for two years, we got married. It wasn't easy at first, but the kids adjusted well and became good friends. Nicole and Felicia became inseparable, because they both had only brothers. Kirk, John, and David all enjoyed sports and played them in school and always got together with friends on weekends to play. John was younger, but that didn't stop him from trying whatever his brothers did. They were the best of friends. John looked up to his big brother and wanted to be just like him. John never called Kirk by his name because it was too hard to pronounce. He called him Brud, and to this day he still does.

Kirk was a very energetic little boy who got into everything and had no fear. As he grew to a toddler, he brought so much joy to my life. He was my first true love and taught me how to love unconditionally. Before I knew it, he was ready to start school. Before the school year started he broke his leg falling off a bicycle and spent three months in a body cast. The doctors thought he would need physical therapy afterward, but within a few days of having the cast removed he was up walking. He was a determined little boy with a lot of life in him. It appeared that nothing would hold him back. As he went through school, he was always determined to do well no matter what he did. He played baseball from tee-ball all the way up to high school. In middle/high school he wanted to branch out and try other sports: basketball, football, and tennis. He loved trying new things that challenged him.

As he was becoming a young man, I realized he liked to be the class clown and joke about everything. He always knew how to make a person laugh. Kirk was always the life of any party we had. He was known to act crazy and have fun with everyone. In high school he met his sweetheart, Ashley, and they dated through the rest of high school. They graduated in June 2008, and in August they found out they were expecting a baby. They came to the house to share the news, and Ashley just cried not knowing what to expect and afraid of becoming a mother. I told her she would do just fine.

It was a total shock to all of us, but Kirk took the news in stride. He was so calm and excited at the same time. He had big plans for his newly expected family. On May 16, 2009, we welcomed my grandson, Mayson Anthony, into the world. Kirk was so proud and excited to be a dad. Mayson was my first and only biological grandbaby. He was such a joy and lived with me a few months after he was born so his parents could save money to get their own place. Mayson was not only spoiled by me but had many aunts and uncles who were always there to help, whether it was to babysit so his parents could work or just to feed him. I remember how he loved to be rocked to sleep. He was such a joy and growing so fast.

Kirk was going to technical school and holding a job at a pizza place so he could support his family. He did everything to ensure his family had everything they needed and more. He landed a job at a bakery in 2011. By the time Kirk was twenty-one, he had rented his first house and bought his first car. I was so proud of what he accomplished in a short time. Kirk worked crazy hours but always made time for his family. The boys always made plans on weekends to play football or baseball with friends and family. Kirk wanted Mayson to see how important family was. He would have his brother, John, along with his cousins Joey and Terry over every Friday night to play video games and hang out. That became a weekly event every Friday night. The boys took turns keeping Mayson occupied. Kirk was a role model and pushed his little brother to stay in school. John had numerous medical problems including asthma, and a birth defect in his brain called Chiara I malformation and underwent surgery in June 2012. He missed a lot of school, and Kirk continued to help him with his schooling and pushed him to do well. Just as Kirk's life seemed to be going in the right direction, that all changed on the evening of July 17, 2012.

I was on my way home from the hospital where my youngest son John had been admitted with some complications from brain surgery he had the month before. He was leaking spinal fluid out of his incision and running a high fever. He was admitted on July 16, 2012, to have the fluid drained every hour which required them to keep him as still as possible so he didn't end up with a severe headache from them draining the fluid. John had a serious infection, and they couldn't determine where it was coming from. His fever spiked to 105 degrees.

I was on my way home to get some clothes so I could stay at the hospital with John when I received a phone call from Ashley. She asked if I had spoken with Kirk that evening. I said no, I had been at the hospital with John all day. Kirk was supposed to pick her up at 8 p.m. and he didn't show up; it was very out of character for him to be late. She tried calling him several times and got no response. I told her to hang tight and I would try to reach him. She called back within a few minutes and said her mom was coming to pick her up but was detoured due to a wreck on the bridge. I decided that Kirk had gotten tied up in traffic and that was why he hadn't picked Ashley up. As my husband drove us home from the hospital, we had to pass the bridge where the wreck happened, and I got this overwhelming feeling and started to cry.

At that moment, I knew my son was involved in the wreck. My motherly instincts knew something was terribly wrong. It was very unlike Kirk to be late or not contact Ashley to let her know what was going on.

Todd came upon the fire police blocking traffic from going on the bridge. He pulled over and explained to the man that our son might be involved in the wreck. He radioed the police on the bridge, and they would allow one of us to walk onto the bridge, so my husband went. Todd explained to the officer that our son and grandson were supposed to pick up his girlfriend at 8 p.m. and never arrived and was unable to be reached by phone. The officer asked Todd to describe our son's vehicle.

The officer and Todd came back down to me as I was waiting in the car, talking to my sister Debbie on the phone, trying to keep myself from thinking the worst. My sister said she would meet me at the hospital. The officer said my son was taken to the hospital, and he asked me to get in his car so he could take my husband and me there.

I sat in the back of the officer's car and just cried. I couldn't speak, as my entire body trembled, not knowing if the boys were injured. The ride to the hospital was only five minutes, but it felt like an hour. I wanted to get to the hospital and see my son and grandson. I questioned the officer about the boys, but he had no information on their condition. I called Ashley and told her to meet me at the hospital because the boys had been involved in a terrible crash. I didn't know much other than they were taken to the hospital. The officer informed me that my grandson Mayson was taken to another hospital.

As we arrived at the hospital, my sister-in-law Karen, who worked there, came out in tears. I knew immediately that something horrible had happened.

She told me Kirk was gone. I screamed and fell to the ground.

I walked into the hospital and waited to speak with an officer and the coroner as my daughter and Ashley arrived. I had to tell them that Kirk died, and Mayson was transported to another hospital. As a mother, you never want to hurt your children, and I had to break her heart and tell her that her oldest brother had died. I wasn't able to comprehend the events of the evening, and how did I expect them to? After Ashley had learned Mayson was taken to a different hospital, the officer transported her there. I waited to go there until I had seen Kirk.

At this point I didn't know what had happened, but my whole life fell apart in the blink of an eye. I met with the state trooper and coroner who informed me that the other driver, Brian, had crossed the center line and hit my son head on. I don't remember much of anything else that evening; it was all a blur. I insisted on seeing my son; I had to see him. In my own mind, I didn't believe what they were saying until I saw him lying lifeless on a bed. I kept asking why my twenty-two-year-old son? Why? All he was doing was picking his girlfriend up from work. I stared at him expecting a joke to come out of his mouth like always. Within a few minutes I realized he was gone. I rubbed my hand down his face and immediately walked out of the room and collapsed on the floor. I cried and kept saying I never got to say goodbye! I never got to tell him I loved him. I kept thinking this can't be happening to me.

I walked outside to gather myself together and received a call from Ashley saying that Mayson didn't survive; my first and only grandson was gone too. I immediately had family drive me to the hospital. Upon arriving, I found that the doctors had already spoken to Ashley and her mother. Mayson was rushed to surgery but didn't survive. I remember walking into his room where my precious three-year-old grandson lay on a bed with only a scratch on his nose. I held his hand as the tears ran down my face. I was having a hard time comprehending everything that had happened that evening, and I felt like I was in a fog. Mayson had just turned three years old in May and celebrated his birthday with a party at my house. It rained all day, but that didn't hinder his party. His daddy bought a bounce house for him and family to enjoy that day, which they did regardless of the rain.

How can someone look so perfect and lifeless at the same time? He was only three years old and had his entire life taken from him. I just didn't understand how he could be gone; he looked so perfect lying on the bed with only a scratch on his face. I remember everyone sitting in the waiting room and nothing was said. We all just cried together. Two of the most important people in my life were gone, and I didn't know why or how.

I had to make arrangements to bury my son and grandson while my youngest son, John, was fighting a severe infection in his body. I prayed to God every day not to take my other son. My sister Debbie and brother Bobby took turns staying at the hospital with me while Todd took care of the house and family who came from Georgia for the funeral. John needed to recover so he could attend the services. After several days of tests, they found the cause of his infection: cellulitis that came from the pneumonia shot he had received in the hospital. With that resolved, we made arrangements for the funeral, which we held off for a week due to the autopsies being performed and a few days for John to be discharged.

Ashley and I chose to bury the boys together, since Kirk always had Mayson by his side. Kirk's love of sports resulted in the decision to bury them in matching jerseys. The funeral home was filled with tons of pictures and videos that showed Kirk's love for life and his son Mayson. As the people lined up to view them, I remember standing there feeling numb. This was the last time I would see them. I didn't want to leave or say goodbye.

I grew angrier as the days turned into weeks, and I wanted to know what had caused the driver to cross the center line. I had to know what happened. I remember all types of scenarios playing over and over in my head. Was the driver texting? Was he speeding? Was he drinking? Who was it? I wanted to know, and no one had answers for me. The only information I was receiving from the police was that the crash was under investigation. As I tried to comprehend the events that had just changed my world forever and make sense of it all, I couldn't eat, sleep or work. My life was a blur, and I didn't know why it was happening to my family and me. My mind was all over the place. I had questions but no answers. All the things they never got to do would go through my mind, and it wasn't fair. Their lives were stripped from them in a moment. Kirk was just starting to get his life on track and working hard for his family. Mayson was his pride and joy, and he never did anything without him by his side. Mayson never got to learn to ride the bicycle he just got for his birthday, never learned to read or go to school. I was so angry at the world.

Three months had passed since the crash when I learned that Brian, the driver who took my firstborn son and grandson, was drunk and drugged. His blood alcohol level was .169 percent, and both cannabis and opiates were found in his bloodstream, which I learned from an insurance agent before the police notified me. It took over three months for the medical blood results to come back. I never expected to hear that, because the original police report said there were no drugs or alcohol suspected. I thought it was an accident, and the thought that it was a preventable crash fueled my anger. How could the police report be filed saying that no drugs or alcohol were suspected? How did the police not suspect alcohol when the driver was double the legal limit? The police report was so hard for me to read, but I had to, since that was all I knew about the accident. I was numb, not knowing what to think. I was so angry and upset, knowing that this could have been prevented. My heart shattered all over again. How can someone be so selfish? Why would anyone drink and do drugs and get behind the wheel?

I just couldn't understand, nor could I forgive. It was not an accident in my eyes. As the days went by I had no ambition to do anything. I wanted answers and wanted to know why the driver was still out on the streets enjoying his life while my life had changed forever. I kept hoping I would wake up from this nightmare. I kept being told by police that the accident was still under investigation. I wanted my son and grandson back, and nobody could give that to me. A mother shouldn't have to bury her twenty-two-year-old child and three-year-old grandchild due to a senseless, selfish act that could have been prevented.

Almost a year had passed, and on June 1, 2014, the driver was finally arrested and put in jail. I was so upset with the justice system for allowing him to be on the streets for a year after their deaths. I continued to ask the status of our case and was told it was under investigation. My boys were gone, and the driver was still out enjoying life while my life had been totally turned upside down.

The driver asked for continuances, and the hearing dragged on for another year. He was supposed to be in court for jury selection but entered a guilty plea to avoid going to trial. In May 2014, he pleaded guilty to two counts of homicide by vehicle with a mental illness (PTSD). I didn't know how to accept the fact that he wanted to claim a mental illness when he should have known right from wrong. I was relieved that the case was over with and I didn't have to go to trial and relive that horrific night that changed my life forever. I didn't agree with his being sentence and claiming mental illness. I felt that was a copout for him and that he wanted people to feel sorry for him. The district attorney assured me that he would receive the highest sentence allowed by law with or without the mental illness. He would receive the highest punishment allowed by law, six to twenty years in prison, and would receive the help he needed. What about my family and me? No one could help us.

During the sentencing hearing in June 2014, I put photos of Kirk and Mayson up for the judge and everyone to see what had been taken from my family. I was unable to read my victim statement; I was shaking uncontrollably just being in the courtroom with the man who took my boys' lives. My daughter Nicole had enough courage to get up in front of everyone and tell how the accident affected our family. The driver sat with his head down. He never showed any remorse for what he had done.

Before the judge handed down the sentence, he asked the driver if he had anything to say. The driver stood up, turned around, and read a letter he had written. He apologized for what happened and said "Not a day goes by that I don't think about Kirk and Mayson, and I hope you can forgive me." I was so upset, and knew I could never forgive him. How do you forgive someone who took the lives of two innocent people because he chose to drink and drive? I felt like I was dying inside. I shook tremendously while holding photographs of my boys. How dare he say that he thinks about them every day! He never showed any remorse from day one and now wanted people to feel sorry for him because he had PTSD. He was pathetic in my eyes for even trying to think people should feel sorry for him. I was the one who lost my son and grandson due to his negligence. The hearing was over, and people expected me to have closure, but I didn't.

In the last three years, my life has been totally shattered, and there are no words that can ease the pain I deal with every day. As the years pass by, I feel as if my life stopped the day they died. I will never see my son, hear his voice or hug him tight. I will never see my grandson grow up, go to school or hear him say "Love you, Ninna," which he always said. I take one day at a time, as I know my son would want me to be happy. So much has happened with our family since the accident occurred. Ashley and John both were committed to mental hospitals after we learned they were harming themselves. Neither of them knew how to handle the pain, so they inflicted pain by cutting themselves. I didn't know how to help them, as I was grieving myself. I tried to stay positive for them, knowing Kirk would want them to continue a happy life.

I can't say our family has moved on, because we all have moments, but I try to turn sadness and emptiness into something positive. The traumatic effect will be with my entire family the rest of our lives. We all get together to remember them on their birthdays and release balloons from their grave. On the date of the accident, we all get together on the bridge and hold signs that say "Don't drink and drive," and release balloons in their memory.

I am touched by the support of my family and friends on keeping their memories alive. Kirk worked with a man who was a member of the Legion Riders. He put together a memorial ride to help defray funeral cost. My husband and I are members of this wonderful group who didn't even know my family but went above and beyond to help. The outpouring community support was amazing. After the first year's ride, we decided to continue the ride each year in memory of them and donate the money to charity. Kirk's life was dedicated to his little boy, so I knew right away I had to do something for children. I was introduced to a charity called Magical Memories, a nonprofit organization that holds an annual Christmas party for children with a terminal or life-threatening illness. I went to their party the same year I lost my boys. It is amazing what this organization puts together for these children. It touched my heart to see these children smile, have a good time, forget about their illness and doctor appointments, and have fun. I knew right then that if I could help families make memories with their children my son would be proud.

All I have left are memories that I cherish with everything I have. I will keep their memories alive until the glorious day we are reunited. People will know what senseless action took my boys' life and how my family has suffered. If I can reach one person in doing this, I will have saved a family from this painful and all-consuming journey called grief. For Kirk and Mayson: Don't drink and drive. If you are going to drink, please have a designated driver.

ROSE HELLER
SUNBURY, PENNSYLVANIA

KIRK MAHAFFEY

MAYSON, KIRK, NINNA & PAPPY

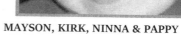

MAYSON & ASHLEY

NICOLE, KIRK & MAYSON

CHAPTER EIGHT

FOREVER TWICE BROKEN

BY DIERDRA ROSE

*My grief journey has no one destination, I
will not "get over it." The understanding that
I don't have to be done is liberating. I will
mourn these deaths the rest of my life.*
-ALAN D. VOLFELT

Beloved Husband, Father, Son, Brother, Friend, and Now Angels ~ Though We Are Parted in Life My Dear Angels, We Will Be Forever Joined in Spirit; A Family's Love Lasts FOREVER.

At the time of Travis' death, I was a single mom of eight children: nineteen-year-old Travis, eighteen-year-old Alex, sixteen-year-old Nathan, fifteen-year-old Brendan, ten-year-old Logan, eight-year-old Emily, seven-year-old Bethany, and six-year-old Courtney. I was a third-year college student at Hennepin Technical College, and employed part-time as a night shift supervisor at Goodwill Industries. With eight children we were not your average family. Needless to say, life was challenging at times and sometimes even somewhat chaotic. But with Travis' help, I was able to breathe a little easier and keep most of my hair too.

Travis was born in Minneapolis, Minnesota, on November 1, 1978, at 9:53 a.m. He was supposed to be a Warlock baby, but he didn't decide to put in an appearance until eight and a half hours after his October 31 due date. Ironically, Halloween would end up being his favorite holiday. Travis weighed seven pounds thirteen ounces and was twenty-two inches long. He was a good-natured, baby and his momma loved him to pieces. Little did I know, though, that in just fifteen months I would give birth to another son, and cut our mommy and Travis time very short, but treasured.

Our family grew to four children in five years. In 1983, I divorced Travis' father and relocated in Long Prairie, Minneapolis, with Travis and his three brothers. As a result, Travis didn't have much kid time. He grew up and matured quite rapidly. By age five, he could not only make a bottle, but change a diaper as well. By age eleven he began babysitting for relatives and neighbors. My siblings didn't see this as a good thing, however, and they weren't impressed by Travis' abilities and often told me that he was being cheated out of his childhood. But if truth be known, I don't know what I would have done without his help.

By 1992, I had met and married my second husband, Donnie, relocated to Mendota Heights, MN, and our family had grown by four more children. Everything seemed to be looking up for us. Travis was able to be a kid again, and for the first time, in what seemed like forever, we were all genuinely happy. I had a loving husband, three beautiful daughters who adored and loved their daddy, and my five sons respected Donnie's authority and looked up to him for guidance. Donnie had a well-respected job and career with the Army (he served in Operation Desert Storm). He was beginning to fulfill a lifelong dream of owning and operating his own automotive repair business.

This new business would in turn enable us to build a home for our, newly formed and happy family. That genuine happiness didn't last long though. On January 24, 1993, our world as we knew it came to an end and was to be no more. At age thirty-one, while home on weekend leave from the Army and exploring our new property and the state snowmobile trail in front of our property on snowmobiles, Donnie and his best friend, Vince, happened upon an airborne snowmobile. The snowmobile collided with Donnie.

He was hit in the chest and mowed over backwards off his snowmobile and left in the cold snow to die. The driver of the snowmobile fled the scene without even stopping. Josh, the sixteen-year-old who was snowmobiling alongside the airborne snow-mobiler, stopped to help.

Donnie was lying on the ground, his face filled with cleat marks from the snowmobile track, and he had multiple compound fractures. The bone in his left wrist was protruding through the skin. His right leg was twisted up behind his neck, his knees were shattered, and both knee bones came through his snow pants.

Both Vince and Josh could see that Donnie was in very bad shape. Vince told Josh to go get help. Josh rode his snowmobile to the nearest house, which, incredibly, belonged to the hit-and-run driver of the other snowmobile. Josh called 911 and reported the collision (not many people carried cell phones back in 1993).

Before returning to the scene of the accident, Josh told the hit-and-run driver that he needed to come back with him to the scene of the accident because Donnie was in bad shape and needed his help. To this the driver replied "Everything that can be done is already being done. My going back there isn't going to help him in any way." Josh returned to the accident site alone. When he got there, Vince was gone and Donnie lay in the cold snow alone. Confused, Josh knelt down next to Donnie and told him to hang on, that help was on the way.

A minute later, Vince drove up the trail in his truck. Knowing that Donnie's survival depended on getting help fast, Vince had left Donnie, ridden his snowmobile down the trail to our property, gotten his truck with four-wheel drive, and drove it back up the snowmobile trail to pick up Donnie. After getting Donnie into his truck, Vince quickly got in the truck and started driving to Little Falls Hospital. At the hospital, doctors found that Donnie's aorta had been torn from his heart and that two vertebrae in his neck were broken. The broken vertebrae caused him to become unconscious after about ninety seconds; several minutes later, as his lungs filled with blood, he drowned in his own blood.

When the police finally arrived at the collision site, on foot with emergency help, they couldn't drive their emergency vehicles down the snowmobile trail. They found no injured body or Josh, who had called in the accident. The only thing there was a snowmobile hood and Donnie's smashed snowmobile.

Police quickly learned who they were looking for. Because the hood of the driver's snowmobile was torn off upon impact, the police were able to track him by the registration number on the side of the hood. The driver knew the police were looking for him; he was listening to them on his police radio scanner. He left his house and went to his friend Bill's house when he heard they were on their way to his residence. Once he arrived at Bill's, he continued to listen to his scanner. He dodged them again by hiding in Bill's barn when he heard they were on their way to Bill's residence, and he had Bill lie about knowing his whereabouts. He managed to elude authorities for four hours before finally turning himself in.

A year later, because of a plea bargain which I was not informed of or even asked about, the charges of drunken criminal vehicular homicide, gross negligence, two counts of criminal vehicular homicide, felony for leaving the scene of an accident, misdemeanor for leaving the scene of an accident, operation of a snowmobile while under the influence of alcohol, operation of a snowmobile with alcohol concentration of .10 or more, careless or reckless operation of a snowmobile, operation of a snowmobile at unreasonable speed, felony evading law enforcement, and felony violation of probation were all dropped.

The driver was sentenced to seven years of probation and two years in the county workhouse, for felony leaving the scene of an accident resulting in death. The judge gave him credit for the one-year house arrest that he spent while he was being tried, so the driver was really made to serve only one of those two years.

In the year he spent in the county workhouse, the driver was allowed to be out on work release from six in the morning to six at night, Monday through Saturday. He only spent weeknights and Sundays in jail. With the driver being allowed to rest and sleep when he returned from his twelve-hour workdays, weeknights were really no biggy for him. The only time he was actually in jail was Sunday. Never mind that he had a blood alcohol content of .238 at the time of the arrest, or was four months into probation for his ninth DWI. Or that eleven years earlier, in 1982, the driver killed a husband and wife in a drunk car crash. One year for murdering Donnie while snowmobiling drunk. Whoop-de-do! Some justice! *Not!*

Three weeks after Donnie's death, Courtney, our youngest child, who was nine and a half months old, came down with respiratory syncytial virus as a result of her being eleven weeks premature at birth and having underdeveloped lungs. She was in a coma for three weeks and in the hospital for almost three months. During the first two weeks of Courtney's coma, the doctors told me that she wasn't going to survive and that I should have her final rights read (Donnie was Catholic) and start making any other final arrangements too. I told the doctor that her father had just been killed three weeks earlier, and I would be damned if they took Courtney too.

She did survive, but has permanent lung damage and is now mentally impaired because her brain was deprived of oxygen for three weeks. She had one hundred percent oxygen saturation all three weeks, but because of the infection in her lungs, they were taking in only fifty-five percent oxygen. She had to relearn all her day-to-day child activities: hold her head up, roll over, sit, crawl, stand, etc. It took two years of occupational and physical therapy for Courtney to relearn enough to get back to the point where she was before she became sick with RSV. Today, Courtney is twenty-four going on thirteen. During Courtney's stay in the hospital, I rarely left her side. Travis, now fourteen, stepped into the man-of-the-house shoes again and took total care of his six younger siblings. He cooked for them, cleaned for them, bathed the youngest siblings and got them dressed daily. He got the older siblings off to school each day before going to school himself.

A neighbor watched my two- and three-year-old daughters and put Logan on the morning bus while Travis was in school. When Courtney came home from the hospital, because of all her needs and the attention she required, taking care of her was a full-time job. I was still in much need of assistance, so Travis never got a reprieve. Instead, he continued to mature. He grew into a kind, loving, caring and thoughtful young man. He would give a total stranger his last dollar if he thought that person needed it more than him. As he grew older, Travis realized that he had the gift of gab, like his momma. He was also wise beyond his years. For these reasons Travis related better to older kids and adults. Because of his kind, thoughtful nature and his being so loving and caring, he left a lasting impression on everyone he met. In fact, Travis never met a person, whose heart he didn't touch. He also became quite the ladies' man. Girls would line up around the block for a chance to go out with Travis.

Travis had many favorites. His favorite color was neon green, his favorite number was seven (for his seven siblings), his favorite hobby was skateboarding. He learned to skateboard when he was only eight years old. My brother Bob, who had taken Travis under his wing after my divorce, taught him the ropes of skateboarding. Uncle Bob quickly became Travis' favorite uncle. He looked up to Bob, who became his role model as well as his confidant. Uncle Bob and Travis became inseparable, doing almost everything together.

A lot of Bob rubbed off on Travis, and like Bob, Travis' favorite holiday soon became Halloween. Bob was artistic and taught Travis how to draw. Their favorite things to draw and collect were skulls and '57 Chevys. Travis' favorite sport was motocross. When he was twelve, Donnie got Travis interested in motocross. Travis raced a neon green 125 Yamaha that was numbered seven. Donnie and Travis had built this bike together from the ground up. Without

Donnie's help, continued training or funds, however, Travis was forced to drop out of the motocross circuit after Donnie's death.

Other favorites of Travis' include his favorite food, tomato soup and grilled cheese sandwiches; his favorite cartoon character was Bart Simpson, and his favorite best friends, Seth and Jake.

In 1994, we relocated to Coon Rapids, Minnesota, where I bought a duplex and occupied both levels. Travis and his four brothers lived upstairs, and I and Travis' three sisters lived downstairs. In September 1994, while attending my cousin's wedding in Kingston, Minnesota, and serving as her wedding photographer, I met a man named Fred who was serving as one of the groomsmen. At the reception we talked and danced together until it was time for me to leave. We exchanged phone numbers and kept in touch. By Christmas of that year, Fred and I had begun dating, and we married ten years later.

Having eight children age two to sixteen had always scared men off. I would go out on first dates with men, at which time I would usually introduce them to my children, but as soon as the men found out that I had eight children, almost never was I asked for a second date. Fred was different, though. My having eight children didn't scare him. He loved my children, and he was a pretty good handyman to have around the house on weekends. There wasn't anything he couldn't fix or do. I was able save money because I no longer was paying repair people to fix anything; Fred fixed everything for me.

Things seemed to be going well for the next four years. I was happy again and so were my children. I liked my part-time job as a supervisor at Goodwill Industries, and I had even gone back to school to further my education. I already had an associate in arts degree and an associate in applied science in accounting technology degree and a computer information systems certificate; I could operate computer programs and applications. But now I had become interested in computer building, maintaining, upgrading, and networking. I went back and started my third year in college. I decided to work toward earning a computer support specialist degree. I was a member of Phi Theta Kappa honor society and maintained a 3.85 GPA.

But one day without notice or warning, the rug once again was pulled out from underneath me. My life and all my happiness were yanked away. My whole world was turned upside down and inside out. Life would never be the same again.

On April 4, 1998, my phone began ringing in the wee hours of the morning. I initially ignored the ringing, but it wouldn't stop. Reluctantly, I answered the phone and without thinking blurted out, "This better be important." After about five minutes of useless back and forth questioning, the man on the other end of the phone asked to speak with "Dierdra Rose."

Now angry and confused, I asked, "Who the hell is this?"

The stern voice on the phone then informed me he was with the Coon Rapids police department. Very solemnly he told me that the police were knocking on my front door, and he needed me to answer it.

Glancing at the clock on my headboard, which said 4 a.m., I hung up and threw the phone on the bed as I went to answer the door. There were two police officers outside. The bigger of the two officers asked, "Dierdra Rose? May we, please come in, ma'am?" I opened the door and waved them into the kitchen. The same officer asked if I had any idea what was going on. Bothered by the fact that the police had awakened me at four in the morning to ask me stupid questions, I arrogantly replied "Which one of my boys is in jail and to which jail do I go to bail him out?" Instead of answering me he asked, "Is there another adult in the house?" Bewildered at the question and the look in his eyes, I quickly said yes, then asked him why he wanted to know. The officer looked down at his notepad and replied, "Ma'am, your son Travis has been in an accident." Horrified at how the officer spoke, I begged him, "Just tell me that he's alive." Mortified that the officer was still looking down at the notepad, but now shuffling his feet, and hadn't answered my question, I again pleaded, "*Please* tell me that my son is alive." The officer finally looked up and looked me straight in the eye. In a low muffled voice, he said, "Ma'am, your son Travis was in a car accident at 2:32 this morning, and he didn't make it. He was killed."

I started screaming for Fred. He got out of bed and before he could even get to the kitchen door, I collapsed on the floor like a baby and screamed, "Travis is *dead!*"

He stood in the doorway looking at me. "What do you mean he's dead?"

I screamed again "He's *dead!*"

I looked up at the officers who obviously had become very uncomfortable. They wouldn't look me in the eye any more. Fred tried comforting me, but all I could do was scream, cry, and pound my fists on the kitchen floor.

Hysterically I screamed, "Someone, *please* tell me it's not true. anyone, *please* tell me Travis is not dead." Finally, I composed myself enough that Fred could lift me off of the floor. With his arms around me, he tried to comfort me as I continued to cry. He began to question the officers. We were told that Travis was the front seat passenger in a car that was driven by a driver who, for whatever reason, lost control of his vehicle, crossed over the median, crashed into a steel utility pole at a speed of sixty-five mph while driving westbound on Hanson Boulevard on the border of Coon Rapids and Andover. The driver and both of his passengers died.

"All three of the boys are dead," the officer repeated.

I looked at him confused and asked who the other two boys were. He told me "Mike and Troy." I knew both boys. Mike was seventeen and ironically was my employee at Goodwill Industries; he was the truck donation attendant. Troy was eighteen and lived on the same street as Mike. All three boys were students at Blaine High School in Blaine, Minnesota. Travis and Troy were seniors, and Mike was a junior. Travis and Troy were six weeks away from graduating. The officer then gave us more details. He told us Mike was the driver of the vehicle and Troy was a passenger in the back seat. He also said they were not sure at the time, but they suspected that alcohol may have played a role in the crash. They told us the boys had all been taken the morgue at Mercy Hospital in Anoka, Minnesota. We were given phone numbers for the hospital and for Mike and Troy's parents. After the officers had finished giving us the rest of the details, as they knew them to be so far, relating to the boy's crash, etc., they got in their cars and left.

I started making phone calls while Fred sat at the kitchen table in stunned silence. The first call I made was to Pastor Perry who led a weekly Bible study class that I attended and was the pastor who re-baptized me (I was only sprinkled as an infant) a month after Donnie's death. I needed his knowledge of death and heaven more than ever right then. I also made calls to my siblings, close friends, and Travis' closest friends. News of Travis and the other two boys spread like wildfire. It was on every local television channel during commercials and on every news broadcast. Television reporters and their news station crews were swarming the crash site, like bees on honey, within twenty minutes after the accident had been reported. All three boys were still inside Mike's car when these reporting crews started to arrive and swarm the crash site. The police had to wrap yellow accident tape around the car windows and windshields because of all the news reporters and their cameras.

"I've got to tell the kids before they turn on the television," I told Fred. He helped me wake them up, and we brought them all into the downstairs living room. They were all puzzled. I looked over at Fred, and he nodded his head. I opened my mouth to speak, but I couldn't say the words. Instead, I broke down and began to cry again. I covered my eyes with the palms of my hands as Fred began to speak.

"There's been an accident," he told them. Alex immediately asked, "What kind of accident?" and then he pretty much asked the same questions that I had asked the police officers. Fred began to cry. Now the kids were all beginning to cry too. I could see the terrified look in their eyes.

Not hearing a reply from either Fred or myself, Alex, in a louder voice, repeated, "What kind of accident?" The kids' eyes were glued to Fred and me as we both cried. Alex, almost yelling now, asked, "Who's been in an accident? Someone we know?"

Both Fred and I nodded our heads.

"Who?" Alex asked.

Fred wiped away the tears from his cheeks and cleared his throat. He blurted out "Travis." Alex stepped back; he seemed confused. All eyes were now open and filled with questions and fear. Fred, more composed than me, began, "Travis was in a car accident this morning with Mike and Troy. Mike was driving, and they crashed. They're all dead."

As the word "dead" slipped from Fred's mouth, the kids all became hysterical. Alex yelled, "Your lying, Fred! Mom, tell me that Fred is lying."

I looked up at Alex and in a very low voice, I said "He's not, Alex. Fred's not lying."

All the kids began asking question after question as they cried. Some of the questions we could answer, others we could not.

As if things weren't bad enough already, I now had to tell Courtney that we had to cancel her birthday party. She didn't seem to mind, and she hung her small head and blurted out, "It's my fault anyway." Puzzled as to what she meant, I asked her what she thought was her fault.

"It's my fault that he is dead," she said between sobs. I hugged her and wiped away the tears streaming down her face.

"Honey, it's not your fault," I told her. "Yes, it is!" she screamed. "It's my fault because it's my birthday." If it wasn't my birthday and Travis wasn't coming to my party, he wouldn't have needed a ride, and he wouldn't have been in Mike's car. He never would have crashed, and he wouldn't be dead."

This was coming out of the mouth of a six-year-old who was mentally impaired. My heart broke worse than it was already broken to hear Courtney blame herself. I pulled her closer to me and reassured her that it was not her fault as I hugged her tight. As you can imagine, from that day on, birthdays for Courtney were very difficult. Not so much now, but for the first ten years or so.

By eight in the morning my house was filled with well-wishers and Travis' friends. Alex, Nathan, and Brendan did their best to be with Travis' friends and to answer their questions. There was so much that we still didn't know yet, but learned in the weeks to come. It became a house in chaos. Everyone seemed to be extending their condolences and asking how they could help all at the same time. I couldn't sit down anywhere because all the seats were taken.

My best girlfriend Lisa came over with her two daughters, Chrissy and Jan. The girls thought they would help out by cooking me breakfast. Jan was mixing eggs for the french toast; she turned on the burner to my panda teakettle that sat on the stove empty. She thought she had turned on the burner to melt butter in the pan for french toast. The heat of the burner melted the yellow plastic butterfly that was on the empty panda teakettle's nose.

Chrissy became distracted by the melting butterfly and burned the bacon. The smoke from the melting plastic and burning bacon set off the kitchen smoke detector and the living room smoke detector as well. By noon, things got to be more than I could handle. People coming, people going, people's loud crying, and the cigarette smoke from everyone smoking became unbearable. My head was buzzing, and I had a horrible, horrible headache.

I yelled "That's it! Everybody get out; please leave now!"

I can remember thinking that because I yelled and made everyone leave, I was now the bad guy, the ungrateful b****. The worst part was that I didn't even care if they thought I had been rude; I was hurting.

My life had just fallen apart in front of my eyes. I didn't want breakfast, I didn't want company, I just wanted to see Travis walk through that door. With nothing else that they could do at the house, Alex, Nathan, and Brendan left with Travis' friends to go to the crash site.

In the sudden quiet, I remembered that Courtney had five little friends who were supposed to be going to Camp Snoopy with us that afternoon. I began calling their parents. I explained to them that we were canceling Courtney's birthday party because of her brother Travis' death that morning. Most of them knew because of the news coverage, and no explanation was needed, and for that I was grateful. Remembering that I needed to call Mike and Troy's parents, I decided to go ahead and make those dreaded calls while I could. After calling Troy's home and exchanging condolences with his mom, Sheila, I called Mike's home and exchanged condolences with his mom, Carrie. When the condolences and small talk were through Carrie told me that Mike's car was insured and she gave me the phone number for the insurance company before hanging up, both of us in tears.

It was almost 3 p.m. when I decided that I needed to be with my son. I called Mercy Hospital and asked for the morgue. Never in my wildest dreams could I ever have imagined I would be living this nightmare again, yet this time it was my son.

A man with a deep and intimidating voice answered the phone. I explained who I was and what I wanted, trying my hardest to hold myself together. The man confirmed that Travis had been brought in early that morning. I quickly interrupted, asking when I could see him and the exact location. After a lengthy and insulting conversation, I was finally told that only medical personnel were allowed inside the morgue. My heart broke again when he explained that my baby, my Travis, was lying on a gurney in a large refrigerated room with many other dead bodies. The thought horrified me.

Anger suddenly took the place of hurt and I tried the last thing I knew to see Travis. I asked the already irritated man, "Don't you need me to come identify his body?" He replied that the police had already identified him by the state I.D. they found in his wallet when they brought him in that morning.

I wanted to sink into this hole of nothingness that I felt rapidly spreading through my body. Travis was dead, and there was nothing I could do, nor could I see him.

Just as I was about to hang up the phone, the man asked where I wanted them to release Travis' body, as they would be releasing it the next morning. The only funeral home I could think of was the one we used for Donnie. So I gave him the name of Gearheart Funeral Home and told him to call them. With that, we said our goodbyes, just as I knew I was about to have to do with Travis.

As I hung up the phone, I turned to see Donnie's parents, Bonita and Dan, coming through the door. They came to give Courtney a birthday gift. As Courtney opened her gift, I began sobbing again, and I told them of Travis' death and explained the details of the crash.

When I had finished, the very first words that came out of Bonita's mouth were "Well, at least, you have other sons. Travis wasn't your only son like Donnie was my only son."

I sat there in disbelief, tears filling my eyes and my heart.

From that point on, Bonita did most of the talking. I spoke only when Bonita asked me a direct question, and Dan just sat there quietly, looking down at his hands folded in his lap. He nervously fiddled with his thumbs. He nodded from time to time as Bonita talked. She was saying all the things that you don't want to say to a grieving parent, especially not one who was only twelve hours into her grief and still in shock. She said Heaven needed another angel. It was God's plan. Everything happens for a reason. Travis is in a better place now, etc.

Then she added, "I know you are a very strong woman. You'll be fine. You got over Donnie's death, no problem. Even with Courtney getting sick and almost dying, you were able to pick up the pieces and put your life back together. You moved on so quickly. I have no doubt in my mind that you will be able to do the same thing with Travis' death."

Because Bonita hadn't a clue about my grief over Donnie, I didn't care to listen to her any more. I tuned her out and withdrew within my mind instead. I thought about heaven and what it must be like, and whether it is as beautiful as you see on television and in books. I wondered if Travis was happy there. Reunited with Donnie, I knew he had to like it in heaven.

I looked down at my watch, and it was 4:05 p.m. and Bonita was still talking. All I could think was, is she done yet? Please, please, will you just shut up and leave?! I can't take your talking any more!

Dan looked up at the clock on the living room wall and then he looked over at Bonita. He said "It's 4:15 p.m." in a soft voice that was so quiet I could barely hear the words he was saying. He continued "If you want to get home [they lived two and a half hours away in Moose Lake] we still have enough time to get ready before having to meet Joe and Sherry for supper. We probably should get a move on." *Yes! Finally!* I screamed in my head. I got up and quickly walked Bonita and Dan to the front door. We exchanged goodbyes, I thanked them for Courtney's gift and swiftly ushered them out the door.

That went well, I told myself. Ummm, yeah right, *Not!* I took a deep breath, exhaled slowly and thought, I am sure glad that's over with. Travis' three sisters were still sitting in the living room. I gathered them and Travis' brother Logan up and by 5 p.m. we were in the car and headed for the crash site. It ended up being only a five-minute drive from the house. I turned onto Hanson Boulevard and instantly my eyes began to swell with tears, and my heart grew heavy. From three blocks away I could see a large group of kids. I knew this must be the spot.

As I continued to drive down Hanson Boulevard and closer to the crash site, I saw more and more kids. They were everywhere; the sidewalk, gathered around a large pole, up in the yard that housed the pole, and some kids had even spilled out into the street. My eyes were now flooded with tears, my stomach tied in knots, and my heart so heavy in my chest that it became difficult for me to breathe. I didn't want my children to see me crying. I was afraid it would scare them before I had even found a place to park. I did my best to keep my face turned away from them as I drove down Hanson Boulevard. I drove three blocks, but there were no parking spots. I made a U-turn and came back up the block. Total pandemonium everywhere.

Not seeing a spot to park, I pulled into the driveway. When we got out of the car, I was trembling. My legs were weak, and I began feeling nauseated. I thought, I can't do this, what was I thinking when I decided to come here! Then I told myself, get a grip, Dierdra! You have to do this for your children. I could no longer hide my tears from them. Logan put his arm around me when he saw the tears streaming down my face. His eyes were filled with terror. As I looked around, I began to panic. I realized that I didn't recognize anyone. The knots in my stomach quickly got tighter, the nauseating feeling tripled and the heaviness in my chest was like something I had never felt this bad before.

I could no longer breathe. My head began to grow lighter and my knees grew even weaker and just as I was thought I was going to faint I saw a friend of Travis' whose name I didn't know, but recognized as someone whom Travis had had over to the house a time or two. He was across the street in the group of kids that spilled out into the street. He waved us over. We weaved through some kids and made our way across the street. Travis' friend now stood in front of what I knew was the steel pole that had taken Travis' life. The friend hugged the kids and then hugged me as he mumbled in my ear, "I am so sorry Mrs. Rose. The crash, their deaths, everything, hits way to close to home and has caught everyone so off guard. How are you holding up? I can't even begin to imagine what you must be going through."

He released me and stepped back, allowing me to get a good look at the pole that killed Travis.

"So this is it?" I said as I reached out and touched the pole. I slowly circled it, and began reading everyone's last respects to the boys. In front of the pole was a half-inch-thick steel plate. There were deep scrape marks on it, and there was a huge dent in the middle of it. It was bent almost to the point of falling off. I knew this was the point of impact. I reached out, my hand trembling, and ran my fingers over the plate, feeling the scrapes and the dent, I looked down at the ground and saw flowers, stuffed animals, candles and other memorials totally surrounding the pole.

As I stood on the edge of the street gazing at all the memorials, I was standing in shattered glass and pieces of what must have been car blinkers. I realized that I hadn't brought any flowers, and moved away from the pole.

"How could this have happened?" I asked. The friend explained, "I'm not sure. We were all at a party having a good time. I didn't see any of them leave. It wasn't until this morning that I heard about the crash. I honestly don't know what happened."

I begged, "Please tell me that I am just having a horrible nightmare. Please pinch me and wake me up." I saw a tear trickle down his cheek as he looked at me and said, "I feel the same way, Mrs. Rose. I think I am going to wake up any second and they'll all be standing here."

Emily spoke up and told me she thought my car was in someone's way. I looked over and saw I was blocking another car from leaving. In a confused state, but knowing that I was in someone's way, I began sobbing as I blurted out, "I forgot flowers. Travis needs flowers. I've got to go get flowers for Travis."

We walked to my car and I quickly got everyone in. I turned to get in myself when the friend reached for my arm and told me "We're going to get through this, Mrs. Rose. All of us Seth, Jake and I will help. We'll take care of you and the kids. It's the least we can do for Travis."

I thanked him and hugged him goodbye. I never did catch the boy's name. I don't remember if I saw him at the funeral, either.

Not really sure where I was going to buy flowers, I decided to make a pit stop at home. I pulled into a driveway. Fred was sitting outside, and he quickly came to open my car door. He asked how I was doing and how things had gone at the crash site as the kids headed into the house, and I got out of the car. I knew I didn't need to really answer the question as to how I was so I told him that it went fine and that I came home because I forgot flowers and needed them to take back to the pole for Travis. I added that I needed to call the funeral home too. My eyes began to swell with tears again. Not sure what to say, Fred silently walked me up the steps and into the house. Once inside, he decided to take the kids to get something to eat so I could call the funeral home in peace. It wasn't until then when I realized I hadn't fed any of them breakfast or lunch.

I looked up the phone number for Gearheart Funeral Home and wrote it on the chalkboard. I took another deep breath and told myself, "You can do this, Dierdra!" I reached for the phone and called the funeral home. A man answered. I told him my name and explained about Travis. I told him that Mercy Hospital's morgue would be calling them to release Travis' body in the morning and that I was also in need of help for a funeral. He extended his condolences and told me that he could help me with funeral arrangements. He told me he would let me know the moment that Travis arrived in the morning and that we could sit down and talk about funeral arrangements then. I thanked the man and said goodbye. That wasn't so hard, I told myself, and you did it without any tears. Now to get Travis some flowers.

Remembering the flower shop that had done Donnie's flowers, it seemed only fitting to use them again, plus it was only two miles down the road. Entering the flower shop without realization of the time, I saw a man sweeping the floor. He glanced up at the clock so I could note that I had only five minutes before they closed. Heartbroken and feeling desperate, I told him that all I needed was a simple bouquet of flowers to take to the crash site where my son had been killed that morning, and I promised that it would take me only a minute.

The florist stopped sweeping, and I knew I had gained his full attention. He told me to take my time, there was no rush, and to let him know if I needed any help. Such a nice man, I thought, just ready to go home but willing to give me all the time I needed to pick out flowers for Travis. As I looked at the flowers, he continued sweeping.

Knowing that I had limited funds, I noticed immediately that none of the arrangements were priced. Hating to interrupt him, I cleared my throat to get his attention. I told him that none of the flowers were priced. I can remember his gentle voice as he looked at me confusedly, and explained that the prices were in their book. He immediately said he would be more than happy to help me if I could tell him how much I wanted to spend and what type of arrangement I was looking for.

As I looked at him, I wanted to scream, *my child is dead*, do you have flowers for that? Knowing that I had to do this, I had to take flowers back to the crash site for Travis, I looked into my purse and realized I had only ten dollars with me. It was at that moment that I wanted to curl up and hide in a corner. Realizing what I was doing from the frantic look on my face, he told me that money was not a problem, and he would be more than honored to have me pick out anything I wanted, and the cost was on him. Tears then began to flow, a total stranger offering such kindness was beyond reason to

141

me, everything was beyond reason to me at that moment in time. He must have seen me looking at the rose bouquet. I remember clearly his words telling me to, please, please take these roses. He held them out and insisted I take them. I accepted the roses as he handed me the bouquet and quickly thanked him for them.

Feeling guilty about not being charged for the roses, I told the florist I would be back tomorrow to pick out some funeral flowers. Instead, he insisted he would be more than happy to stay late if I wanted to pick out flowers now. I knew I wasn't ready to pick out flowers for Travis; how could I be, would I ever be? Picking out flowers made my son's death real and final!! Against my feelings, I decided to stay and pick out flowers to get it over with and out of the way so as to have one less thing I had to worry about later.

After locking the door, the florist led me to a chair at a desk where he patiently watched me struggle just to keep the tears back and try to look through a book of sample arrangements for memorials that he had done. I was adamant about not wanting Travis' flowers to look cheap, but explained I was on a tight budget. Patiently and calmly he explained that we would find something in my price range that I liked, and he would make sure they would look as nice, if not nicer than the arrangements in the book.

As I began turning the pages, I realized that I was going to need flowers from Travis' siblings as well as from me. All I could think of was that Travis' favorite color was neon green without realizing that I had blurted that out loud. The florist assured me that flowers could be dyed any color of my choosing.

From Travis' siblings, I ordered a spray to be placed on his casket. It had yellow roses with seven neon-green lilies randomly placed, one for each of Travis' siblings, and a white ribbon with "In Memory of Our Beloved Brother and Gone, But Never Forgotten" written in gold lettering. I picked out a praying angel that reminded me of Travis to sit inside the casket spray. From myself, I ordered a blooming peace lily with a yellow ribbon that read "Beloved Son and FOREVER in My Heart" in green lettering. I ordered a wreath of white roses, too. In the middle of the wreath, there were miniature neon-green roses in the shape of a cross and a green ribbon that read "Travis" and "FOREVER Young" in white lettering. I also ordered four balloons each one saying something different. I nearly fainted when the florist gave me a total for my order; I had ordered two hundred and twelve dollars' worth of flowers. Too ashamed to say I couldn't afford that much, I just thanked the florist, hugged him, and left for the crash site.

I will forever remember his kindness when I needed it most.

Not wanting to deal with the mob of kids who had been at the crash site earlier, I was very relieved when I arrived to see that most of the kids had left. Only a few friends remained. I pulled up and parked across the street. Crossing the street, I stopped in front of the pole. A couple of the friends who remained came over to give me their condolences. Thanking them, I knelt down with Travis' roses. I rearranged the flowers and stuffed animals, making room for the roses. I carefully laid them out one by one. With every move I made, my heart shattered a piece at a time as if they were cutting my very soul.

After I laid the last rose in place, I again noticed the shattered glass and broken blinker plastic in the street. I quickly picked up pieces of the debris and placed it in some of the cellophane from the roses, then carefully folded the cellophane and gently tucked it in the pocket of my sweater. I gazed up, and noticing the pole for the first time, I read all the tributes that Travis' friends had written.

Wanting to write a message of my own, I stood up and quietly asked the boy standing next to me if I could borrow his marker. I wrote "I Love You, Travis. Always Have and Always Will, FOREVER!" Staring up at the words I had just written, I kissed my fingers, placed them on the pole, and repeated the words out loud as I touched each word slowly. Blowing a kiss to the sky, I repeated "I love you, Travis. Always have and always will, forever." I handed the marker back to the boy and quickly crossed the street to my car. I got inside and gazed over at the pole one last time. I sat there, shaking my head.

I must have drifted off. I'm not sure how long I sat there with my engine running, but I do know it was long enough for the boy with the marker to become concerned. He crossed the street, knocked on my car window, which was down slightly, and asked if I was all right. Embarrassed, I explained that I was fine. With tears filling my eyes and soul, I quickly drove away.

Fred was home alone when I came up the steps and through the front door. He quickly came to the doorway with a worried look on his face. He hugged me as I explained my experience at the florist and then at the crash site. Just talking was tiring, yet I knew he was grieving too. After asking him where the kids were and realizing they were all with friends and comfortably accounted for, I felt a sigh of relief escape my lips. All I wanted was to be alone and sleep. I kissed Fred, walked to my bedroom and shut the door. I lay down fully dressed, and dozed off right away.

I didn't wake up until the next morning when Fred knocked on my door around 9 a.m., and said "Gearheart Funeral Home is on the phone." I quickly picked up the phone next to the bed. The gentleman told me that Travis was there if I wanted to see him. Immediately sitting up in bed, I answered "YES." He quickly explained that Travis would have to be cleaned up first and he would call me back shortly.

I got up and went into the kitchen to tell Fred, then quickly went back in my room and changed into clean, unwrinkled clothes. I decided to call Mindy and Shelly, the two girls Travis had been keeping company with, to see if either of them wanted go to the funeral home with me. I knew I was going to need all the support I could get. Getting no answer at Mindy's, I called Shelly. Her mother, Betty, answered the phone so I asked her if either she or Shelly would please go with me. She said they would both be right over. When they arrived, I was surprised to see Shelly's younger sister Jessie accompanying them. The funeral home called about an hour later. I asked if I could bring a couple of friends and my camera, to which they readily agreed. I gathered up my camera and we all headed for the funeral home, driving in separate cars.

We were greeted at the door by a very small yet compassionate gentleman. He shook our hands and introduced himself as Samuel. He said, "You must be Travis' mom," as he looked at me clutching my camera. I nodded. Samuel extended his condolences as he led us to a small chapel. "There's no hurry, please take as much time as you need," he said as he opened the chapel door.

Not ready to see my dead son, Shelly and Betty each took one of my arms and we walked down the aisle toward Travis together; Jessie followed behind us. Halfway down the aisle, I stopped, and we all began crying. Travis was lying on a gurney. He was dressed in a clean white T-shirt and had a white sheet draped over him. Only his head and the top of his chest were exposed. He had fresh red lacerations around his mouth and on his forehead and a large gash above his right eye.

I reached out and caressed his face, my hands trembling. All I could do was sob and say, "Oh, Travis." I laid my face down next to his and our cheeks touched. Tears were running down my cheek and spilling onto Travis'. I just stood there with my face on his cheek, hugging his chest. I kept thinking how good he looked, thinking he definitely didn't look like he should be dead.

I didn't see Travis' injuries from his chest down. He was an organ donor, though the only viable organs were his corneas and the long bones in his legs, which is what was donated. After a long while I lifted my head, placing my hands on Travis' cheeks. I kissed his injuries and repeated, "Oh, Travis. What have you done? How am I going to survive without you?"

I remember rubbing his arm over and over through the white sheet. Deciding to take a couple of final pictures of Travis and his beautiful face, I walked over and picked up my camera. When I finished taking pictures, I excused myself to go speak with Samuel about Travis' funeral. After finalizing arrangements, I returned to the chapel to find the others had left, and Travis and I were alone.

I made my way down the aisle to see Travis one last time before leaving. I felt my breathing become shallower with every step, as if at any moment I might just stop breathing completely. In my mind and heart, at that moment I was okay with that.

The next day I got a call early in the morning from the Coon Rapids Police Department. They had a few more details as to what had transpired that fateful Friday evening that ultimately led up to the crash and Travis' death. I cringed as I prepared myself for whatever the officer was about to tell me. Had I not been through enough? I had just planned my son's funeral; he's lying cold and lifeless on a gurney. How much more do you want from me, I thought, as I listened to the voice explain the details they didn't have earlier.

I was told that there was a keg party held in Andover and hosted by Jack, a spoiled little rich boy, who was a seventeen-year-old minor. The party was attended by about seventy-five to one hundred minors. They were unsure who had supplied the three kegs of beer; Jack wasn't talking. Jack's parents were out of town for the weekend, so there was no adult supervision.

Apparently Mike got into a fight at about 1:30 a.m. He was sticking up for an unpopular boy who was considered to be very uncool. He made quite a scene and Jack asked him to leave. Stating that he was pretty buzzed, Mike asked if he could just pass out in his car until he sobered up a bit. Jack told him no, he needed to leave immediately.

Travis and Troy were nearby and overheard Jack and Mike's conversation. Travis decided to ride with Mike to make sure he was okay to drive and got home safely. Troy just wanted a ride back to the trailer park where he and Mike lived. Neither Travis nor Troy had driver's licenses, so Mike drove. It was unclear why Mike was traveling westbound on Hanson Boulevard, since all three boys lived in the opposite direction. The blood alcohol content came back on all three boys. Travis was .02, Troy .04, and Mike .10. The police told me they would keep me posted as new details became available.

I spoke to both of the other mothers, telling them of the new details as the police had explained them. They had already spoken with the police, so they knew everything I knew. Carrie told me that they had notified State Farm of the accident and that Mike's insurance had a one hundred thousand-dollar liability limit for each boy's wrongful death. She gave me a claim number and said that if I had any further questions I should call State Farm and give them the claim number. The conversation was short and informative, something only grieving mothers could understand at that time. There was no small talk as before, only tears.

In light of this new information that the police had just shared, Fred and I decided that it was time to call State Farm. We couldn't wait until after the funeral; this needed to be handled now. I called State Farm and asked to speak with the person or persons assigned to Mike's claim, and gave them the claim number.

I was connected to a woman who had no empathy for the accident and most certainly not for me. As we talked, she told me that State Farm's position on the claim was that they were not liable for Travis' wrongful death because Travis was negligent. He got in the car with a drunk driver and unfortunately he paid the ultimate price for his negligence; he died.

I sat there dumbfounded, holding the phone in my hand, not believing she could be serious. I responded angrily with words that just came spilling out of my mouth, threatening words telling her how lucky she was that this conversation was over the phone and not in person. She said she was sorry I felt that way and if there were no further questions she was going to hang up. And that's exactly what she did. I wasn't even able to get any other questions out before she rudely hung up on me. Fred and I decide that I needed to contact a lawyer.

I called, Jim, my family attorney whom I had used for fourteen years. I explained the situation and all the details of the accident. Jim agreed to represent me in a case against State Farm for Travis' wrongful death. He explained that he knew Jack's (the minor who hosted the party) family very well; that he personally knew the parents' net worth, and explained that he could not, however, represent me in a case against them because it would be a conflict of interest. He graciously gave me the name and number of a firm that he believed could help with my case.

Disappointed, I decided not to use Jim at all. I would later contact the firm whose number Jim had given me. It would cost me *only* one-third of any settlement that might be received, and nothing at all if there was no settlement.

In the end (eleven months later), because of some kind of umbrella insurance policy that Jack's parents had, they were not held liable for the party that Jack hosted. They were not liable for anyone at the party, or any of their actions that happened once they left the party or their property. They were not responsible for Mike getting drunk on their property, getting kicked off the property by Jack, driving drunk, crashing into the pole, or the deaths of Travis and Troy.

State Farm, however, lost their case and had to pay the one hundred thousand-dollar settlement for Travis' wrongful death. After paying the attorney, I had approximately sixty-six thousand dollars for my son's life. No justice, just a small lump sum. I put the money in trust funds for Travis' siblings until they were twenty-one. All have now collected their trust funds except Courtney.

As if I didn't have enough on my plate already, the day before Travis' funeral I got a letter from the Morrison County district attorney. The driver who had killed Donnie hadn't learned his lesson yet. He was being sentenced to two years in prison for violating his probation by receiving yet another DWI. I would be notified of his sentencing hearing if I wanted to give another victim impact statement.

On Wednesday, April 8, 1998, at 1 p.m. I said goodbye to my son for the last time. It's a date that will be forever burned in my heart. Because I was exhausted physically, emotionally and mentally, I don't remember much about the actual funeral. The funeral home had the pictures of Travis and his personal effects placed as I requested, and the songs that were picked were played between eulogies as designed. The florist did a beautiful job with the flowers I had ordered what now seemed like an eternity ago, but was actually only days. The arrangements looked much nicer than I had envisioned they would. I was pleased.

Travis had many friends, and I can recall that there was standing room only. Seth and Jake gave a combined eulogy, as did Betty and Shelly; my nephew Byran, Alex and Nathan did their eulogies individually. I can remember the seemingly long hours it took to make decisions I didn't want to make, that no mother should ever have to make. And I vividly remembered that when I looked at the card inside the memorial flower arrangements that I had gotten from the flower shop, it read, "Paid in full. Our sincerest condolences for the loss of your son, Travis." I sobbed as I read the card. The rest is all a blur; a horrible nightmare that has become my journey.

A luncheon was held after the cemetery, but I decided not to go. I knew that my siblings and other relatives would think badly of my not going, but that didn't bother me; I didn't care anymore. I didn't care about a lot of things anymore. The only thing I cared about was the fact that Travis was gone and that I would *never* see him again.

Because Travis was to be cremated, he wouldn't actually be laid to rest for two more days. When it came time for his ashes to be buried, I at first refused to go. I didn't want Travis buried. I wanted him home with me as he should be. But because Shelly and Betty had several burial plots, they decided that Travis would be buried in one. I went along with his burial only because I didn't want to come off as being selfish and ungrateful. I decided that it wasn't fair if I made Travis' siblings miss his burial just because I wasn't going. So I called and asked Pastor Perry if he minded stopping by and giving them a ride. He agreed. Fred and Pastor Perry both tried desperately to change my mind. But I was adamant about not going.

Everyone, including Fred, left to go the cemetery. After everyone had left and given me time to think alone, I decided that if I didn't go to Travis' burial I would regret it the rest of my life. I knew deep down that I would never forgive myself and resent the fact that I didn't go to watch him laid to rest. So at the last minute, even though I wasn't properly dressed, I decided to go for myself and for Travis.

I was the last person to arrive at the cemetery. Everyone was standing around a small hole in the ground on the edge of the cemetery driveway as I entered the gate. Everyone's eyes were on me as I pulled in, parked and got out of my car. I stood out like a sore thumb, arriving as late as I did. Pastor Perry said a final prayer as Logan set Travis' ashes into the shallow grave.

In the months to come I found it too painful to go visit Travis at the cemetery. It was easier just to stay in bed. Travis died in April. I didn't go visit him till his first birthday in heaven in November.

A couple of weeks after Travis' funeral I asked to meet with the coroner. I needed to know if my son suffered and how long it took before he gasped his last breath. It was at this meeting that I saw the extent of all Travis' injuries throughout his body as I looked at the pictures taken by the coroner during the autopsy. Each picture showed a different injury. The injuries all had a ruler next to them to measure their size. The last picture showed Travis' heart with a huge hole in it. His aorta had been torn from his heart. The hole looked big enough to put your fist through. How sadly ironic that Travis would die from the same injury as Donnie. Their aortas were both ripped from their hearts, causing them both to drown in their own blood. It took several minutes for each of them to take their last breaths.

Travis shattered what is known as the St. Peter's bone in his skull. Donnie snapped two vertebrae in his neck. Both injuries caused them to become unconscious. But it took about ninety seconds before they went unconscious.

I asked the coroner "Be honest, did Travis suffer before he went unconscious?"

She softly but firmly answered "Yes, Mrs. Rose he, did." When Donnie died I was lied to and told if it was any consolation, that Donnie was dead before he hit the ground. The police and the county attorney both told me this. A year later, I found it to be a horrible lie. Donnie had lived for several minutes. I questioned the county attorney and asked him, "Donnie wasn't dead before he hit the ground, was he?" It was then that I was told Donnie hadn't died immediately.

I asked, "Why was I lied to? What gave you and the police the right to play God and lie to me?"

"We only wanted to spare you from undue grief," he said. This is something that I have never told Donnie's parents or his sister, Kellie.

I took three weeks off from both work and school, thinking that I would be better by the end of three weeks. I was wrong. I wasn't better; in fact, I got worse. I couldn't even get out of bed. I had lost all desire to live. I requested additional time off from both, but was told three weeks was the maximum bereavement time allowed for the death of a child. Because of my mental state, I ended up quitting both my job and school. As if I weren't having a hard enough time trying to deal with the loss of Travis, my siblings for weeks to come criticized me for the circus I had made out of Travis' funeral. They called me cheap, so cheap that I put my son in a welfare casket. They said I looked like I was hosting a garden party because I dressed the girls in floral dresses. I poured on phony tears for attention and sympathy every time a well-wisher came up to me to extend their condolences. My sister Jane was so furious that the florist had provided their memorials for Travis, at no cost to me, that she remarked, "No matter what, Dierdra, somehow you always come out smelling like a rose."

I think her real problem was that she was jealous of their generosity and compassion, something she has never experienced because of her "I'm better than you" attitude. She further said that all the kids at Travis' funeral weren't really his friends, they were just kids who wanted a free pass to get out of school early or kids who wanted to see the "monster on display" because I didn't put restorative makeup on Travis' bruised face.

In the months to come they would continue bad-mouthing me for how I handled Travis' memorial money. They said I got rich off my son's death and I stole money from MADD. That particular statement came about because Samuel suggested that I put "In lieu of flowers, memorials preferred to MADD" in Travis' obituary. Not wanting to come off as being greedy, and being so exhausted and overwhelmed, I agreed to almost every suggestion Samuel threw my way. I just wanted to be done so I could go home and be alone.

Mike's parents donated his car to MADD, which put it on display at Blaine High School three weeks after the crash. With all of Travis' siblings, I attended MADD's display at the high school that day and I gave their director, LaDonna, the donations received from Travis' funeral that were made out to MADD. She had been hounding me for them for three weeks. The total was three hundred and ninety-five dollars. LaDonna looked at what I had handed her, and without even counting it, she asked if that was all I had for them. I told her that those were all the checks that were made out to MADD and all the cash that I had received. I kept the checks that were made out to myself or my children. She looked at me, shook her head, and rudely walked away. Travis' brothers and I were asked to speak in front of the students who attended MADD's display. But having just been insulted by LaDonna, I lost all respect for MADD and refused to be a speaker for them.

The icing on the cake would come several months later when I, Sheila and Mike's dad, Al, were all asked to write a short article on how the boys' death had impacted our lives. My article was titled "Law and Justice." LaDonna didn't like my wording and totally rewrote the whole article. She then had the nerve to put my name on it. I haven't participated in MADD ever since.

Today, my siblings still call me cheap because Travis' grave is marked by a six-by-twelve-inch patio block that I personalized with paint, permanent marker, and lacquer. There is no headstone, partly because I can't afford one, but mostly because I am still stuck in the angry stage of grief and I will *never* accept that Travis is dead. To me, a headstone signifies closure, which is something I will *never* have. Until you have walked in my shoes, don't judge my journey.

I hated God. I blamed him for both Donnie's and Travis' deaths. And while I know that he didn't cause their deaths, I know that he didn't stop them either. Being brought up in a strict Baptist family, I was always taught there was absolutely nothing that God couldn't stop. But not only did he not stop Donnie's and Travis' deaths, he left them to suffer immensely and to drown in their blood. What kind of God does that? I was also taught that God never gives you more burden to bear than you can carry on your shoulders at one time. Couldn't he see that my knees were buckling?

As the months went on, my friends began to drop like flies. They never called me anymore, they never invited me to join them in outings anymore. There were no more invitations to their houses. If I called them, they were too busy to talk. If I asked them to come over or to a movie or something, they always had other plans. Even Fred eventually stopped supporting me. Every time I needed to talk about Travis and his wrongful death, Fred would say, "Do I have to listen to this again? I've been listening to it for so long now. It's time that you get over it and move on."

Travis' death made Donnie's seem like a picnic. In the eighteen years since, I have been hospitalized seven time — three for suicide attempts. I've had thirty-five electroconvulsive therapy treatments that left me with permanent brain damage and unemployable. I have three college degrees but I am unemployable. I now live on disability, and have become known as the CrAzY lady.

I have no interest in things that I did before Travis died. Bowling, gardening, computers, photography, flea markets, garage sales, rummage sales, antiques; all interests are gone. All that remains of me is an empty shell that is forced to get up day to day and go through the sad and ever emotional motions of existing.

In conclusion I say this: there was no justice served in either Donnie or Travis' death. The driver who killed Donnie basically got away with murder, and with Travis there was no judge, jury or process; I was never given my day in court. Was Donnie's or Travis' death an accident? Not by my definition of the word. They were needless tragedies, caused by drinking and driving.

Just six short weeks after Travis' tragic death, the Coon Rapids Police Department informed me that rather than waste more time and money on an investigation that was going nowhere, they were permanently closing the case. No criminal charges were ever brought against Jack's brother-in-law, the adult who supplied the alcohol and ultimately responsible for Travis' needless death.

My heart is broken, my life forever changed. I am left with many unanswered questions. Travis, Mike, and Troy are not here to answer my questions. I was told that to pursue the case would be a total waste of time and money. I wonder who determines the time and sets the price limits that a police department can spend on a case? At what point does the pursuit of justice become a waste of time? And ultimately, it leaves me to wonder if I were more well known or had more money, like Jack's parents and brother-in-law, would this investigation have remained open?

For the past eighteen years, I have been trying to cope with the same nightmare that I did when Donnie was killed twenty-three years ago. I said back then that there was no justice in our legal system, and unfortunately I'm still saying it today. How long will our laws be allowed to protect the person who chooses to drink and drive? How long will our society turn the other cheek when an adult supplies alcohol to minors in the misdirected belief that "if I know what they are doing, I can take care of the situation?" Whose son, daughter, or spouse must be the next victim? Which will be the one to see the case pursued to the end, no matter the time or cost? Will I ever get closure? I'm not certain, but most likely not. The one thing that is for certain is having suffered the devastating losses of Donnie and Travis for almost a quarter of a century now, I am and always will be "FOREVER, twice broken!"

DIERDRA ROSE
COON RAPIDS, MINNESOTA

TRAVIS D. MCNAMARA
(11/01/78 - 04/04/98)

DONALD W.E. PRATT
(06/13/61 - 01/24/93)

DIERDRA'S BIRTHDAY – 6 days before Travis' death

FOUR GENERATIONS (1993)

FAMILY CHRISTMAS CARD 2015

Killed by a Drunk Driver

DRUNK DRIVING IS NO ACCIDENT !

Donnie
6/13/61 - 1/24/93

Travis
11/01/78 - 4/04/98

DON'T Drink & Drive !!!

In Loving Memory

Travis Daniel McNamara

November 1, 1978 - April 4, 1998

DONNIE & DIERDRA

A mother's grief is as
timeless as her love.
-DR. JOANNE CACCIATORE

DON'T TELL ME
Unknown

Please don't tell me you know how I feel,
Unless you have lost your child too.
Please don't tell me my broken heart will heal,
Because that is just not true.
Please don't tell me my son is in a better place,
Though it is true, I want him here with me.
Don't tell me someday I'll hear his voice, see his face,
Beyond today I cannot see.
Don't tell me it is time to move on,
Because I cannot.
Don't tell me to face the fact he is gone,
Because denial is something I can't stop.
Don't tell me to be thankful for the time I had,
Because I wanted more.
Don't tell me when I am my old self you will be glad,
I'll never be as I was before.
What you can tell me is you will be here for me,
That you will listen when I talk of my child.
You can share with me my precious memories,
You can even cry with me for a while.
And please don't hesitate to say his name,
Because it is something I long to hear every day.
Friend please realize that I can never be the same,
But if you stand by me,
You may like the new person I become someday.

CHAPTER NINE

SHATTERED HEARTS,

UNBREAKABLE SOULS

BY GINA LANCE

Laugh when you can. Apologize when you should. Let go of what you can't change. Love deeply and forgive quickly. Take chances and give your everything. Life is too short to be anything but happy. You have to take the good with the bad.
- AUTHOR UNKNOWN

Around 2:30 in the morning I woke suddenly from my sleep, sat straight up and said: "I'm pregnant." I had been taking tests, but like my prior pregnancies, they were continuously negative. I had one miscarriage in recent months. I just knew I was pregnant but couldn't remember what woke me to know this. I took another test, and it was positive. I put the test results on the bathroom cabinet and left it for my husband, Allan, that morning. This would be our third child, as our firstborn was a boy, Travis. I went back to sleep with such calm.

God blessed us with our precious baby girl Ashlyn on December 20, 1995. I loved her fat rolls on her legs, her sweet face, the way she begged for food like a baby bird, and how she was so sweet with her mannerisms. I remember her dad just studying her little face, proud of his little girl. Our life wasn't perfect, but we had our two precious children, and they were the highlight of our lives.

Ashlyn was so precious as a baby. She was such a content baby. The only time she cried was when she was hungry. I couldn't eat enough when I was pregnant, and knew why after she entered our world. Not only was she sweet in her mannerisms, smiled and laughed all the time, but she was very independent, absolutely loved animals, and was very advanced at everything for her age. She said, "I love you, Daddy," at four and a half months. She and Allan had a special relationship from the beginning. It was so sweet and adoring to watch.

When she was a baby, I thought she would be sweet but shy. She wasn't a shy child at all. She was so happy and outgoing. So silly and friendly, saying "hi" to strangers at stores and making little friends at restaurants. She always rooted for the underdog and was a total animal lover from the start. She would tell her dad and me, when we told her not to pick up bugs, "But I just love it." Her dad would get concerned that she would pick up a spider or snake. He doted on her from day one and would just study her sweet face for hours. He was always watching her with such pride.

He loved all his kids, and with Travis being his first little one and a boy, they were close as well. Ashlyn was our first girl, and she was a messy little thing from the start. She would get dirty as soon as I dressed her up, her desk at school was easy to spot, her room at home was hopeless. She couldn't find anything if it were clean, she claimed. Her purse looked the same. She liked clothes, even though she had started wearing pretty much the same outfits over and over in her teens. I would have had her buried in that outfit if she hadn't had a dress hung on her bedroom door and hadn't asked about her other sandal the very last time I saw her precious face or heard her sweet voice that night. She had done her chores and was getting her outfit ready for school the next day.

I had little nicknames for Ashlyn. I called her Babygirl, Bubbles, Skittles, Lollipop, and several other silly, sweet names. As a teen she gained the nickname Bugsy for her big brown eyes. She liked that nickname a lot. I mostly called her Babygirl and still do. Bubbles fits because she was bubbly, and the song "Bubbly," by Colbie Caillat, is the song I think of when thinking of her and when my kids were little.

When Ashlyn was one, Allan and I divorced. He went on to marry and have two more children, Sarah and Chase. I remarried after an eight-year-long relationship and had three stepchildren, Andrew, Anthony, and Adam. Travis and Ashlyn loved their siblings. Growing up and playing with them was an adventure. All my boys treated Ashlyn so sweetly because she was the only girl. She admitted as a teen that she thought she was something special when little. Sarah and Chase moved out of town with their mom after their parents' divorce, both still really young. They stayed with us for six months before moving, which all the kids enjoyed.

Before their teen years, my second marriage ended as well. Travis and Ashlyn remained very close even as teens. They were each other's go-to person in hard times and for advice. Allan ended up moving out of town later as well when Ashlyn was a preteen, but visits and calls were as often as possible, and we worked together to make that happen. The teen years were much different than the younger years. Ashlyn wasn't as outgoing and didn't have the same confidence. She missed many loved ones who had moved away or passed away including my mom, who died in 2008. We both grieved, especially Ashlyn, to the point of emotional and health problems, causing her grades and attitude with adults to change, especially when some of them lacked the skills or care to deal with a preteen with such problems. Instead, Ashlyn got labeled by new teachers who didn't know her before as a bad kid with an attitude. Rebellious she was, but there was an underlying reason. I told them she was grieving her favorite granny (called her Good Granny) whom she saw just about every day, and whom she had watched deteriorate with cancer. That is hard for anyone, especially the first time you experience someone you are close to dying in front of your eyes.

Ashlyn became more distant, and it was evident that she missed the loved ones who had moved away as well. She wanted to sleep most of the time, didn't want to go to school which she normally loved, stopped reading which she also loved, started passing out and having migraines, and self-harming herself along with other bad habits. The worst was to get high. It was a way of escaping her pain. It was years before her grief and depression started to get better, but she was still different. She slowly started being happy again, but was very emotional and distant to me although we had always been so very close.

She once said, after apologizing for hurting my feelings and making being a single parent so hard, that she didn't understand why God took everyone she loved away from her. That was when I knew why she was so distant with me. Life became easier, though the hard days would still rear their ugly head from time to time. I was still the bad guy looking out for her and often saying no to the things she wanted to do.

Later she realized why I did what I did. She gave me a heartfelt apology and hug just weeks before that final day. She said she was sorry but was young and was still going to do things that hurt me, but that it wouldn't be intentional. Many things we shared in the last few years, especially the last few months, were special mother-daughter moments that mean so very much. I know our love is strong and unbreakable.

I stop and close my eyes to take in those memories of how it was when she was here. It's still not the same, but as close as I get anymore. Oh, how we would dance and sing in the car when we both liked a song. Otherwise, it was radio war, which she won more than she lost. "Forever 22" by Taylor Swift was the last song I remember us singing one day after I picked her up from school. I remembered thinking how I hoped she would always keep her youthfulness. However, she never made it to age twenty-two.

Her picture on her headstone is what she looked like just about every day. American Eagle jeans, Sperry shoes, and a blue Hollister jacket, mix-matched colorful socks, and she had to have her hair so straight most every day. I had her buried in the outfit she had laid out for school the next day. The school day she only attended in other's thoughts and memories. Her seat in every class was empty, and the hallways were filled with saddened teens shaken up by the news of another teen from their school killed in a wreck.

Thursday, May 9, 2013, three days before Mother's Day, was a fairly normal day except for the fact that I had a bad sinus infection. I decided to lie down as soon as Ashlyn and I got home for the second time around 7 p.m. I fell asleep knowing that Ashlyn was supposed to be at home, as she did not have permission to go anywhere that night. Ben, a very good friend, woke me up about twenty minutes later telling me she was gone. I looked at him in confusion as he told me that he had seen her walk outside at 8:09 p.m. When she didn't come back in by 8:22, he started to look for her. After about ten minutes he decided to wake me up.

I jumped up and immediately tried to contact her by text. There was no response from texts that I continually sent, and then I just stopped because I knew she would have already responded. As I stood outside in the driveway shortly after looking for her at home, I felt a sudden overwhelming feeling of her being gone. It is hard to explain, but it stopped me immediately. That feeling happened right at the time of the wreck.

I was frantic; I needed to find my Ashlyn. I looked for her in several places, returning home a few times during the search. I was so worried that I couldn't think clearly. I knew she wasn't conscious, but I couldn't quite shake that distant feeling either. I was trying just to get to her.

Even though I felt distant from her, I didn't know she had passed away yet. I just couldn't and wouldn't think that, no matter the feeling I was having. She communicated by telepathy while I was in our driveway, shortly before my making police report. I hadn't taken it seriously and didn't connect it to the wreck as I hadn't heard about a wreck yet.

I returned home to get a call from Travis about Ashlyn's friend being in a wreck. The word was that her friend had been killed and people were trying to figure out who the other girl in wreck was. I screamed to Travis, "It's Ashlyn!" I screamed for Ben, helpless and needing to find out more. I yelled and begged him to hurry, feeling that I couldn't drive.

During the earlier telepathic communication, I felt what Ashlyn felt, and heard her thoughts in my mind. I felt she wasn't conscious but knew what was going on around her. There were three males and the one in the middle was evil, and he directed it toward Ashlyn. He kept looking at her and she felt his evilness, too. I will never forget that evil feeling. Once you've felt an evil presence, you will never forget it. I only vaguely saw but strongly felt that there was a female friend in the distance. Ashlyn felt concerned for her. Her last thought that I felt and heard were "I just wanted to see my friend. I just wanted to see my friend." After those words, the experience was over.

Ben and I left the house to go to the hospital in search of answers; we saw the officer to whom I had made the missing person report on our way. He was parked at a church talking to another officer, so we pulled in to find out anything we could. This was when my worst nightmare came true, as they told us it was a blonde who was killed. I screamed, "My daughter is the blonde!" The officer made a phone call, and they had us follow them very slowly to the hospital. Ashlyn was being transported to the emergency room to be pronounced dead. I knew as we followed that my life was forever changed, and my heart was aching with a reality that I didn't want to face.

Later we would find out what happened that horrid night. Ashlyn received a text from a friend, also seventeen, asking her if she wanted to go with her to the nearby Walmart. They decided while texting that Ashlyn would meet her down the road from where we lived, at the church, around 8:15 p.m. Ashlyn knew the driver through other people. He had asked her out when she was in the tenth grade, but she had a boyfriend at the time. When he found out that Ashlyn and her boyfriend had broken up, he continually texted her, asking her out, to which she repeatedly said no. She had expressed her concerns to someone just a day before, saying that he was really starting to bother her, and she was getting concerned. To this day, I do not know if Ashlyn had any idea that he was going to be the driver when she agreed to go with her friend to Walmart.

He had three other passengers with him, including Ashlyn's friend when they picked her up. As her friend told me, the girls went inside to use the restroom when they got to Walmart, while the cousin of the eighteen-year-old driver went inside to purchase canned duster. Meanwhile, the driver and her friend's boyfriend smoked a joint together. When everyone was back at the vehicle, the plan to take Ashlyn back home got changed. The nineteen-year-old driver insisted that Ashlyn sit up front, exchanging seats with his cousin, before leaving the parking lot. Ashlyn ended up in the front passenger seat.

They were heading out into the country to Flat Rock, a place where young people have hung out for years. However, they never made it to Flat Rock and Ashlyn didn't make it home that night. The driver decided to huff the canned air as he was driving. As the passengers screamed for him to stop huffing, he wouldn't, and then decided to leave his lane at the posted speed, crossed the opposite lane, went down a ditch, through a fence, and stopped in a cow pasture. Yes, he stopped, and my baby girl was not hurt at this time. However, that evil monster decided the ride wasn't over yet.

He accelerated at a high level of speed, going through an open gate into another area of the pasture. Next in his path of destruction was a descending hill and a creek with a tree. He could have stopped, but he never chose to use his brakes again. His path didn't have twists and turns, and he wasn't doing doughnuts. No, it wasn't a joyride as the local paper described; it was almost a straight line, leaving the Blazer mangled against a tree at the creek's edge. The impact of the front end of that old Chevy Blazer was all but even or straight in the middle. All the damage was on the front passenger side where he had insisted my baby girl sit just minutes earlier.

Ashlyn and two of the other passengers were unconscious upon impact. The driver and Ashlyn's seventeen-year-old female friend were still conscious. Her immediate reaction was to escape the wreckage and get away from the driver. She climbed over the back seat where she had been sitting and through the back hatch, falling to the ground. Before she had a chance to get out of the seat, the driver grabbed one of her legs, and she yelled "ReRe, *let go!*" and he let go. When she hit the ground, she realized her leg was hurt and she couldn't walk, so she crawled through the cow pasture yelling for help repeatedly. She was heard by a neighbor, who alerted her husband.

The husband ran to the field yelling that he was coming. When he got to the fence, the driver stopped him, saying everyone was fine, and asked for a phone to call his dad. Before she was heard by the wife and the husband who came, the driver was telling Ashlyn's friend to "SHUT UP." He was going back and forth from where she crawled, upsetting her, then back to the wreckage looking for a cell phone. He had no regard for the passengers and offered no help. Thinking only of himself and wanting a phone not to call for help but to call his dad to help him. What was his dad going to do? Instead of asking the first person there to help for the same reason, he should have been asking if that person called 911 and told him about his seriously injured passengers. The man had already called 911, and he didn't let the driver keep him from checking on everyone else. He found out from the conscious female friend that there were three other victims, and what their names were.

It was hard to see in the vehicle without climbing in, because the front end ran up the side of the tree which had been uprooted like it had been hit by straight-line winds, although even straight-line winds would have had trouble uprooting the tree at 75 to 89 mph. The tire tracks went straight to the tree, which wouldn't have been straight had the driver not been conscious. He consciously accelerated at a high rate of speed from the stopping point in the field through the open gate and downhill to the large tree.

When the first state trooper arrived, he was told by the driver that there were only four of them in the wreck. But there were five. My Ashlyn was the last one, and wasn't found until the trooper went up to the passenger side. She was in such a position that she was hard to see, and her jacket that was sitting on her shoulders was now lying on top of her. I believe the driver put her jacket over the top of her, and intentionally lied about how many passengers were in the vehicle.

In the following days and month I had a feeling that her jacket and phone, along with the evil feeling about the driver, was Ashlyn trying to tell me something. Ashlyn's phone still hadn't been found. I believe it was found and there was important information on it.

This crash doesn't sound like an accident, does it? The answer is *no* because it was intentional. No impaired driving crash is an accident to begin with. It is a choice that one makes knowing the possible outcome. An outcome that mangles and kills but isn't considered a violent crime. Is it because a crash happens so quickly that we don't consider it violent? I hardly think that is the reason. If I got drunk and shot a person before he or she had knowledge of what was happening, that would be still be considered a violent crime. I would be arrested and charged with aggravated assault with a deadly weapon, attempted murder, or even murder if death was the result. So what is the difference? That's the question that plays over and over in my mind.

The driver had no regard for human life, always thinking only of himself. That is evident, with his assaulting them all like he did, and his actions after the crash. The wreck was immediately investigated as a murder. An autopsy was ordered which kept me from being able to see and hold Ashlyn before the autopsy. For many reasons, it was thought to be a possible cover-up for another crime. I was told that was the reason for the autopsy, and they didn't want possible DNA contamination.

I was so distraught with the word that Ashlyn was dead that I don't remember who the two officers were who told me and Ben in the chapel. I remember the room but can't remember their faces, only the shock and mental anguish. There is no way to describe my screams that followed.

That following Sunday, Mother's Day, I saw Ashlyn's lifeless body on that table for the first time since that horrific night. I did her makeup and my friend fixed her hair for the visitation that day. It was hard, but I asked God for strength and felt his help. I made it through with my will to do that last thing for her, because I loved her so, and with help from a friend and God.

Later that day I had to see her in that coffin. This is how I spend my Mother's Day, realizing that the next day we would be burying my sweet baby girl. It was a packed funeral home for visitation and the service. There was a huge procession leading from our town almost through two counties. The school excused students who wanted to attend the service.

There were several nice flowers, pictures, bible donations, and figurines sent. Some people just wanted to give me a hug. Some didn't know what to say. Many saw me from a distance but never could bring themselves to walk up to me. A few apologized for it later. They said it was the look on my face. A look of pure grief. I still don't remember much of the visitation or funeral. I don't have as much of the grief look now, but it lasted for over two years. It was very noticeable for over a year. I saw it myself. It's hard to hide.

The most amazing tribute to Ashlyn was that her complete funeral costs and half of her huge headstone were paid for by friends, family, neighbors, and even people from other areas who had heard about her and our loss. The news portrayed her beautifully. I declined any interviews, mainly because I was not in a position to do so.

Her dad and I had broken hearts and disbelief. I remember the look on his face. We were helpless. He was distant, but went to her casket to look upon her there and pat her hand the same as me.

I still am in disbelief that she was killed and is forever seventeen. I know it's true, but I can't truly accept it. I just miss her so! How can this be?

The driver's bond was set at two hundred and fifty thousand dollars, because he is a murderer and because he had family in Mexico, which made him a flight risk. He was arrested four months after the crash and immediately asked for a bond reduction. The judge reduced it to one hundred and twenty-five thousand dollars. He did have to wear an ankle monitor, which was of small consolation to me.

In my opinion, the defending attorney did not build a good case against the driver, nor did they expound on the violent details about how my child died. The attorney who was supposed to be representing Ashlyn, however, did bring up the driver's family as having filed multiple bankruptcies and that the driver's dad was of bad character, and that his dad's green card would expire the next year. It felt to me like the district attorney's office seemed to give up on the case after that. They seemed so serious and ready to pursue a tough case against the impaired driver when we first talked. They never let on that they had no real intention of strongly pursuing the case. I thought they were mad at his actions and going to fight for justice; impaired driving *is* against the law.

After that, I started hearing excuses, and there were many. The witnesses started dropping like flies, no one wanted to testify. One witness was the driver's cousin. He wasn't going to talk and wasn't even questioned until jailed sometime later. All he said to investigators was something to the effect of "He is my cousin." I took that to mean "I know what happened, it is incriminating, and I'm not going to tell on my cousin." The other two witnesses, the driver's best friend and his girlfriend, were pregnant before the plea deal and later had a daughter.

Ashlyn's friend was connected through her boyfriend and was the only reason Ashlyn was in the vehicle. Obviously, Ashlyn should have chosen her company more wisely.

The district attorney's office called a meeting and talked other victims out of testifying. It was a meeting to which I refused to attend; they could never convince me not to stand up for my daughter's right to live. We had support (not that I would have ever dreamed we needed it) until after that meeting with the two victims. It's shameful and wrong how an attorney would scare two witnesses into not testifying.

The driver served only ten months: approximately two months before bonding out after reduction and the other months after a plea deal on the mere eleven of his twenty-nine month sentencing. The only reason the driver wasn't charged with murder was that he was driving impaired. He smoked pot right before driving and huffed canned air while driving. He wrecked intentionally, having been in complete control of the vehicle, leaving the road at the posted speed, stopped in the field, then started back up again, accelerating and never braking again until my child had fatal wounds from his striking that tree on her side. How is that not murder?

He was given a year of house arrest after leaving the local jail. I saw him at my workplace soon after he was released. As I write this part of Ashlyn's story, the driver is getting off house arrest. I can't even go freely in the town I've lived in my whole life without the fear and possibility that I will see him. It doesn't affect him, because he doesn't hurt to see me, nor is he reminded of anything painful. It hurts the surviving victims and their loved ones.

The driver was not made to pay for a funeral or fix damage to property. He didn't lose his life, and he didn't lose a loved one. He isn't being forced by the district attorney to do anything in Ashlyn's memory or to pay restitution to her family. He was given a small fine and served a pitiful little sentence, both of which were a slap in the face to a grieving mother.

He lost his license for a while, although he will probably drive anyway and probably already has, and has a felony on his record. None of that compares to being murdered or having a loved one murdered. Especially your child. How could this monster intentionally crash, killing my child, and serve only ten months in the local jail?

How does our government not feel more responsibility to protect and serve? It comes down to a budget and people who just don't care unless something directly affects them. Why don't they realize that at any point their loved one or they themselves could be victim of such a crime? I truly believe that the sympathy lies more with the guilty driver than the victims, because so many lawmakers, judges, and even officers drive impaired daily.

How is the driver not in prison for life? Why does he have all the rights and I have none? The district attorney didn't care about anything I had to say and didn't add one thing I asked to be added to any possible plea deal. She and the investigators took away my right to see and hold my child that night, and had me sign papers for an autopsy because the crash was being investigated as intentional from the start. They then used the fact that not enough blood was drawn for all necessary testing to be done as an excuse to give him a plea deal.

When I stood up for justice, I was made out to be the bad guy by the driver's family and the few friends he had, and unbelievably also by the district attorney, who was up for re-election. I got a petition circulating with over a thousand signatures, so the plea deal was stopped. That was only after the election though, as she lost in our town but won in another town in our district, so she was re-elected. Not long after, the plea deal saw the light of day. I wasn't even given twenty-four hour's notice to be in court; the driver and his family knew before I did.

I was so upset at the call that I had to have Ben, who had been there for me since that horrible night, come to where I sat immobile in a parking lot. I was on my way to the cemetery to take Ashlyn's decorations for fair week, her absolute favorite time of year.

Not only did the district attorney rule for the plea deal, but she refused to close the case even though the driver had been convicted. Yes, you read that right. I'm being denied papers I have a legal right to by a district attorney who is supposed to be fighting for victims and their loved ones. One has to wonder what she has to hide. Why would she give him a plea deal without considering or adding anything for Ashlyn's family or in her memory, and then refuse me, her mother, the case file and in doing so stop my civil suit against the driver?

I paid a lot of money for my lawyer who was incompetent, and who added another lawyer to help him and then charged me double until I spoke up about the billing. I was then back down to one lawyer. He stopped even sending me a bill and letting me know what he was doing. He wouldn't respond to the district attorney by certified mail like I had asked, and instead ended up working with her by phone because she was supposedly going to share part of the case file.

There was no need for a meeting, and I wasn't even notified about a meeting between my lawyer and the district attorney until about an hour before, when I was at work. I knew what the outcome would be, and also that I couldn't make it there in time. More important, I wasn't willing to let her upset me again. I was being told that a meeting would be set up to discuss my wanting to see the case file, not to actually let me see it.

While my lawyer was conversing via phone calls and not through letters as I had asked, he stopped sending correspondence to me regarding his work on the suit he was hired for. He communicated only by phone, asking the same things and getting nothing done. After I refused to attend a meeting I was notified of only an hour prior while at work, the claim was that part of the file was going to be shared. I believe that to be a total lie.

The week the driver got the plea deal, Ashlyn's flowers and other things around her stone were torn up, and several heavy items were thrown long distances. Flowers close by were pulled out of the ground. It had been done by a person who seemed to be in a hurry and didn't get to do a whole lot. Nonetheless, it was a cruel, disrespectful, evil thing to do. The driver's family was mad about what I said in court, especially about his never apologizing. I mentioned after court that he was right there in court without any remorse or an apology. That angered them, but I wasn't supposed to be angry at what he had done, in their minds. My daughter lost her life on this earth at seventeen, and I have to serve the rest of mine. Her siblings lost a sister and their dad suffered along with me, then died only days after her. Who should be angry?

I read the Bible over and over, making sure that I couldn't just run him over with my car for murdering my child in cold blood. I didn't like my answer, but I did accept it, I guess. I was also led through many verses about my child's salvation. I am very content with my answer, even though that still for a while wasn't enough. Then later I asked nonverbally for an answer from God, something so specific that it couldn't be denied. God showed me exactly what I had asked within seconds. I asked for a second confirmation, and then promised that the third one would stop my doubt. Within seconds of asking, I hushed upon that third one and promised I wouldn't doubt it or worry. Ashly is okay; she is in paradise. That is most important above anything.

Ashlyn's favorite quote, at the beginning of this story, is sweet and gives me comfort, but I don't feel very forgiving. I don't feel a need to forgive someone who doesn't have remorse. To have remorse you have first to admit you did something wrong. Then you would have to feel bad for what you did. If you don't, then how are you forgivable? God's forgiveness is not without this, and I'm told to forgive as God forgives. Someday I may forgive the driver's stupidity, because he isn't Christian and obviously wasn't raised right. As of today, *no*!

The anger and rage still appear when I think of what happened to her and know that it was one hundred percent preventable. That same anger is fueled daily by the injustice of the law and those who are put in office to enforce it. I still feel very responsible for fighting for her. To me, she is still seventeen and should be home every night. She should have been a senior in high school and graduated with the rest of her class, but she didn't. I can't imagine her older than seventeen. I don't know what life could have held for her. I still have a bedroom with her things in it, even though I have had to move from the last place we lived together with our last memories up to that night. I still want her to be there and in her bedroom asleep as she should have been that night.

If only we could just go back to that night and make everything all right. If only she hadn't left with a text from her friend; if only they had brought her right back as planned, if only she hadn't been in that seat; if only, if only. The whys and what-ifs will drive you slowly crazy. I have watched others her age go to prom, graduate, go to college, get married, have children, get their own place, start jobs, etc. All I can do is be sad, jealous, wonder, and try to be happy for them while I miss my baby girl so terribly.

My mind has never been the same. I was overwhelmed mentally, physically, and emotionally to the point of breaking. I really don't know how I survived; I don't know how any parent survives something so horrific that takes his or her child away forever. The truth is that some don't. Her dad died of a heart attack within a week. Others commit suicide, and some of us merely exist. Many of us suffer from severe grief and posttraumatic stress disorder. Grief and depression, though often confused, are two different things.

Many struggle with working and taking care of our other kids and even ourselves. We can't function or find much joy in anything and are drowning in our pain, our grief. Child loss brings many emotionally damaging thoughts that add to our grief. All those hopes and dreams for that one child I carried in my body, gave birth to, took care of from day one, and watched grow into a beautiful, silly seventeen-year old, gone in a moment. Each loss is as unique as the relationship. I am often in the numb mode just to work and function day to day. I have to remove myself from the grief as much as possible when I have to be okay, and that requires down time to be the new me that I can't let everyone else see each day. It is something I can't really escape, but no one else wants to see or be uncomfortable around me. For a long time I couldn't go a minute without thinking about her and being in misery.

As time has passed, I'm forced to attempt to be okay. I've gone back to work full-time and keep busy most of the time. There are still times when I feel overwhelmed with grief and her absence. The fact that my precious Ashlyn was murdered at seventeen and is gone from here forever is too much to comprehend. It mentally and emotionally stops me in my tracks, no matter where I am. I feel guilty for trying to hide my pain because it is like I'm being fake and trying to forget her to save myself. I know nothing will ever make me forget her or stop this hurt.

As I put the final touches on this story of my Ashlyn's life and how she was so violently ripped out of my life, it is her *third* anniversary in heaven today. Three years that I can't even imagine, I survived. There are so many emotions I feel every day, as if I ride a never-ending rollercoaster. However, on this day they are felt more deeply, more acutely, as if they penetrate my very soul. It is on this day and other holidays that I pull out the cards that she always made or bought me for every holiday during her short life. I look at them each year without her, along with the saved and now treasured keepsakes from her earlier years. I continue to feel her love and I know she is with me. I have never felt as loved by anyone as I have by her. I am sure this will be my life until I see Ashlyn, and we are together again. Now all I have is dread, confusion and pain. Time isn't my friend; I have nothing to look forward to.

I still live in disbelief of so many things. I miss her and all that could have been. Knowing that the man responsible could come to my workplace or pass me on the street, and there is nothing I can do, feeds my anxiety daily. The disbelief in the justice system for not making Ashlyn's life matter and allowing a killer to walk free with a mere slap on the hand to kill again. The realization that I will never see her marry or have children shatters my heart time and time again. It is still unbelievable to me that driving impaired is the same as using a deadly weapon to kill someone and yet is not treated as such. It is Certainly not punished as murder in the eyes of the law. Impaired driving has become an epidemic, one that is preventable and a conscious choice made without regard to the aftermath or the domino effect it leaves in its wake. Let's not let this continue. We all need to make some noise against impaired driving and stand united and loud for all those who have lost their lives, and their loved ones left behind. Help save lives and shattered hearts, for Ashlyn and all the other sons, daughters, mothers, fathers, siblings, friends who walk this journey every day.

DO NOT DRIVE IMPAIRED.

GINA LANCE
MCMINNVILLE, TN

In memory of Ashlyn Barnes
(Daughter of Gina Lance)
12/20/95 ~ 5/09/13

SARAH, PA, ASHLYN, ALLAN, TRAVIS & CHASE

"Hello," a song by Evanescence released on their album titled Fallen in 2003, was written by Amy Lee about the loss of her sister. She passed in 1987 at the age of three from an unknown illness. This song has never been performed live in concert. I can understand why.

Playground school bell rings again,
Rain clouds come to play again,
Has no one told you she's not breathing?
Hello, I'm your mind giving you someone to talk to,
Hello...

If I smile and don't believe,
Soon I know I'll wake from this dream,
Don't try to fix me, I'm not broken,
Hello, I'm the lie, living for you so you can hide,
Don't cry...

Suddenly I know I'm not sleeping,
Hello, I'm still here,
All that's left of yesterday.

ASHLYN, GINA & TRAVIS

GINA & ASHLYN

TRAVIS & GINA

CHAPTER TEN

EMERALD GREEN BALLOONS

BY LAURA G. HERRON-SMITH

*The most painful goodbyes are the one that
are never said....and never explained.*
-AUTHOR UNKNOWN

It was, for my kids and me, a fairly normal Friday afternoon. I had three teenage boys, Donny, Bryan, and Robert, my stepson, and my little girl, Chelsey, who had just turned seven. They rode the bus home from school and tumbled in the door, all excited. The boys were all talking at the same time about what they wanted to do for Halloween, while Chelsey quietly began to play.

Halloween fell on Sunday that year, which meant trick-or-treating on Saturday. I had not been feeling well the entire day. I had a horrible migraine and was very seriously considering going to bed to try to sleep it off. We discussed what the boys wanted to do and what I would be willing to let them do. I just wanted to get them all fed and calm so I could go to bed. I managed to fix dinner and was in my room. That is when the telephone began to ring. It was still early in the evening, around 5:30 p.m. It was October 29, 1999. I will always remember that date and the phone call.

I answered the phone. It was my beautiful, blonde-haired, blue-eyed oldest niece, Monica Renee Rachford Trammell. She was just a few months away from turning thirty-one. Monica, as an adult, was one of the few people I was very close to. My mother had married Monica's grandpa, Pops, when she was almost three. As a young child, she was not at all like any other kids her age. She didn't play with dolls like other little girls. She was a tomboy and would rather be tagging along with me outside. She was cool, always wore her jeans, cowgirl boots, and a vest with a cowgirl hat.

At three years old she knew so much about rock 'n' roll and had already been to see many famous rock concerts! She loved Rod Stewart's song, "Wake Up, Maggie." We would put his album on the old turntable and stand her on an upside-down milk crate with a badminton racket for her guitar. There in the black light she would sing her little heart out for us, enjoying herself and her music.

"Hey! Aunt Laura, I need a ride home from the bar. I am drunk," she said, laughing. That has to be one of the things that I immediately missed when she was killed: the way she walked into my home, always loudly greeting everyone with "Hey!" I already knew what bar she was at. Her mom, Karen, was my older sister, and was the bartender there. Monica had gotten off work and went to hang out with her mom and have a couple of beers. She sounded quite inebriated.

"Monica, my car isn't running! The boys are going to work on it tomorrow," I replied to her. I hated telling her no, but I was unable to help her.

She said," It's okay. I will just call the cab company. But Sunday is Halloween and we need to hang out, because it has been too long."

I told her, "Absolutely. I will be up and ready by one o'clock and at your house for sure."

We hung up with smooches and "I love you" with what I assumed were intact plans for Sunday afternoon. Halloween was Monica's favorite holiday. The last thing I said was "I love you!" No one could have convinced me that it would be the last words I would ever speak to her. At the same time, I am so grateful that they were the last words I said to her!

I finally went to bed around 7 p.m. The migraine was making me sick to my stomach. The boys were watching Chelsey for me, along with her dad, David, my ex-husband. I assumed that all was well. About 8 p.m. my son Bryan came in and asked if he could go to town for a pop and cigarettes with one of his friends. He said, "I will be right back, Mom."

Bryan and Monica had a very close bond. They were very close as family and as best friends. They understood each other in a way that the rest of us didn't. They both had some issues with alcohol and drugs. They had been talking about how they needed help and that if one would, the other would agree to go to detox and rehab. They were very serious about supporting each other and agreed that Monday would be the day they would get on the phone and make arrangements. He asked me what Monica had wanted on the phone, and I told him she was at the bar, drunk, and needed a ride home. He asked me if she had a ride and I told him, "Yes, she is going to call a cab." "Okay, Mom," he said. "I love you, and I will only go straight to the store and back."

Bang! Bang! Bang! I woke to a loud pounding on the door. As I opened my eyes, I saw red and blue lights flashing off the walls of my bedroom. The rest of the house was quiet, with everyone sound asleep. I glanced at the clock to see what time it was: the red numbers on the digital clock said 2 a.m. I immediately thought of Bryan. David and I made it to the door at the same time. My head was still pounding, and it took all I had not to throw up on the sheriff's deputy as he patiently waited for us to get the door open.

The deputy asked," Do you have a son, Bryan?"

My stomach instantly lurched with the thought that something horrible had happened to Bryan. "Yes, we do. Is he okay?" I asked with knots growing in my throat. "Yes, ma'am. He is fine, but we do have him in custody. He and his friend had climbed in the window at his friend's house and the sister called dispatch, thinking they were burglars. We need one of you to come downtown and get him."

I persuaded David to go in his truck because my car was not running. David and Bryan came home an hour later. David was really angry, because he had gotten a ticket for Bryan being out past curfew. Bryan apologized for scaring me so badly. Of course I forgave him, and sent him straight to bed with a stern warning to not do that ever again. My anger had slipped into relief and thoughts of "I know I raised that boy better." I had no idea that it was only a precursor to the horrible events to come.

The next day, David and the boys had my car fixed and running. I was excited about the plans I had made with Monica and spending Halloween Day, October 31, 1999, with her. Nothing special had happened that Saturday. The weather was still cloudy with scattered showers throughout the day. The migraine that had tormented me was gone and I felt much better. I remember it as being just another day for all of us and nothing exceptional. I did laundry, and got the house cleaned up so I would not have to worry about anything while I spent time with Monica. I made sure that David would be around to watch Chelsey and the boys the next day, and I was ready to go.

I slept in that Sunday. I woke up around 11 a.m., got my coffee and just relaxed for a bit before taking a shower and getting dressed. I was thinking about the afternoon with Monica and wondering what we would do. I was sure that it would include beer and maybe a joint or two, lots of music, and since Karen didn't have to work, then hopefully she would be able to hang out with us.

I was in my bathroom and had just finished putting on my makeup, preparing to dry my hair. I heard the phone ring several times. I yelled for one of the boys to answer it so I could finish getting ready. About two minutes later, my youngest son, Robert, came into my room. He walked over to me, and I could see that something was terribly wrong. I asked him who had called.

From that moment forward my life, our lives, and my family's lives changed in such a traumatic and horrible way. "Mom, it was Aunt Karen, and she said you need to get hold of Pops and Grandma. The police want y'all to meet them at the police department. They think Monica is dead."

The emotional feelings I felt swelling up in me were emphatically shoved back down, because there would be time for that later if it were Monica. It just could not be her, though, because we had plans. We had just talked Friday evening. I stood there in shock and complete disbelief. I knew I could not have possibly heard right. Then I grew angry in my denial, and I began to yell loudly at the top of my lungs at my already crying stepson, telling him that I knew it was Halloween and we play jokes and prank each other, but, there was nothing funny about this.

Robert, with his tender heart, was still sobbing, and said to me, "Momma, it isn't a joke. It is real; Aunt Karen was crying." I grabbed him and hugged him, my heart breaking that I had lashed out at him, and apologized profusely. We were both crying at that point. I did my best to console and comfort him, telling him that it would be all right, that none of them should worry, because it couldn't be true. It couldn't be. It just couldn't.

I forced my legs to move forward, and went to the living room and picked up the phone to call my parents and relay the worst possible message a person could ever have to give to anyone, especially a loved one. Mom answered with her usual "Hello." I told her what I knew, and that Karen had called me, saying she needed us to meet her at the police station. She said, "*Oh, no!* We watched that on the news Friday evening, and we had no idea it was Monica! All Channel 7 said was that an unidentified woman had been in the truck, and she had drowned. We will be right there to get you." The boys and Chelsey were all looking at me. I could see the questions on their faces, and all of them were in shock. I hung the receiver up, and I prayed, "Father God, please do not let this be true. Please, let it not be Monica."

The drive to the police department in Altus, Oklahoma, was a long eight miles, with only small exchanges about hoping they were wrong. All I could think was, "She called me, and I couldn't help her." In my mind I was denying it, and at the same time I was telling myself it was my fault. If I had gone and picked her up, she would still be alive. No, wait, she can't be dead. This is just a horrible mistake. I couldn't convince myself either way. We arrived a little after one o'clock, the time I was supposed to be with Monica. Not this way God, not this way.

At the police station, the lady at the window showed us to a small room, maybe eight by ten feet. There were those ugly brown, metal folding chairs. The four of us took a seat to wait for the detective. None of us said a word as we waited. We were afraid that if we did, then it would be true.

Detective Robin Gorman came in quietly and unfolded a chair to sit down. He looked very weary. His clothes were wrinkled, and it was obvious that he had not gotten much sleep. He held out a wallet-size photo of a long-haired blonde woman on a morgue table with an autopsy "Y" stitched on her chest. He solemnly asked," Is this Monica?" The silence as we all nodded was deafening and heart-wrenching. I looked over as a tear rolled down my daddy's cheek. I had never seen him cry, and I never saw him cry again. That was when the cold, hard reality of what had just been said really hit me, and I started to sob uncontrollably. It was my fault. I was responsible for Monica dying in that truck at the hands of a total stranger! I had to leave the room to get control of myself.

Detective Gorman began to tell us what facts he knew. On Friday evening, Monica got off work and was at the bar. She was drunk and trying to find a ride home. A man she had been talking to in the bar volunteered to give her a ride. They made plans to be at one of the local restaurants to have dinner with Karen, and my sister would take her home. Karen was counting out her money drawer to end her shift, but couldn't leave just yet.

The drive to the restaurant was about a mile or so to the west, and back to the north about four miles, maybe five miles straight north. For some reason, that man took a detour and went through the Altus reservoir, which is in the shape of a figure eight. There are three entrances and exits. Two of them are on the west side. The third, on the south side, runs into the middle of the figure eight.

The weather on that Friday night was cold, and it was raining. Not a hard rain, but a slow and steady, continuous rain. Daylight savings time was about to change, and it was already getting dark. The man, Robert, was married with children. He lived in Hollis, Oklahoma. At the time, he and his wife were separated.

Robert took the south entrance, where it curves into the center. Testimony at the trial by Officer Pogue with Oklahoma Highway Patrol, revealed that as the driver took the curve just yards from the entrance, he was already doing seventy miles per hour according to the skid marks. He was about halfway in the middle when he lost control and went off into the dark water on the west side in his pickup truck. He claimed that Monica had grabbed his steering wheel. Somehow, in his drunken state, he was able to open the back sliding window and escape from the vehicle. His testimony stated that he didn't even try to save Monica as the truck went down fifteen feet to the bottom of the reservoir.

He was found two hours later walking in the rain by an off-duty Altus police officer. I have never known who that off-duty officer was. He made the call to dispatch for the wrecker to get the truck out of the water. By this time the underwater current had carried the truck south, with Monica in it, unable to escape.

I am uncertain as to when the newscast from Lawton and all the emergency vehicles made it to the reservoir. Detective Gorman said removing the truck took six and a half hours for the divers, first to locate it and then retrieve it from the water. Robert still hadn't mentioned Monica being in the truck. They had no sense of urgency, believing they were after an empty vehicle. Finally, after two hours of walking around the crash scene, Robert finally said,

"You have to get it out, Monica is in there." The level of urgency immediately went to frantic searching and the arrest of Robert.

Detective Gorman told us that when the truck was removed from the reservoir, he wouldn't allow it to be opened in front of the media and onlookers out of respect for Monica. He demanded that it be taken to the Altus police garage. His story was so difficult for him that he had to leave the room three times to regain his composure so he could continue. This case affected Detective Gorman so horribly that he retired not long after he finished the investigation. He did appear in court for his witness testimony. He was at Monica's funeral. I can remember looking at my parents and my sister and expecting one of them to say it wasn't true. But I never got those reassurances.

At the garage, they opened the truck to remove Monica's lifeless body. The detective said that the water poured out as they gained entry. He then offered more details, such as how swollen she was and purple from being under the water for so long. Monica was black-tagged as a Jane Doe, and her body was automatically sent to Oklahoma City for an autopsy. She had no form of identification with her. There was no way for them to contact her family. Cellphones were around then, but were very expensive and not everyone owned one like they do now.

I still do not know how they were able to identify her body or find out who she was so they could call Karen. I wonder to this day if maybe at some point Monica had been arrested and they had her fingerprints in the system. I don't suppose that it matters now.

I am not certain of Robert's blood alcohol level, though it was in the range of .275 percent. I will never forget Monica's, because it was .333 percent. When the truck hit the water, it was going very fast and Monica most likely passed out and never knew anything. Evidently she had not grabbed the steering wheel, as Robert said. The prosecution stated that if Monica grabbed the wheel, the vehicle would have gone to the east. I have always been amazed at how quickly a drunk driver who has injured or killed someone will blame the victim and others for their horrid decision.

Her funeral at Kinkannon's Funeral Home was several days later. We had to wait for her body to go through the red tape politics of being released, and then find out how to get her home from the city for her funeral. I remember going through the motions with my sister and parents as we decided on her casket, the pallbearers, and the music that would be played, and just feeling numb. I had cried so much, and it seemed that each new person I saw or family member would restart the flow of tears. I was starting to believe that I would never be able to stop crying.

Monica had worked at Subway and a convenience store. Both stores are on the main roads in downtown Altus. She had met what seemed like the entire town through her jobs, and it was very apparent that all the people thought kindly of her. I walked into the standing-room-only chapel for my beautiful niece's funeral. People from all levels of society came to show their respect, from the gutter to the upper echelon. Monica was loved. I remember walking up to her casket and looking down at her dimples. She hated her dimples. I wanted to touch her. I wanted to reach in, pull her out and wake her up. As I slipped my hand over hers, I was taken aback at how cold she was. I expected her to be warm. I wanted her to wake up and say, "Hey! What are y'all doing?" I slipped my hearts necklace in her hand, kissed her icy forehead, and forced myself to walk away from the casket, in tears again.

Monica had two children, a boy, and girl, Colby and Tawney. For her children and the others, there was a balloon release of emerald green balloons at the graveside. Emerald green was Monica's favorite color. Her father rented an emerald green Jaguar, her favorite car, to drive from the airport in Oklahoma City for his goodbye to his daughter. As we all stood watching, the emerald-green balloons lazily crept higher into the sky. The balloons clustered up into what appeared, to those who saw it, as an angel. The funeral home employees were loading flower arrangements and plants as they prepared to lower her casket when Colby walked up and put his little hand on it. I had never known a pain such as what swept over me when I witnessed him saying his last goodbye to his mother. Tawney stood by and watched him. Their blonde hair was shining and their blue eyes were full of tears.

I could not fathom that Monica was no longer going to call me, or that we would never see each other again, not here on earth. I have shared this story many times over the last eight years. So now the years have gone by, some slowly and some too quickly. All of our lives have slowly changed to a new normal of some sort. I chose to go to rehab in March 2000 because of my choice of self-medicating my pain. I sobered up, and I cleaned up. I did relapse for a year in 2005-2006 when my last marriage ended, and my dad had a massive stroke that paralyzed him on the left side. He passed away on Saturday, May 13, 2006. The next day was Sunday, Mother's Day, and my birthday. A month earlier my best friend woke up and found her husband lying in the hall. He had a stroke on the right side. My son Bryan has spent most of the last ten, almost eleven years in and out of the penitentiary, mostly in.

I have diligently worked hard for my recovery. It has not been easy. It is the only way I have been able to be a voice for Monica. It is also the way that I have been able to face the challenges in my life and not just control but overcome. I have shared my story so that Monica would have a voice and her death would not be in vain at the hands of a drunken driver. I have conquered most of my anger and resentment with her murderer. His felony assault with a deadly weapon was dropped to involuntary manslaughter. He was ordered to pay two thousand five hundred dollars in court costs and fines and given probation. But he never saw a day behind bars. He even moved to Colorado with his wife and kids. There is still a bench warrant for his arrest—he owes one hundred eighty-four dollars on his fines.

In some aspects, I feel that I have made a feeble attempt to make my amends to Monica. I have shared the survivor guilt that I am still slowly healing from. The PTSD flare-ups that I have are still sometimes crippling. I shared with her kids what their mom was like and how much she loved her now-grown children, hoping that they would know what really happened and to answer the many questions they had. Colby now has a sweet little girl with blonde hair and blue eyes. She is named after her grandma, Harley Renee. Tawney and her fiancé, Corey, have a newborn son. His name is Knight. They also have a new baby on the way.

I share this story now, hoping that you, the reader, will know that healing will take place. I honestly tell you, it is a long and grueling journey, uphill. It is most definitely not in our time, but God's. I share Monica's story in hopes that someone will choose not to drive drunk after reading it. I share it in the hope that if only one life is saved or one person makes a healthy choice not to drink and drive, then Monica's voice has been heard, and she has saved lives through her own death. Our family dynamics have changed. Not all the changes have been negative; however, the bond we once had is no longer the same. There are some who choose to drink, and that is their choice. My only prayer is that we don't get another phone call to go and identify another body.

Please, don't drink or use drugs and drive.

LAURA G. HERRON-SMITH
MANGUM, OKLAHOMA

MONICA RACHFORD-TRAMMELL   **LAURA G. HERRON-SMITH**

TAWNEY D. TRAMMELL & COLBY TRAMMELL

CHAPTER ELEVEN

THE MIRACULOUS NIGHT

A Story of Survival, Determination & Faith
BY MICHELLE LAWSON

Miracles happen when you replace tears by prayer and anxiety by faith. -UNKNOWN

In order to tell you my story, I have to share some of my life with you in order for you to understand what I go through every day; what I see, how I feel and what my daughter Faithlynn goes through. My mother raised me as a single parent. My father was in the military, and after being together eight years they divorced. I was two years old. Things weren't easy growing up. We moved from Camp Lejeune in Jacksonville, North Carolina, to Kokomo, Indiana, to live with my grandparents. My grandma passed away July 1, 1985, and with my grandpa being blind we continued to live there to help him. I loved living there and I was completely happy. I felt like I had everything, a family, nice home, and friends.

When I turned twelve, a family dispute started. I'm still not sure what it was all about, but in the end my mother and I had to leave our home and the only family I knew. I can't explain the heartache I felt in having to leave my grandfather. I was not allowed to have any contact with him or my aunts, uncles and cousins. My mom did the best she could and made sure I had food in my stomach, clothes on my back, and shelter. After living in a couple of different places we finally settled down in a home my mother bought in March 1996. I lived three blocks from the junior high school and we were located in the downtown area. There were also a few kids who lived on our street. The police station was nearby as well. My dream from the time I was two years old was to be a police officer or go into the military. When I turned fourteen I joined the Kokomo Police Cadets. I worked hard and became a lieutenant. I also studied hard in school and stayed out of trouble.

A couple of years later, in October 1998, my mom suffered a heart attack and underwent a six-bypass surgery. By Thanksgiving she was home and everything was back to normal. Christmas passed and the new year began. On February 16 my mom, a friend of hers, and I went out to eat at my favorite restaurant. When we got home I had started cleaning my room when Jedidiah, someone I knew from school, stopped by to see if I wanted to go with him to his aunt's house. She lived about ten to fifteen minutes from us. My mother was leaving shortly because she was involved with the Emergency Management Association, an organization that prepares applications of existing facilities, materiel, equipment and personnel during an emergency, in such a manner that lives may be saved, health and efficiency maintained, and property protected. She had to go take care of some things, and said I could go but had to be back by 8 p.m. I really didn't want to go because I wanted to finish cleaning my room, but I figured I needed a break so I went.

I vaguely remember Jedidiah's aunt's house. It smelled like incense when we walked in. Beads were hanging from the doorways, and in the living room there was a brown carpet hung on the wall and shelves with little trinkets. It was like entering a time capsule of the 1970s. When we left we were pushing for time. I looked down and saw the green glow of the dash light and saw that it was 7:57. I was late. He was driving fast, but we were still ten minutes from my house. I told him to slow down but he didn't. The next thing I remember was seeing a cornfield and a lady covering me with a blanket. She smelled so good, like lilacs. Her hair was pure white, her eyes were crystal-blue, almost transparent. When she spoke, her lips didn't move, but I could hear her sweet voice. She told me that I would be okay and she kissed my forehead. To this day, I believe she was my guardian angel. There was no cornfield, no woman or anyone who had covered me up.

I was rushed to a local hospital and transported by ambulance to Methodist Hospital in Indianapolis, Indiana, a ninety-minute drive away. Because of my involvement with the police cadets and many of the officers knowing my mom, by the time I got to the hospital, there was my mom, her friend, and two rooms full of friends, extended family, and many police officers.

The result of the accident was that I had many aches and pains, short and long-term memory loss, road rash on my back and face, and my brain shifted from one side to the other, causing a traumatic brain injury. I spent two and a half weeks in a coma and had to learn to do everything all over again. I had to learn to talk, walk, dress myself, eat; I mean *everything*! It was horrible. I felt normal and I felt like I knew what I was doing, but when it came out I was doing it all wrong.

I went from a sophomore in high school to a first grader. When I heard the doctor say this to my mom, I could feel myself cry but I didn't have any tears. I had lost the ability to cry as well or to show emotion when it was appropriate. From that point on, I listened to the doctor as much as I could. I wanted to know who I was and how others perceived me.

When I returned to school it was different. When I did class work with the teacher and made a mistake, I would do it over until I got it right even though it made me sick and tired. I recognized the kids' faces but I couldn't remember their names. Some of the kids said I was fine and that I was faking my head injuries. I believe that people are afraid of what they cannot see. I just ignored them, even though it hurt deeply. I didn't have time to focus on rumors. I learned who my true friends were. I lost most of my closest friends, and the ones I weren't close to were the ones who became my "guardians."

It's sad to say, but because of what happened, Jedidiah got bullied so badly that when I returned to school it only got worse and he had to drop out. I was so far behind academically that I had to stay after school and attend summer school to catch up on my credits so I could graduate with my class. I attended normal classes for my electives, but I had to take my regular classes in a special education setting. It helped me but I was embarrassed to leave class to get the extra help I needed. I was determined that I was going to be as normal as I could be and that I was going to graduate on time.

The summer between my junior and senior year I ended up pregnant. That was a disappointment that I bestowed not only on myself but my mother as well. My mom was there for me and helped me to make the best of the situation. On April 21, 2001, I welcomed a beautiful baby girl, Faithlynn, into the world. She weighed seven pounds and thirteen ounces, and was twenty-one and a half inches long. She had olive skin and was perfect from head to toe.

My mom watched her while I attended school. I graduated June 8, 2001. Faithlynn and my family were there to cheer me on as I walked across the stage. It was such a happy moment in my life. During this time I worked at GNC and Motel 6. I stayed with my mom for about a year so I could get a job, and my license, and be able to support my daughter. On April 17, 2002, Faithlynn and I moved into our own apartment. Faithlynn was such a happy baby and was on time with all her developmental milestones.

When Faithlynn was three and a half, my boyfriend, Zach, and I got a house together in August 2004. Faith was so happy. At the age of two she could count to ten and knew most of her colors. I got her into preschool and she loved it. I had homeschooled her, but this gave her the opportunity to help with her social skills. The first year in preschool they taught her how to write her name and she was starting to read.

A short time after we moved into our house I found out I was pregnant. I kept thinking how perfect our life was. I was so excited.

When I found out I was going to have a boy, Zach wanted to pick out the name, since I had named Faithlynn. He picked the name Haden Allen. On May 10, 2005, after thirteen hours of pain and false labor, Haden was born by cesarean. He weighed six pounds and was twenty inches long. As the year passed I noticed that he was not like Faithlynn in his mentality. He seemed to be somewhat slower and he didn't meet most of the child development stages. When he was a little over three I found out that he had fluid behind his ears and needed tubes to drain it. The doctors also felt that he had ADD/ADHD, but couldn't test him until he started school.

In April 2007, I started a part-time security job so I could help with our finances but also be able to do things with the kids. In September I was promoted to full time. It was rough, because they were split shifts, but I had a set schedule every week which was nice. At least I knew when I had to work so I could schedule Haden's many doctor appointments around my work. Because of the split shifts, I missed a lot of their school functions. In December my boss changed the schedule so that I worked the day shift and he had the night shift which was awesome. Faithlynn had been asking if I would take her to the Christmas concert, and now I would be able to.

On December 11, 2008, I went to work, so did Zach, and the kids went to school. Faithlynn was seven and Haden three. Zach had decided to go coyote hunting after work, and when I got off I picked Faith up from school and got Haden off the bus. We hurriedly got homework done, ate and changed, and made it to the concert on time. I was exhausted. My work day had started at 4 a.m. that morning so I tried to relax, but Haden wanted to be everywhere and he only got worse once the program started. Halfway through the program, my friend Tatonya said that Faith could ride home with her and her family. So Haden and I left. We went and got a drink and drove through We Care Park and looked at the Christmas lights.

When I pulled up at home Tatonya called, so I left again to go get Faith. I was facing west as I pulled up to Tatonya's house. Her house sits on the north side of the road. I left the car running with Haden in his car seat, and stepped out to get Faith. She and her best friend, Takaya, were hyped up from the concert. Since I didn't have to work the next day, I told them I would take them through Highland Park to see the Christmas lights, and if we had time I would also take them through We Care Park. It was 7:10 p.m. by the time we were leaving, and Takaya had to be back home by 8, so we were pushed for time.

As I was trying to get the kids to hurry I walked to the driver's side of the car which was on the roadside. I could see a vehicle approaching two blocks down the road, heading east. I looked behind me and saw Takaya on the sidewalk and Faithlynn at the front door of the house coming out. I glanced back at the car and it was coming down the middle of the road toward me pretty fast. I looked at the girls and Faithlynn was running toward me, laughing. I yelled "NO!" I went to grab her, but her silk dress slipped through my hands. She hadn't even made it to the driver's side of the car when the car swerved and hit her head on.

It all went by me in slow motion. I saw Faithlynn get thrown into the air and landing on her back on the hood of the car that hit her. Her legs flew up in the air as her head hit the windshield. The windshield cracked and Faith's eyes were open, as big as baseballs. I saw her yell "MOM!" but I couldn't hear her, although the road was deathly quiet.

It happened in a flash and I was by her side. I don't remember walking or running to her; I was just there. She was lying curled in a fetal position on the other side of the road half of a city block down, by an alley under a street light. I was absolutely numb and in shock. Faith lay there quietly and kept shutting her eyes every few seconds. I just sat by her, not knowing what to do. I couldn't talk. I couldn't think. Then I started to scream bloody murder. Only then did she start to rock and moan.

I looked around; there was no one in sight. I couldn't remember my friend's name or the name of my mom's friend who lived next door to my friend. I started to pray, and remembered my cellphone. I called 911. The dispatcher told me that I had to calm down and stop screaming. I had to be calm for Faith and help her. I told the dispatcher the street name and she said help was on the way and we hung up. I felt all alone. It was still so quiet and dark. It seemed to take the ambulance forever to get there. I just kept praying, asking God to forgive me for my sins and to please not take my daughter from me. I wasn't ready for her to go. There was still so much I had to teach her about Him; God and about life.

I could hear sirens in the distance. People started to gather around and I heard someone say, "Don't move her! Get something to cover her up with." I took off my work coat and covered her with it. I was in complete shock as to what was going on, what I had just witnessed. I just couldn't believe what I had seen. This was my baby, my child. I had no idea if she was going to survive or not.

I kept looking back at my car, trying to see Haden. Was he okay? Was he crying? Did he see what happened? He needed his mommy, but I couldn't move from Faith's side. I was frozen in fear.

When the fire truck pulled up I looked behind me and I could see the woman who hit my baby. She had her hands over her mouth, talking to an officer. I stood up so the firefighter could have room to work on Faith. I started to walk over to my car; people stared but didn't say a word. The red and blue lights were flashing everywhere. I looked up at Tatonya's house and she was standing at the door with her husband. The look on their faces was one of horror. I felt like crawling in a hole and dying. I looked over at the cop. Tatonya ran up to me and said they had Haden inside the house and that they would keep him until family came. I just looked at her and said "Thank you."

I looked over at the ambulance as they were loading Faith in. I reached my hand out to her and asked the medic if I could ride with her. He told me I couldn't. I remember thinking to myself, "Why can't I go? That is my daughter. What if something happens? She needs her mommy!" I looked all around as I turned in a circle. When I had turned a full 180 degrees my eyes met the officer's. He looked like he was about to cry, and this scared me that much more. He said he would give me a ride to St. Joseph Hospital. I was grateful, because at that moment I was ready to run. I just wanted to sprint as fast as I could and get to the hospital. I could picture myself running behind the ambulance as it took Faithlynn.

I couldn't take my car because it was blocked by emergency vehicles, and I was far from being in the state of mind to drive. The officer cleared his seat off and I got in. I had to wait a minute for him to let another officer know. I looked at the green dashboard lights, the computer in the middle, and then down to the floorboard thinking about Faithlynn and all the what-ifs. When the officer returned to the car, I pulled myself out of my thoughts and called my mom. She was in complete shock, but told me to hang tight and that she would make some phone calls and that I should not lose my faith in God. She told me that she was going to get a prayer chain going and that she loved me and she would try to find a ride to the hospital.

The ride to the hospital seemed to take forever. The officer didn't say anything to me, but then what could he say? I think he was praying silently along with me.

When we got to the hospital I went to the bathroom. I wanted to drown myself in my tears as I stood looking in the mirror, trying to collect my thoughts of what had just happened. I knew I couldn't stay. I had to get to Faith. So I took a deep breath and walked out into the hall. My friend Jessica showed up first. Friends were rushing in the door. They had heard what had happened. They kept trying to get hold of Zach, but no one could reach him.

I was able to go back to see Faith. I walked through a door and it was bright. Faith was lying there in her red silk dress. She had only one of her sparkly silver shoes on, and her sock was covered in blood. The doctor said they were going to airlift her to Methodist

Hospital. I asked if I could go with her and he said no. I didn't know how I was going to get there. No one could get hold of Zach, and my car was involved in a crime so I wasn't able to take it. I walked into the waiting room and I told everyone what was going on. Jessica said she could take me to her brother's house; he was Zach's best friend, and then her sister-in-law would give me a ride to the hospital. I just wanted to be with Faithlynn. I wanted to hold her and I wanted to hear her voice. I wanted Haden to be with me.

As I watched the helicopter land, I saw the medics go into the hospital to get Faith. I hurried with Jessica to her car. We made it to her brother's house quickly and I got into Rachel's van. This was the longest car ride of my life. Driving down that long stretch of Highway 31, I thought back to the time when I had been injured and wondered how my mother did it when I had been injured. I felt for Rachel. She was driving as fast as she could without getting pulled over or in a wreck. We were silent a quarter of the way there but I couldn't take it any longer. I had to talk, but I also just wanted to be lost in my thoughts and alone. I tried to call Zach; still no answer. I called my pastor. He and his wife were at the hospital around the block with his mother-in-law. He said he would try to make it over there. Making phone calls to get prayers helped to pass the time.

Faith was at the hospital when we arrived and they already had her in a room, preparing her for tests. I had to wait to go back because they were taking her for a CAT scan. My pastor showed up and prayed with me. He couldn't stay, but he said he would be back and that he or Evelyn would call.

I'm not sure when Zach showed up, but he was there when I was allowed to go back to see Faith. She looked like an angel. Her faced glowed. The doctor came in and said she had swelling and bleeding on the brain and that they were going to have to put a pressure monitor in her head. Zach and I stood there in horror as they shaved a small patch of the hair on the right side of her head and inserted a small box.

We were able to stay with her for a short while and then were asked to leave so they could get her admitted into a room. They admitted her into the pediatric intensive care unit, room 2, the exact room I had been in years before. This made it a little more difficult for my mom when she got there. She stayed for a while and then said she would come up later on Friday.

There were quite a few people who came to the hospital to support us. We also found out that the woman who hit Faith had been drinking and that she had a child with her in the car. I was furious, and had all kinds of emotions running through me, and once again all the what-ifs. After everyone left, I sat in the recliner next to Faith and Zach sat on her other side. I was still in shock and unable to cry, but crying on the inside. It was hard to close my eyes. Every time I did, I would see Faith on the hood of the car, yelling my name. I finally just closed my eyes, but I could hear everything around me. All kinds of scenarios kept going through my head. What if I did this, what if this happened, what if it was me, would I have been able to survive another hit to the head? Why couldn't it have been me?

On Friday, friends and family stopped by for most of the day. My brother Matt got word of what was happening and called from Iraq. Wow! That was awesome. Matt told me he was praying for us and so were all of his buddies.

On Saturday, Zach's grandparents brought Haden up so we could see him. Did I ever miss my little boy! He was fine and being taken care of, and I knew Faith needed me more than ever at this time. The doctors still had her in a sedated coma. She was on a breathing machine and had all these tubes and wires hooked up to her. I couldn't help but wonder if she was going to wake up from the coma. So many thoughts; was she going to make it?

Zach went home and got some things for me because I wasn't going to leave my baby's side. Sunday came and the doctors took her off the breathing machine. She was able to breathe on her own. A few hours later she started coming to. Zach was next to her talking to her and telling her that he needed his fishing buddy to wake up, that she had slept long enough. He went to give her a hug and she opened her eyes and told him she loved him. He told her he loved her and that her breath stank; she smiled.

Four long days in a coma not knowing if she was going to wake up or not. I had done a lot of praying and pleading with God. I couldn't help but think about my mom and how she must have felt when I was in a coma for two and a half weeks. I was just so excited and relieved that Faith was awake and breathing on her own.

On Monday they moved her to the pediatric floor and started therapy. They worked with her on her speech and physical needs. I used Faith's therapy time to rest. I would walk around the hospital and as soon as Faith started doing better she would go on walks with me. I showed her where the pharmacy and library were and where the indoor playground was. She liked our time together, and she especially liked the fish aquariums they had there. Zach had been staying at the hospital with us but we decided he needed to go home, because he had to continue to work; we still had bills to pay. The parents and staff at Faithlynn's school gave us two hundred dollars to help with food, gas and some other expenses. Zach came up as often as he could. Toward the end of the week, I had used the phone at the nurse's station when I overheard Faith's doctor saying that Faith had a moderate to mild traumatic brain injury. I was furious. They had known this and didn't tell me.

Faith was discharged two days before Christmas. She had spent eleven days in the hospital. I was so relieved that we would finally get back to some sort of normal. I was excited to get home and back with Zach and Haden. We were ready, but Faithlynn needed some accommodations at home. Our insurance wouldn't pay for a shower chair, so the hospital gave us one. We also had to get a non-slip mat for the tub and a shower hose. She had to be careful walking because she was still off balance. She would still have to go in for physical and occupational therapy.

I stayed home with Faithlynn until after the new year. I had been off for a month. The fear of her going back to school and my returning to work was overwhelming. I was afraid that something would happen to her and I would be unable to get to her.

The drunk driver filed for a bond hearing in January. I started a petition to stop her. She had only been in jail a little over a month. I looked her up on the internet and found out that she was forty years old and had two kids who were in trouble with the law. It was apparent from what I saw that she liked to party and drink. I had over five hundred signatures and a letter for the judge hoping to keep her in jail. The judge denied her request and scheduled a hearing in April and then a sentencing hearing in June. While snooping around the courthouse I found out that the drunk driver had previous DUI charges, one in 1991 and then another in 1992. In 1994 she was charged with driving on a suspended license. When she hit Faith her blood alcohol content was .09 percent and she had her thirteen-month-old grandson in the car. She was sentenced to three years, but served only fifteen months and lost her license for a total of nine months. When she got out of jail she moved in with her parents and struggled to find a job. She was sentenced to pay thirty thousand dollars in restitution, but she struggles to pay that. I tried to appear in court every time she had to go because of her not paying, but it takes so much out of me mentally and physically. Besides, I felt that the judge just gave her a slap on the wrist. I lost my faith in him and in the judicial system. To this day the drunk driver has shown no remorse and I don't think she ever will. She will never understand what I went through.

Faith has experienced difficulties. She has mild cognitive memory loss, short and long-term memory loss, behavior problems and some balancing problems. She suffers with depression, anxiety, and shows signs of ADD/ADHD and is very defiant at times. It is very frustrating, because the doctor says that every little problem she has is caused by the brain injury. It would be nice if they would classify some things so I would know how to help her better. As a parent with a child experiencing the sequel of a head injury, it is very challenging, not to mention having a brain injury myself. Our journey has not been easy, but we take every day as it comes. The crash occurred over seven years ago and it is the toughest thing I have ever had to deal with. Even though Faith has overcome a lot of the effects of the crash, we still deal with her defiant issues. Her temper used to be so bad at times that she hit me; she would scream and show no respect. It was really hard to see her like this. It's not how we raised her, and it is hard to define whether it is the brain injury or just age-related. She has done a lot better the last couple of years and has really matured. She is in the tenth grade now and has accomplished a lot academically. She has received fourteen credits already toward her high school diploma. She needs forty-six to graduate. Faithlynn is an honor roll student and wants to go to college at Ball State to become a veterinarian. Her interests are gymnastics and modeling as well as volleyball, fishing, hunting and camping.

Haden has done a lot better. He still remembers the accident and is very cautious when we are around streets and vehicles. He is in the fifth grade and loves playing football, hanging out with his friends and attending church functions. His goals are to continue football and one day play professionally, go into the military as a working dog handler, and become a firefighter.

I feel so very blessed to have both of my children with me, but I wish that night had never happened, but it did, and as a result I have met some really awesome people along the way, people whom I probably would never had met if it wasn't for that night. But I have also witnessed horrible things as well; things that never would have bothered me as much if that tragic night had never happened. If you are reading this and you drink and drive, drive impaired, or know someone who does, please don't. Tell them not to. The consequences are nothing but a lifetime of pain and heartache, no matter the outcome.

MICHELLE LAWSON
KOKOMO, INDIANA

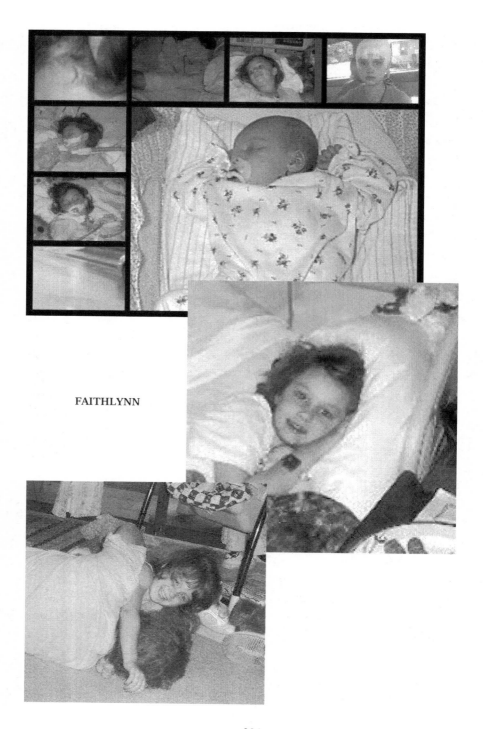

FAITHLYNN

GREAT GREAT GRANDMA BETTY, FAITHLYNN & HADEN

**ZACH, FAITHLYNN
HADEN & MICHELLE**

FAITHLYNN & MICHELLE

FAITHLYNN & GIZMO

FAITHLYNN RECEIVING TURNAROUND
ACHIEVEMENT AWARD (2015)

ZACH & FAITHLYNN (2015)

MICHELLE, HADEN, FAITHLYNN & ZACH

FAITHLYNN & HADEN

CHAPTER TWELVE

CHANGED FOREVER

BY BRIDGET MCWHORTER

To the world you may be just one person,
but to one person you may be the world.
-BRANDI SYNDER

I am a very blessed wife and the mother of two beautiful girls. My girls have always been happy and full of life. Kasi is my oldest by almost six years, and she is very smart and active. Kasi was born June 18, 2000, and Mackenzie April 6, 2006. As my youngest, Mackenzie is so full of life, and she is definitely a social butterfly. I knew that she was going to enjoy school because she was going to have time with her friends and make many new friends. I was right. Mackenzie was making so many new friends at preschool. She was becoming really good friends with Kailyn, a girl in her class and from the same town. The girls would ride the bus together to our town from school. They started playing at the park each day after preschool if time allowed. The girls were becoming great friends. They had playdates at each other's houses. Nikki, Kailyn's mom, and I would spend time together while the girls played. Nikki, Kailyn, Lincoln (Kailyn's brother), Mackenzie and I took a few day trips together as well. It was so nice to see Mackenzie enjoying her friend.

One day while at Kailyn's house, I was talking about going to Chicago to watch Oprah in her final season. I wanted to go, but I wasn't sure what to do about child care and Mackenzie's field trip. I knew I would be gone Thursday and Friday. My husband was going to take Thursday off work to spend the day with Mackenzie on her field trip. I mentioned that I still needed to make arrangements for Friday during the school day since Mackenzie didn't have preschool on Fridays. Nikki volunteered to watch Mackenzie during the day. She offered to come to our house, get Kasi on the bus, and then watch Mackenzie. It was the perfect solution. Mackenzie and Kailyn were going to have another playdate together.

The time came for my trip to Chicago, which was going to be a nice time with family and just a nice little vacation. The two days went by so fast. On Friday morning, October 8, 2010, I received a phone call from Nikki asking me if I could watch Kailyn and Lincoln that coming Sunday so she could go on a motorcycle ride with her husband. She also wanted to make sure that it was okay that she took a check to the bank in a town about twenty minutes from my house. Nikki had assured me that Kasi was on the bus heading to school and the girls were playing at my house. They were going to travel to Belle Plaine, Iowa, to deposit her husband's payroll check. They were then going to Nikki's house in Keystone (we lived in the country outside of Keystone) where Tim would pick Mackenzie up after school.

That same day my mom, my aunt, my cousin, and I were traveling back home from Chicago, a long four-hour drive, after a great couple of days of shopping, sightseeing, and watching the taping of Oprah. I was extremely tired because we had packed as much fun as possible in the two days we spent in Chicago. I was about to take a nap on the trip home, as we were still about three hours away from home. It was going to be a nice nap before seeing my family again. My husband and two beautiful daughters were waiting for me to come home. It was going to be so nice to see them and hear about what they had been doing the past couple of days.

As I was getting comfortable for my nap, my phone rang. I was a little perplexed by the name that showed up, Rebecca Duwa. My mind started turning. Do I answer the phone or ignore it and go to sleep? Why is she calling me? I don't talk to her much. Maybe it is important since she is calling me. I guess I will answer her call. I will be able to sleep after we are done talking. I never could have imagined how much that phone call on the afternoon of Friday, October 8, 2010, would change my day and life forever.

When I answered, she said they couldn't get hold of my husband, Tim. I informed her that he was probably still at work, and I wondered what was going on. She began to tell me that there was an accident. All she knew was that Nikki, the "friend" who was watching my daughter, was being airlifted to the hospital. They also thought that Lincoln, Nicole's son, didn't make it. She had no response regarding what was going on with my daughter, Mackenzie, or her friend Kailyn. She had no information as to the extent of anyone's injuries except that poor little Lincoln didn't make it. She didn't tell me anything about the crash except that Nikki totaled the van.

After this mind-blowing phone call, I had to call my husband to tell him the horrible yet vague information that I had just learned. I also had to make the call through tears and before telling my family in the vehicle any information. They learned the information as I told Tim over the phone everything that I knew, which wasn't much. Tim was thankfully not at work anymore. He was on his way home, but he still had some exits left to be able to make it to the hospital without having to turn around. He told me he had a feeling that something bad was going to happen that day. We were both extremely worried about our baby girl.

My mind turned to being a mom and managing the situation as best I could, since I was still at least two hours away from the hospital. I knew that Tim would need support at the hospital. I called my brother, Chad, who had just finished his day of teaching at a high school in Cedar Rapids. He was going to travel to be with

Tim and Mackenzie at the hospital, but mostly to support Tim. I then made phone calls to arrange somewhere for my older daughter, Kasi, to go after school, which was a time crunch. I received the first phone call from Rebecca after school was already out. I was very appreciative to have such good friends who were there to help during this horrible situation. I wanted to get Kasi, but she was another forty-five minutes past the hospital. It would have taken an extra hour and a half to get her as well. I needed to get to my baby girl, Mackenzie, as soon as possible. She was only four years old, and she needed her mom by her side.

The next two hours seemed never-ending. My mom was driving as fast as she could without being out of control. She worked for a clinic that performed many surgeries at St. Luke's Hospital, where Mackenzie was taken after the crash. My mom made phone calls to try to find out information from someone as to the condition of my daughter. Chad called to keep me updated, but he did not know much except that Mackenzie wasn't moving or talking. They were also taking her up to x-rays.

Wow, did that make my mind go a thousand miles a minute. What if she never walked again? My beautiful, happy-go-lucky girl would have to face a reality that no one wants to see happen to her baby. Why wasn't she talking? Would she be doing better if her mommy was with her? Why did I go on this trip? This would never have happened if I had stayed home with my baby girl. Why did I leave my family? Why was I not there for my baby girl? What kind of mother was I?

We finally arrived at the hospital. The last two-hour drive seemed to take forever, but now I was frozen in the waiting room. I decided to wait for my mom to park the car and walk back with me. Her physical and emotional support was going to help me with the walk to Mackenzie's room in the emergency room. As I waited, I saw Shane, Nikki's husband, and a couple of women with him. They were coming toward me. Shane and I embraced. He told me that Lincoln didn't make it, and I gave him my condolences. Shane updated me on Kailyn's and Nikki's condition. Kailyn was about to get numerous stitches on her shoulder and some staples in her head from being ejected from the van. Nikki was about to have surgery for some internal bleeding. Then the ultimate blow came. Shane told me that Nikki was drunk when she wrecked the van. Her blood alcohol level was .131 percent, which is almost twice the legal limit. He also didn't want me to say anything, because he didn't want the small town that we lived in to talk about it.

I was in complete and utter shock. My daughter was in this hospital not talking and not moving, all because Nikki had been drinking. I had to tell my husband about the crash, and now I had to tell him why the crash happened. How was I going to do this? It was just one more piece of information that rocked my world all in one day. I was just going through the motions as I walked to my daughter's hospital room.

When I reached Mackenzie's room, the words just came out of my mouth about Nikki's being drunk. My husband, Tim, was furious. I could only look at Mackenzie, and touch her. She was still not moving or talking, but I was finally there to see her with my own eyes.

Her hair looked so different; it was stained with blood, and all snarled. She had cuts all over her face, legs, and arms. Tim and Chad informed me that she had a broken collarbone. Mackenzie also had blood in her bruised lungs. She was going to be transported to a hospital about thirty minutes away to be better monitored because they were concerned about the bruised lungs with blood in them. I had barely made it to her bedside, and we were already starting the process for her to be transferred somewhere else.

Before we left, I knew I had to see Kailyn see how she was doing, because she was an innocent little girl like my little girl. I also knew that her dad was suffering the loss of her brother, dealing with his injured wife, and dealing with the information that his wife was drunk and killed his son. Kailyn was just across the hallway from Mackenzie's room, so I would not have to be gone long. Kailyn was about to have her stitches put in when I saw her. She had large gashes on her shoulder blade from the glass cutting her precious little body while being thrown from the vehicle. I asked how she was doing. The poor little girl told me that her brother was dead. She also told me that no one had been wearing seat belts, which was yet another blow. Up to this point, I had not known for sure how the girls received all their injuries, but it was clear now why; they had been thrown out of the van. My heart was breaking all over again with every new detail I was learning. I also had more information that I was going to have to share with Tim once again. I wished her the best and went back to my little girl.

When I got back to her room, it was time to get Mackenzie into the ambulance. Tim was going to ride in the back with her, and I was going to ride in the passenger seat. My mom was going to get Kasi and take her home for the night.

On the way to the ambulance, we were informed that we would be admitted through the emergency room as if Mackenzie had not been seen yet, which meant more medical personnel poking and prodding her for a second time. The drive seemed longer than the two-hour drive, but we finally made it to the new hospital. We were brought in just like they said, as if she was a new patient. We spent hours in the emergency room before finally being taken to her private room in the children's wing. I knew it was going to be a long night watching over my baby girl. She was still not speaking much or moving much.

Tim and I were getting mixed text messages from different people about details of the crash and the investigation. People were saying so many different things that it was hard to keep all the different theories and stories straight. We finally had to stop reading and replying to the text messages and just focus on what was important: Mackenzie! Neither Tim nor I got much sleep that night, as we wanted to make sure that Mackenzie was okay and resting comfortably.

The next day was long as well, but it brought us more comfort. Mackenzie started off with some x-rays to check on her lungs, which showed not much change and even a little progress. We had some friends stop by to bring Mackenzie some stuffed animals to make her feel better. One of them was even able to make Mackenzie smile and laugh, which was a huge success. The nurse even convinced Mackenzie to take a bath and let her start to untangle her tangled mess of hair.

Mackenzie was starting to get that glow back in her face especially after her sister, Kasi, and grandma came to visit. Mackenzie even traveled down the hall of the children's wing to the arts and crafts area to do some coloring. It was great progress for her. The long part of the day was meeting with the Department of Human Services to speak about Mackenzie and the details of the crash. We also then learned that we were going to be required to have a home visit with the Department of Human Services worker once Mackenzie was released from the hospital. It was one more thing that we should not have ever had to encounter, but the crash was just starting to change our lives forever.

Thankfully, Mackenzie was released on Sunday morning after being in the hospital for about forty-eight hours. The past two days seemed like weeks going through a rollercoaster of events and emotions. She was excited to go home and stop to see Kailyn on the way home. She wanted to see for herself that her friend was okay. I think she also wanted to see the only other person who knew everything she had experienced a couple of days earlier. It was nice to see the girls together again. They smiled when they saw each other.

We did learn some shocking news: Shane had recovered a receipt that showed where and when Nikki had purchased the alcohol that she drank before the crash. The visit was short as Mackenzie wanted to get home before going to her sister's basketball game later that afternoon. Mackenzie was not going to let this crash, scars, or broken bone stop her from living her life.

The ride home was very emotional. We had to drive past the location of the crash for the first time, even though there would be many trips past the crash site as it was less than a mile from our house. Even as hard as it was, both Tim and I needed to stop and walk around the area. We walked along the road and saw where it had all started. Since it was on a gravel road, we could see the swerve marks on the road. We could see where the van first went into the ditch. We also saw where part of the van had dug into the ground; we would later find out that when the back end of the van dug in, it flipped end over end.

After seeing the crash site from the gravel road, we decided to venture into the ditch to get a closer look. While we were walking, we found an empty alcohol bottle, so we knew that what Shane had told us was true. It was so hard to see where your child endured the most horrific experience in her short little life so far. It was also wonderful knowing that while she was in the vehicle that caused so much damage, she was still here. The walk and experience were full of emotions, from overwhelming anger to heart-wrenching to extreme gratitude.

The basketball game was hard, because it was the first time when we were going to have to answer questions face-to-face with people from the community. I thought we would have a lot of questions and comments, since we received many different messages while in the hospital with our injured daughter. It was a definite eye-opener, as people knew as much information about the crash and alcohol as we knew. It seemed like some of them knew more information than we did at this point. Why should people in the public know more about a car crash that involved my daughter? One person even asked me if Nikki had been drinking. I was surprised, since we were asked not to speak about the alcohol. As to how they knew the information, some of them told me that Shane had told them, which logistically made sense since Kailyn was released the day before. But it was confusing because he asked us not to speak about the alcohol. I remember being grateful that not too many people were asking questions, so I was able to get through the basketball game pretty well. That night I offered to help Shane by getting pictures printed for him to use for Lincoln's memorial service, which was to be held on Monday. Since I was driving to the same town as the hospital that Nikki was at to get the pictures, I decided to stop and see Nikki for myself. The visit didn't consist of much, because she was in a coma, but her sister did give me a medical update. I was also able to forgive her at that moment while I was still being the strong person and not letting myself feel anything.

The next obstacle would be getting Mackenzie safely through her first day back at school, which was also the same day as Lincoln's memorial service in town. I decided to drive her to school that morning and speak to her teacher. Her teacher had been wonderful, and contacted us over the weekend to see if she could do anything to help. I spoke to her about the sling that Mackenzie had to wear for her broken collarbone. She offered to speak to the other students about being extra careful around Mackenzie, so no one would bump into her and make it hurt. It was reassuring to have such a wonderful teacher for her during preschool. I was a nervous wreck because of having to leave her, but if she was that strong at four years old, then how could I hold her back? Unfortunately, her strength diminished in the following years.

After taking Mackenzie to school, I was going to help Shane give Kailyn a bath and get ready for her baby brother's memorial service. How was I going to handle being around the crash and sadness all day? I knew I had to put Kailyn as a priority and focus on that poor little girl to get me through the day. I would have to view her like it was my daughter to give me the strength to do what I needed. It broke my heart to see all the stitches on her back while I helped her get ready that morning. No child should have to go through what they did, much less at such a young age.

Once I was done helping get Kailyn ready, it was time to attend the memorial service. I had never been to such a young person's memorial service before, and I hope that I never have to again.

I should not have looked at the physical body that was left because it looked nothing like the Lincoln. Again, I turned my focus to Kailyn and her family to help in any way that I could, to keep myself physically and mentally busy. When it was over, people were talking and giving condolences.

At the memorial service I learned that not many people knew Mackenzie was even in the car crash, much less anything about her injuries. How many other people didn't know? It had been in the newspaper and on the news. After the service, I went to someone's house with Shane and Kailyn for the luncheon. It was there that Shane and I made arrangements for Kailyn to come home with me for a little while so he could have some time with his family. I was shocked when he talked about going to the bar, because alcohol was the reason his son was no longer with us. I was more than happy to take Kailyn to make sure she was in a safe environment. We stayed at the luncheon until Mackenzie finished with preschool, so we could all go the house together.

The ride home was the hardest experience of the past three days and maybe even my life so far. We had to travel a different path to our house because the girls did not want to go past the spot where the crash happened. We had to take gravel roads to get to my house, which is the same type of road as they drove on the day of the crash. The girls insisted that I drive very slowly, which made me realize that Nikki had been driving too fast.

The hardest part of the drive home was listening to the conversation of two beautiful and innocent little girls in the backseat. They were talking about the crash. They were both talking about how they did a couple of somersaults (rolled twice) and then a flip in the air (end over end). Kailyn then asked Mackenzie if she remembered being right next to the van. Kailyn told Mackenzie that she had been almost touching the van from where she landed. I knew that once again I had to remain strong and not react, even though I heard the most horrible thing that I have heard since the original phone call just a few days before.

The girls had a great afternoon talking and playing as much as they could with their injuries. I truly felt that they would need each other in the coming days, weeks, and months, because they were the only two alive who could remember what happened that day. Unfortunately, a divide slowly began to creep between the families over the next days, weeks, months, and years.

We knew we had to start looking out for what was best for Mackenzie and our family. It all became clear after speaking to the detective about the alcohol bottle we found when we walked through the crash site that first time, and the receipt from the convenience store where Nikki purchased the alcohol that Shane told us about. The Department of Human Services had an agent come to our house to make sure that we were a safe family and had a safe home for Mackenzie. They had to get involved because of the details of the crash. At least we knew they were coming, because we had to meet with the agent at the hospital before Mackenzie was discharged. It was after those meetings and all the rumors going around that we decided to look out for our family, not speak about the crash in public, and hire a lawyer. I probably could have done the legal research to aid in a lawsuit with the insurance companies, but I honestly did not want that added stress. So we hired a lawyer to handle any and all insurance settlements and bills.

I finally lost my strength and let the emotions roll out the week after the crash. I remember that time vividly. Early in the day, I learned just how Nikki had purchased the alcohol she drank that day. She was at a convenience store in Belle Plaine, the town she was supposedly depositing her husband's payroll check. She left all three kids in the car to go into the store. She was looking at a twenty-four pack of beer in the cooler, but she decided on a six-pack of tall boys, which is equal to twelve regular beers. The detective put together a timeline of events that day. Nikki took the kids to Belle Plaine after calling me that morning about 8 a.m. She took the children to two different parks in Belle Plaine. She purchased the alcohol around noon. She traveled back to my house although they were supposed to go to her house. Nikki fed the kids lunch, and then Kailyn and Mackenzie went outside to play on the trampoline. While they were outside, Nikki most likely had been in the house drinking the alcohol. The crash happened about 2:30 p.m.

Later that same day, I received a phone call from someone who was going to help us with a thank-you dinner we had planned for the emergency personnel and neighbors who helped our baby girl that day. I left the house, because I didn't want my family to see all my emotions come out all at once. All of the emotions from the last seven days just came out now. I was yelling and crying at the same time. My husband, Tim, came out to comfort me and to learn what the phone call was about. I had finally reached my emotional breaking point. I just couldn't handle any more rumors or shocking facts from that horrific day. I needed to let it all out.

October brought many different things, but the main thing I did was go to visit Nikki after she woke up. We also went to see her as a family once as well. The visits were very hard for me. I wanted to hear what she had to say, and after a long time, I realized that what I wanted most was an apology. Nikki cried many times about Lincoln's death. She told me she had driven a few times with Lincoln riding on her lap in town. I was in disbelief, because why was she telling me this? And why had I not seen who she really was in all the times we had spent together the last few months?

Also during October, Mackenzie was able to remove the arm sling that she had to wear for her broken collarbone. She was also able to start using her arm more and more to play like she used to before the crash. Near the end of the month, I was hit with more bad news: my uncle died from a brain infection. While I was attending his funeral out of state, Nikki was released from the hospital. My husband had a hard time watching Shane, Nikki, and Kailyn walking around on Halloween like nothing had happened just twenty-three days before. We were both beside ourselves as to why she was able to be released from the hospital without being arrested. How had she not been arrested? When was she going to be arrested? It is not fair that she just received a large payout from their insurance company for the loss of their son, walking around like nothing happened, and we were living with a different child who was now riddled with anxiety.

Mackenzie started counseling, which lasted years. Her separation anxiety was so bad that she slept with us every night for over five years. She also would not go into a room alone, so someone had to be with her at all times. She never worried about where we were going before, but now you had to tell her every place you were going if we went running errands.

She had never asked questions about death, but she brought it up on a regular basis for weeks after the crash. She spoke about Lincoln's death and asked questions about what happened to him after he died. My heart would break a little bit every day, seeing her worried all the time and asking these questions, which we answered honestly. Why did I not see what Nikki was, to prevent this horrible crash from changing my little girl and our family? I didn't protect my baby girl that day, and now she would forever be changed. How could I let this happen? On top of trying to parent a child with anxiety and asking many difficult questions, I also had a ton of guilt and questions that I asked myself every day.

There were so many different things to adjust to and stress about after the crash, but we were about to experience something no one should have to deal with. We never knew that the criminal charges and court process would bring so many different emotions over the next months and years. We went through Mackenzie being interviewed at the hospital with a person who had experience asking children questions while detectives were behind a double-sided mirror. I am sure it was more nerve-wracking for me then it was for her. I spoke with the detective before the interview and told him what I knew about the crash from Mackenzie talking about it as I did. We discussed where Mackenzie said she was sitting, and he looked very shocked. I could only guess it was because of the window they believed she was thrown out of during the crash. To this day, he has never told me which window.

Before Mackenzie and I left that day, I asked the detective to show me pictures of the van. He told me that we weren't supposed to see them because they were viewed as evidence, and the defense could have it thrown out of court if they're tampered with. I knew it would be emotional seeing the van, but I wanted someone to walk me through what happened, where everyone was sitting, and what windows they believed everyone were thrown out of. I will never get to see it or know exactly what facts the detectives found.

On May 10, 2011, Nikki was finally arrested for the events of the crash. She was charged with six different counts, and was looking at a maximum of ninety-six years if she was found guilty for everything. She had to serve her mandatory night in the county jail before her arraignment the next morning. I attended the arraignment. Nikki looked at me and told me that she knew I was the one behind her getting arrested and some other choice words. The judge even told her lawyer to watch his client and that she was not allowed to speak to the victim. The arraignment proceeded and in the end, Nikki was released on her own recognizance, because she had no prior arrest record.

I was crushed because I was told before the arraignment that one judge would release her and another judge would increase her bail, which would mean that she would most likely not be released before the trial. I was hoping until we walked in that she would be held in jail. Of course, Nikki did not take the judge's advice, and she said something to me as she was walking out of the courtroom. I could not hear what she said, but at that point it didn't matter to me. It felt like the walls were caving in on me with the judge letting her go.

The district attorney met with me and went through the process of what would most likely happen next. He did tell me that there would be some changes throughout the process due to hearings and continuances. I was still trying to process my feelings about the decision when I left the courthouse. As I left the courthouse, I was asked to do an interview for a local news channel.

The interview was fairly short and not too hard, but I am sure I felt that way because I was still a little numb and sorting through my feelings. It was kind or surreal watching myself answer questions on the news that night. And then the waiting game began.

There were a few different hearings in between Nikki switching lawyers four different times. Every time there was a new lawyer, a continuance was soon to follow. We would get our hopes up only to have them crushed with all the delays and postponed hearings. During this time, we would have people tell us to get over it and move on (which we started hearing weeks after the crash, even from some family members). Three years after the crash, her lawyer wanted her tested for competency to stand trial, which again was a possible huge setback for us. After hearings and scheduling, she was tested weeks later. The doctor found her incompetent to stand trial due to either her bipolar disorder, the brain injury that occurred in the crash, or a combination of the two. Nikki was closely monitored by doctors to make sure that she was following the doctor's orders to regain her competency. Again, we just waited and waited, because she would not be tested for at least another year.

Well, that year came and went. It was two years after her first testing and a little less than five years after the crash before she was tested for competency again. The doctor said she was worse than two years earlier, and would never regain competency to stand trial. We were crushed, to say the least. How could someone kill her son and injure two innocent children and not go to a courtroom? How could she do so much damage to people's lives and emotions, and nothing was going to happen? Why does she get to live as if nothing happened?

During the two years between her first and second competency hearings, I figured out that what I wanted the most out of the court case was the chance to speak at Nikki's sentencing hearing. I wanted Nikki to have to sit in her courtroom chair and listen to what she had done to my family, how she had changed our lives, and especially how she had changed Mackenzie forever through my victim's impact statement. I wanted her to know that she did affect all of our lives forever. She changed so much for us. We went with our now anxiety-ridden child sleeping with my husband and I or our older daughter for over five years. We dealt with new situations, with Mackenzie now having anxiety that we had never experienced before. We dealt with emotions that no one should ever have to go through, from right after the crash all the way up to today. We remember the anniversary of the car crash every year, which is a date that we will never forget. As of today, the case has been dismissed. Nikki is living free with her new husband. Even though she was found incompetent due to her low cognitive level, she is living like any other free person in America. She served only one night in jail for her horrible choices that day. To the best of my knowledge, Kailyn is living with her dad, Shane, with visitation with Nikki.

My family has learned to keep moving forward from the event that forever changed our lives. Mackenzie is currently ten years old and still lives with her anxiety every day of her life, which I am sure she will have forever. Mackenzie will forever have the physical scars left on her face from the glass that cut her as she was thrown from the van that day. However, she is a happy young girl living life as normally as she can. She loves to go swimming, fishing, boating, and playing with her friends. Mackenzie really loves to play basketball. She plays with a team from her school at tournaments. Mackenzie also plays for a traveling AAU team, Team Iowa, and Kasi also plays basketball for Team Iowa.

Kasi is now fifteen years old and has her school permit. She is practicing and playing basketball as much as she can because she loves the game so much. They are both living every day by going to school, doing homework, participating in sports, and just being kids. I am truly blessed to have them both here and happy! We work through any situations that come about on a daily basis, and we all continue to learn how to help Mackenzie with the different issues that her anxiety brings.

I am currently speaking to groups about what happened that day, so I can hopefully make a difference in someone's life. I am also an adult leader of a youth group at our local high school that helps the students bring awareness to things that affect teenagers every day like drunken driving, drug use, suicide, tobacco use, etc. The group also spreads positive messages throughout the school. It has been fulfilling to help these students and speak to different groups, because I feel like I am using this horrific event to help others.

We look forward to what great things our daughters will experience and accomplish in their lives. Kasi would love to play basketball in college. She wants to become a neurologist to learn more about the brain and to help as many people as possible. Mackenzie wants to continue to play basketball and grow as a player. She loves to go camping and be outdoors. We will plan many camping weekends, because the peace of the outdoors seems to help her. Mackenzie has said she would like to be a teacher, but she has plenty of time to make that decision. I know they are both going to grow into wonderfully accomplished women who will live life to the fullest!

BRIDGET MCWHORTER
KEYSTONE, IOWA

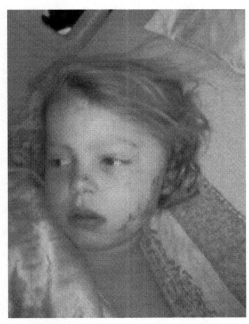

MACKENZIE ONE DAY AFTER THE CRASH

MACKENZIE & BRIDGET

CHAPTER THIRTEEN

THE DAY MY HEART

STOPPED BEATING

BY SONYA POINDEXTER

*There is an hour, a minute - you will
remember it forever - when you know
instinctively on the basis of the most
inconsequential evidence, that something is
wrong. You don't know - can't know - that it
is the first of a series of "wrongful" events
that will culminate in the utter devastation
of your life as you have known it.*
-JOYCE CAROL OATES

Losing a child is a pain that is indescribable. It leaves a scar that never goes away. You spend the rest of your life looking for and wishing for what might have been. Always wondering who he would be now, who he would have married and how many children he would have had. It's a future that comes to a screeching halt when your child's life ends too soon. It's a heartache no parent should have to endure.

In April 1987, I married my husband Steve. He came as a package deal with two boys whom I love as my own. We lived in a four-bedroom house in Randleman, North Carolina, a small, quaint town. It's the type of town where everyone knows your name. We were very happy there. Together, Steve and I had five more boys, each different in his own way. I felt blessed and knew it until that fateful day that took my son Nicholas away and shook my faith to its very core. Our son's names are Jarrod, Stephen, Jeffrey, Nicholas, Dustin, Zachary, and Jacob. Nicholas, my second birth son, was born on September 22, 1989, the day Hurricane Hugo came through the Carolinas. He weighed nine pounds two ounces and was twenty-one inches long. Nicholas had a head full of dark brown hair and blue eyes. He was the middle child in our family of all boys except for me.

Our family was big and often loud, as one can only imagine with seven boys. We were a family who loved doing things together. We spent many Saturdays at the zoo. Each boy had a different animal he liked the best. We also loved to go to Jordan Lake in Pittsboro, North Carolina, for the weekend or just spend the day having a cookout and swimming. The boys were always competing against one another to see who could swim the farthest or stay under water the longest.

Nicholas lived to play sports. It didn't matter what the sport was, he always had to be the best. The boys grew up playing recreation ball all year long. In the spring they played baseball, in summer they played soccer, in the fall they played football, and in winter they played basketball. Nicholas loved football and baseball the best and excelled at both. He could and did play all positions.

As Nicholas got older he became the protector for his brothers and friends. His favorite saying to them was "I can mess with you, but nobody else can." He always took up for the underdog, or the kids being bullied. He didn't back down from a fight and most of the time he would win. There were a lot of people scared of him because they knew the consequences of making him mad.

Nicholas was an honor student his entire time in school. Learning came easy for him. He never studied, and would have all his homework done before he came home from school. He loved to learn and all his teachers would remark about how good a student he was. I remember a time the teacher called because he was caught swinging from the beams in the classroom. So even though he was a good student, he loved to have fun and he made time to be the class clown.

Nicholas had talked about going to college but decided he wanted to go into the Marines instead. He had signed all his papers and was ready for boot camp. He would be leaving in September 2009, so he was spending that last summer having fun with his family and friends. How I wish now that he had left earlier. He was ready to fight for his country and was excited to see what the next chapter of his life was going to be. He had no fear. He was not afraid of anything. Nicholas had a job with Domino's delivering pizza so he would have spending money till it was time to leave for boot camp. He loved to deliver pizza and meet different people. He never met a stranger and was always happy. He had a way of making each day a new adventure.

In July 2009, we still had five boys living at home, twenty-year-old Jeffrey, nineteen-year-old Nicholas, seventeen-year-old Dustin, fifteen-year-old Zachary, and eleven-year-old Jacob. We had a four-bedroom home. Jeffrey and Nicholas shared a room, Dustin and Zachary also shared, and Jacob, being the baby of the family, had his own room. Our house was always full of their friends playing ball in the yard, swimming in the pool, or just hanging out in the garage playing pool and listening to music. It was nothing to find three or four extra boys asleep in the bedrooms. Feeding them was a challenge. I hated to grocery shop and it seemed like all our money went to Walmart for food. We had to buy groceries every three or four days. Boys sure put the food away. I remember I used to tell them I was going to put a jar out and take up donations so I could afford to feed them all.

On Thursday, July 2, 2009, Jeffrey left to go to Myrtle Beach, South Carolina, with his girlfriend and her family for his twenty-first birthday. Before he left, he and Nicholas spent time in the backyard throwing the football around and goofing off. Nicholas kept jumping in and out of the pool as he asked Jeffrey what he wanted for his birthday, and they talked about a movie they both wanted to see. Jeffrey's girlfriend arrived and it was time for him to leave. Nicholas told him goodbye and said he would see him for his party on Sunday, July 5.

Friday, July 3, 2009, started out like every other day of the summer. With Jeffrey gone, the other boys slept late, and after lunch their friends started showing up. They swam in the pool with the radio turned up loud. After swimming for a while, they played pool in the garage. Nicholas told me that he and Dustin were going to go out with their friends. Around 8 p.m. they got ready to leave. As they were leaving, they gave me a hug and said they would see me in the morning. I told them goodbye and that I loved them, and Nicholas said, "I love you too, Mom." I told them to stay out of trouble and to be careful. Nicholas said "Don't worry, Mom. I love you and will see you in the morning." But morning never came for Nicholas. If only I had known that would be the last time I would see him alive, I would never have let him leave the house that night.

Dustin and Nicholas decided to go to Greensboro with their friends to a party. Alcohol was served even though all the boys were underage. I was told by their friends that Nicholas and Dustin each had a beer or two. After a while they decided to leave with their friend Josh, since he hadn't had any alcohol. They had every intention of going home. But on their way Nicholas received a text message from a girl he had been dating off and on. She wanted him to come see her at another party. Nicholas at first told her no. He told her he wanted to go home, but for reasons we still don't know he changed his mind and went to the party. His friend Josh said he dropped Nicholas and Dustin off around 3:45 a.m.

My husband, Steve, and I and our two younger sons, Zachary and Jacob, were asleep along with my niece, Julie, who was spending the night with us, when we were startled awake by the phone ringing. I checked caller I.D. I didn't answer the first couple of calls because I didn't know the number. I let the calls go to voicemail. No message was left. My cellphone then started ringing, and it was the same number that had called the house phone. I had a bad feeling in the pit of my stomach. I just knew something was wrong. Oh, how I wish I had been wrong.

I answered the phone and it was my seventeen-year-old son Dustin screaming, "He's dead, he's dead, Mama! Nicholas is dead!"

I remember yelling at him to shut up. "What are you talking about? Who told you Nicholas was dead? Please stop saying that, you don't know what you are talking about!"

Dustin kept crying and screaming, "He's dead, he's dead. I know he's dead, I saw him, Mama. Mom you need to get here now, please come now!" I asked him where they were. He said he didn't know and hung up the phone.

I was screaming and telling my husband we needed to go. He asked why, and I told him that Dustin said Nicholas was dead. He jumped up out of the bed saying, "Let's go."

But we had no idea where to go. What do you do when you have no idea where to go or what to do? I tried calling Dustin back on his cell, but it went straight to voicemail. I called four or five more times. Something finally told me to call the number that called my cellphone a few minutes earlier. I called, and a fireman answered. He told me there had been a bad car wreck and gave us directions on how to get to the crash site.

With Steve driving and me giving directions, we headed that way. I was crying and saying that it couldn't be true. Dustin just didn't know what he is talking about, he's only a child, and he doesn't know anything about someone being dead. How does he know anything like this? I kept thinking that this couldn't be happening. It just had to be a very bad dream. Oh, how I wish it really had been a dream.

My husband tried to get me to calm down and said, "Let's not worry until we know what's going on." How am I supposed to not worry? I was sitting in the van, going crazy.

As we drove down Highway 311 we saw flashing red lights in the distance. Oh, no! This is not a dream, it's a nightmare. As we approached the road the fireman had given us directions to, we saw an ambulance and fire truck with their lights flashing parked in the church parking lot. There was a group of firemen standing around talking and looking into the sky. Steve and I jumped out of the van and went over to where they were, and a fireman stopped us. I asked him what was going on and he said that there was a bad wreck around the curve. He proceeded to tell us that one person was airlifted to Baptist Hospital in Winston-Salem and there was still one person left in the car. I asked him who was in the helicopter and who was in the car.

"I am sorry, but I cannot tell you anything at this time. You will have to talk to the police," he said. I told him we were going to the wreck.

We ran to the van, jumped in, and drove about a mile down the road. As we started around the curve, we came upon a line of emergency vehicles: fire trucks, ambulances, police cars and tow trucks. There were so many emergency vehicles with their flashing lights that it looked almost like daylight. As we got out of the van we saw a little red car that seemed to be growing out of a huge oak tree. It was just a mangled piece of metal. My mind was telling me that it was a mistake. There was no way my son was dead, because we didn't know anybody who drove a car like that.

I stumbled out of the van and ran toward the mangled car. I had to know the truth. I needed to know who was in that car. A group of firemen stopped me from getting to the car. They said they couldn't let me near the car until the police said it was okay.

Out of the darkness my son Dustin came running to me. He was crying and yelling again that Nicholas was dead, and was still in the car. I yelled at him to shut up, and to quit saying that because it was not true. It couldn't be true; we did not know anybody who drove a car like that. We stood on the side of the road, not talking, each of us lost in our own thoughts.

How did this happen? Whose car was this? Who went to the hospital? Are they okay? Why won't they tell us anything, and what was Dustin talking about? My husband, Dustin and I stood on the side of the road for what seemed like hours but probably was only thirty to forty-five minutes. My stepson Stephen and his wife showed up and stood there with us as we waited. I kept looking at the car that appeared attached to the tree. The firemen were standing guard, not letting anybody close to it. All I could tell was that there was somebody in the car, covered in a white sheet that had blood all over it. I kept thinking, it is not true, I don't know anybody who drives that kind of car and I don't know anybody who lives on this street, so there is not any reason for Nicholas to be here.

A highway patrol officer came walking toward us, carrying something in his hands. He was holding Nicholas' wallet in one hand and his driver's license in the other.

He looked at us and asked "Is this your son in this picture?"

We all said yes. He looked at me and said, "I am sorry, he is dead." He handed me the wallet, driver's license and cellphone and walked away. I chased after him, yelling that he was lying because we didn't anyone who drove a car like that.

The officer said, "Yes, ma'am, it is him. I took your son Dustin up to the car when I got here, and he identified your son and the driver."

I fell to my knees screaming, "Nooooooo! My son is not dead, and I don't believe you! He can't be. He said he would be home in the morning. Morning is almost here. He will be home soon."

I stood there holding my son's belongings, wondering what we were supposed to do now. I ran after the officer and yelled at him, "What am I supposed to do now?" He just stood there staring at me for a moment and then said, "Follow the ambulance to the hospital."

The police officer came back to where we were standing and told us he needed Dustin to write a statement on what had happened. Dustin said that he and Nicholas went to a party to meet up with some friends down the street from where the crash was. The party was for this guy who was celebrating his twenty-first birthday. Dustin was in the house and didn't see him or Nicholas leave. The officer looked at me and said for us to not let Dustin drive, because he could still smell alcohol on him and that he could tell he had been drinking. My thoughts were, "Really, you're worried about Dustin driving after drinking but not worried that you took a seventeen-year-old to a wrecked car to identify his dead brother. And you don't seem to be worried about the drunk underage kids you told to leave and go home. You let them drive off knowing they had been drinking. Wasn't one wreck enough?"

Since Nicholas was pronounced dead, the wreck was being investigated as a crime scene. Nicholas was left sitting in that car covered in a bloody sheet while pictures were taken and marks on the road measured. After what felt like forever, my son's body was finally removed from the car and placed in the ambulance. We followed the ambulance, and on the way we had to make phone calls that no parent should ever have to make.

Nicholas' oldest brother, Jarrod, was in Virginia visiting family with his wife and daughter and had a five-hour drive home. Jeffrey was at the beach with his girlfriend's family, and the youngest two were at home waiting to find out what was going on. How do you tell your children that their brother and protector is dead? I had to call his cousins, uncles, and his grandmother. How do you make all these calls? What are you supposed to say?

My husband, stepson, and I were met at the hospital by our good friends, who were like second parents to Nicholas. The head nurse took us to a plain, ugly white room and told us to have a seat and that she would be back in a moment. She returned a few minutes later with a doctor who told us he was sorry that Nicholas didn't make it; he was killed instantly.

He said we could see him but that he wouldn't recommend it. I wanted to see him, because there wasn't anything that Mama couldn't fix. My husband and friends made the choice that we wouldn't see him and that we needed to remember him the way he was. I will always regret that I didn't see him. He was my son; why didn't I see him? Why did I let them make that choice for me? Next, we had to make a choice of which funeral home to send him to when all I wanted was to take my son home.

Nicholas was an organ donor, but our local hospital was not able to do organ donation, so he was sent to Durham, an hour and a half away. He was left in the car so long; he was only able to donate his eyes and some bone and tissue. Nicholas was able to help four people with his choice of being an organ donor. I received a letter saying that his eyes gave sight to two people and that his tissue was used to help a thirty-year-old man and a sixteen-year-old girl to walk again. At least some good came out of this tragedy.

I was told by some of the kids and the police officer that the kids were celebrating the birthday of the drunk driver, who was to turn twenty-one on Sunday, July 5. The wreck happened early Saturday morning. Why couldn't he have just waited? Why celebrate early? We were told that my son was a passenger in a Dodge Neon, driven by the drunk driver. For reasons we don't know, he and Nicholas left the party and went to the dead end road, turned around and started back down the road, speeding. The drunk driver lost control, ran off the left side, and hit two mailboxes. He came back across the road, hit a large boulder and went airborne, hitting a tree head-on. According to the police, he was doing 135 mph on impact when he hit the tree.

Nicholas died instantly, and the drunk driver was airlifted to the hospital. His blood alcohol level was .219 percent almost two hours after the wreck. He spent his twenty-first birthday in the hospital knowing that he had killed my son. He suffered acid burns from where the battery exploded, and lost part of his foot from the track on the bottom of the seat. Nicholas died from massive internal injuries, head trauma and a broken neck.

My husband and I decided to hold off a day for Nicholas' viewing, because we didn't want it to be on his brother Jeffrey's birthday. So on July 7, we had his viewing at the local funeral home. There were many flowers and over sixty potted plants. So many people wanted to say goodbye that it seemed like the line was miles long. The funeral home lined us up so that everybody could just walk by and see us. Jeffrey stood at the head of his brother's casket, trying to protect him in death when he couldn't in life. This went on for hours. I think everybody in our town and surrounding towns came to say goodbye.

On July 8 at 10 a.m. we saw our son for the last time. It would be the last time I would be able to touch, kiss, and tell him that I loved him. I begged them to let me stay with him. I kept thinking that there was no way I could leave. How could I let them close the casket and lock my son away from me? At the church, there were so many people that there was no place left to sit or stand. Nicholas' brothers and friends told stories about him and all the wild and crazy things he had done.

This is a short letter his best friend, Patrick, wrote and read to the church.

"People say that a friend is someone you trust and care about, someone you respect and love. Nicholas was much more than that. Nicholas is someone who was more than life itself. Nicholas was someone who meant the world to me. He was there for me when I was hurt, mad or just lonely. Nicholas was a young man who took the world head-on every day. No matter the situation, Nicholas always found a way to find the good in it. Nicholas was a person who was very respected and loved. He was also feared by many, not because he was a bully but because he was scared of nothing or no one. They say my friend was taken by force of the impact, but I refused to believe it because my Nicholas couldn't be stopped or defeated by anyone or anything on this earth. Nicholas' mental strength was beyond words. I love you and will never ever forget you."

I will never forget this young man and the words he had to say about my son.

As we were leaving the church behind the hearse, all I could think was that I wished it was me instead. How was I supposed to leave my son in a hole in the ground? I still have nightmares after all this time. How am I supposed to move on? I can't do this.

The drunk driver was placed in jail under a ten thousand dollar bond. Is that all my child's life was worth? When he got out on bail, he continued to go to parties and drink and post pictures online. Life wasn't fair. How could he be out partying when he killed my son? When he finally went to court, he was placed on house arrest. While on house arrest he failed multiple drug tests. His excuse was that he used the drugs to help him deal with what had happened. So I guess we all should be on drugs so we can deal with the death of Nicholas. I wish I had something to help me understand how to deal with his death.

The driver was taken back to jail and placed on another ten thousand dollar bond. In North Carolina if you violate house arrest and are able to post bond, you get out of jail and are able to continue with your life. No more house arrest, no court date for violating, nothing; so much for justice for the victim. It seems like as long as you have money the law treats you differently. His family posted bond again so he got to Christmas shop and spend the holidays with his family and friends, and we got to decorate a grave.

For two and a half years we had to go to court every three months to hear what the drunk driver had been up to. He got his high school equivalency, which was court-ordered, had a job and got engaged. It wasn't fair; my son was dead because of him, and yet he was going on with his life. He was facing nine years in prison. The charges were involuntary manslaughter, felony death by motor vehicle, reckless driving with wanton disregard, exceeding safe speed, driving while impaired, driving left of center, and driving after consuming under age twenty-one.

The police officer didn't do his job. He didn't pick up the blood sample from the hospital within ten days, and the hospital destroyed it. The officer said he was sorry but his wife was pregnant with their first child and having problems, and he forgot. Really, you forget to do your job? The drunk driver was found guilty of felony death by motor vehicle. He received sixteen months out of the nine years he could have gotten. He is now married, working, and the father to a little girl. Nicholas had his life taken away, and my son's killer gets to continue with his. It's not fair.

The drunk driver got out of prison on March 30, 2013. I suffered a heart attack that day, and my heart is truly broken. My health has continued to go downhill since Nicholas was killed. I now suffer from major depression and I am scared for my other children. If I hear a siren, I start calling all the boys to make sure they are all right.

We have lost so many friends who think we should be over it. They can't deal with us always talking about Nicholas. We were told that we need to let him go and that we are hurting our other children. But I will never be over it, nor quit talking about him.

My husband and I now go to the DUI checkpoints and take food and drinks for the officers to have during their breaks. I hope that with our being there the officers will be more alert and we can stop another family from going through the pain and heartache we now live with every day.

What I wouldn't give for just one more day, one more hour to see Nicholas smile, hear his laugh, to be able to feel his arms around me, giving me a big hug. *I want my son back. I need my son to complete my family.*

SONYA POINDEXTER
RANDLEMAN, NORTH CAROLINA

NICHOLAS POINDEXTER

NIECE RHYLEAH VISITING NICHOLAS

CHAPTER FOURTEEN

FROM THE HEART OF A BROTHER

BY JEFFREY POINDEXTER

Because I have a brother,
I'll always have a friend.
-ANONYMOUS

My brother Nicholas Adam Poindexter was born on September 22, 1989. I was fourteen months old at the time and for as long as I can remember he was always there. We shared a room up until the day he died. We had so many late night talks about girls we liked and about what we wanted to be when we grew up. We would always have our long talks after everybody else was asleep. I miss our time together and the many jokes we played on our other brothers. I knew that no matter what, I could always count on him if I needed him. He excelled in everything he did; whether it was school or sports, or anything else he put his mind to, he never quit.

Everything changed the morning of July 4, 2009. I was at the beach celebrating my twenty-first birthday. I received a phone call around 5 a.m. I heard my phone and I just let it ring, because I thought it was my phone alarm. A couple of minutes later I got up and saw that it was my dad who had called. I had a bad feeling about that call. Why would he call this early if everything was okay? I called him back, and he was crying. I couldn't understand him. He kept saying somebody was dead. I asked him what he had said, and I heard "Nicholas is dead!"

Within minutes, my girlfriend, Heather, and I were packed up and on the road heading back to Randleman, North Carolina, where we lived. Ten minutes later my phone rang again; it was Nicholas' best friend, Patrick. He was also crying. He asked me if I had heard that my brother Nicholas was dead. I told him that my dad had called but didn't tell me what had happened. Patrick then told me. He said Nicholas died in a car wreck. I flipped out. I couldn't stop crying.

About an hour into our four-hour drive, my older brother called and told me what had happened. He said the drunk driver hit a tree head-on at 135 mph, and that Nicholas died instantly. I cried all the way home, with my girlfriend driving and trying to comfort me.

When I arrived home there were so many people there that it was hard to get into the driveway. I got out of the car and walked up to where my mom was. She had been crying so hard that her eyes were almost swollen shut. All I could do was hold her and tell her how much I loved her. I couldn't tell her everything would be all right, because it wouldn't. I knew she would never see her son again and I would never see my brother alive again.

I went to the backyard where my other brothers and dad were; they were all crying. I looked at the pool, remembering that it was the last place I had seen Nicholas alive. Before I had left we were throwing the football and Nicholas was shooting basketball in the pool goal. I had told him, "I'll see you Sunday at my birthday party." He said, "Okay, bye, I love you."

I walked inside and went to our room. As I walked in, I looked over at his bed, praying he would be there laughing at me for crying and calling me a baby, but he wasn't. I didn't know what to do; I just sat on his bed and continued to cry. My older brother Stephen came and sat beside me and told me how the hospital thought the seat belt had crushed his chest and that he had head injuries.

Later on that day, my little brother Dustin, who was seventeen and had been at the party, told me everything he knew. He told me that Josh had dropped them off around 3:45 a.m. and the drunk driver and Nicholas had left the party, and then they heard a crash down the road. My brother and two of Nicholas' so-called friends ran up to the wrecked car. They saw Nicholas in the car, dead. The two friends then left my little brother Dustin, all by himself with his dead brother and the injured driver, because they were scared of getting caught by the police. Great friends, right? Nicholas considered them friends. But when his life was taken, all they worried about was getting in trouble for underage drinking. Dustin told me he saw Nicholas lying in the car with his hands straight out in front of him like he was trying to stop the tree. I didn't know how Dustin was holding it together.

My brothers and I went to where the car was taken. I saw the car and I was in shock. Looking at the car, it seemed to me that the driver should have died, but he didn't. There was nothing left of the front end of the car. On Nicholas' side, the door was dented and the glass broken, but everything else was in better shape than the driver's side. There were no scratches or anything. The side mirror was even still there. I remember Nicholas' blood splattered all over the dash, and the airbag was drenched. I got sick to my stomach. I went through the car and found the back to his phone, and I cleaned out his seat, getting all the trash and glass out. I put the seat belt that had been cut and was covered in his blood around the seat to make it look like a bow. I reached into the floorboard, looking for the battery to his phone, and I stuck my hand in my brother's blood. I started to cry, wishing it was all a dream. Please let me wake up.

We went to the crash site and walked the road, and saw where the car had left the road and taken out two mailboxes. The drunk driver never once hit the brakes. He then came back across the road and hit a boulder that was estimated to weigh close to five hundred pounds, splitting it apart and throwing part of it through a van's window two houses over. It sent the car airborne and into a tree, wrapping it around the tree on the driver's side. So why did the driver live? You could see parts of the transmission on the ground, oil and fragment of red paint all over the place. I cried so hard, knowing that was the last place my little brother saw on this earth and took his last breath. At the funeral home for Nicholas' viewing, I stood beside him. Everyone said it looked like I was still trying to protect him. I wish I could have protected him. I wish I had been in that car instead of him. I was not supposed to bury my little brother. He was supposed to bury me!

The day of Nicholas' funeral, his friends told me to look at the old water tower in town. Somebody had climbed it and painted it in memory of him. We went inside the funeral home, and Nicholas looked so peaceful lying there. Everybody told him goodbye, and then it was just my parents left standing there. They didn't know what to do or how to move away and leave him there. When we got to the church there were hundreds of people there to say goodbye to Nicholas.

NICHOLAS' NIECE RHYLEAH

After the funeral, we went back out to the crash site and placed a wooden cross that my little brother Dustin had made and was signed by all of Nicholas' friends. We placed it against the tree where Nicholas had taken his last breath.

It took two and a half years before the drunk driver was sentenced for killing my brother. Because of the officer's mistake in not picking up the blood sample from the hospital in time, he was sentenced to only sixteen months in prison. But my brother was sentenced to death. Nicholas was taken from me because of a choice a drunk driver made. How am I supposed to go on, knowing I will never see him again?

It's now been six years, and the pain has not gotten any better. His friends are still drinking, driving and forgetting that their friend was killed by a drunk driver. I want what happened to Nicholas to be remembered, and for others to learn from his death. The only positive thing that has come out of this nightmare is that I have started a Don't Drink and Drive page on Facebook. It is for victims to share their stories and tell how they have learned to cope with the deaths of their loved ones. It helps me, knowing I use Nicholas' story to try to save lives.

JEFFREY POINDEXTER
RANDLEMAN, NORTH CAROLINA

NICHOLAS POINDEXTER

CHAPTER FIFTEEN

I WATCHED MY BROTHER DIE

BY DUSTIN POINDEXTER

Sometimes being a brother is even better than being a superhero. –MARC BROWN

Blurred by tears of pain, I saw Nicholas breathe his last breath. Braced against the dashboard were both of his bloody arms stretched out to prevent a collision with the windshield. I was helpless as I watched my brother pass away. As I learned that night, you have only one life, so make every day better than the last, because you never know when it will be your last.

On the Fourth of July, 2009, my brother was involved in a fatal crash. He was the passenger in a car that collided with an oak tree at 135 mph. Although the intoxicated driver was severely injured, he managed to survive. Enjoying the thrill of going fast, my brother had been quick to jump at the chance to ride in this car. Glass and shrapnel covered the ground at my feet where I stood looking at my brother's lifeless body. I remember praying and wishing that it was a dream, that he was still alive. Helpless but hopeful, I ran to his side only to see that he was nonresponsive. My legs trembled and my knees hit the ground. With my eyes closed, all I remember is a police officer picking me up and forcing me to the side of the road. I was crying like a baby as the weight of a million worlds came crashing down on my shoulders. Reaching for my phone, I dreaded calling my parents. With every ring, my heart sank deeper. Waking my mom at 4:30 in the morning was bad enough, but to have to tell her that her son was dead was almost impossible. I couldn't tell her what happened, I just told her she had to come. Awaiting her arrival, all I could imagine was how she and my dad would feel.

Covered under a white sheet was nineteen years of excitement that came to an end in less than a minute. My parents couldn't see that it was my brother under the sheet. But seeing the car, they expected the worst. As they learned the truth, I watched my mother fall to the ground, screaming "Nooooooooo!" Having no idea what was going through her mind, I could only imagine. Comforting me yet hysterically sobbing, my mom kept telling me it would be okay. Lit by the lights, I could see my father's face. Holding his tears back, staying strong for my mom, my father kept to himself. Even though I couldn't stop it, I felt like it was my fault. The thought of "what if" ran back and forth in my mind. I thought of how I could fix it, but I knew that nothing I said or did would bring my brother back.

Every few days I relive that night in my head. I'll never forget that horrifying night. Until that night, I had never gone through life thinking about the consequences of my actions. Since then I have realized that everyone has regrets, some worse than others, but life will go on. My brother always said, "Life is too short, so live it up while you can." I live every day by his words.

DUSTIN POINDEXTER
RANDLEMAN, NORTH CAROLINA

DUSTIN, SONYA & STEVE POINDEXTER

CHAPTER SIXTEEN

FROM FEAR TO FORGIVENESS

BY NICOLE RAMOS

*The scars you share become lighthouses
for other people who are headed to the
same rocks you hit. —JOHN ACUFF*

I was born and raised in Southern California. I grew up with two brothers in the same house, but I have three more brothers and two sisters from my father's side. I grew up with all boys in our neighborhood. We played football, stickball, cops and robbers, and rode our bikes all over town. I loved to swim in our pool, body surf in the ocean, and jump on our trampoline. My stepdad got me interested in softball at the age of five. I fell in love with the sport and bonded with my female teammates. I played softball for fifteen years, and then after I graduated from college I decided I was not ready to give up the game. I started coaching at the college level and then began to study the game and pursue my master's degree. When I got pregnant with my second child, I decided to leave the college scene and stay closer to home.

With a daughter who was active competitively in soccer and softball and another on the way, I could not divide my time between work and family. Audrey, Elijah and I moved to a town fifteen miles away to get a fresh and new life. I started teaching at the junior high and coaching at the high school. We bought into the Friday Night Lights culture at Permian High in Odessa, Texas, and were immediately welcomed to the Mojo family. We all went to the college, junior high, and high school volleyball, basketball, football and softball games. Our family was involved in athletics all day, every day. My husband, Tommy, is a college softball coach, so we support his team and all of their athletic events.

When Audrey was going into junior high and Elijah was entering Pre-K they were both going to be involved in sports year round. Most of our days consisted of practice, travel and games.

I decided it was again time for me to make a shift in my profession so I could watch my children grow. I left the junior high and high school position to teach Pre-K. This was a huge jump, from college to high school and junior high, but I loved spending time with the little ones. I taught Pre-K at our church for five years. Our summers consisted of visiting family and one family vacation when all the kids, including my three stepchildren, would load up in our Suburban and travel to a national park, camp, go to a theme park, or to the beach. Our five children look forward to hiking, swimming, and horseback riding, exploring and making new memories together. Our busy schedules usually keep us from all being together at the same time. We really look forward to our summer vacations and creating memories.

In mid-October our family was stretched in all different directions. My husband and I coached a 14-U traveling softball team that had just played in a Think Pink tournament. We paid off our Suburban the month before, and were spending our first month without a car payment buying a new stereo for it. I remember how exciting it was to try out the bluetooth feature and all the extras it had. The previous stereo had shorted out after a full glass of sweet tea fell out of the cup holder and soaked the stereo. The buttons stuck in, and it would not allow you to change the channel, and if it did, it would scan until you turned it off. Audrey became the permanent DJ with her auxiliary cord and iPod. She was toward the end of her junior high volleyball season and preparing for the all-city tournament. Elijah was enjoying his first season of flag football by mimicking what the Permian boys do Friday nights. Tommy had just finished his fall scrimmages and started the recruiting season. I was wrapping up our Red Ribbon Week celebration on campus by taking down my decorated door and transitioning to spiders, candy corn and monsters, preparing for Halloween.

On Friday, October 25, after the school bell rang our family rushed from school life to the weekend athletic life. I picked up Elijah and then Audrey from school. Tommy was in Las Vegas recruiting prospective student-athletes for the next school year. When we made it home, Audrey got all dressed up in her best outfit to attend her first Halloween party. Honestly, I was very hesitant to let her go, because she had a volleyball tournament, and there was going to be a large group of kids from her school. She ended up going, but we had to lay down the law on what time she would be home. After dropping Audrey off around 7 p.m. I decided to have some one-on-one time with Elijah. We went to Target to shop for his Halloween costume, candy and pumpkins. We got back home, tried on his wolverine costume, and took a picture to post on Instagram and Facebook for my family to see. Elijah was starting to get sleepy around 9 p.m. so he changed into his pajamas, but I told him he couldn't go to sleep because we still had to pick up Audrey.

Around 9:30, Audrey asked if she could stay until 10:15. I told her no, because Eli was already getting cranky and 10 p.m. was our agreement. Elijah was in his pajamas and fell asleep in the Suburban before we were halfway to Audrey's friend's house.

The house was way out in the country. It was very dark, but I could see about fifty kids out on the front lawn waiting for their parents to pick them up. I couldn't tell if Audrey was outside so I parked, opened the door and went around the backside of the Suburban but then I saw the interior lights come on. Audrey was climbing into the passenger seat. I got back in the driver's seat, looked in the back to check on Elijah, clicked my seatbelt on and put the vehicle in drive. My daughter began to tell me all the drama that had happened at the party. She was flipping through her phone and continuing on with all the details. I was not very familiar with the area, but I could see a store sign that was on the street I needed to get to. I made a left at the stop sign and noticed that the speed limit was very high, and thought, "I must be on the highway." I started to accelerate and checked my approximation to the store I was looking for so I could make another left turn to head back to town.

I saw a vehicle coming toward us, and then to my surprise I saw a small car moving onto the shoulder like it was going to pass on the shoulder. In my head I thought, "What an idiot." The small car hit the rear passenger side of the Lincoln, sending it into a spin. At this point I saw the headlights staring right into our windshield. What came out of my mouth was "OH!" The next words would have been profanity. My yell caught my daughter's attention, and she looked up right before the loudest sound I've ever heard: the sound of metal crimping and grinding, and then came absolute silence. Everything went black, and I accepted death right then and there. I was at peace, and then a white fleck flew across my field of vision and I followed it. Then black became brown, the noise returned but, over and over again, our Suburban rolled into a ditch on the side of the road.

Dust and smoke filled the car, and so did the smell of burning plastic and gas. I remember moaning, "Ouch, ouch," and then I heard my daughter screaming, and soon my son followed. That is when I remember my brain becoming clear and focused on getting out of the car. The sound of my children screaming brought me absolute joy and peace.

I was hanging in my seatbelt because our Suburban had landed on the driver's side. I tried to undo my seatbelt but my right wrist was broken. Bones were bundled up under the skin like a rainbow. I asked if my daughter knew where her phone was; I could not see mine. She said no, but then asked me to call OnStar. Our rearview mirror was hanging off the windshield with wires all over the place.

My son started screaming, "Call 911!" After my own failure in getting my seatbelt off, I asked my daughter if she could get out. She said yes. She used the middle console to bear weight to break her window with her elbow and butt. She climbed off the vehicle and started screaming for help.

I started to wiggle around, and then I felt my foot hanging in a direction that it should not be hanging. I could feel my khakis getting heavier from soaking up blood. Audrey returned and I asked if she could get Eli out of the backseat. I could hear him wiggling around in the back seat. When he made his way across the front seat, I could see blood running down his face. He was crying when his big sister reached in to pull him from the wreckage. That was the last time I would see them until six days after the wreck.

Two men came to the passenger side of the car and I could hear one of them cussing. I told him I had a broken arm and leg but other than that I was okay. I was not in any pain and speaking clear as day. I asked if he had a knife to cut me out of my seatbelt so I wouldn't have to hang anymore. He took off, yelling at others, and returned to bust out the back window and climb past the third row and back seat to approach me from behind. After he cut my seatbelt, I asked if he could try to help get me out. I tried pushing with my left leg because of the hanging foot problem but couldn't get very far because the steering wheel and dashboard were in my lap. I wanted to see if he could release my seat so I could scoot or lean back to go out the vehicle the way he came in. He did not feel comfortable moving me anymore, so he decided to wait until help got there.

When he got out I asked if he could call my husband, because no one was going to be at the hospital for my children. I could hear him outside the vehicle making that phone call, saying, "Dude, it's not good...." I tried to tell him I'm fine, just make sure someone is there at the hospital for the kids. I could hear sirens in the distance. It felt like an eternity. The first thing I heard was an officer yelling, "Does anyone know where the driver of this vehicle is?!?" The first thought that popped into my head was that someone got ejected. Then I heard him say as he approached my vehicle, "Is this one DOA [dead on arrival]?"

It took the firemen over an hour to secure my vehicle and cut me out. Once I was out of the vehicle they cut off all my clothing and tried to strap me onto a stretcher as the helicopter waited to take me to the emergency room. The medic asked if I could put my leg down because it was sticking straight up in the air. I had some pain while they were getting me out of the vehicle, and feared that my foot was going to fall off when they tried to get me out of the wreckage. I thought my hip and butt were cramping from staying in an awkward position for so long.

When I got to the emergency room I saw my sister-in-law. She was crying. I asked if she had seen the kids and she told me they were in the same hospital, and that my ex-husband was there for Audrey. I was being poked, prodded, questioned, x-rayed, and then the doctor came in. My sister-in-law, Brenda, and former softball player Dina, who was now a DPS officer, were in the room when the doctor explained my extensive list of injuries and reported that I needed to have surgery right then and there. I remember being in shock, because I was sure that the arm and leg were my only injuries and I would be out of there quickly. I asked if they could call my mother in California to let her know. As I was spitting out phone numbers, they wheeled me to the operating room.

What I didn't know was that Tommy had contacted a friend who lived near the crash site. When they tried to put Audrey in an ambulance with the driver of the truck and his ten-day-old baby, she noticed he had blood running down his face and she asked to wait for the next ambulance to ride with her brother. Our friend rode with our two children in the ambulance to the hospital. Tommy had called all of his family within an hour's distance from us. My son and a three-year-old little girl who was in the truck were airlifted to Covenant Children's Hospital in Lubbock, Texas.

Audrey walked out of the emergency room in borrowed scrubs and barefoot, because her clothes had been cut off at the scene and her shoes were soaked in blood. Tommy's identical twin and other family members headed to Lubbock to be there for Elijah. They thought he could have internal bleeding. Tommy left the softball fields in Las Vegas in shock to try to contact my family and change his flight home.

When I woke up from surgery, everything was a blur except the metal bars that were sticking out of my leg. I anticipated seeing Brenda, but instead it was two of my good friends who were very upset. I asked where Brenda was and they explained that she had gone to Lubbock to be with Elijah. This is when I learned that Elijah needed stitches and staples to his head from the cuts. This made sense, because I remembered the way he looked like crawling over my seat. I didn't know that he was classified as serious because of possible internal injuries from the seatbelt.

My father and stepfather were some of the people I saw that day with the most worried faces. I tried to reassure them that everything was going to be okay; bones heal. When my mother flew in from California the next day, the doctor explained to her the extent of my injuries. I had an open pilon fracture on my right ankle, which means it was crushed. The first surgery was to try to clean the site of bone fragment and debris. They put an external fixator, which looked like a kickstand from my old childhood bicycle, to keep my leg the same length. The doctor told my mom before they rolled me back for surgery they were not sure if they were going to be able to save my leg. They were going to try because I was so young (thirty-two) but it just depended on how much bone loss there was. My hip needed to be plated and I was going to have pins in my arm to stabilize my wrist. I spent five days in critical care and a total of twelve days in the hospital.

After my second round of surgeries, I found out that the car that hit the truck was a drunk driver who left the scene on foot. His face and name were exposed by local media so anyone who knew who or where he was could come forward with information. Cody was his name and I resented the fact that he took off on foot, leaving seven injured people. He continued running even after he heard Audrey scream for help. He left the man who pleaded for help for his wife, three-year-old, and ten-day-old baby.

He hid out there in the dark country until about 3 a.m. He knocked on a door to ask to use the phone and for a ride home. He left his car at the scene and never went to the wrecking yard to claim it. All his belongings were still in there. When Tommy came home, he went to the wrecking yard to take pictures of our vehicles and saw Cody's mail and other items left on the passenger seat like the DPS officers were going through his glovebox. Sure enough, it was Cody's full name and address in that gold Kia Optima that hit the black Lincoln. The car still smelled of alcohol days after the wreck.

It was recommended that I be placed in a nursing home because I was going to be bedridden for several months. I was non-weight bearing on three out of four limbs. I needed a physical therapist to help me sit up and learn how to use a slide board. I needed to have my dressings changed on my wounds, rolled so I didn't get bedsores, bathed, given medication and fed. My mother knew that she could not physically handle all that so she went with Tommy to tour nursing homes so I could leave the hospital.

Audrey and Elijah were not allowed to visit me in the hospital, so I thought moving to a facility where they could visit would be the best situation. My mom returned from the tours to notify me that I could not get into the good nursing homes because there were age requirements. The homes that I could get into were not up to par for my mother and she thought the kids would not want to go there to visit.

Needless to say, we decided that I would come home. My father built me a ramp so I could enter my own home. I had to arrive in an ambulance because I could not use the slide board to get from my wheelchair into my SUV.

We cleared the dining room and moved in a hospital bed, bedside commode, and a TV tray to hold my belongings. I was bathed a few feet away in the kitchen. I hid behind a shower curtain hanging on a portable clothes rack to do my duties. Anyone who was in the living room or playroom knew I was done when I moved the curtain and sprayed. It was so embarrassing because I had become so helpless. I had to be sponge-bathed by Audrey and my mother, wear a bib when I ate because I was not left handed, and had to eat in my bed. My mother decided to move in indefinitely to take on all of my duties. She carted my kids to and from school and athletic activities. My father and mother had not been under the same roof since I was an infant. Now these ex-spouses would have to deal with each other and care for me like I was an infant.

My mother and father's snide comments to each other were entertaining and frustrating at the same time. I started reading books and binge watching Netflix on my iPad. If I didn't feel like talking or eating that day, I rolled over to face the wall and acted like I was asleep. I would cry and try to conceal the sniffling because I really did not want to differentiate between the emotional and physical pain.

I had so many people calling, texting, emailing, Facebooking, fundraising, and stopping by to visit me that I just wanted to be alone. I wanted to try to process all that had happened without having to filter it with a smile and a happy ending. I tried to be thankful that we had all lived, and were only dealing with broken bones, but anger started to bubble inside. I wanted Cody, the driver, to know what it felt like to be broken and in constant pain. I wanted his children to draw pictures of him in a wheelchair. I thought about making a visit to that address on the envelope left in the gold Kia Optima. I wanted him to look me in the face. I wanted him to know what he walked away from that night: kids screaming, two women who were so broken that they might not be the same again, a man holding his newborn with blood running down his face, crying to his wife, who was unconscious in a ditch. I wanted Cody to get the six-figure bills that were being sent to my house right before Thanksgiving. I wanted him debating what Christmas was going to look like for his children. Honestly, I didn't mind the pain, I just didn't think it was fair that he was not injured and might not be caught because of how many wrongs he had done.

The car he was driving was not registered in his name. He had purchased it with cash a month before and did not have it insured. My attorney told me that he would not be pursued because he didn't have enough assets and would probably file bankruptcy and I wouldn't get anything. The investigating DPS officer had, in my opinion, done a poor job investigating the crash. In fact, it took two weeks to get a crash report, one that was filled with many lies.

The first crash report was based on the driver of the Lincoln. He said that a vehicle came into his lane, which caused him to hit his brakes, and then the Kia Optima rear-ended him on the rear passenger side, which sent him into my lane to hit me. I lost my cool when I realized that people were trying to cover themselves. I called the DPS officer to tell him that there were mistakes in his report and that it needed to be amended. He basically said I can reword it, but it was my word against his. That sent me into a downward spiral, because I wanted the truth to be told. Basically, Cody, the driver of the Kia Optima was at fault because he was driving too close to the Lincoln. It was amended with a phantom car causing the Lincoln to hit the brake, which led to the initial crash and then the second crash. I was so infuriated that the truth would not be told and little was going to be done to find Cody.

I wondered how I was going to be able to keep up with all these bills, three medical insurances, two hospitals, our car insurance, and an attorney. It wasn't even a month before I was back in the emergency room with a staph infection in my left leg from an open wound. This was my first time out of the house and not in an ambulance. I was treated twice the weekend after Thanksgiving because the infection was spreading to the pins in my arm and the incision site on my hip. I was freaking out because if it had reached the bone in my arm, they would have to cut away bone and replace all the hardware in my body. I should have been out Christmas shopping with my mother-in-law and sister-in-law. It was a tradition that after Thanksgiving dinner we got all the kids in the family to look through ads and make wish lists. We would all get the gifts loaded up, and hit stores all night and the next day. We would nap and then hit the rest of the sales later that weekend. Now I was not only not able to go out shopping, I was racking up more medical bills. The best part about this weekend was that I figured out that I was able to transfer from my wheelchair to my mom's car. I would finally be able to get out of the house once in a while.

Soon after that my mother recommended that I take a trip with her to the grocery store. I recall that the sun was out and it felt really good to be able to contribute to the weekly grocery shopping. We pulled into a handicapped spot and were contemplating how to get me into the motorized grocery cart. As my mother opened the door, a lady in a truck pulled up behind our car and rolled down her window to yell, "I can't see your placard! Are you handicapped?"

My mother proceeded to tell her in a matter of fact way, that she was not handicapped but I was. The lady pulled off and ended up parking in the handicapped spot directly in front of us. At this time my mother was walking into the store to bring me the cart to see if I could slide from the car to the cart. When the lady got out of the truck she proceeded to attack my mother. "It looks like you can walk just fine!" My mom lost her cool as she was riding the cart back to the car, and yelled back, "I already told you, it's not me that's handicapped, it's my daughter! Oh, and you look like you can walk just fine yourself!" I could hear and see all of this going down because I had the door open, anxious to transfer to my first motorized cart. By the time I made it into the store I was so furious. I wanted to shout out through the grocery store, "Here I am, the young handicapped lady from whom you needed proof to park in the handicapped spot. Would you like to see my scars? Would you like my trauma surgeon's phone number or diagnosis?"

What was supposed to be an exciting and liberating experience ended up being the first time I was judged and made to feel different. My mother felt horrible, because she had such good intentions for my first outing, but I just wanted to return to my bed and deal with how the world was going to view me. I guess the old me would be judged as athletic, strong, a fighter, hard worker, and funny. Now I would be seen as fragile, damaged, needy, and wrecked. Wrecked can describe what happened that night, or how I felt inside, or how my body was.

December was always a busy but exciting month for our family. First it was my birthday, then my father, brother, and then Elijah all in the same week. This month we tried to fake normal excitement. I did not get to bake my son's cake, throw him a party, or fill his piñata. Instead, we bought a store cake and went to the local pizzeria and arcade to celebrate. I was in a wheelchair wearing a nightgown and dealing with the public again. Luckily, I was surrounded by a few friends and their kids. This was my first attempt to try to explain why I had bars sticking out of my arm and if it hurt, and so on.

I sat there at the table looking at the half-eaten cake while the kids were in the arcade, thinking things might never be the same. My participation in holidays, birthdays, anniversaries and vacations would be altered, and I didn't quite know for how long.

I started doing more physical therapy at home to prepare me for the strides to come. I started marching while sitting at the edge of my bed, using putty to get my fingers in my right hand to become more usable. Eventually I was released to start to bear weight on my left leg, because the hip x-rays came back good. I used a walker with a platform for my right arm to rest on in order to try to get up out of bed. I had to raise my hospital bed all the way up to the highest position so there was not much work for me to do. I remember being absolutely scared that I would fall or put weight on my right foot, which was still trying to grow new bone, and scared that I just couldn't do it.

On my first attempt my legs shook and I immediately fell back on the bed. I had no balance or strength but I did not further hurt myself. I repeated sitting and standing on one leg several times a day. I lowered the bed a little bit each time, giving the quivering leg a real workout. Just before Christmas I had to go back into the operating room to get the hardware off my right arm and put into a cast that went just above my elbow. The cast inhibited my slide board operations and using the platform on the walker. I felt like I had taken a small step backwards. I was in more pain being in a cast, and my hand, fingers and arm hurt almost constantly. I started taking more pain medication, which led to other medications so I could sleep through the night.

I eventually started using the walker for transfers and could finally get rid of the slide board, which left me with several marks from being pinched and my very first fall all the way to the ground. I would now rely on my one leg instead of a plastic board to move my larger than normal body from object to object. I felt like I would be able to transfer on my own using the walker, which means going to the bathroom without asking for someone to wake up and help me in the middle of the night. Needless to say, I stumbled twice and accidentally put weight on my right foot, which still had a few months to go before I was supposed to do that.

Our church puts on a family event the weekend before the kids get out for Christmas break. There are hayrides to look at Christmas lights, a bonfire, hot chocolate, kettle corn, and a fabulous candlelight service. This year I arrived in a wheelchair and wore a nightgown instead of a hospital gown so I could attend church service for the first time. I covered my hardware with a blanket and saw many familiar faces. I wanted to shy away, but I knew they had been praying for us and providing us with so much support. I sat in the back where there was room for my wheelchair. When they stood to participate in praise and worship I sat there wishing I could stand. I felt every song with every bone and started to cry. I felt that I was being selfish because of my suffering.

That night I figured out I wouldn't be in back forever; I would stand again, and be able to raise my hand, and I would continue to live. Sitting in the back definitely changed my perspective in many ways. There was hope that I would heal, not in my time but God's. I needed to be patient and focus on the process.

Christmas was a time we usually spent with extended family, either with a trip to California to be with my family or just down the road with Tommy's family. That Christmas I did not do any shopping, because I tried to do some online shopping but became very irritated with the process. Tommy and my mom did the shopping. The kids put the tree up and tried to decorate the house. I saw the first snow from my bed through the dining room window and the kids brought me icicles from the backyard.

I thought about the last time we had taken our family picture in the backyard in the snow. We built a snowman and tried to get the two dogs in the picture as well. I took many trips back and forth to the camera on the tripod because one dog was looking and the other wasn't, or Elijah was making a silly face.

That winter, as if things were not tossed around enough, our black lab, Chico, passed away. He suffered for a while, but I could not look at him from my bedside like that anymore. Tommy had to take Chico to the vet, to watch him go limp. He tried to keep it together to tell the kids and tell me. I was not only upset that we had lost a family member of nine years, but that I could not be there to hold him. Emotions ran high for the next few days for our entire family. I started feeling guilty and anxious, and started curling up in the bed facing the wall to cry myself to sleep. As the year came to a close, I was still angry, full of revenge, pain, and fear. Our family was emotionally drained with all of the changes that we were still trying to get accustomed to.

When the new year began, I wanted only a better year than the previous one. January was a month of steadfast. I anxiously waited for restrictions to be removed so I could gain more liberties. Standing up and sitting transitioned into using one leg and a walker to move around a few steps. I was able to get into the kids' bathroom and sit on a bench and shower with a plastic bag on my cast. I tried to shower with one arm and the removable shower head. This was one of the first things that made me feel like I was becoming normal again. I started writing in a journal led by devotionals that were brought to me from the prayer team at church. My writings were so different from what I typed on my phone in a locked diary app.

I loosened my obsessive internet search for Cody, the driver, that had peaked during early December. My need for Cody to experience my pain faded, but I still yearned for him to know the repercussions of his decision to get behind the wheel intoxicated. During the waiting periods between x-ray results and doctor appointments, I really looked forward to returning to my classroom. I started looking at lesson plans for after spring break.

I was looking forward to February so I could start traditional physical therapy. When I walked into the physical therapy office I was greeted with a warm welcome because I had just been treated for ACL reconstruction on my left knee. I knew that it was going to be a long and hard road to recovery, but I was excited to move forward. I spent almost two and a half hours three times a week in that office treating my hip, wrist and ankle. I entered the first day with a walker and a support for my right arm. It wasn't long before I was using a quad cane and then a traditional cane. My wrist and fingers were the most painful for the first couple of weeks, but progressed very quickly. My hip was very limited in range of motion but the leg was strong. My right leg was very weak and the ankle was in constant pain. I had my scars pulled on and my range of motion pushed to the point where I thought I was going to pass out. I would leave the table with a full body imprint of sweat. I wondered how long I was going to be like this.

When I returned to my doctor with improvements, he released me to start driving again. This was nerve wracking and liberating at the same time. I drove a short distance from the ball fields to

Chick-Fil-A and realized that this was going to be a process. I could hardly hold my foot on the brake because of pain. I knew that I was close, but needed more time to heal. Once I felt confident that I was capable to drive safely, I told my mom that she could go home.

Tommy wanted me to attend his athletic banquet and visit with people I hadn't seen in about six months. I wanted to go buy a new blouse for this event and headed to the store. I picked out a couple of options that I thought would go with a long skirt that I already owned. I knew that I would have to cover up the scars on my ankle and left leg where I had an open wound. An associate helped me, opened a dressing room, and told me she would be back to see if I needed anything else. I had on sweats and a T-shirt and hobbled in with my cane. I attempted to try on the blouses and then looked in the mirror. Once I saw myself, I broke down and cried right there in the dressing room. I saw scars everywhere. I would have to be covered up head to toe for everyone's comfort. I didn't want the wreck to be the only conversation that night.

I lost complete control and could not leave the dressing room because I was blotchy red, my nose was running, and I was crying uncontrollably. I literally could not stop. I texted my mom to tell her what was going on, to get up enough courage to exit the store. I left the clothes in the dressing room and stared at the ground as I made my exit. Before I made it past the register, the associate asked if I was okay. The only thing I could get out was "It's just too soon to be doing this." I was ashamed of what I looked like and knew that these scars were never going away. They would always be a reminder of what I had been through. I wasn't sure if I was ready to face some of these hidden feelings alone, without my mother.

I cannot express what my mom sacrificed to be here for me and my family. She was to come and visit us the week after the wreck. She was going to take Audrey to her first concert in San Antonio to see her favorite singer, Selena Gomez, the day before Halloween. She had to cancel her roundtrip flight to be there six days earlier to pick up the pieces of our wrecked family. Three weeks after the wreck she was supposed to go on a trip to Costa Rica with my aunt. Those plans were canceled and her trip was given to a friend of my aunt because she could not change her prepaid vacation. She was away from her own bed, dogs, husband and son for four months. She was forced to live with her ex-husband. She dealt with my emotional and physical pain. She guided us through the processing of bills and insurance notifications. Without my mom, my family would not have been able to move on as quickly as we did. I would have been stuck in a nursing home and probably would not have progressed as quickly or as well as I did. Her sacrifices will never be forgotten.

I continued physical therapy until June. The kids were out of school, and I felt confident driving and walking short distances with a cane. We decided to stay in California at her house for a month. I joined a gym to keep up my physical therapy exercises and got in her pool every day to stretch and exercise. I made a trip to Disneyland in a wheelchair and was limited to certain rides that I was confident I could transfer onto. I knew that being pushed around the park in a wheelchair was going to be difficult, but I didn't think it would bring up all sorts of emotions that I thought were buried months earlier. I started to get angry again. I was suffering from nightmares of meeting Cody through a mutual friend or bumping into each other in a public place. My biggest fears were how I was going to react when we met face to face. Would I seek vengeance? Would I freeze? Would I act like nothing had happened, try to gain his trust, and then tell him who I was?

So many scenarios went on and on in my dreams. The worst dream I had was that I was walking with my two children and a man followed us up to our front door. When I turned to try to defend myself, all I had was my cane. I poked it at the man but it did not help. I remember feeling so helpless because I could not run from the situation or defend myself and my children. This feeling returned the day I took a trip to the beach. I thought that this trip would rejuvenate my peace and stillness. The beach is a place where I used to go to cleanse my soul. I would think about how large the ocean is and how small I am. It would put into perspective how little my worries really are in the grand scheme of things. I would let the waves take me as they willed. I would learn to let go and ride the waves. But this trip would not fill me with peace. It filled me with fear and anxiety. I had a hard time walking with a cane on the sand. My balance was challenged by the pounding waves and I fell. I decided to just go with it and get in the water. I swam for about thirty minutes and then decided to try to get out. This is when everything started to turn for the worse. With my back to the waves, I struggled to get out with the water below my waist. I got down on my belly and tried to get as close to the beach as I could. I tried to stand up, but got thrown down by the oncoming waves four times before I stood up.

My friend and Audrey saw that I was struggling and brought me my cane. I was covered in sand from head to toe and completely embarrassed. I didn't attempt to swim the rest of the day. I sat in my beach chair watching Audrey learn how to boogie board and Elijah build sandcastles. When Elijah ran toward the water to jump over the little waves, I feared that I could not get to the water fast enough if something were to happen, and my challenge to be in the ocean would conquer me again. I felt as helpless as I did in my dream. I knew that my physical limitations were taking a toll on my confidence and self-worth.

After our trip to California, I returned home for more x-rays to see if healing was taking place. My doctor was impressed with my improvement, but wouldn't release me back to work. I asked to start some sort of water therapy because being in my mother's pool every day seemed to be easier and less painful. I put in for a leave of absence and would not be returning to work that school year. I joined the local YMCA because they had a water aerobics class and a water arthritis class that were held three times a week. I spent six to ten hours a week in the water working on balance and range of motion on my hip and ankle. Just before my one-year checkup, I remember feeling frustrated because I had come a long way but was not even close to where I wanted to be. This would be the last exam with my trauma surgeon. They would not continue regular x-rays, which led me to believe that all the healing was done. I was still in constant pain and very limited. I tried pushing a cart in place of a walking device in the grocery store, but this caused swelling and I would be miserable the rest of the day. I had a hard time coping with the new me.

Recently I started feeling pain while working out in the water, which had never happened before. I pushed through the pain until I was on a road trip with Tommy and his team. I started to feel grinding and locking in the ankle. I could not put any pressure on my ankle and was in tears. I knew something was wrong, so I went to urgent care to get x-rays. I thought they were going to tell me a screw was out of place and needed to be fixed. But the x-ray showed a nonunion—gaps in my leg that never healed. I called home to my doctor only to find that he was no longer practicing in my area. I came home from this road trip in a tremendous amount of pain and with no doctor.

I had to jump through the insurance hoops to get a referral to see a new orthopedic surgeon. He sent me for a CT scan and two weeks later I would be given the news. My hardware was out of place and I had several sites of nonunion. I would be referred to a foot and ankle specialist. At this point I was in so much pain I begged for an amputation. My new surgeon is the first doctor to look at my ankle and give me hope. We planned for removal of the hardware and a bone graft to fill in the nonunion sites, and if the ankle joint was not stable, new hardware would be added. He took bone marrow from the center of my femur and had bone from donors to fill in my ankle. This procedure will put me back to a non-weight-bearing status to give the bone time to heal. He also felt hopeful that we could address the damage to the joint after I recover from this procedure, which would take about a year. I walked out of his office feeling that there was hope that I might be able to walk normally again and take some stress off of my hip. Hopefully, after my ankle is fixed I can get my hip replacement. I know that I have a long recovery road, and my faith in healing has had many ups and downs, but for once I feel like there is hope to return to my old self.

My emotional relationship with Cody, the driver, has evolved. I still keep up with him through social media every now and then. I long for the chance to be able to impact his life. I want him to know that his actions changed my life forever, along with those who surround me. Even with a possibility of healing there has been a tear in my trust for law enforcement, lawyers, and insurance. I have a wonderful support system at home and in California and online. Without a place to vent my current mood or emotions, I would have already given up. Knowing that there are people out there feeling the same way and in much worse situations helps me try to stay strong to give them a voice. I talk to many young adults and teens about the importance of making good decisions and how quickly life can change. On the night of the wreck, things could have been completely avoided if Cody had just decided to call for a ride home after drinking, instead of causing a head-on collision.

I am grateful to be able to have survived to witness to those around me. I believe that night we had perfect bad timing. If we are half a second too soon or too late, our wreck becomes fatal. The newborn in the truck that hit us was due the night of the wreck. If the mother had still been pregnant with him, he would not have survived. I am thankful for what we still have, although it is hard to not look back on what I thought I would have had. Our planned vacations, school trips, athletic seasons, church and career activities have drastically changed because of that night. I honestly hope that one day I can look back at all this and feel confident enough to share our story to help someone change for the better. I want those who feel they are not going to make it, or want to quit, to realize that it will get better. It's like my scars that I see every day in the mirror; they will fade but never go away. They will remind me of where I've been and how strong I can be.

NICOLE RAMOS
ODESSA, TEXAS

AUDREY GARCIA, NICOLE RAMOS & ELIJAH RAMOS

Not every day is beautiful, but
there is beauty in every day.
LYNDA CHELDELIN FELL

CHAPTER SEVENTEEN

GOODNIGHT, I LOVE YOU,

SWEET DREAMS

BY SANDRA RAWLINGS

*In the night of death, Hope sees a star and
listening love can hear the rustle of a wing.*
-ROBERT GREEN INGERSOLL

I think the beginning of this nightmare starts early in life. You're a child with no cares in the world. You have a nice home, brothers and sisters, friends. As you get older you think about what you'd like to do when you grow up, whom you might marry, how many children you might have. You've been taught right from wrong, how to take care of yourself and others, never expecting that anything would devastate your dreams for the future.

I was born and raised in Cleveland, Ohio. I had two brothers and a sister. I had a nice family, nice home, great neighborhood. I graduated from high school and was dating a classmate named Rick. Three years later we were married.

We eventually had three children: Jennifer was the oldest, Tiffany is my middle child, and my son Bradley. Tiffany was the usual twelve-year-old girl. She loved music and clothes, and was just beginning to like boys. She had gone through that pudgy stage, and had just become taller and thinner. I could tell she was feeling

273

so happy and more confident about herself. She was absolutely beautiful. As the middle child, she was very loving and caring. Unfortunately, things changed after my son Brad was born. Rick and I were having problems and separated in late 1980, and divorced in 1983. I was a single mother living in Cleveland with three children aged six months, two years, and four years. I remember standing there watching them sleep, then starting to cry, wondering how I was going to handle this on my own. I knew my parents would help me if needed, which they did many times.

A couple of years later I met a widower with twin sons. Things seemed to be going well. His sons and my children were around the same age and they got along very well. I still lived in Cleveland and they were going to start busing the children to school. I decided to sell my home, as he asked us to come and live with him and his boys. So my three children and I were living at his home in Parma, a suburb of Cleveland. I thought this was it. I would have a family again, better schools; everyone seemed happy. The children were all involved in music, drama clubs, cheerleading, choirs. In the beginning I thought this was how a family should be.

After a while, things started to change. He drank too much at times and he was verbally abusive which turned physical. I stayed even after he had thrown me against a car and I needed stitches and had a concussion. On New Year's Eve in 1991, he was choking me by the back door. I then left with my children and went to live with my parents back in Cleveland. I left most of my things at his house in Parma. This was somewhat difficult, since we didn't have all of our things and I had to drive back and forth to take my kids to and from school.

It was snowing one day that January, and Tiffany and Brad wanted to go sledding. They had so much fun, so I promised them we would continue to come back. On the way back from my mother's, we were hit by a drunk driver who broadsided us as he was pulling out of a bar. There was damage to the right side of the car where Tiffany had been sitting. It wasn't too bad, but the door was pushed in and it had bruised her leg. Unfortunately, I don't know what happened with the drunk driver. My mother came to pick us up, and at that time my car was being towed and the police were still with the driver.

My children spent every other weekend at their father's. He lived in Maple Heights on Warrensville Center Road. As they got older, Jennifer started not wanting to go. She had other plans with friends. Jennifer went along for the ride as I took Tiffany and Brad there on Friday night, January 25, 1991. Tiffany and Brad walked to the side door, but Tiffany put her suitcase down and came running back to the car. I rolled the window down and asked if something was wrong. She said, "No, Mom. I just wanted to tell you I love you and give you one more kiss." Little did I know that would be the last time I would get one last kiss.

On Saturday I had a party to go to. I didn't really feel like going and while there I was wishing I had an excuse to leave. When I was at the party, I called their dad's house around 3:45 and talked with Tiffany. I told her I thought I should pick her up, because her leg was still hurting her from Tuesday, but she said she didn't want to come home. She said, "Please, Mom, let me stay. I'm having fun." I told her okay, not knowing that would be the last time I would ever talk to Tiffany.

Two hours later there was a knock on the door. It was my older daughter, Jennifer, and my sister, Robin. When I saw the looks on their faces, I knew something was wrong. Tiffany had been hit by a car, and we had to get to Meridia Suburban Hospital in Beachwood where she had been taken. We did not yet know how badly she was injured. As we scrambled to get our things together and were deciding how to get there, all I could think about was how badly she might be hurt, that she needed me, what could be wrong, maybe she had a broken leg. I was thinking maybe it was just broken bones; my mind didn't go any farther to anything life threatening. That ride took around forty-five minutes, because we got a little lost, but it was the longest ride of my life. I was scared, and my heart was beating out of my chest. All I knew was that I had to get to Tiffany as quickly as possible.

When we arrived, I was not allowed to see her as they were trying to determine the extent of her injuries. They came out occasionally with an update. I knew she had a broken leg, broken pelvis, and was unconscious. Sitting there pacing, waiting for some kind of news was pure torture. After a couple of hours, they said I could see her, but only for a few minutes. They took me down a hallway and I saw her lying on a stretcher with the helicopter waiting outside the door. I will never forget how she looked, lying there, not moving, tubes down her throat, IVs and monitors everywhere. I had just seen her less than twenty-four hours ago, and she was fine. How could this be? Is this really happening? She had to be airlifted to Rainbow Babies & Children's Hospital in Cleveland. I kissed her and told her I loved her, and she was taken away. I asked if I could be with her in the helicopter but was told no, and that I should meet them at the next hospital.

Again, another long ride to Rainbow Babies & Children's Hospital. At this point I knew this was very serious. When we arrived at the hospital, I again was not able to see her. Finally a nurse let me into the room, but told me I had only a minute. There was Tiffany lying on the bed. I noticed that her eyes kept opening and closing. They said it was probably due to brain injuries and possibly small strokes. That was the only movement she made.

After some time and their evaluation, they escorted me, my mother and sister to a room where a doctor was waiting. The doctor told me she was very seriously injured and they didn't expect her to make it through the night. The doctor said she had a broken leg and pelvis, a broken neck at C5/6 that would leave her paralyzed, damage to her lungs and severe head trauma. She died on impact but was brought back by the medics. Unfortunately, too much time had gone by without any oxygen. She had extensive damage to her brain.

I remember my sister grabbing me as I slid down the wall to the floor. Tiffany would never be the little girl that she was. Those words cut like a knife. She was the most loving, sweet, beautiful child. How could this be? Not Tiffany, not my child. Why? What had I done wrong that caused this terrible thing to happen to Tiffany?

I was finally taken to her room in intensive care. My beautiful daughter was lying there lifeless. She remained on life support for twenty-six days. There were so many tests and consultations. At times, things looked positive and there was hope. On other days things looked much worse, and any hope seemed lost. I took notes every day of what the doctors and nurses told me. I was still in a state of shock, so I couldn't remember from day to day what was happening. Tests were constantly done, trying to determine if there was even a slight chance for her. I learned how to do some therapy to keep her muscles toned so atrophy wouldn't set in. We had to keep her shoes on, and continue to move her legs and arms. They inserted a feeding tube because it seemed like some of her other bodily functions were working.

The worst day was when they had to replace and drill another hole in her skull to put in another cranial monitor. I remember they wouldn't let me see her afterward because she was "restless." My God, what did that mean? I asked if they sedated her for that, and they told me no, she wouldn't feel anything. Did her restlessness mean that she did? To this day, that still bothers me. The nursing notes said, "Tiffany cries; please talk to her when you are doing things to her." Did she hear us? Did she still feel our touch? Was part of Tiffany still there?

Tiffany loved music, and Madonna and Janet Jackson were popular at the time. They were her favorites. I had her cassette player and her earphones and I would let her listen to her music. She carried that player with her everywhere she went. I talked to her, asking her to give me a sign that she knew I was there. I asked her to move a finger, open her eyes, I would pinch her toes, but there weren't any movements. I stayed there for twenty-six days, sleeping in the parents' lounge. I didn't ever want her alone in case she woke up. All I wanted was for her to open her beautiful eyes. I prayed and prayed for what I knew had to be a miracle to save her. I went to the chapel and wrote all my feelings and prayers down every day in a journal they had at the altar. I prayed God would take me so she could live.

Tiffany also contracted an infection called MRSA while in the hospital. One day I went to go into her room and they stopped me. She was behind a closed glass door and we now had to wear robes and masks when we were visiting here. What else could possibly happen? After many tests and consultations, they determined that she was deteriorating. They tried to remove the breathing tube to see if she could breathe on her own, but there were just a couple of faint tries. Her eyes were no longer dilating.

On February 19, they declared her brain dead. They wanted to disconnect life support on February 22, but that was my father's birthday. When he was a child, my dad's sister died on his birthday. I couldn't do that to him again. We changed the date to February 21, 1991. Tiffany had one nurse named Sue who was so special. She would sit with me and gently explain the severity of Tiffany's injuries. She washed Tiffany's hair, and treated her as if it was her child. That day, when saying goodbye, I looked all over for Sue. She wasn't there that day. I will never know why; maybe she chose to stay away for personal reasons, but I desperately wanted her there.

I remember them telling everyone they could come in to say goodbye. My family, friends, her dad's family, doctors, and nurses were all there. They took Tiffany's bed into a private room. I asked if I could be with her, and they said it was better if I waited outside. Why couldn't I hold her, talk with her? I was there for her first breath; why couldn't I be there for her last? On that day, at 3:05 p.m. the doctor came out and said Tiffany's heart had stopped beating. It had been only three minutes so that showed how badly she had been injured. She was gone forever.

My sister cleaned out Tiffany's room, taking all her personal items, stuffed animals she had received, balloons, flowers, pictures. I couldn't do it. I remember riding home that day watching everyone driving to work, waiting at bus stops. How could their lives be going on as if nothing had happened? My world, as I knew it, had come to an end. It would never be normal again.

We had to make the decision as to whether to donate any of Tiffany's organs. All other family members, my parents, sister, and my ex-husband were fine with it. I, on the other hand, was having such a difficult time. They explained how they would keep her on life support and then take her into surgery to remove what they could use. I couldn't do it. I told them, "You're going to kill her," but they said she was already brain dead. I told them I couldn't let them take her apart. So we did not donate organs from Tiffany.

To this day, I regret that. When I hear other stories, or the subject comes up, I get so emotional. If only someone had her heart, her eyes, I would be so happy. Tiffany could have saved someone or even a couple of people. She would have loved that. She always wanted to help people. We once gave our hamburger from Burger King to a homeless man on a corner because Tiffany wanted to help him. I feel like I let her down, along with someone who might have benefited from all that Tiffany had to give. I've been told to accept that I made the best decision I could at that time. The thought of Tiffany's heart beating for someone to save their life or Tiffany's beautiful eyes allowing someone the ability to see would give me so much comfort. If someone told me they were confused about what choice to make, I would tell them my story, and hopefully that with their decision.

From that point we had to make arrangements for her funeral. How was I going to get through this? They took my sister, mother and myself into a room filled with caskets. As we were looking, someone came in and told the director we would need a regular size casket, not one for a child, because she was taller than they had originally thought. I remember just staring at him, not believing what was going on. I chose a silver one with a white interior and a pretty flower pattern. They wanted to know which vault I wanted. One is good for ten years, the other was good for thirty. Of course I chose the best, because you're talking about my baby. I also wanted the thickest plush blanket, because she was always cold.

On to the cemetery at the end of February. It's snowing in Ohio and nothing looks attractive, especially when you're deciding where you want your twelve-year-old daughter buried. The first plot was right along a busy street, and I told them I didn't want her there. Someone mentioned another cemetery I hadn't been to, called Sunset Memorial. There I found a place at the top of a road in the shape of a heart near the trees. I have always associated hearts with her, because she dotted the "i" in her name with a heart.

We were to arrive at the funeral home early the day of the viewing. They had called and asked if we had a shawl we could bring so they could cover the bruises in Tiffany's arms from the IVs. Someone also came up the stairs and showed me two fingers and asked what polish color I wanted for her. Being in the state of shock that I was, I just pointed to one, not even really knowing what color it was. I also had to order a crown of flowers. Since they had put the two monitors in her skull, the funeral home had to pull the hair from the back of her head up to the top to cover them and then place the circle of flowers on her. She looked like an angel.

I don't remember much about the funeral. Singing Angels, a children's singing group that my daughters were in, sang songs. I remember a bagpipe playing, a police escort, and miles and miles of cars. I do remember that at the cemetery, when it was time for us to leave, I wouldn't walk away. I couldn't leave her there alone in the cold and the snow.

Today I still have some of Tiffany's things. Her small box that was in her desk at school, with pencils, pens, some coins, a hair clip, lip gloss. Her pillow, sealed in a bag, never to be taken out again. The cast that was taken off her leg. Her Barbie dolls, some of which were lovingly handed down to my two granddaughters and my niece, telling them they had to take special care of them. I have some of her clothes, her favorite things, some she had just gotten for Christmas the month before and never wore. Her robe she wore on Christmas morning. I had all of them at one time, but have since given some away. Every time I tried to look at them to sort them out, I would fall apart and close the boxes.

I eventually gave some to a friend I worked with for her daughter. I handed the bag to her in the parking lot, but couldn't let go. I felt I was giving part of Tiffany away. I started to cry, and she sensed what was going on, took the bag and quickly walked away. I sat in my car for about an hour and just cried. I also don't live in the same house or neighborhood where she grew up. I don't have her room to go into that felt so familiar. I don't have the yard she played in, the sidewalk where she rode her bicycle. There are no places nearby that bring back memories of things she did as a child. It feels like I'm living in a completely different world.

The crash could have been avoided. The man who hit Tiffany had a blood alcohol content of .198 percent. In court, they stated that .198 percent, with his height and weight, was equal to twelve shots or beers in a two-hour period. He had been at the racetrack and was on the way home with his girlfriend.

It was Saturday, January 26, 1991. Tiffany's stepmom had sent her and her stepsister Aimee and another child to the store across the street. Her father lived on the four-lane street, Warrensville Center Road in Maple Heights, across from a shopping mall. My son Brad was watching out the window. The other two children made it to the curb, but Tiffany was a few steps behind and did not. She was three steps from the sidewalk. He hit her, she went onto the hood, onto the windshield, flipped in the air and landed on top of his station wagon. He kept driving with her on top of his car in the luggage rack. Neither he nor his girlfriend knew he had hit someone. A police car saw what happened and followed him, and he finally stopped. In court, they said it was the distance of about two football fields.

When the driver put on his brakes to stop, he saw Tiffany's leg fall down over the windshield. When asked if he had known he hit someone, he said he thought he had run over a log in the road. How does a ninety-pound twelve-year-old girl who went up over your windshield, cracking it, feel like you ran over a log? His girlfriend didn't know they hit anyone either. Later it was said that they were also eating food they had just picked up while they were driving home.

To make matters even worse, if it could get any worse, Tiffany's ten-year-old brother Brad was watching out the window. He had just said, "Dad, here they come," when he saw and heard the car hit her. They said the noise was so loud that it sounded as if two cars had crashed; this was in the winter with the house closed up. Brad and my ex-husband, who was barefoot in the January snow, chased the car down the street. Brad called my mother and 911 before he went out the door. My son didn't tell me until he was in junior high school that he had tried to climb on top of the car to get to Tiffany to help her, but the police got him down and put him in the back of a police car with locked doors. He cried and tried to get out. I am still devastated about that. I realize they probably didn't want him right there when they were working on her, and didn't want him to move her, but there was this ten-year-old little boy who had just witnessed his sister being hit by a car, alone and helpless.

I have a friend who also lost a daughter. Her daughter died instantly, unlike Tiffany being on life support. We've talked about that, which way we thought might be easier. I feel God knew I needed time for me to accept that Tiffany was leaving us. It gave me the time to touch her, talk to her. I said I didn't know how I could have handled getting to the hospital and finding out she was gone. My friend thinks that it would have been too difficult seeing your child lying there for twenty-six days. Either way, it seemed to happen the way our families needed it to. It still is the most devastating and difficult thing any parent ever has to go through.

The trial wasn't until October 1991, nine months after the crash. It lasted over two weeks. At one point they tried to declare a mistrial because I was upset about something they had said and ran out of the courtroom. I guess the door slammed, and that was enough. They had informed me before the trial started that I wasn't allowed to cry or show any emotion, because it would influence the jury. The driver sat outside the courtroom during breaks, looking at the newspaper and betting on horse races. I could only watch in disbelief. His girlfriend followed me into the restroom once and tried to start a fight by making comments about the crash. That probably was another way for them to declare a mistrial if I had reacted. He was finally found guilty of aggravated vehicular homicide. He was sentenced to four to ten years, and his license was taken away for life.

The drunk driver never said he was sorry, and when asked if he still drank, he replied, "Yes, I do." They let him spend Thanksgiving, Christmas and New Year's with his family before he started his sentence. I went to the parole board each year to try to prevent his release. After serving eight years, he was released because the law had changed and the most you could serve was five years. My question is, and always will be, does he feel guilty, does he remember her on her birthday, on the crash date, on the day she passed away? Does he drive even though his license has been taken away for life? I heard rumors he received some type of degree while attending school in prison. Should I be happy that maybe he's a better person and won't hurt anyone else? Should I be angry that Tiffany didn't even make it out of sixth grade? Never to attend junior high or high school? No first date, proms, cheerleading, a wedding, her children. She, our family and all who knew her have been cheated out of so much. We will never see or know who Tiffany would have become.

So many lives have changed or were affected by this tragedy, from family members to friends and acquaintances. Her brother Brad went through some very bad times. He was so close to her, and he was so lost. He would reenact how she flipped in the air and landed on top of the car. He wanted those memories to go away. I cried, and I said, "I'm your mother and I'm supposed to make things better and fix things, but I can't ever take that away, and I'm so sorry." As a teenager, Brad saw another girl being struck by a car in front of the high school. He went into a downward spiral. He talked about suicide and how he'd never forget what he saw. He just wanted to die. I would sit next to him on his bed for hours as he listened to music, stared at Tiffany's picture and talked about ways he could end it all. I've never heard anyone talk like that before. I was petrified I was going to lose another child. He finally came to me and said he needed help. I called Oakview Behavioral Health Center and was told they had a bed open. Taking him there and having to leave him with his belt and shoelaces in my hand to get the help he desperately needed was so emotional and very difficult. This crash had totally devastated our family. Brad still has some bad days, but is now married and has three wonderful children.

My daughter Jennifer was different. She kept everything inside and to this day still doesn't talk much about losing her sister. It came out years later that before Tiffany got out of the car that evening, Jennifer said something negative to her. Her friends told me that Jennifer still feels guilty and thinks that Tiffany didn't know that she loved her. I still don't know what was said, and maybe it's better that I don't. Jennifer is also married and has four wonderful children. She moved to California within the last couple of years, which was difficult for me with her, her husband, and four grandchildren moving so far away. It had been her lifelong dream to live there, so I was happy for them. She is a nurse and decided to go into that profession so she could help others at the worst time of their lives. She had already lived through a nightmare and hoped that she can show compassion for those in similar situations. She visited recently and wanted to see Tiffany's hospital records that I have. She said at the time of the crash that she was a fourteen-year-old girl who only knew that her sister had been severely injured. Now that she is an adult and a nurse, after reading the records she said, "Mom, this is really bad. Her injuries were very severe; she had no brain function." It helped to hear my daughter confirm and explain some of the things I questioned.

My ex-husband, Tiffany's father, had a very difficult time. He felt guilty for her being sent to the store. She was hit right in front of his driveway, so every time he backed out of his driveway he drove over the site of the crash. He had said that if he hadn't left and divorced me, she wouldn't have been there and it wouldn't ever have happened. He was absolutely crushed. He always felt guilty. He was a smoker and continued to smoke very heavily. He passed away last year in April. He wanted to be buried with Tiffany, so he was cremated and placed in the same plot with his daughter. He was only sixty-two.

Years later, my son and daughter told me how they felt I had abandoned them. I didn't realize how they were feeling. Since I had lost one child, they thought I would be closer to them but I wasn't there for them when they needed me most. I was in such a state of shock that I could barely function. A counselor told me to take one day at a time. I told him I couldn't even get through a day. He then said to take one hour at a time. That's what I did. I would look at the clock and think about just getting through the next hour. I feel terrible about that, and now that my children are adults with children of their own, I think they understand.

After four months of still living with my parents, I decided I needed to find a new place to live that was close to my children's schools. I wanted them to still attend the schools they went to while living in Parma. I didn't want them to lose their friends after just losing their sister. I found a duplex right across the street from Valley Forge High School in Parma. There was a single man (Rick) with twin teenage daughters and a son in college living in the other apartment. We talked and became friends. I was still grieving and not being able to function day to day very well. Rick jumped in and took over. He made my children dinner, took them to their activities, did my grocery shopping. Whatever my children or I needed, he did. He once said, "I just want to make you smile once a day." He saw me at my worst. Times my family didn't even know about. Yes, I did take pills once. I didn't take enough to kill myself, I just wanted the pain to stop. Little by little Rick eventually got me to go to a movie with him, and out to a restaurant. Things I thought I couldn't do because Tiffany had died. How could I have fun; that's not possible. Five years later we were married, and we still are nineteen years later.

I had worked in the admissions office of a college in Berea, Ohio, a job I loved, for eight years. After Tiffany passed away, I was off work for nine months. When I went back, I thought I was doing well. Keeping up with my work, getting there on time, etc. Then one day they came to me with a box and said they wanted me to pack up my things and be gone before everyone came back from lunch. They said I wasn't as productive as I used to be, so they let me go. I was in shock again. I lost my daughter, lost my job, and still had two other children. Also, no medical insurance, which petrified me because Tiffany's bills were so outrageous, being in ICU for twenty-six days. One day I was sitting at a red light looking at a bank's operation center. I told myself that they must have a job I could do there. I went in and applied and started a data entry position. I was there two years and then applied for a job at Continental Airlines, the best job I would ever have.

I've been on antidepressants since Tiffany's death. I now have anxiety and panic attacks. I constantly live in fear. I am so afraid that I will lose someone else because I now know things can happen in an instant. No one really understands that constant fear, only others who have lost a child. I was in so much pain. It's strange, you can't see it, you have no bodily injury, but my whole body hurt. I truly and painfully hurt. It felt like someone had reached into my chest, grabbed my heart and ripped it out of my body. I needed help. I didn't know how to get through this alone. I had no idea where or how to even start to get a new normal back for my two other children. The MADD organization helped me through the trial, and I became an active member. I started speaking at our

Justice Center to drunk drivers who had to attend victim awareness meetings. I also spoke in other cities at their police stations and courts. I have to tell you that it was one of the most difficult things to do. Standing in front of hundreds of strangers and telling your heart-wrenching story is almost unbearable. I would always ask Tiffany for help to get me through. Many times I would break down, turn around to try to get myself back together, and then continue speaking.

After a couple of years, a high school asked me to talk to the seniors before prom. These students came into the auditorium smiling, laughing, happy, their prom was that weekend and school was finally over. That all changed when I started speaking and showed my video, which includes music and pictures showing Tiffany's twelve short years of life. Then you could hear a pin drop. The school brought a casket, with Tiffany's picture in it, into the auditorium. After my speech, they had to sign the Prom Promise and put it in the coffin. These students cried, hugged me, told me I saved their lives that day. I was making a difference.

I continued that for over ten years. Friends would ask why I would put myself through that. They said, "You always cry and get a headache. Why would you want to do that?" I responded, "But you don't see these kids, they were listening." I had big football players who came into the auditorium looking like nothing was going to bother them. They left crying, saying they couldn't imagine their mother onstage telling a story like mine. My thought was, if I save one person today then it's worth it.

Another group I joined was The Compassionate Friends. They were so open, and it was comforting to hear other parents say and describe things I was thinking and feeling, and to know I wasn't going crazy. There is help out there, though I know at times it is so hard to reach for it.

During my grieving process I started my job with Continental Airlines. I believe Tiffany helped me get that job. I had to fly to New York for the interview, and I was never really a confident person. I put on my skirt and jacket, flew to New York and had the best interview I ever had. I felt strong, relaxed, and they loved me. I had my dream job. Because of that, I have been able to travel all over the world. I thank Tiffany all the time and always find heart-shaped shells or rocks to bring home. Through working at for the airlines, I have met so many wonderful people who became a support group for me. They are like a second family. I have also helped others through their tragedies by talking about my experience.

In the days at the hospital and talking with family and friends, we learned a couple of things that were very strange. Tiffany had told her friends she wouldn't be in school Monday. They asked her why, and she said she would probably have a broken leg or something like that. Also, her stepmom walked past the girls' room the night before and saw Tiffany lying on the bed on her back and holding flowers. She asked her what she was doing, and she said just playing and pretending she was dead. And finally, the school brought her things from her desk and some artwork. The last picture she drew in school had a blue sky, trees with snow on them and a fence with a gate that says "Welcome." As strange as that seems, it looks like the fence and gate at Sunset Memorial where she is buried.

Something else has happened over the years that I believe was somehow God, the universe, or Tiffany making some hard days easier for me. All of us who have lost children know that all the dates associated with them are difficult and bring back memories. Tiffany was hit on January 26. My grandson's birthday is January 20. Tiffany's angel date is February 21; another grandson's birthday is February 28. Christmas is always difficult but one granddaughter's birthday is December 26. Tiffany's birthday is November 19, and two of my grandsons' birthdays are November 11 and 22. I also have another grandson and granddaughter who have birthdays in October, and Tiffany loved Halloween. Every bad day associated with Tiffany has a day to celebrate within a week. To me this isn't a coincidence. It's a miracle.

Recently I've decided to make memory lockets for people who have lost children. I think it somehow brings them some comfort and something to hold onto. I see these pictures and sad stories and just feel that I want to do something. Tiffany would love that I am reaching out to other parents. It does get better; you learn how to live again because you have to. Twenty-five years later, there isn't a day that goes by that I don't think of Tiffany. I can now look at her pictures and videos, and smile with a tear in my eye even though my heart is still broken. I still have days when something will happen, a song, the old neighborhood, her friends, a wedding, that will bring back that unbearable pain again.

It's not as severe as it was, it doesn't happen as often as it did before, and I wouldn't want it to stop completely. I have those feelings because I loved my daughter Tiffany so much, and her life was taken away by a drunk driver. I will take those days of pain and heartache; I have them because I had twelve wonderful years of fun, laughter, love and memories with my angel.

As you read these stories, these awful, unbearable events about lives changed forever, remember that these things all happened because in that one moment someone made the wrong choice to drink and drive. Would you want to be responsible for destroying so many lives and maybe your own? It took me years, one hour and one step at a time. Sometimes you take four steps backwards, but somehow you get the strength to keep moving forward. As my angel said each night, "Goodnight, I Love You. Sweet dreams."

SANDRA RAWLINGS
LAGRANGE, OHIO

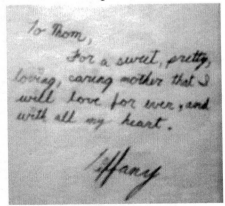

A NOTE TIFFANY LEFT FOR HER MOM

TIFFANY & SANDRA

TIFFANY CLAWSON

TIFFANY, BRADLEY, JENNIFER

BRADLEY & TIFFANY

TIFFANY CLAWSON

TIFFANY, BRADLEY, JENNIFER

FOR THE LOVE OF TIFFANY
Tiffany Lyn Clawson 11/19/78 - 2-21/91

By Sandra Clawson (Rawlings) – February 1992

Well, That awful day is here again
I can't believe it's been a year
Who would have known last Christmas Day
that just a month later,
a drunk driver would take your life away

It's not the same without you here
There's so much sadness and so many tears
I tried so hard to save you
But, there was nothing I could do

I know you understood and
heard the things I said to you
I know you knew I was there,
Praying and caring for you,
playing your favorite songs,
sitting with you all night long

How could this happen?
In an instant so many lives were changed
all our hopes and dreams for our
family and future have been rearranged

I have so many wonderful memories and
souvenirs of times of you and me
Now, my memories consist of what I did
on those specials days that used to be

I brought to the cemetery something for you
Things I never thought I would have to do
Flowers that will soon wilt, a deflated balloon
all brought to someone who died too soon

Now I look for wreaths or flowers
to bring to your grave
I feel in total disbelief and sick at those times
But I try so hard to be strong and be brave

That's all I can do for you now
I fight to keep your memory alive
And hope that all of those who love you
will be able to survive

Tiffany, you were such a special child
you gave so much and had so much more to give
I promise for you I will try again to live
Right now I feel as I'm just existing in this world
That I do not want to be part of, not without you

The pain of thinking I have to live the rest of my life
without you being a part of it is unbearable
All I can do now is try to make it through
One day at a time and remember in my heart
You will always be mine

I Love you and miss you so much Tiffany
Goodnight, sweet dreams. Love you
to the moon and back.
– Mom

THE LAST PICTURE TIFFANY DREW

CHAPTER EIGHTEEN

AN EAGLE AT HEART

BY NICOLE RIBALKIN

I look up to the sky and talk to you. What I wouldn't give to hear your voice. I miss your laughter, I miss everything about you.
-AUTHOR UNKNOWN

It was a January night in 2003 when I met Rafael at a night club in Kelowna, British Columbia. He came to Canada for five months to learn how to speak English, and we met during the last two months he was in Kelowna. I was out dancing with a friend and spotted him standing near the dance floor with one of his friends. I knew in that moment that I had to meet him. Rafa was a tall, dark and handsome Latino man. He was the man I had dreamed my whole life to marry. When we met that night we believed that the stars were aligned between us because our eyes locked while the music played on. I was so happy that he asked for my phone number, yet I was nervous about going on our first date together. His handsome face was the only face I saw that night on our first date. He had the most amazing smile I had ever seen and his eyes would sparkle when he talked. His laugh was contagious, and when he spoke to me in Spanish he made my heart melt.

As we began to learn more about each other, we fell deeply in love. Rafael loved playing soccer and he excelled as the goalie; he enjoyed watching soccer just as much. His favorite Mexican soccer team is called Aguilas; the translation in English is Eagles. One of his favorite pastimes was playing his guitar and composing songs. Rafael wrote two songs for me. One is called "It's Up to You" and the other is called "Brandy," my middle name. He would serenade his songs to me. I loved when he sang to me; he made me feel so special. You could also find him studying all the time as he loved to learn something new every day. Kindness soared out of him; he was the type of guy who wore his heart on his sleeve.

Rafa, a fun-loving and caring guy, volunteered to model for a charity event in Mexico. My dream of dating a super sexy model became a reality. The modeling event was to help raise money for a devastating earthquake in his city. He also co-hosted for radio stations in Mexico for different events. Rafa told me that when he was younger he would enter competitions for swimming, biking and ping-pong. He always won.

Family and friends were always number one in Rafa's life; they meant the world to him. Spending time with him was absolutely amazing. While getting to know Rafa, I spoke to my parents about him and told them I wanted them to meet him one day. When I brought Rafa over to my parents' house to introduce him to them, they thought he was a very kind and respectful man. He also met my friends, and they said that he was a very nice guy.

When he told me that his study permit was going to be finished at the end of February 2003 and that he had to return to Mexico, I was sad. I thought I would never see him again, until he asked me to wait for him. We had a long-distance relationship until we could be together again in person. We would sit up late talking for hours on the computer and we would count down the days until we could be reunited.

While we were apart I worked at three different jobs for three months straight, only getting one or two days off to save up money faster to buy my plane ticket to Mexico. I took a three-week vacation in the summer of 2003 after not seeing him for almost four months. I flew to Colima, Mexico, to see him again and to meet his family for the first time. My stomach was full of butterflies; I was so excited to see Rafa again, and at the same time I was nervous because I was meeting his family.

After I went through customs at the Manzanillo airport I grabbed my luggage and there I was shaking excitedly to see him waiting for me behind the closed tinted glass doors. As I approached him I jumped into his arms and he lifted me up; it was one of those sweet movie moments when two people are reunited. It was the best feeling ever to see him again after what seemed like an eternity talking on computers for communication. The drive back to his home was very hot and humid, but that didn't matter because I was with the man I loved.

When we arrived at his house, his immediate family was there waiting to meet me. They were all so kind, and we got along great. I couldn't speak any Spanish at the time, so Rafa had to translate everything. We then went to his grandma's house, and the rest of his family was there waiting to meet me. He had a big family, and they put me to the test to try to remember all their names. Rafa would whisper their names to me to help. He showed me his home town, and took me to see the most active volcano in Mexico. It was an amazing sight to see, and what made it even more amazing is that I got to see it with him.

We went to beaches and he held onto me in the ocean, as the waves were strong and they kept pulling me back with them. He took me to flea markets and I bought some traditional Mexican clothes and souvenirs. We ate at traditional Mexican restaurants and went to a park called Piedra de Lisa. The tradition was to slide down a smooth rock and it meant you would return to Mexico again. We slid down it together a few times. We had so much fun together that I didn't want my vacation to end. It was so hard to leave; all I wanted to do was hold him and never let go. But I had to return home and go back to work so I could save money to see Rafa again. We promised to wait for each other and to continue our long-distance relationship.

One day when we were talking on the computer Rafa had some exciting news to tell me. He said he was applying for a work visa to live and work in Canada. I was so excited when he told me the news. He moved to Toronto in September 2003. Although he was still far away from me, I was happy he was in Canada. He set out to live there for six months, because the work visa was for him to live there first. He flew me out there to see him for a short trip. He showed me the restaurant where he worked at. We explored the CN Tower, saw Niagara Falls, and took some fun pictures at the Ripley's Believe It or Not Museum. After Rafa had lived in Toronto for six months he flew back to Mexico to spend Christmas with his family. He then moved to Vancouver in February 2004 for six months, and I lived with him for three of the six.

On June 24, 2004, out of the blue we decided to make our love official and we got married by the justice of the peace in Vancouver. My family was surprised about the news when I told them, yet they were happy for us because we were in love. In September I moved to Mexico and got a job teaching English as a second language at one of the best universities in the city. Rafa worked in social communications at another university.

On June 30, 2005, my parents flew down and attended our second wedding ceremony. Rafa looked so handsome in his suit, waiting for me to walk to the front of the church with my dad. I'll never forget the smile he had on his face; he was grinning from ear to ear. I got to marry the man of my dreams twice; I was on cloud nine. Two weddings to Rafael to be remembered forever. We then went on a short honeymoon in Guanajuato, Mexico. We went on a bus tour of the city, and when we went to the Calle de Besos (kissing street) we asked another couple to take a picture of us kissing. It was a beautiful moment that I will never forget.

In 2007 I started feeling sick, so Rafa took me to the doctor and we found out that we were going to have a baby. Rafa and I were so excited about the wonderful surprise coming into our lives. He took care of me so well, always making sure that I was okay and getting to work safely. I started to have contractions at thirty-one weeks and Rafael took me to the hospital to make sure our baby and I were going to be okay. The doctors managed to stop the contractions and they had me on bed rest for seven days. Rafa would wheel me around in a wheelchair when I wanted to get out of bed; he was extra cautious with everything I wanted to do. We were going to fly back to Canada so that our baby would be born there. But our baby had other plans. I experienced early contractions yet a second time, and at thirty-three weeks there was no stopping them this time. On January 29, 2008, Rafa and I became parents to a beautiful and healthy baby boy named Tyrel Rafael. I'm proud that my son has my husband's name. Rafa was so happy to see Tyrel for the first time, as was I. He was so dedicated to him. His face would light up every time he held him close, he was so proud to be a dad. We were happy new parents, and we had a lot of great plans for our future as a family together.

Four months after our son was born we decided to move back to Canada to raise our son. Rafa and I moved into my parents' house until we could save enough money to rent a place on our own. About three months after living with my parents, we found a place to rent. Rafa then got a job as a drywaller. It wasn't his ideal job, but he took what he could get until he could find a job working in the communications field at a college or university.

What mattered most was that he knew he was supporting our son and putting a roof over us to stay safe. We decided to purchase a condo instead of renting an apartment. Our new place was the place we could call home, the place where memories were made together as a family of three. The first three years of our son's life were amazing. We took turns in the pool with him at his swimming lessons. I watched Rafa with Tyrel in the water, seeing how much fun they had together and how happy he was. Rafa spoke to Tyrel in Spanish, because he wanted Tyrel to be bilingual. He taught him how to walk and how to kick a soccer ball. I could keep talking about all the wonderful times we spent together, but then this would become a long novel.

Tuesday, March 1, 2011, was the day my world stopped. It was the day I never got to see the love of my life again. The day my son lost his beloved father. The day I felt that I had died with him. I spoke to my husband after work that day at 3:30 p.m. to ask him if I should take our son grocery shopping or if he wanted us to go all together that evening. He said we would go in the evening, and then he told me his boss had invited all the employees to go to a pub for a while after work. Rafa said he would stay only for half an hour. He told me he loved me and I told him that I loved him too. *Never* in a million years did I think those sweet words "I love you" would be the last time I would hear his sweet voice.

I went about as usual, picking up our son from daycare and then cooked dinner at home. As I was cooking dinner I looked at the clock and saw that half an hour had turned into two hours and dinner was getting cold. I called Rafa to tell him that our son and I were going to start eating dinner, but there was no answer. I thought that maybe he was driving home and couldn't answer the phone. He would always text me to say when he was on his way home, but because I didn't receive a text from him that's when I started to worry.

Seven p.m. came around and I was putting our son to bed. I continued to call Rafa but there was still no answer. I called my best friend around 9:30 p.m., telling her I was worried. She said, "Don't worry, Nicole. He will be home soon." I started to get an awful feeling deep down inside my gut that was telling me that something horrible had happened, because it was not like him not to text or call me. He always came home after work.

I kept looking out the living room window for his car, and for a moment I saw a car that looked like his. I waited and waited but he didn't come up from the underground parking lot because it wasn't his car that I saw. I tried to go to sleep, telling myself that Rafa probably stayed the night at the house of one of the guys he worked with, but the gut-wrenching feeling in my stomach kept me awake, worrying nonstop. I continued to call Rafa's phone over and over again, but it went straight to voicemail.

At 1 a.m. I got the horrible phone call to let the police into my condo. I told them my son was sleeping. They said, "Please come to the lobby and let us in."

I was crying and shaking uncontrollably on the elevator ride up to the third floor. I knew then that it was bad news.

They asked if they could see Rafa's passport, and then they said, "Your husband is deceased."

I screamed "NO, NO, NO! That's not true."

They said they were terribly sorry but it was true. My screams woke up Tyrel, and one police officer went into his room to check on him. Can you imagine a three-year-old waking up to see a police officer in his room and not knowing why she was the one trying to get him back to sleep? I never thought I would lose the love of my life at such a young age; he had turned thirty-one two weeks before the crash. I was in complete shock.

Getting this horrible news all by myself is a nightmare that will never go away. I couldn't believe what I had just heard. I couldn't process the words "Your husband is deceased." I felt angry, sad, lost, confused, shocked, empty, lonely, and brokenhearted. The list of pain goes on and on.

I didn't know how I was going to tell our son that his dad was never going to walk through the front door again and that he would never be able to run into his arms again. I wondered how I would mend my son's heart. All of our hopes and dreams for the future had been taken away from us as a family. Within a blink of an eye, my world and my life had been torn apart, thrown upside down and shredded into a million pieces.

I will never get the chance to tell Rafa that I love him again, never get to hold him in my arms, see his gorgeous smile and hear his laugh. My son was robbed of his father. He will never get to play soccer with his dad or learn Spanish from him. He will never be able to dance to his dad playing the guitar anymore. He will never get more than the first three years of his life to spend quality time together. His dad will never get to see him graduate from school or go to his wedding.

I then asked how it happened. The police said my husband's coworker was driving his car, drunk. She crossed the centerline, heading toward oncoming traffic, and crashed into a Peterbilt truck. For some reason she was driving in the direction to go to Merritt instead of driving back to Kelowna from their job site in Penticton. My heart was pounding with rage toward her. I felt a hatred enter my body that I had never felt toward someone before. I began to wonder why she was driving Rafa's car, especially driving drunk. I then found out she had only a leaner's license, so that made it even worse. The horrible news had me running to the bathroom and vomiting.

The police asked who they could call to come over to be with me, so they called my parents and my best friend, Carrie. They came over right away, hugging me as I cried. They were all crying and in complete shock, just as I was. I was up all night after getting the worst news of my life. Carrie and I kept trying to call my husband's boss to tell him what had happened, but he didn't answer. We figured he had the ringer off so he could sleep, because he had to work the next day. We finally got hold of him early in the morning to tell him that Rafa had been killed by his coworker in a drunk driving car crash. I then had to call Rafael's parents in Mexico, and I asked them to connect on Skype so we could talk. A friend who was also Mexican came over to our place and helped me tell his family the tragic news of their son's death. As my friend Luis was telling my husband's family the most painful news ever, I was crying and shaking uncontrollably. I will never forget hearing my mother-in-law scream, and the look on her face is forever in my mind. It's the look you never want to see on someone's face or for them to feel the pain of losing their son.

A couple of days after my husband's death, I found out that the police were gathering evidence and starting a criminal investigation against the driver. In the meantime, I was planning my husband's memorial. I wasn't supposed to plan his memorial at such a young age. We were supposed to spend the rest of our lives together; just shy of eight years of marriage wasn't enough for me. I had two memorials for Rafael, one in Canada and the other one in Mexico where he is from.

Before the memorial in Canada, I went to view his body at the funeral home. Seeing my husband's lifeless body lying there was a pain forever wedged deeply into my soul, and the image of his face is forever etched in my mind. The touch of his cold body is something I will never forget. His fingers had the look one gets when you stay in the bath too long. He didn't look like my husband Rafa; he just didn't have the same look that he used to have. The funeral home had asked me for a collared shirt to cover his neck, because the impact from crashing into the truck forced my husband's head through the windshield. According to the coroner's report, he died of exsanguination from severe laceration of the internal jugular vein that was the consequence of a drinking and driving motor vehicle accident. They tried to revive him in the ambulance and at the nearest hospital, but it was too late; he had lost too much blood to survive. Apparently his seatbelt wasn't on. If it was, he might have stood a chance of surviving.

Everything was ready for my husband's memorial in Canada. I didn't want it to be ready, because I wanted to hold onto the thought that he was still alive. I wasn't ready to say goodbye. Rafael had told me that if anything were to ever happen to him, he wanted to be cremated and for me to bring his ashes back to Mexico. I had two urns made, a small urn for my son and me to keep and the bigger urn to take back to Mexico. His ashes were taken to the church in Kelowna first to be blessed. The drive to the church was very difficult; my heart was pounding, my hands were shaking and sweating at the same time and tears were pouring from my eyes.

When we arrived at the church it was completely full of family, friends, and coworkers. The drunk driver didn't go, plus she was not welcome there. My son was only three years old at the time and he was asking me why the picture of his dad wasn't talking to him. The tears flowed down from my eyes, my heart was broken into a million pieces, and it was aching for my son.

I wrote Rafael's eulogy, but I didn't have the strength to read it. I had someone read it in English and someone read it in Spanish. I had it read in Spanish because we had a live stream video for his family and friends to see the memorial. I also had a video of all the happy memories we had captured in photos, and we played it at the memorial. That is a day I will never forget, the hardest day in my life; the day tears from my eyes flowed like an ocean.

Having to fly back to Mexico with his ashes was extremely hard and horrifying; I felt so guilty that I could only bring Rafa back to his family in an urn and not alive in person, walking through the door to give his family hugs and kisses. The security in the Mexico City airport wanted to open his urn, even though they saw the document said I was bringing my husband's ashes back home. I had to wait thirty minutes for the security to make their decision on what they were going to do. It was tough. I was crying and trying to take care of my son at the same time, while begging them not to open his urn. Eventually they spoke to someone higher up and they were told to only take a swab of his urn for precaution. I understand that they were only doing their job, but in that moment it was excruciating knowing they might open the urn. I didn't want to see his ashes in that way.

When we arrived to Colima, we had to go straight to the funeral home and we had to be with his ashes all night. It was a long trip to fly there, and then difficult to stay up all night with a three-year-old. My son and I were getting exhausted, so my father-in-law took us back to the house so we could sleep. Since I have epilepsy, if I didn't get enough sleep from all the stress it could have caused a seizure.

The next day we had Rafael's second church memorial. Again the church was full; all his family and friends in Mexico were there. Tyrel and I stood at the church doors with Rafa's immediate family before his memorial began. When the church bells rang, it began. Rafa's mom carried his ashes, with his dad's hands on the urn and mine as well. We walked together to the front of the church to bring Rafa to the priest for blessings and prayers. I was crying and shaking uncontrollably once again. To have two memorials was extremely difficult. To say goodbye to him twice was torture. Rafael's ashes were then laid to rest in a crypt in the church. We put family pictures with his urn, and a rosary. When Rafa's dad closed the crypt door, that's when my heart sank to my feet. Reality slapped me when the key locked the door. In that moment I knew this was a living nightmare. I wanted to unlock the door and put him back together again. But it just wasn't possible. I couldn't stop crying as all the family and friends gave me hugs.

The man I loved so dearly can never be in my arms again. I will never get to kiss his sweet lips again. For the next nine days they had prayer sessions for Rafael. I was so disoriented that I pinched myself trying to wake up from this nightmare. I also caught myself looking around and trying to find him. I thought maybe he was taking care of our son in the house somewhere, but he wasn't there in person. It came time when my son and I had to fly back home to Canada. It was extremely hard to leave Rafa's mom during such a tragic time, but I had to return home. I had to try to go back to work to try to pay bills and keep a roof over my son and me.

My criminal lawyer had contacted me to say that the court dates were all set up to take place in Merritt, two to three hours from Kelowna. It was finally time to fight for justice. I needed to see the driver go to jail; I didn't want her to get away with killing my husband. The trial was scheduled for five days, but it was over in three. The first two days I was struggling to go to the trial, because I didn't want to see the driver's face, so my parents went for me. My mom told me that on the second day of the trial, which was Tuesday, it looked as though it might wrap up on Wednesday. So that's when I decided to try to be brave and stand strong, because this was to fight for justice for my husband.

When we arrived at the courthouse, the driver was standing outside with her lawyer, her mom and her boyfriend, all smoking together. They saw my parents get out of the truck first, then they saw me get out of the truck. I think they didn't expect to see me there, since I wasn't there for the first two days of the trial. I was hoping that my being there would make her even more nervous.

I don't regret going at all. In fact, I am glad I went because I got to read my very powerful and emotional victim impact statement. I truly believe that I moved the judge with my words and that it helped to give her a jail sentence. She was charged with committing an offense of dangerous driving causing death and committing an offense that caused an accident resulting in death. She also received three years of probation for criminal driving. She was sentenced to fifteen months in a women's correctional jail, but sadly for me she got out after a short five months. I told my friends and family that I had fought hard to keep her behind bars, so why was the justice system letting me down? Why did they let her out when she still didn't know right from wrong? It was like a knife to my heart all over again.

Everyone told me that I should try to look at in a different way, that at least she spent some time behind bars, because most first offenders don't go to jail, which is true. But I wanted her to serve her full sentence. She had a baby before she went to jail, and I'm pretty sure she planned that in order to keep herself out of jail or get a shorter sentence. She didn't want to take full responsibility for her actions nor was she remorseful. My husband got a life sentence and she got out of jail after a short five months, one year probation and three years driving probation. In my eyes there's no justice in that! My husband's life was worth way more than that. She should be behind bars for the rest of her life. I also had a civil lawsuit against her, and I had to attend a discovery examination. The examination only lasted for two hours, but it felt like it lasted all day long. Having another lawyer asking me questions about my life before, during and after the crash was extremely unnerving. My hands were shaking and my palms felt sweaty. It almost felt like I was the one on trial, but I wasn't, I was there to seek justice.

Having to deal with both trials at the same time was more than one could possibly bear, along with the bills piling up; I still have a hard time to this present day to pay for everything. No matter what, between the criminal suit and the civil suit, it will never bring back the love of my life, Rafa. It will never take the pain away; it is the type of excoriating pain that I struggle with on a daily basis and it will follow me for the rest of my life.

Four years after his death, it still hurts like it happened yesterday. I cry every time I visit his cross; I get all nervous and shaky. I want him back!!! I want my husband back; my son wants his dad back. During the four years without him, I had to learn how to become really strong for my son. I would put on one of those "I'm okay" faces when really I was not okay in the least. I will never be the person I once was. I have taken on a different identity that defines the person I am now.

I was really weak inside and I wanted to die, I didn't want to go on living. I felt guilty to eat food, guilty to breathe in air, guilty to see the sun shining in my dark and gray new life. Deep down I knew I couldn't die, because I didn't want my son to grow up without both his parents. I couldn't commit suicide, because I have a beautiful son to take care of who needs me as much as I need him.

I still struggle to this day with thoughts of wanting to die when I feel depressed and unhappy that I will never see Rafa again and that I'm dissatisfied with my job. But I know deep down inside I won't take the path to end my life. Instead I go to the gym and exercise to release as much stress as I can. I've had countless sleepless nights, and nights when I cry myself to sleep. Nights when I'm scared to go to sleep because he's not here physically to protect Tyrel and me anymore. I have become Tyrel's number one protector here on earth since the day Rafa was killed.

I will always miss my beloved husband like crazy, and I made a vow to my son and myself to always keep his memory alive and try to keep fighting to stop people from drinking and driving.

They say time heals. But does it really heal? I think time helps you find ways to deal with the pain. My heart will forever be missing pieces, therefore it will never be fully healed.

Until I see you again, my love, fly like an eagle and protect us from above.

I ask everyone to please not drink and drive, because it will affect you and your loved ones for the rest of your life.

NICOLE RIBALKIN
MERRITT, BRITISH COLUMBIA, CANADA

NICOLE & RAFAEL

RAFAEL HEREDIA CARDENAS

CHAPTER NINETEEN

FORGIVENESS: FROM

VENGEANCE TO JUSTICE

BY SUSAN RILEY

Please notice the joy I feel when someone acknowledges she is real. And she is my child... still. Please see how she becomes alive in me again, how she becomes part of my present, and part of yours when you invite me to speak of her freely. Her name... Karly. And she existed.
-JENNIFER MITCHELL

After almost five years, there are still times when I am literally overcome with grief. My head and heart hurt, my stomach churns, pictures of Randy and the truck on top of him in his bed fill my mind and I can't make them stop. I just want to scream!

In 1978, my husband and I sold our house in Texas, quit our jobs, and made a move to northern California. We had been married almost six years. We had dogs and cats, but no children so we started on a great adventure. We were so young and so hopeful for the future! I was a rookie special education teacher and my husband was good at a lot of things like welding and machining.

We loaded up a rental truck along with the cats, having flown the dogs out there, and drove off into the sunset.

I got a job teaching, but after a year I was laid off. I applied for a job at the Sonoma State School for the Developmentally Disabled. It was scary for me, as I had limited experience with children with severe disabilities, but I was willing to try, and I soon found that I had so much love for these children. There was a teacher's aide named Ginny LaVine who had worked there for several years, and she became my mentor. I learned so much from her. I began to see these children as very special individuals.

One of my students was Randy Williams. He had been just a normal kid, playing baseball and helping his single mom care for his younger sister Stacy, until the night that there was a car crash involving a drunk driver. Suddenly, eight-year-old Randy was brain injured, in a wheelchair, in an institution for the mentally retarded. He had suffered a traumatic closed head brain injury and was in a semi-comatose state for months. He had a tracheotomy tube in his throat and was often fed with a nasogastric tube.

As time went by I was able to get some amazing responses from him, and came to realize that this boy in the badly damaged body possessed strength and a sense of humor, a working mind in a badly damaged body. He had the clearest and most expressive blue eyes. I fell in love with this kid! And when my husband met him, it was like there was an almost instantaneous bond between them. One minute my husband was taking Christmas pictures for me to send to families of the children I taught, and the next minute he and Randy were rolling around on a mat and laughing their heads off. My husband, who had been very hesitant to come to my workplace where the children were all so different, was so transformed by this child that he became a citizen's advocate for him.

Randy's mom was a waitress in town, and she rarely visited. I am certain that it was very difficult for her to see her son in this condition, but she was willing to let me take her daughter, Stacy, to visit on weekends. Stacy enjoyed reading to Randy, and taking him on walks around the beautiful campus. Randy's face would just light up when he saw his little sister!

Eventually we discovered that Randy could communicate using eye blinks for yes and no. That was a tremendous breakthrough that led to a significant change in how the people who worked with him viewed him. I was trying my best to get these kids out into the community more often. We planned trips on the ferry to San Francisco; to Bodega Bay, where the Alfred Hitchcock movie *The Birds* was filmed, and even to Los Angeles via airplane to participate in the California Special Olympics! It was on this trip when Randy met his hero, Henry Winkler, *the Fonz!* Though the picture I took of them with Randy's huge grin and his medal from wheelchair bowling around his neck, and the Fonz smiling down at him, has been lost, I can still see that scene in my mind. And I treasure that memory.

Through advocacy, my husband and I were able to get the doctors to remove the trach tube, and get Randy moved from the institution to a group home in nearby Napa. Randy finally was going to public school again for the first time since the crash! At about this time Randy's mother decided to move back to Oregon, and she began the process of giving up her parental rights. We immediately retained a lawyer and petitioned the court for guardianship and permission to move him to Texas, as we were planning to move back home. We got custody, and I am not sure who was happier. Ceryl, my husband, was the only father figure Randy had ever had. I have to say that many family members and friends were very shocked, questioning our sanity because of our decision to take on such a medically fragile child, though with time they came to love Randy just as we did.

In 1981, we moved back to Texas, and in 1982 Randy joined us. During the next few years Randy lived with us, and lived in a state school here while attending a public high school, where he graduated to a standing ovation! With a happy heart, Randy welcomed brother Ben Riley in 1985 and sister Erin Riley in 1988. He adored them both from the day they were born, though he kept a special place in his heart for his little sister Stacy, whom he had not seen since 1981.

After graduation he moved to a group home where he lived for the rest of his life. Randy made friends, had a ready smile, was always willing to laugh at jokes. He had a fondness for cute cheerleaders and ice cream! He lived life to the fullest and was a favorite of all who worked with him. He attended a day program and stole their hearts as well.

And then on a Saturday night in June 2010, I received a phone call that would shatter our world. I was sitting at home when my phone rang at about 10:30 p.m. Having two young adult children, I was always a bit nervous when they were out. Seeing that the call was from the hospital, my heart just stopped. But never in my wildest dreams would I have ever imagined the news I received that night. Randy had been sleeping in his bed in his group home when a nineteen-year-old drunk driver crashed into Randy's bedroom, and his truck came to a stop on top of Randy. Randy had been transported to the trauma center and was in the ICU.

The driver had hit a motorcyclist, and in trying to get away, he lost control of his mother's truck and went through a wood privacy fence and crashed through the wall of Randy's bedroom. He then ran on foot from the scene, leaving Randy under the truck. According to witnesses and media reports, the driver exited the truck and disappeared into a neighbor's yard. The first officer on the scene happened to be the husband of a friend of mine. He followed and located the suspect hiding in a yard down the block. He smelled of alcohol and resisted arrest, resulting in the officer having to use a taser on him. He was cuffed, taken to a hospital for a blood draw, and booked into the Travis County Jail.

During this time I understood that the group home staff were busy making sure all the other clients were accounted for and safe.

Randy was transported to Brackenridge Hospital and placed in the ICU. By the time I was called, he was already being evaluated and treated for his injuries, which were extensive. The truck had landed on his body, crushing his legs and hips. He had also sustained a blow to the head that later was determined to have caused a bleed in his brain. By the time I arrived there, he had been given massive amounts of pain medication and was hooked up to assorted monitoring equipment and was receiving oxygen.

Randy was a very tough man, having survived the crash when he was only a child, coming out of a comatose state after months when no one expected him to survive. And so we were hopeful that he would once again prove the doctors wrong! He was reasonably alert for the next five days, responding to us and to the nurses and doctors using eye blinks (one for yes and two for no) to answer questions.

Sadly, the brain bleeding worsened, and Randy was too weak physically to survive any surgery, much less to survive the kinds of surgeries that would be necessary to ensure his survival. The doctors contemplated amputating both legs at the hips. Randy went crazy when they told him that. He looked at me with his beautiful baby blue eyes, and I could feel the pain and terror in his gaze. The doctor explained that there was only a tiny chance that he would live through the surgery, and that he would not be able to return to his home, but would have to go to a nursing home to live out the rest of his life. Randy's eyes began blinking and blinking and blinking: No! No! No!

I met with the doctors via a conference call, and they were in agreement that to proceed with treatment under the circumstances would only cause him intense pain and suffering for no reason.

I had been able to locate Randy's birth sister, Stacy. She was still in Oregon and was able to put me in contact with his birth mother, who had returned to California. Stacy and I were in almost constant contact during the days Randy hovered near death in the ICU. Together with Randy's guardian from Family Eldercare and a representative from hospice, we as a family made the decision to let him go. It was one of the absolutely hardest decisions I have ever been involved in making. It tore my heart to shreds, and it has never healed. Sadly, I am unsure if it ever will.

On that hot summer evening a number of people gathered to say our goodbyes to Randy. He was alert and calm. Staff members from his group home were there; the wonderful director of his day habilitation program was there as well. My husband and I were there, along with both of our adult children. Randy seemed in good spirits, and was responsive. We were all able to tell him how much we loved him, and we talked about all the good times and good people in his life. Although he was receiving pain medication, the only other thing medically that he was receiving was an oxygen push. By this time his body was beginning to shut down, not processing nutrients and such. The hospice chaplain was there as well. It was time to let Randy go.

The only thing the nurse did was disconnect the oxygen drip. At the time it seemed to me that it was not so much pulling the plug as it was releasing him from the pain, releasing him from the body that had been broken thirty-five long years ago. We had given him permission to continue on his journey in a form that was once again healthy and whole. No more wheelchair, but a pair of wings.

It took only about a minute for Randy to exit that broken body. As we who loved him grieved, I could not help but *believe* that he was experiencing a sense of relief. The morning after Randy died, his grandfather in Oregon, after being told of Randy's death, died only a few hours later. I am certain there was a grand reunion in Heaven of a grandson and grandfather who had not seen each other in over three decades.

We opted for cremation and arranged for his ashes to be shipped to his sister, Stacy. We did the local obituary notice, as well as one in the newspaper in Sonoma, California, where we had first met him. There were television interviews that I gave while still in a daze from the whole situation. There was a service to plan. I had a young friend who became a minister and I contacted him to ask if he would officiate at the memorial service. His name is David Lillard, and I will forever be grateful to him for the beautiful and insightful sermon he wrote for the service: "As recorded in the book of James, *What is your life? For it is a mist, which for a little while appears, and then disappears* (James 4:14). However, we are gathered under the most horrible of circumstances; that a man, who was robbed in his youth, by the act of a drunk driver, would also, by another drunk driver, be robbed of his life."

Randy Jordan Williams bore the consequences of the poor decisions of his fellow man. And sadly, in our society he was not the first, nor will he be the last, to lose his life because of drunk driving. No, the poor decision that took him from us will also take many others before either this day is done or this year has passed. In a nation of plenty and in the land of liberty, it is a shame that so many of our brothers, sisters, mothers, fathers and children should die from something so preventable. That with our technology, our sophistication, our "wisdom" we can still be so...so...stupid. Solomon said succinctly, *"Drinking too much makes you loud and foolish. It is stupid to get drunk"* (Proverbs 20:1).

If a foreign army killed or maimed as many as die each year from drunk driving, we would rage. But we don't. As a nation we just lower our gaze and mumble "What a shame." And a shame it is, a shame on us. Randy's death tragically shows that you are not safe from a drunk driver, either in the streets of your city, or the security of your home. He would want his death to be a wake-up call to all who would listen. Drunk driving kills, and it is still a very big problem. Drunk driving's consequences are not somewhere in the future, they are with us today and we feel them now.

Randy was known for his baby blue eyes. And it was through those baby blues that he communicated with the world. Left quadriplegic at the age of eight, he became, as he would say, "a bright boy in a bad body." He lived challenges that few could ever imagine. To sample the life Randy lived, go a day or even a few minutes communicating with the world around you by using one blink for yes and two blinks for no. See if you can do that with the grace and good cheer that he did.

Randy was something special. He joked that if he ever wrote a book, it would be a best seller, full of all the secrets that people had confided in him, either knowingly or unknowingly! Of course, he ventured to guess that he could make even more money if he just threatened to publish it. Randy truly loved people. He was always interested in what was going on in the lives of others. He had a mind like a steel trap! If you met Randy, he would remember you. He was genuinely and sincerely interested in you, even more so if you were a cheerleader. No one who met Randy was a stranger for long. His body could not hold him back from life. He graduated from Manor High School and received his diploma to a standing ovation. He competed in the Special Olympics in Los Angeles at UCLA. He even met Henry Winkler, *the Fonz*!

Randy was unique, and yet the example of a great truth that people are trying to find. Life is not about the clothing, the cars, the job, or the jewelry. Life is about you overcoming the challenges and connecting with others. It is his example of living that gives us strength in celebrating his life. Only in seeing the beauty of his life can we hope to make sense of his death.

Randy teaches us gratitude. In the past, we would not have had the medical technology or know-how to help a person in Randy's condition. In years past we might not have had the medical compassion or the resources to help him, but now we do and we did. So many people had a hand in helping Randy. From the doctors and nurses to his caregivers and his guardians, and his adopted and true family, he allowed us to give. We were able to understand that *it is more blessed to give than to receive* (Acts 20:35). No one who gave of their time or themselves ever did so in vain.

Randy teaches us persistence. He was nearly written off as a child, but because of his determination to connect, he connected. It was his patience and persistence that gave him the strength to communicate with us. He had to wait for us to understand him. He knew what he was thinking, and he knew what we were saying. He had to wait for us to build a bridge to him, and so he waited. You could not live Randy's life in his body without a mental toughness to push you toward your goals. You couldn't do half the things Randy did without perseverance and dogged determination.

Randy teaches us forgiveness. If anyone had the right to hate, to be bitter, to be angry, it was Randy. But if you knew him, you know that that was not him. He was joyful and happy. He would light up at the sight of a friend, and always enjoyed a good joke. Randy was unencumbered by a past that would cripple a weaker person. He lived the command to *love your enemies, bless them that curse you, do good to them that hate you, and pray for them that despitefully use you and persecute you* (Matthew 5:44). He had made peace with what had happened, and had he survived, he no doubt would have done so again.

Randy teaches us love. He was at the full mercy of those around him. He had no monetary gifts to give, no powers to bestow. He was the essence of humanity. What he accomplished, he did with the assistance of others. So how did he accomplish so much? How did he get so many people to help? He loved them and they loved him back. He was honest genuine and caring. I would say that what you see is what you get, but with Randy it was the opposite: you got a lot more than what you saw.

Randy didn't let a day go to waste. He didn't know his life would end when it did. And truthfully, neither do we. We celebrate his life because it is a life worth emulating. We can honor him by learning the lessons he taught, and by living them. God has not given us to know the full rhyme or reason of this world, only to know that this world is not all there is and that *No one can please God without faith, for whomever comes to God must have faith that God exists and rewards those who seek him* (Hebrews 11:6). Randy has gone on, and soon we shall follow. Let us walk joyfully, uprightly, and courageously to that new shore, as Randy did.

The day hab program that Randy attended offered to let us have the service there so that his friends with developmental disabilities could take part in saying goodbye. The day dawned sunny and mild as we gathered for the service and balloon release for Randy Jordan Williams, son, brother, uncle, friend.

There were pictures of Randy, and a book that chronicled his life in pictures. There were balloons with messages written on them. There were many tears. I read the following message that his sister, Stacy, had asked me to read:

First of all, I want to apologize for not being there in person to read this myself. Randy Jordan Williams, I want you to know that growing up as kids you meant so much to me. You were my only sibling and we were only thirteen months apart. You taught me everything: from how to walk, talk, play, ride bikes, and we even climbed trees together. You were not only my brother, you were my best friend. When I was seven and you were eight, we were in the first car accident together where a drunk driver hit us. I felt like a part of me was missing. With mom being a single mother and working to support us and you in the hospital, I felt so lost and scared without my big brother around to take care of me. It is very hard for me to write this without crying. I feel like you got cheated out of life by two different drunk drivers. I am sorry we got separated by so many miles. I wish I could have been a part of your life. I want to personally thank Susan, Ceryl, Erin and Ben for taking my brother in as a part of their family. I also want to thank Diana Gale from Family Eldercare, Ross House, and the people at Life Skills Dayhab Program that had a part in Randy's life. Even a special thanks to the wonderful people on Facebook and to the people with MADD. Randy, I want you to know that you will always be in my thoughts, prayers, and dreams… until we meet again.

Your sister always,

Stacy Joleen Willams

There were people in attendance who had not seen Randy for years, including teachers from years gone by, giving testament to the incredible impact that Randy had had on their lives. Some of his friends with developmental disabilities spoke, including one who said, "I will miss Randy a lot. He was my friend. He laughed at my jokes. They should put the man who drove drunk and killed my friend. They should put him under the jail."

For the first few days I was in a daze, and I was almost unable to sleep. When I would sleep I would awake from nightmares of Randy as the truck landed on him. Randy, who already knew what damage could be done.... Randy, who had already lived this once in his life.... I wondered how this could happen to him again. And I tried in vain to sleep, to find peace, to escape the pain.

The nineteen-year-old driver was found to have a blood alcohol level of almost twice the legal limit. He was released on a very low bond before Randy died, so the proposed charges were driving while intoxicated, two counts of intoxication assault, and resisting arrest. It took eleven and a half months for a grand jury to finally increase the charges to intoxication manslaughter.

During that year I put my job plans on hold. To be honest, I was in no condition to work a real job. Many days it was all I could do to get out of bed, provided that I had even made it to bed at all. I became immersed in the virtual world of Facebook. I spent hours playing virtual games because they were mindless, just like me. Farmville was an escape from my real world.

In retrospect, I realized that I withdrew from the world. I withdrew from friends who really did not much care for the person I had become. A few friends hung with me, but many more were very vocal in expressing their opinion that I should be over it by now. I had to reroute my trips to town because I would burst into tears if I inadvertently drove past the crash site. The sight of the building repairs and repaired fence where the new boards had not yet weathered were enough to send my senses reeling.

The sadness and the unrelenting questions that rolled like a tape looping through my head led me to seek solace in my writing. I journaled obsessively and even tried my hand at a few poems. Many were consigned to the trash can if, upon rereading, they made no sense to me, though I think now that my writing at the time mirrored the depression and the confusion in my brain. In plain language, I became a basket case. I had so many questions; we all did. Our lives had been irrevocably changed by you, Randy; by your existence in our lives, and now by your untimely departure from our lives, and especially by the manner of that departure. We were all grieving in our own way.

My daughter, Erin, had been unsure of what she wanted to do with her life. At age twenty-three she lost her beloved brother, and shortly after that she made a decision to go to college in pursuit of a degree that would allow her to become a Registered Nurse. Since that time she has worked and attended school part time, taking the numerous prerequisites that will soon allow her to apply to nursing school. I am happy for her, and I am certain that Randy would be very proud of her hard work and diligence.

I worked only short-term jobs, and was prone to melting down at work. Though I was retired, I had planned to work for some additional years, but that plan was yet another casualty of the drunk driving crash. The financial impact of these situations upon the survivors is something that almost seems crass to mention, but it exists!

Another factor was the need for me to be in court monthly for years, and to meet with the prosecutor regularly as well. Employers seem more willing to accommodate persons who have worked for them for a while, but less likely to even consider hiring someone who comes with such baggage, no matter how qualified they are for the job; at least that was my experience and perception. Over time, I have become thankful for jobs that are seasonal in nature and that allowed me flexibility to be in court when necessary, and I have come to terms with the fact that I might never again hold down a real full-time job.

The next twenty-six months were fraught with a lot of frustration for me. The court dates were physically and emotionally tiring. Sitting in a courtroom with the man who killed Randy, and his family, was actually painful to the point of physical symptoms like difficulty breathing and nausea. Neither the man nor his family ever looked at me, not once in all those months. I had meeting after meeting with the prosecutors, and spent time with a very caring victim's advocate, Carmen Castro. This woman dried my tears, listened without judgment to my ranting and raving, and never once left me to attend a court date without her support.

During this period of time one of the things I struggled with was *forgiveness*. David Lillard's words at Randy's memorial service would pop into my head at the most random times. At the beginning of the court process I had more compassion for the young man being accused of killing Randy than I would have later in the process. I had had almost a year to work through my anger, and in the meetings with the prosecutors I started out advocating for education and rehabilitation for the young man. He was young. He had not been in trouble with the law before. He was not a repeat DWI offender.

As time went on, and there was no resolution for what seemed like forever, I became bitter, and I wavered in my forgiveness for him. Listening to his lawyer ask for a reduction in the bond from what the grand jury had recommended, asking the court to suspend a curfew that had been imposed by the probation department as a part of his bond requirements for the reason "He doesn't have time after work to hang out with his friends," and the constant continuances month after month after month were almost more than I could take. One of my most constant complaints/rants was on the subject of speedy trials. This experience left me with the sad knowledge that nothing in the court system is speedy. Justice is not swift, nor is it blind. Money (and connections) talk, even in our justice system.

One example was the trial of a young lady with strong political connections. Our trial date had been set and was bumped so that this trial could happen sooner. Then after this trial was over our trial date was again bumped because her lawyer (who was also defending the driver who killed Randy) argued that he could not get a fair trial because of the public outcry over the lightness of the sentence given to this young lady.

She had hit and killed a pedestrian. She left the body lying in a residential area and denied having hit the victim, even though there was physical evidence on her car. She denied having been drinking, although bar security footage showed otherwise. She received a few months in the county jail and a ten-year probated sentence.

Our case never went to trial. The prosecutor was replaced by a different one about three months short of three years after Randy was killed. This new prosecutor pushed for a plea agreement. And for several months it was back and forth. His lawyer asked for probation. The prosecutor asked for the maximum of twenty years. His lawyer countered with four years. It was like a hellish poker game.

I had pressed for a trial. Even if a jury gave him probation, I wanted him to have to see the pictures and hear exactly what he had done, since I was fairly sure that he had little recollection of the crash. I wanted him to internalize the havoc he had caused by taking the life of a truly innocent man.

The "game" continued until finally an agreement was hammered out. The driver got a sentence of nine years in prison. Because the vehicle was declared a deadly weapon, he would be eligible for parole after serving half of the nine-year sentence, rather than the standard quarter of the sentence. The day of the sentencing finally arrived. I had asked if it was possible for Randy's sister Stacy in Oregon to give her impact statement via Skype, and they arranged for that to happen. I was very nervous. I should have been comfortable in that courtroom, as I had spent many hours there over the last twenty-five months, but I wasn't. This is what I said:

Mr. S., I am in awe at the audacity of you and your lawyers to wait three years before getting down to business and ending this mess. In June 2010, you made some really bad choices and those resulted in the death of a truly innocent man. At numerous points you could have made a choice

322

that would have avoided this entire situation. You were underage and drinking, made no arrangements for a sober driver, called no one sober to give you a ride, called no taxi, did not sleep it off but chose to get in your mama's truck. Randy had been in a crash with a drunk driver when he was eight that ended all chances of a normal life. He became a quadriplegic, unable to walk/talk/take care of his own basic needs. He became a child, and later a man, with a good heart and soul, trapped in a body that no longer did his bidding. He battled demons that would have killed a weaker person, and went on for thirty-five years to touch the lives of hundreds of people who came to know him. He taught people many things and made them better people for having known him. He never gave up on life. He loved everyone. He taught us appreciation for what we have. He gave people hope. He smiled and laughed and lived, even in his broken body. Randy had the most expressive blue eyes and they spoke volumes. He communicated with eye blinks, one for yes and two for no.

He graduated from Manor High School to a standing ovation. He lived his life the best he could for thirty-five years from a wheelchair. He loved his sisters and his brother. He touched the lives of people whose names I will never know. And your choices, Mr. S., finally took his life. As he lay under your truck in his bed at his group home, I can only imagine the terror he felt as you ran away and left him there like a bag of garbage. As he lay in the bed at the ICU, with legs crushed from the weight of the truck, as doctors determined the almost negligible possibility of survival if they amputated both legs at the hips, as family and friends cried, as he bled inside his brain. This man would have forgiven you. I am trying to do so, but it is very hard. It is heart-wrenching. You may have gotten a deal for nine years, and you and your family may think that is harsh, but what Randy got was death, and what we got was a life sentence without him. Randy's birth sister in Oregon has his ashes, but she will never have the opportunity to hug her brother again. His nieces and nephews will never meet him. Randy's death leaves a huge hole in all our hearts.

With your time incarcerated in prison, I hope that you will reflect on the pain and horror that your choices caused for Randy and those who love him. Mr. S., I hope that your family is thankful that you are going to prison, rather than dead. I hope you realize that your mom could have had to sit in the ICU with you while you breathed your last breath. Or she could have been getting a call and having to identify your battered and dead body at some cold morgue. Forgiveness will come from me when you have served your time and have changed your ways. Randy is proof positive that these things can happen more than once. I want you to heed the warning and change how you make your choices. I hope that you will share your story so that other young people can learn from it and senseless deaths can be avoided. Because if you do not make those changes, you will sooner or later be dead or back in a courtroom, and no one will have sympathy for you if you do this again. You have been given a gift, to have the opportunity to change your life. Please do not squander it.

Randy's sister, Stacy, spoke of having had dreams of seeing him again and of the tattoo that she had that was done with some of his ashes mixed in so that she would carry him with her always.

After the impact statements were given, Mr. S.'s lawyer asked that his client be able to meet with us prior to the sentencing and we agreed. We met in the jury room with no lawyers present, just him and my family. What happened then is nothing I could have imagined in my wildest dreams. He told us that he knew in his heart that he deserved the sentence he was about to receive, and more. He said he wished he could bring Randy back. He told us that his family had held prayer vigils every night for Randy and the motorcyclist who had been injured in the crash. He told us that his lawyer had cautioned him and his family to not look at us in the courtroom, and to show no emotion.

My husband told him that his road in prison would be hard but that he was young enough to be strong and to change his life if he truly desired to do so. I handed Mr. S. tissues from my purse, as he was crying in earnest by this time. That seemed to make him cry even more. I told him that the proof to me would be in how he chose to live his life from that point forward. He had owned his choices and was going to pay for them. Our daughter, Erin, told him that he looked like he needed a hug, and when he stood, she and I hugged him and my husband shook his hand.

After he was sentenced and led from the courtroom to begin serving his sentence, we cried; and waited for the room to clear before we left. When we finally exited we were surprised to find this young man's family lined up outside the courtroom door. As we came out each one hugged us and whispered their condolences on Randy's death. I did not know until that point that the driver's mother did not even speak English, His sister translated my response to her after she told me in English, "I am so sorry for the loss of your son. We pray for you every day." That she had gone to the trouble to learn what she wanted to express in English touched my heart. At that moment I knew that my quest to find forgiveness had truly begun. We all hugged one another and cried. I like to think that Randy would have been extremely pleased at this unlikely turn of events.

The reporter from Fox News was there to capture this moment on film, and as I turned around I saw that the cameraman had tears rolling down his face as he was filming. The story ran on the evening and nightly news with the tagline "You will never believe what happened after this man was sentenced in the drunk driving death of a disabled Austin man."

Despite my good intentions and having told this young man that I would write to him, I procrastinated. I followed his location as best I could on the Texas Criminal Justice website, and tried to write a letter. Many letters were started and consigned to the trash. I had very conflicted thoughts about what I wanted to say to him.

I had thought that the closure from the court proceedings would bring me, if not peace, then at least some measure of acceptance. As I have been told, "You expected too much!" And that was true to an extent, as I had hoped that I would once again find "myself," that I could find the "normal" that I had once had. The acceptance came with strings attached.

One of the most difficult strings was a loss of innocence. Once a person has endured the loss of a child, there is the fear lurking in the back of your mind that if the unthinkable had happened once, then who was I to be so arrogant as to think that it would not, could not happen again? Randy's life, injury, and death seemed proof to me that there was a pattern in nature. Randy's life and death was proof that lightning can strike twice in the same place. I had, and truth be told, still have severe anxiety every day about the safety of my adult children. The lack of control of things in my life and the lives of the people I love has caused many problems for me and for those people whom I love.

I pray daily for family and friends, for myself, and for the young man in prison for the death of our Randy. My prayers seem to reflect my life over the last five years: prayers for peace, comfort, strength, health and healing (physical, mental, emotional and spiritual), good choices. Searching for things that are very elusive in my world has become an almost daily quest. I used to joke that I had never prayed much until I had children, but I had no idea until I had lost one how important prayer would become for my sanity.

Grief is never a straight line; at least it has not been for me. Some days are good and filled with appreciation for what I have — my life, my children, my memories, the friends I have made on this journey. Those are days when I can see and enjoy the world around me! The sun on my face and the companionship of my animals can bring me great comfort and joy. Other days I am right back at square one, missing Randy and filled with the regrets of a lifetime, and drawn into the darkness of a tortured mind. The "what ifs" seem to suck the life right out of me at times. My mind has a mind of its own, and I am rarely in control. I am coming slowly to accept all these things as a part of my life now.

A few weeks ago I finally obtained the driver's prison I.D. number and address, and was determined to make another attempt to write him a letter. I was in the local Dollar General store when I was drawn to a card that said "Challenges are never easy — but they always make you stronger." The sentiment of this card seemed applicable for the young man in prison as well as to me and my life, though I also have thought when hearing other versions of this, "I am strong enough already!" and *"No more*, please!"

In my letter I told him that although our lives became irrevocably intertwined in June 2010, I really knew very little about him as a person and that I hoped that our correspondence would remedy that. I really hope that he will also come to know Randy. I apologized for the length of time it had taken for me to write. I expressed my hope that he would learn from this experience and be willing to share his story with others so that they might not end up in a similar situation. I mailed the card/letter and wondered "Will he write me back?" and waited. Knowing that letters had to be screened before delivery at the prison, I was unsure as to how long I would have to wait for an answer, or even if I would ever receive an answer at all.

Two weeks later I opened my mailbox to see a letter with neat handwriting addressed to me. I rushed into the house and just held the letter, looking at it, and almost scared to open it. It seemed that my healing depended on this letter in some strange way. I once thought that forgiveness was a one-way street, but I was learning that it was much more.

I had been struggling to write this story, and to find the words to express what this loss had meant to me and to my family in an attempt to help others in similar situations, but there seemed to be an important piece missing in the equation, just as there was a piece missing from my heart. As I gazed at that letter, I suddenly realized that the missing link was not Randy, because he will forever be in my heart and my memories, but was the young man who had made a very bad choice to drive while intoxicated.

I opened the letter. It was long, a total of four pages. Like many people of his age, he printed in easily readable script. I had told him that I was writing a story about forgiveness, and with his response I knew that the story was not just about our family, nor just about Randy, but also about this young man, age nineteen at the time of the crash but now almost twenty-five, and his family. I had said from the very beginning of this sad journey that there were no winners in a situation like this, but at the time I had not yet figured out the truth, and yet also the untruth of that statement. This letter was to reveal to me how right and yet how wrong I was in my thinking. One thing I had known since the meeting with the driver, José, prior to his sentencing was that he had a religious upbringing. In his letter, he thanked me for the forgiveness I had shown to him. He said that God had given him the courage to change for his victims and their families, as well as for his own family.

José wrote that the most difficult thing for him, besides facing the victims and families, was learning to forgive himself for his actions. He said, "I felt like I was living a lie, trying to hide all the pain, anger, confusion that was bottled up inside me. I would think to myself, why couldn't I have been the one to die and not Randy? Should I have been sentenced to death?" He came to realize that he should not question, but to find out what his purpose in life is. "There is no restitution, no act that I can do to fill that empty space in your family and heal the pain I have caused. I can only promise to carry your son in my memory and to do good things in honor of him. I will carry my cross until the Lord carries me home," he wrote. I will be sending him a picture of Randy, not to further pour salt in his wounds, but in the hope of helping him to heal.

I pray that this young man will carry through on his vision of finishing his education, taking over his father's business one day, having a family and children, and carrying this story to young people who need to hear it. It is a story that needs to be written about and told, as do all our stories. Though I hate the saying "All things happen for a reason," I do think that through Randy's death there are people whose lives have been or will be saved. And for a child who was never expected to be able to do anything after the initial drunk driving crash, Randy has had a great impact on many, many lives, not the least of which was mine. Unexpectedly, one of those lives might just be a young man from West Texas who is learning lessons he never wanted to, but accepting those lessons with gratitude and grace.

There are a few things I wish to add. One is that I hope the healing results in my becoming a better and less bitter person. I have checked into places where I can share Randy's story in the hope of making a difference. I have met many very brave and strong people during this journey, many from Facebook grief groups, who share their stores on a regular basis, and I had despaired at ever being able to do that on a face-to-face basis. I am so thankful for these people who have believed in me, comforted me, cried with me, and encouraged me. I know that each story is different and that every drunk driver also has his or her own story. But I was reminded recently by my husband that maybe I had been searching for "vengeance," but calling it "justice." If José can own up to what he did, then certainly I can as well.

Just because someone drives drunk does not make them a horrible person. It makes them a person who needs to make better choices. What they do with their lives after the crash, if they were blessed enough to survive the crash, is what counts. As humans, we all make choices that we may regret. I wish for all people to realize that "There but by the grace of God go I."

Whether we choose to write or save animals, speak to groups, foster pets or children, be a friend, feed the homeless, listen to or check in on the elderly, save the environment, create art, take photographs. To make positive contributions to the world in which we live, with love and the memory of our loved ones in our heart, will promote our own mental and physical health. The journey of grief is not easy, nor is it painless, but sharing our stories and our love for those we have lost can make our lives more fulfilling, and make the ache more bearable. Channeling your energy and your emotions into things that are truly important can do wonders for your perspective.

Pick something close to your heart or something your loved one would be happy to see you doing. Be kind, especially to yourself! Healing seems to be promoted by helping others. When making those pesky decisions in life now, I always ask myself, "What would Randy do/think/be proud of me for doing?"

Never leave important things unsaid. Life is fragile and uncertain. We have all learned this from our experiences. The pain of loss will be with me for the rest of my earthly existence, though with time I have come to realize that the memories are priceless, and I take the time to revel in the incredible ability to close my eyes and relive those moments in my life that, if not perfect, at least seem to hold the glimmer of the magic of times past, and the hope for a brighter future. Hold tight to those moments in your past and in your current life!

I wish for all of us the ability to struggle through the darkness and find our way once again into the light, carrying with us the memories of loved ones who are no longer bound by earthly constraints.

SUSAN RILEY
BUDA, TEXAS

RANDY WILLIAMS & SUSAN RILEY

SUSAN RILEY & RANDY WILLIAMS

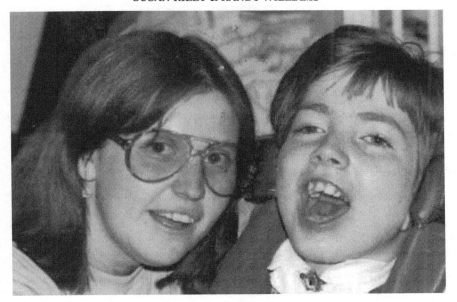

RANDY WILLIAMS

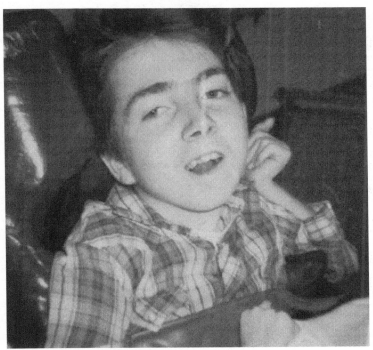

RANDY WILLIAMS

CHAPTER TWENTY

THE DOMINO EFFECT
ETHAN'S STORY
BY LEANNE SALTAR

For the rest of my life, I will keep searching
for moments full of you...
-AUTHOR UNKNOWN

I married Steve Saltar on May 28, 1988, and we began our new life together. Life was good, and we were happy, both working and adjusting nicely to married life. To me, the only thing that was missing was children, a family. On August 1, 1991, our dreams came true, and Ruby Jo was born. An amazing bundle of joy who delighted us daily. Two years later on December 15, 1993, we were blessed again, this time with the most handsome baby boy. We named this precious one Ethan Cody Bleu Saltar. He loved his sister from day one, as she did him. I vividly remember watching them play, bursting with more love than I had ever known possible.

We have always been a close family and when younger the kids were active in Girl Scouts, Boy Scouts, and sports. Ethan played football from the time he was in second grade until he reached high school. We were told by several of his coaches starting at an early age that he was a natural, and if he stayed in football he would go pro someday. While other kids were watching cartoons,

Ethan could be found watching NFL classic football games played way before his time in black and white.

Their childhood was made up of many fond memories that I carry with me always. As the kids got older, and we moved the location of the diagnostic lab where I was working, they pressured me to move them to schools closer to home and our neighborhood. I had always kept them in schools closer to the diagnostic lab I have worked at for the last twenty-six years. The kids started their new schools, and soon we learned that Ruby Jo would have her first child, Zane. Ethan started acting out because he was upset that we did not ground Ruby Jo for becoming a young mother. He often told me that we expected him to be Mr. Perfect, and she could get away with anything. Zane was born July 29, 2007. Once Zane was here, Ethan was a proud uncle and loved his nephew with all his heart. He would do anything for him except let him in his bedroom.

Ethan was a social butterfly and had a big heart. He often brought home four-legged strays, along with some two-legged ones. I was not impressed with some of the kids my son chose to befriend. In 2008, we moved into our current home, a fresh start for all of us.

My kids were coming home with more stray kids. It seemed as though I was always ushering kids out of my house after they overstayed their welcome. I had never met so many homeless teenage kids and runaways until we moved here, and we were only a few miles from the old house and in the same county. It was a different school district with higher property taxes and bigger homes. As we settled in, things got better, and some of their friends changed again. Once again we found out that Ruby Jo was expecting, and on September 11, 2009, Elijah Josiah was born. Ethan was still playing football and going to school, but also learned that it was easy to ditch in high school. The kids he hung around with did not have much adult supervision, so anytime they were caught out after curfew or needed a ride somewhere, I was the only mom who picked them up.

Ethan made some mistakes, but every adult who knew him would say that out of all the teenage boys who hung around with their kids, Ethan was always polite and lent a helping hand with anything they needed. For some reason, about this time I had a nagging feeling that one of Ethan's friends was going to take him away from me. I did not know how, where or why, or even who it would be. It became an ever-present feeling that I just could not shake. I knew he was a good kid, but would one of them convince him to do something illegal, and he would end up in jail? Would one of them hurt him on purpose and just leave him somewhere? I did not know, but this feeling nagged at me for at least six months to a year before that fateful day. Ethan and I had discussed this and argued on the night of Friday, September 17, 2010, before our nightmare began. He assured me his friends loved him and would never do anything to hurt him. He added "Besides Mom, most of my friends I have known almost my whole life," and went on to list some of them.

One of his friends had stopped by that night to ask him to go out after I had already asked him to stay home. I knew I had to work the next day and did not want to worry about where he was, what he was doing, and if he was safe or not. Ethan told his friend he was grounded and could not leave the house. I found that out by chance when I was talking to the boy's sister-in-law. She told me Ethan had told the boy he could not go out because his mom had grounded him. This was so unlike him, as even though Ethan was a good boy, he was also headstrong and at sixteen years old, six feet two inches and two hundred and twenty pounds, he usually did what he wanted. I have never been so proud of my teenage son than I was at that moment.

On Saturday, September 18, 2010, I was leaving for work at the lab. I had made arrangements with my parents to pick the kids up to take them to my sister's house to celebrate my niece's and Elijah's first birthdays with the rest of the family. Before I left for work, I asked Ethan to make sure he did his chores, including the dreaded dishes. I told him I loved him and walked out the door. Little did I know that would be the last time I would see my beloved son alive. My parents showed up to pick them up, and Mom surprised Ethan and let him drive her Lincoln Town Car for the very first and last time. He had always begged her to drive it, and now that he had his learner's permit she decided to let him drive to his aunt's house a few miles away.

Unbeknownst to me, that evening after Grandma and Grandpa dropped them off at home, Ethan made plans to go out with his friends Wes and Danny to a party. Ruby Jo told me as Ethan ran out the door that since she could not go with him, he should come back and give her a hug. He did, and she lent him some money. As he left he told her, "Don't worry, I will be back, I promise."

I worked my shift and returned home between 11 p.m. and midnight, as Saturdays were my swing shift hours. Ruby and the boys were in bed, and Steve was away in another state at a training session to begin his new career as an over-the-road trucker. I did my routine and hit the desktop computer for a night of Facebook games and man-bashing Steve's cousin Brett and an old friend of ours named Frank. It was all in fun; they would send me woman-bashing jokes and comments, and I would return the favor. I realized it was getting late and started to worry about Ethan. I excused myself from the computer and told the guys I was going to watch a movie and wait for my son to get home.

At the time, I did not know which group of friends he was with, but I decided I would start calling around. I started with Danny, one of Ethan's best friends; I cannot remember why now, but I could not get hold of him. I really could not even remember who I tried that night, but I did not find Ethan. I turned on the TV and started watching a Queen Latifah movie, *Just Wright*. I ended up falling asleep in my chair. Something woke me up between 3:30 and 4 a.m. I worried and wondered, but finished watching the movie. I waited for a call from Ethan or for him to come home. It was not unusual for Ethan to stay out late, but he never spent the night at anyone's house. He told me he did not feel safe staying overnight at anyone's house. To this day, I still believe that when Ethan passed away, he came home to check on me, and that was what woke me up.

The crash occurred at approximately 1:54 a.m. on Sunday, September 19, 2010. According to the police, Ethan was in the back passenger seat, and one of Ethan's best friends was driving. The driver's girlfriend, Amanda, who was twenty-two, was in the front passenger seat. Amanda owned the Ford Explorer but was too drunk to stand up, much less drive, so she gave her keys to her seventeen-year-old boyfriend, Ethan's good friend, who was also drunk and drugged. The driver was seventeen and had only a learner's permit which, in Colorado, makes it illegal to operate a motor vehicle without an adult in the car or to transport any other teenagers not related to the driver.

We were also told by the police that there were a total of three people in the car at the time of the accident; they had just dropped off two other passengers right before the crash occurred. They were eastbound on 80th Avenue in Westminster at a higher rate of speed than was permitted. The driver was moving the steering wheel back and forth, messing around, when they hit the railroad tracks. They blew out a tire and rolled the vehicle. The Explorer landed at 80th Avenue and Stuart Street with Ethan lying behind the vehicle. For some reason he was not wearing his seatbelt, so he was ejected. Not having his seatbelt on was very unlike Ethan, who always told his sister and anyone else in the car "Buckle up, Buttercup." He was my seatbelt guard instead of school crossing guard. Later we would find out why Ethan, my seatbelt guard, didn't have on his seatbelt.

We found out later that Ethan was sitting in the cargo area, which didn't have a seatbelt. Amanda's arm was unmovable under the Explorer, and they transported her to the hospital. At the time of the crash, Amanda had a two-year-old daughter who was living with her mother, who just happened to be a defense attorney. Amanda has had four of ten surgeries to correct her arm. I have not followed her recovery, as I feel she was partly to blame for my son's death. She purchased the alcohol and whatever drugs the kids had taken, and gave her boyfriend, who had only a learner's permit, the keys to drive her car.

The driver was not injured as far as I know, and there were no other cars involved in the crash. We are not sure where they were going, but we have been told they were going to another party. We have also been told they were bringing Ethan home and were heading in the right direction for that.

So many things just didn't add up at the time, but all I knew at that moment was that my son was dead, and my heart and soul ached to have him in my arms one more time. My mind was not comprehending any of this, as if I were numb. I think back now to Ethan's funeral, and I feel like it was not me there. As if I was watching everything from above, outside of my body, the weight of the world now firmly planted on my shoulders.

I first learned of the accident from one of the teenagers who had been dropped off right before the crash. She called me about 5:15 a.m. When the phone rang, I assumed it was Ethan calling me for a ride home. I was wrong. The girl on the other end of the line asked me if I was Ethan's mom. I did not understand her, so I asked her to repeat what she said. She asked me again if I was Ethan's mom. I told her I was, and asked where he was. She proceeded to tell me that Amanda had been in an accident, and they thought Ethan was with her, but he didn't make it. He was gone. I asked her what she meant by "gone," and to which hospital Ethan had been taken. With this information, I found the number to the hospital and got through to someone who took my information and said they would call me back. After just a few minutes, which seemed like hours to me, the hospital's chaplain called to inform me that the John Doe had been identified as my beloved sixteen-year-old son Ethan Cody Bleu Saltar.

As I was hanging up the phone, a couple of Adams County sheriff deputies knocked on my door. They asked me if I was Mrs. Saltar, and I said yes, but I needed them to leave because I knew why they were here. They asked me what I meant, and I told them they were here to tell me my son was dead, and they needed to leave. They would not leave and asked me if they could come in, I did let them in. They asked if anyone else was home, and I told them my daughter Ethan's sister was downstairs. At that point I woke Ruby Jo up and called my mother with the devastating news. One of the sheriff's officers was looking around my house with his flashlight for some reason, which made matters worse. I kept asking them to leave. I told them I needed to be alone, but they would not leave until either the victims advocate got here or my family did. When the victims advocate arrived, I sent them away also, because I needed to be with only my family. I needed time to try to process the last few hours. My heart was breaking over and over, leaving a big empty hole with every thought that entered my mind.

I know that they knew who Ethan was at 3 a.m. that morning but did not notify me until 5:30. Ethan had left his wallet in my van, because a few weeks earlier he had almost lost his identification and learner's permit, so they had him listed as a John Doe. My son died in the operating room at 3:40 a.m. September 19, 2010. I asked the deputies who came to the door when I could see my son, and they told me once they released his body to the coroner. Later that morning my nephew's girlfriend called the coroner's office and asked when we could see him and identify his body. I knew as well as she did that a family member would have to identify him. However, they told her they already had a positive identification on him. Confused, she asked the voice on the phone if none of the family had identified him, and since he arrived as a John Doe, how they knew who he was. After going back and forth, they finally said they had pulled him up on the computer by his fingerprints.

I was not allowed to see my only son for the last time until Friday, September 24, the morning of his funeral. My heart was shattered again as the pain became increasingly more unbearable. Steve was in another state for a truck driving job, and his phone did not work there. The deputies told me they would help us get hold of him by sending someone from the police department out there. I called all the phone numbers of people from whom he had borrowed their cellphone to call me, and left him a message to call me back. The company recruiting him would not even pay his way home on the Greyhound bus, so amidst everything else, we had to come up with the money to get Steve home for his son's funeral.

On Sunday morning by 7 a.m. my family, friends and neighbors had gathered at our house, mourning the loss of Ethan. My middle sister brought my mom out to be with us and took the boys back to her house, trying to shelter them from the dark cloud of grief that now hung over our home. Mom did not think Dad could handle losing his youngest grandson and best friend, as he called him a week later at his memorial, so she left him home that day. Zane had just turned three years old, and Elijah had turned one just days before. We were hoping we could find a way to tell them in a way that they could understand that their beloved Uncle Ethan would not be coming home. Unfortunately, Zane overheard someone say that Ethan was dead, so we did not get them whisked away fast enough. How do you explain to two young boys that their uncle was taken before his time? Yes, Ethan made a choice that night, and it was a bad one, but how many times have you made a bad decision in your life? Did you pay for it with your life?

We had Ethan's memorial service on September 24, 2010. The service was beautiful; my Uncle Dan presided over it. My great-nephew was only seven years old when Ethan was taken from us, but he got up to the pulpit and spoke of his cousin very quickly but with a lot of love. My nephew Aaron, who had contacted MADD right away after the crash, got up and gave all of Ethan's friends his cellphone number and told them to call him no matter what time of day or night it was if they needed a ride home.

When I saw the school's guidance counselor, he was holding a red manila folder. He was very nervous and apprehensive about telling me what the folder contained; he said he did not even know how to approach me. He explained to me the assignment he had given Ethan the Thursday before his death. The assignment was to draw a picture of what you think your headstone would say if you died that day. He asked if I wanted it, given the circumstances. I told him I needed to see it and needed to have anything my son had created or even touched. It was so surreal to see the date of his funeral, knowing after I saw it that in just three short days my son would be dead and life as I knew it would be over. Inside the folder was a drawing of a normal headstone and it had a cross on it and said, "Ethan Saltar - In loving memory, beloved son, and uncle" with the dates December 15, 1993, to September 16, 2010.

After the service was over and we started to head for the reception only a few miles away. Steve came to me and told me he wanted to ride with his cousin Brett. I told him that was fine, and I would meet him at the hall. Little did I know at the time that Steve had the only set of keys to our van. Luckily for me, my sister Laurie and nephew Adam had stayed behind to make sure I was okay, and they took me to the hall. They quickly got the keys from Steve and went back for the van. As I walked in I was talking with family and friends when Ethan's football coach, Julio, whisked me away to make sure I ate. I remember I filled my plate and picked at it. Food was not what I needed or wanted at the time. Once I sat at the table, I did not move until it was time to go. Ruby Jo and Ethan's pediatrician, Dr. Knott, showed up and sat with me the whole time. Looking back now, I know Ethan was truly loved and touched a lot of people's lives, but at that moment I felt nothing but a dull ache deep inside, an emptiness I could never explain. This was not how my life was meant to be I was not supposed to be the mother at the roadside memorial. I had preached to my kids every day never to get in a car with anyone who had been drinking!

You will recall from earlier in the story that Ethan left our house with his friends Wes and Danny, and the boys went to one party and left it to go to another. The second party is where Ethan met up with his good friend the seventeen-year-old driver and the driver's girlfriend, Amanda. Ethan changed cars when he left the second party; according to some, he switched cars with one of his best childhood friends, Jeremiah. Ethan went with the driver, and Amanda and Jeremiah went with Wes. Ethan had grown up with these kids, and even I knew that seemed unlikely, because Wes hated Jeremiah and would never give him a ride anywhere. Knowing this, there is an unofficial side to our story that makes sense to us. I believe this is the side of our living nightmare that is true. We were told by Amanda's brother and his girlfriend that three other people were in the Explorer that night, and three of them ran from the scene of the accident. They told us that Amanda kept asking about Jeremiah but never mentioned Ethan's name after the accident. Jeremiah, who claimed to be Ethan's best friend, ran away that night and left my son for dead. The other two were Doc and his girlfriend Ehran, who had called me in the early morning hours to tell me my son was dead, and life as I knew it was over.

There were six people in the Explorer that fateful night, forcing Ethan to sit in the cargo area, giving up his seatbelt to the very ones who ran away and left him. Jeremiah began by denying that he was in in the car. As mentioned earlier, it was said that he had gone with Wes. He created that story by calling his sister in the early hours of the morning saying that Wes had threatened to beat him up and kicked him out of the car somewhere. Jeremiah's father worked nights, so his sister went to the driver's house to get his mom out of bed to pick up her brother, Jeremiah, about a mile or two from the crash site. She found him disoriented, scared and hiding in some bushes in a gas station parking lot across from a farmer's field. The story we have heard is that Jeremiah was on probation and had some drugs in his pocket that night and Eric had a warrant for his arrest. My nephew and others remember Jeremiah having unexplained bruises, plus complaining about his ribs hurting, to which he made up an excuse, saying he got mad and punched a wall.

My three nephews and Ruby Jo seemed pulled to the scene of the crash and needed to see where it all took place. They talked to the neighbors living around there. Ruby was on the street corner just walking around when she was approached by a middle-aged lady asking her what they were doing there and what had happened. Ruby Jo explained that there had been a car crash that took her brother's life, and she didn't think the driver and other passengers were injured. The lady, who turned out to be Amanda's mother, got closer and yelled at Ruby Jo that the other passenger just happened to be her daughter and that she was injured in the crash. Ruby Jo told her, "My brother is dead; he paid with his life." The lady kept talking, saying that her daughter had a daughter at home waiting for her, as if Ethan's life didn't matter because he had no children. Everyone who knows Amanda, and she herself will tell you that her mother and father were raising her two-year-old daughter while Amanda was out partying most of the time. Ruby asked her, "What about my sons whom Ethan was helping to raise?" I wish I could have been there that day to tell her that being her mother did not make her daughter's life any more important than Ethan's life. They were both people who had people who loved them and depended on them for many reasons. They both mattered; the big difference was that Amanda started this domino effect by supplying the alcohol and drugs, and she was alive; my only son was dead.

When the detectives came to the house Monday morning, September 20, 2010, they told us there had been four different accidents that same night, all involving alcohol, and I believe they all had fatalities. We asked them about Amanda and what charges she would incur. They were livid with my daughter for suggesting she should even face any charges, as she was considered a victim. We demanded that they do an investigation as to who purchased the alcohol, as Ethan and the driver were not old enough. The detectives told us they would do an investigation. We talked to them about other kids being in the car, and they told us that as far as they were concerned no one else had been in the car that night. That is also when we found out that Amanda's mother was a well-known defense attorney in Westminster and Adams County, with a specialty in DUI cases. She had instructed her daughter not to admit any guilt or fault in the case.

We knew right then that we would need to fight to get her charged with anything. I demanded that when her case came up it would be moved out of Adams County, as her mother knew the judges and staff at the courthouse. The best they would do was have a judge from Jefferson County rule over the case. I spent many hours online researching different charges that I felt should apply to her, and emailing the Adams County district attorney, asking him if he would charge her with them. He denied all charges except for four contributing to the delinquency of a minor, but they could not prove she supplied any alcohol to Ethan. The charges were for the driver/boyfriend, Jeremiah, Eric, and Ehran. The only ones who filled out victim's impact statements for her case were me, my family and the driver's parents. The other parents would not fill them out. Jeremiah's dad, who always said Ethan was like a son to him, told me to let go and move on because they were just kids. This was the second time in our friendship that this man had said something to me that was so offensive that I do not call him a friend anymore.

The district attorney and her office kept us informed every step of the way in the driver's case. They valued our opinions, and even sat up a family meeting informing us of the charges they were planning on filing. They knew we were concerned not only with justice for Ethan but also making sure the driver got the help he needed. The driver admitted guilt and was put on suicide watch from the very beginning. I knew I had to do what I thought Ethan would want me to. I owed it to my son to not only get justice but to make sure two lives weren't lost. We asked the district attorney from the beginning to try the driver as a juvenile and also to make sure he got mental health and drug/alcohol counseling. We agreed to the district attorney's offer of a four-year sentence in a juvenile detention center. We knew that if prosecuted as an adult he would not get any of the counseling we as a family felt was important to the rest of his life.

On March 17, 2011, the judge sentenced the driver as a juvenile to six years in a juvenile detention center with the provision that if he got into any trouble while incarcerated, he would be moved to an adult facility and do a sixteen-year sentence, eight years for each victim in the car. The judge was livid with the district attorney's office and told him that the judge was the only one in charge of handing down the sentence, and that he alone would set the term. The driver was incarcerated from September 19, 2010, until approximately September 17, 2014. Unbeknownst to us, once Amanda was sentenced the driver appealed his sentence, and it was dropped to the four years we had originally agreed upon, but also time served, which was not given in the previous sentence.

Our family was never informed or included in the appeal or any decisions made in it. I felt that since we had stood by the driver and his family, we should have been informed by his family or the justice system. It was a big shock and even larger disappointment to us when we were informed that he was not even going to do the four years we had agreed to. As for Amanda, she pleaded not guilty and asked for a jury trial. When all her court dates began, we somehow managed to catch the same elevator as her as we were leaving one day. It would not have been so awkward if she had apologized to us or admitted any guilt in Ethan's death. She never said a word and only looked at the picture of Ethan on the front of my shirt and looked down at the floor.

Finally one day, after many court dates, the district attorney gave us an apology letter from her, and she changed her plea to guilty. At her sentencing sometime in October or November of 2011, she gave a speech apologizing to us for Ethan's death. She was given only ninety days in jail and eight years of probation. The judge told her she had to have proof of a forty-hour workweek job and take childrearing and family classes. She was *never* charged with anything having to do with Ethan's death.

As our family walked out of the courthouse that day, I saw Amanda walk past, and finally reached out to her. I told her I appreciated her apology and hugged her. Her mother continued walking and waited across the driveway. Her father came back, I am sure, to protect his daughter if needed and he also apologized to me. I cannot say I truly forgive her, but as I told her that day, I needed to hear her apologize and admit her guilt in the death of my son, Ethan Cody Bleu Saltar. No, he did not have his own children, but does that make him any less of a person? Does that mean his life did not mean anything to anybody? His life meant a lot to a lot of people and left a hole in many hearts, young and old.

Life has had many twists and turns since September 19, 2010, some good and some bad. Many times I have told people that my life will never be better than okay again. My husband and I were separated from November 2011 through October 2015 for many reasons. In the aftermath of a traumatic death, people grieve differently, and sometimes it is hard for one person to understand another person's grief, especially when you are both so wrapped up in your own. Steve grieves quietly and does not want to talk about this painful time in our lives. Ruby Jo and I are open grievers; talking about Ethan is all I want to do. Broken relationships and families are just a minor part of the domino effect from one person who decides to drink and drive and affects so many lives.

On November 13, 2014, Ruby Jo gave birth to her third child, my only granddaughter, Amiyah Bleu. I never wanted a granddaughter and was not sure what I would do with one after having had two grandsons. After meeting Amiyah Bleu for the first time, I know she had been handpicked by her uncle Ethan Cody Bleu as a gift from God himself. Ruby Jo named her Amiyah, meaning midnight rain in Japanese, and Bleu after her uncle. After sometime Ruby Jo had realized that the name Amiyah also included our MADD victims advocate Maya, who helped us through our courtroom experience. Amiyah has given our life a little more sunshine on grief-clouded days.

Some time ago I found Ethan's MySpace page. There was a place where it asked who you most wanted to meet. Ethan answered "Jesus." I am so proud to have been his mother and still take comfort in those times when there is no comfort, feeling that he is resting in the arms of the person whom he wanted to meet most — Jesus. I am determined to tell Ethan's story and keep his memory alive. If I can stop even one person from drinking and driving and keep another family from grieving at a streetside memorial pole, I have honored my son and his memory. In honor of Ethan, please do not drink and drive.

LEANNE SALTAR
DENVER, COLORADO

STEVE, ETHAN, RUBY JO, LEANNE & ZANE SALTAR

AMIYAH BLEU, ELIJAH, & ZANE

ETHAN & ZANE

ETHAN & LEANNE

ZANE, RUBYJO, AMIYAH BLEU & ELIJAH

ETHAN, LEANNE & ZANE

A POEM FOR ETHAN SALTAR
By Aaron Hudson

The loss of you has brought us all great sorrow,
I'm not sure how we'll face tomorrow.
A pain unlike any I've ever felt,
When you were young you made our heart's melt.
For a while you were on the wrong track,
With the help of your family you were on your way back.
For such a short life you left an undullable mark,
Everyone says stuff like this brings positive spark.
I am positive that you wouldn't want us to hurt this much,
Who knew this would pack such a punch?
Just know you made your whole family proud,
We'll think of you every time we see a cloud.
Wonderful kid becoming a great man,
I hope the man upstairs has great plans.

I love you, bro. Rest in peace.

HOW DO I SAY GOODBYE?
By Ruby Jo Saltar

How do I say goodbye to a brother
that I love as much as you?
I still cannot believe you're gone,
I'm still hoping it isn't true.
Wishing this heartache was just a dream
from which I'd wake up and find
you're still here, in life, with us
or if not... somehow time we could rewind.
For I don't know how to do it.
how to say goodbye to a brother like you.
There's almost no one who's shared as much of my life
who knows me as well as you.
I often think upon the memories we shared
when we were very young.
You teased me, played with me and laughed with me
when our lives had just begun.
When we shared simple thoughts and simple dreams
and were lost in childhood's plans
dreaming up our next adventures
in the vivid ways only children can.
And as we grew up there were more special moments...

CHAPTER TWENTY-ONE

ONCE UPON A TIME

BY JONI SMITHHART

*It was almost like a reverse nightmare, like
when you wake up from a nightmare,
you're so relieved. I woke up into a
nightmare. -NED VIZINNI*

It started with a photo posted on Facebook. It was a Friday evening, October 3, 2014. I had been hanging out in my bedroom, enjoying the peace and quiet, after a long day at work. Bored, scrolling through my newsfeed, I found my eyes locked on what once had been a vehicle. Twisted metal, like a discarded soda can on the highway; the car was a horrific sight. I didn't need to read the attached caption to know that someone had lost her life. "Rankin County, MS : Two people dead and one person injured in a head-on crash along Highway 469," announced a news station out of Jackson, Mississippi. The location of the crash sent me into instant panic mode, because the majority of my family and friends live in Rankin County.

Dialing my mother's number, I tried to slow my speeding heart. Mom answered and reassured me that everyone was safe and sound, as far as she knew. That night, as I struggled to fall asleep, I couldn't shake a weird, uneasy feeling. Dozing off around 10 p.m., I didn't sleep long. Jolted awake by the ringing of my cellphone, my eyes had barely opened when I heard my mother's voice spilling words that I wasn't ready to hear. "Kimberly's dead; she was killed in that wreck tonight," she blurted. Oh, how I long to unhear those words, to be able to erase that night from history. How I yearn to go back in time, to be able to call my niece and beg her to just stay home and watch movies or something. Instead, it is just plain me here, writing on the eve of what would have been Kimberly's nineteenth birthday, with no superpowers and no time machines, stuck clinging to my memories and my anger.

I feel slightly guilty for being chosen to tell her story, for I am merely one of the many who are hurting and wanting her back. Kimberly meant the world to so many. In order to explain what was lost the day she was killed, I must somehow do the undoable, and find a way to describe how special she really was. Kimberly was her parents' first child. She was the first surviving grandchild on both sides of her family. She was the little girl who made my sister and me aunts. She was the moon and the stars to her younger sister Gabby. She was more than just a daughter to her mom; she was a partner. She was a confidante and comedian to whoever needed it, never failing to say something hilarious and inappropriate to make someone laugh, even as a young child. She was a loyal friend to many. If someone was messing with her family or friends, she was that person's worst enemy, halfway out the door to go beat them up before she even heard the ending of the story.

At the time of my writing, it has been four months, two weeks, and two days since Kimberly Copelan died at the hands of an impaired driver. As tempting as it is to fill these pages with my opinions about the evils of drunk driving, I cannot do that; I must do what I set out to do, to tell the story of Kimberly in a way that will allow her to be remembered for who she was, not just for what became of her. "She had the soul of a gypsy, the heart of a hippie, the spirit of a fairy..." -Unknown.

Kimberly was born on February 21, 1996. I will never forget standing outside the nursery window, gazing excitedly through the glass at this squirming little thing with bright eyes and perfect, pink skin. Her father, my older brother Jimmy, had hugged me proudly from behind. He and Kimberly's mother Stacy were very young, only seventeen and eighteen at the time of her birth. Renting a small apartment only a few miles from my mother's home, they took Kimberly home and set out to raise her. I remember visiting the day Stacy and Kimberly were discharged from the hospital. She was wearing a tiny pink dress with a bonnet, and I just sat there holding her, in awe. Only months before Kimberly's birth, my family had buried an infant who would have been Kimberly's cousin Jackelyn. With the pain of that loss still very raw, being able to hold Kimberly, to touch her warm little cheek, was an amazing blessing, bittersweet. My mom had to force me to put Kimberly down that day; I am certain I would have sat there holding her forever.

From the very beginning, Kimberly spent a great deal of time at our house, being cared for by my mother, or her Mamaw, as Kimberly grew to call her. To say that this child was spoiled would be an understatement. There wasn't a lot of money to go around at the time, but my mom would have moved mountains to give Kimberly what she wanted. All the toddler Kimberly had to do was rub her little hand down my mom's cheek and ask sweetly for something in a store, and it was hers. I remember my new favorite hobby becoming shopping for "my baby," just as soon as I was old enough to work and earn money. I will never forget the pride I felt as I pushed Kimberly through Walmart in a cart, letting her choose toys. I even put things on layaway that I couldn't afford to give her immediately.

Kimberly was a great source of joy for our family; the love we felt for her is really indescribable. A chubby kid with an overbite and crazy red hair that sprang straight up from her head, she kept everyone laughing. There was never a dull moment once she learned to speak; she was so funny. For her parents, the early years were very hard. Having rushed into getting married and starting a family, they realized quickly how challenging adult life could be. They relied on my mom's help to care for Kimberly while they both worked full-time jobs. Struggling to get along and make ends meet, they did the best they could. Hard work began to pay off in 1998, when they purchased their first home on Garland Avenue in Jackson, Mississippi. I remember seeing the pride on my brother's face the day they moved into the home. It was a small, two-bedroom fixer-upper, but it was theirs.

Kimberly had her father wrapped around her little finger. A difficult child, she often threw tantrums and was not easy to deal with, but he did well with her in his own laid-back, gentle way. Things were far from perfect, though. For not a day was this child's life easy. Her parents worked tirelessly to provide for her, but it never seemed to be quite enough; her clothes were always a little too snug. Being young and experiencing freedom for the first time, Jimmy and Stacy also wanted to have fun and party. There were always lots of people in and out of the home, and my mother worried constantly about Kimberly's well-being.

When Kimberly was six years old, the couple decided to move to California. Stacy had relatives there, and I believe they felt that the drastic change in scenery would improve their rocky marriage. I sit here now and reflect on that day, smiling at the memory of little Kimberly selling her Barbie Jeep that wouldn't fit into their truck. She told me that she wanted ten bucks, but refused to accept a ten dollar bill, demanding instead ten singles. The image of their little family, packed inside a blue Toyota 4Runner, along with all their possessions, is still vivid in my mind. That day was difficult for us all; it was heartbreaking for everyone to see them go.

Things in California were not as Jimmy and Stacy had hoped, so they did not stay gone long. Returning only months after moving, Kimberly was thrilled to be back near her family and friends in school. By this time her grades had begun to slide; she struggled to read, and that caused her to have difficulties with all subjects. She was held back in the first grade.

On December 21, 2003, Kimberly's sister Gabrielle, or "Gabby" was born. Gabby was a wish come true for Kimberly. From the time she could talk, she had asked for a sibling. I remember Kimberly waking up from a nap when she was little, and excitedly exclaiming "I had a dream I had a whole *bunch* of sisters," gesturing dramatically with her hands. Well, that dream never came true, but she was happy with just one live baby doll to play with. Kimberly was an amazing help with Gabby, taking her role as big sister very seriously, always there to make sure that she was properly taken care of.

When Gabby was only seven months old, the family moved once again, but this time their father was not included in the moving plans. There was no farewell gathering this time; Stacy boarded a bus with my two nieces and headed back to California without telling anyone. My brother was devastated. He had no idea where his daughters were. He began receiving phone calls from Kimberly, begging him to come get her. I remember him crying, saying that he would if he only knew where to go. Losing his children just broke Jimmy emotionally. He began to spiral rapidly downhill. He abused substances and threatened suicide.

Unbeknownst to anyone in our family, Stacy, Kimberly, and Gabby were staying in a homeless shelter in San Diego, California. It was there that Kimberly was sexually assaulted. She was nine years old. Kimberly wanted to be safely at home with her dad more than anything, and he would have done anything in the world to be with her.

I remember the day Kimberly told her dad where they were. He had me rush him home to stuff a few clothes into a backpack, and we sped away to the bus station, with only moments to spare before departure. I was driving so fast, but never fast enough, according to Jimmy. He was so excited that he could barely function as he boarded that bus, headed to see his daughters. In 2006, Stacy returned to Mississippi with the girls. Kimberly's performance in school deteriorated further; she just couldn't keep up as she once again transferred schools. Her parents reconciled briefly, but it wasn't long before history repeated itself. The couple went their separate ways, finally divorcing, and Jimmy ended up serving a year in the county jail. He moved into my home upon his release. He worked hard to pay off fines and stay off drugs. Stacy let him keep the girls at my house on weekends, and things were going well. Jimmy began to complain that he was feeling overwhelmed with stress and having some anger issues. He began going to a local clinic, was diagnosed with bipolar disorder, and prescribed medication. It was around this time when things once again started to fall apart for him. Moving out of my house, he switched jobs and began abusing his medication.

On May 29, 2009, Kimberly's world was turned upside down when her father passed away in his sleep at the age of twenty-nine. Outwardly, she seemed to cope well with his death, but inside she was dying. In entire life, all she had wanted was to be with her dad. Always a daddy's girl, she had dreamed of him coming through for her and getting a place for them to live together.

Seven months after losing her father, Kimberly attempted suicide, taking the exact combination of medications that had been found in her dad's postmortem toxicology report. She was treated briefly at a psychiatric facility in Hattiesburg, Mississippi. Shortly after being discharged, she dropped out of school after failing the seventh grade twice. She then stayed home, caring for her little sister while their mother attended college and worked.

In November 2011, Kimberly entered Camp Shelby's Youth Challenge Program. This was a very hard time for both her and her mother, made obvious from the endless letters Kimberly wrote begging her mother to pick her up. She was very angry about being forced to participate in this program. One can only assume that she was worried about her sister and wanted to be near her friends. Thankfully, her mother practiced tough love and forced Kimberly to stay and finish the program. The entire family was proud of her when she graduated, but most important, Kimberly was proud of herself. She was quoted as saying, "Thank you for making me do this, Mom."

Returning home, Kimberly again took over as full-time caregiver to Gabby while their mother worked and attended college. If anyone were to ask any member of Kimberly's family, or any one of her friends what they remember most about Kimberly, they would say they remember how amazingly dedicated she was to caring for her sister. Gabby was Kimberly's number one priority. Of course, being a teenager, Kimberly didn't always babysit without complaint, but she did it nonetheless, taking Gabby wherever she went. She even had Gabby's name tattooed proudly on her wrist.

In 2013, Kimberly moved into my home after being asked to leave by her mother's landlord. I was excited to have her near, eager to spend time with her. When I looked at her face I saw my brother, whom I missed terribly. I was amazed at how grown-up she had become. Trying to be the "cool aunt," I allowed her to have lots of friends over. I can close my eyes now and still hear their laughter radiating from my living room.

Kimberly lived with me only briefly. She had begun experimenting with drugs and alcohol, and ended up being arrested. Doing what she felt was best, her mother had her placed into a long-term treatment center.

While there, Kimberly progressed, finally beginning to talk about the loss of her father. For the first time since losing him, she began to make plans, such as attending college. She got her first job in September 2014, at a café called Frog Heads. Her mother proudly tells the story about how Kimberly got hired there. While she was being interviewed, the manager asked why he should hire her. "Because you need me," she asserted with a smile. The manager said it was the best response he had ever heard. That statement says a lot about Kimberly's personality. I feel that she had more character from the day she was born than the rest of the world combined. She was strong-willed, even as a baby, and she had no problem going after what she wanted.

Although Kimberly momentarily strayed down the wrong path, in the end she had begun to find her way. The day she died, she received her very first paycheck. Impressing her mother, she eagerly paid her fines. With the money that was left, she purchased matching silver "Big Sister" and "Little Sister" bracelets for herself and Gabby. She then picked up her boyfriend, Josh, in Bay Saint Louis, Mississippi, planning to enjoy an evening at the state fair in Jackson. Kimberly had been really excited about this trip to the fair; she had not been able to go for several years prior to that. Planning to pick up Kimberly's best friend, Casidi, the couple were traveling on Highway 469 in Pearl. Receiving news that Casidi had found another ride, they turned around and headed to Jackson. I can imagine what the two were doing, undoubtedly listening to music and laughing as they made the trip. If that were the case, their laughter was cut short when the forty-year-old driver veered into their lane, hitting them head-on as they turned a curve. It was said that they never knew what hit them. I sit here and imagine the horror that transpired inside that vehicle. I worry that they suffered, because we were never told whether or not they died instantly.

Kimberly's mother Stacy was an EMT. She was called into the conference room at work and informed by a stranger that her daughter was dead. She broke down, lashing out at everyone there, insisting that it wasn't true, that her daughter was going to the fair. She told me later that going home and telling Gabby that her sister was dead was the hardest thing she had ever done, and that "As a mother, I am not supposed to hurt my child. But here I was breaking her heart."

Stacy then called my sister Jessica, Kimberly's favorite aunt, to break the news to her. When I arrived at her home about twelve hours later, Jessica was still in a heap on the floor, sobbing uncontrollably. I will never forget her voice just chanting, "She's dead, Joni; she's dead; she's dead." Over the years, Jessica and Kimberly had become extremely close, having more than just an aunt-niece relationship, but also a deep friendship. Over the next few days, everyone had to concentrate on holding themselves together for Jessica, because she was in pieces. Trying to help, I decided to take my youngest niece, Jessica's daughter Jordan, and my children to the fair, to get them out of the house and keep them occupied, because I knew they too were hurting. As soon as we arrived, I knew I had made a huge mistake. Standing there watching as carefree teenagers stood in line to board rides that Kimberly never got to ride, I struggled to keep my lip from trembling. I wanted so badly to run up to each young girl and just beg all of them to be careful driving home. I couldn't stop worrying about my sister, and bought her a T-shirt with Kimberly's name airbrushed on it.

When I arrived home to give her that shirt, Jessica was crying again, but this time repeating different words. "He was drunk, Joni; he was drunk."

Kimberly's wake was held the following day. She had an open casket. I remember walking into the room and being overwhelmed by the sounds of people talking. Their voices were all running together, sounding to me like the buzzing of bees. I saw people mingling in small groups and couldn't understand their dry eyes. As I approached Kimberly for the first time, the tears that I had been holding in for days exploded onto my face. I am not sure why I had expected to see my niece lying there, but that was not at all the case. It was like standing over a stranger. The entire shape of her face looked different, swollen to the point of being unrecognizable. Her always rosy cheeks were dull. Her hair was styled nothing like the way she had always worn it. She was dressed very modestly and very un-Kimberly like, attired in a long-sleeved shirt, covered with a cotton jacket type thing. Our beautiful, glowing Kimberly looked like a forty-year-old woman.

My sister came to stand beside me, rubbing Kimberly's broken cheek, the same cheek that I had gently rubbed that day she had left the hospital, so long ago. I remember looking back to see my nine-year-old son Triston standing behind me, crying. I had seen him cry many times, but never like that. On the wall, hanging up high for all to see, there was a video playing, showing the endless number of "selfies" that Kimberly had taken, accompanied by beautiful music. As I turned to watch, it felt as though I had sunk onto the floor. The chubby kid with the messy hair had grown into a drop-dead gorgeous young woman while I hadn't been paying attention. That night we were given red ribbons to pin to our shirts. As we wrestled ourselves away from Kimberly's broken body at the conclusion of her wake, we felt hatred for the man who stole her from us.

The funeral was held the following morning. Re-pinning our red ribbons, we gathered around Kimberly's body to pray and say our goodbyes. As I stood there, I said my own personal prayer, silently praying that Kimberly was with her daddy, where she had always wanted to be.

Watching my mom say goodbye to her oldest granddaughter was unbearable. She leaned down, shaking as she kissed her and said "I love you." When it came my turn, all I could do was sob, as my sister stood and held me. I couldn't walk away, because I knew that once I did, I would never see Kimberly again. I squeezed her arm, cried, and told her that I loved her.

I get very emotional, even now, when I reflect back on her funeral. I wish so badly that it would have been different. The minister who officiated had not known Kimberly. I kept waiting for some words of comfort, but all he had to offer was the verse "Like water spilled on the ground, which cannot be recovered, so we must die," which he repeated several times. It is true, yes, death is inevitable; but two teenagers with their entire lives ahead of them did not have to die like they did. Several others spoke, but nobody seemed to give the eulogy that Kimberly deserved. My sister Jessica posted the following message on Kimberly's wall after her funeral:

"Kimberly, there are so many things that I regret now that you're gone. So many things I miss. I always told you that I loved you, but I'm not sure if you understood the extent of that love. I don't know if you ever understood how much I respected you as a person. You were beautiful and terrifyingly fearless. And even though that lack of fear made me want to shake you sometimes, I had a deep respect for it. I also regret not speaking at your funeral. You weren't simply a hammer. You were a beautifully undeniable force of nature. You gave your all to your relationships, even when someone didn't deserve it. You understood loyalty and rarely second-guessed your decisions. And even though your life was rarely easy and would have broken many people long ago, you never gave up. You believed in hope and never let your head down. And you were also compassionate and talented enough to give others hope too. I miss you so much, and would happily trade the rest of my days, just to bring you back for one more day. You would be able to accomplish so much in just that one day. Your personality was like a rainbow, and no one can ever even come close to being as special as you were."

Jessica had known Kimberly more than anyone else in the world, but she had not been strong enough to say those beautiful words at her funeral.

Recently my sister and I visited Kimberly's gravesite, which doesn't have a headstone yet. She was laid to rest right beside her father. As we stood there, I remembered an occasion, not too long ago, when Kimberly had stood beside us in that same spot, missing her daddy, as we told her stories about him to make her laugh. The fact that both father and daughter are now gone is just impossible to fathom. The finality of it is so painfully frustrating.

During the first few months preceding Kimberly's death, I felt numb with anger. It took six weeks for the impaired driver to be arrested; six weeks for Kimberly's family to envision him home, safe and sound, enjoying precious time with his family. I had nearly gone crazy, praying for an arrest. When that day finally came, I was shocked at the emptiness I felt. There was still nothing to celebrate; she was still dead. We are currently awaiting the day when he will go before the grand jury, and just praying that justice is served, that the system doesn't let Kimberly down as everyone else in her short life did. While speaking to my oldest brother, Jamie, recently, he reflected on Kimberly and her father by saying the following: "When I looked at Kimberly my heart broke, because I saw Jimmy in every way and I miss him so dearly. My life will never be the same in so many ways, but I know neither of them would want us to stay sad." He, like so many in our family, are normally hesitant to speak about what happened, because it's simply too painful. Both Jamie and I are faced with not only our grief, but the grief of our children. Kimberly was always so good to her little cousins, and they are lost without her.

As for little Gabby, who just turned eleven, she is hanging in there, trying to adjust to her new life as an only child. You can see the pain in her eyes, though, even as she smiles. I suppose that her mother has been trying to keep her busy; they have taken a couple of trips in the last few months. "It's just so sad, because we started doing all this fun stuff *after* she died, so she didn't get to do it with us," she told me the other night. Kimberly was buried wearing her "Big Sister" bracelet, and I have no doubt that Gabby will cherish the matching bracelet until the day she too goes home to be with their dad.

JONI SMITHHART
COLUMBIA, MISSISSIPPI

MISTAKES WE MAKE
Written in memory of Brandon Thomas
Performed by Alex Xses Meulenbeld
https://youtu.be/_WHw-FKP9qo

Mistakes we make, ya, ya, ya
Every day we wake alive we are bound to make mistakes
It's up to us the choice we are willing to make,
I've has misfortune head my way
I've had people die who were too young to be taken
And it ain't fair cause the good die young
The bad die old, the rest of us gradually become cold
My heart weeps for the lost ones
And beats for the parents who lost their daughters and sons
They saying life ain't just, becomes more true,
That death takes one of our youth
(damn) it gets dark as we stop trying
Can't hear over the sounds of the wounded crying
Life will only get harsher as we lose faith
It's all a test it kills to test our mind state
We walk alone through the dark dungeon
Wanderin' aimlessly, looking for a better something
Becoming more weak when our loved ones fall
It's hurting so deep pushing our back against a wall
But every time we lose someone, we gain knowledge,
Become stronger, can't break, more solid, you better not hop in that truck
You've had too much, you're putting your whole life in a rut
So What, as the truck door slams shut with a bang
Shifts into gear, he's ready, had enough of these lames
Pulls out the drive and he almost hits a car
Whew close, his friends shouting for him to stop
But he ain't hear them, the radio is on full blast
It's cold outside, the heats blowing turned to the max
Floors the gas, the snow leaves proof of his tracks
He's gone too far so now he ain't never going back, 122 on highway 22
It's December 6th, of two thousand one two,
He swerves wide and sideswipes a few
One turns and rolls the other had no time to move,
Shoulda listened he got a whole town blue
As the Chevy slams headfirst into Brandon's Subaru
My heart goes out to his family and friends
It's been a year and it still hurts to no end
His life was a shooting star among the heavens

365

And though it was short, he still blessed us all with his presence
It wasn't fair but we have to hold on
He wouldn't want us to hurt and I'm sorry for his mom
Just remember that your son was a knight
His armor was strong and you can see him every night,
Each star celebrates Brandon's life
And though it is dark the stars will forever bring light
Remember his smile, remember his game, remember his style and we will
never forget his face
Remember his name, remember his cars, remember his flame,
forever remembered among the stars
Our dead are never to us, until we have forgotten them
Remember that and he will always live, rest in peace

KIMBERLY COPELAN

CHAPTER TWENTY-TWO

THE GREATEST GIFT

BRANDON'S STORY

BY KIM THOMAS

*If tears could build a stairway and memories
a lane, I would walk right up to Heaven and
bring you home again. - AUTHOR UNKNOWN*

On October 24, 1992, in Lethbridge, Alberta I was given the first of the two most amazing gifts anyone could ever receive. A beautiful daughter was born to my husband and me, and we named her Kayla, the first child in our family. For me, everything that I had been before changed, and I became someone new, someone amazing: a mother. The person I used to be was no longer anywhere to be found. I can remember taking Kayla to the park and watching her play in the sand. Sitting there on that park bench, I thought to myself how nice it would be if she had a sibling, a friend, someone who would always be by her side and would always have her back. Soon my wish was granted. I was given the second most amazing gift anyone could ever imagine. A tiny son was born to us on October 8, 1995, in Fort Macleod, Alberta. Our second child was five weeks early and entered this world with such a small cry. Brandon Stanley Walter Thomas; we laughed because his name was longer than he was. I knew Brandon would be our last child, as I suffered terribly during both of my pregnancies. I was truly blessed and wished for nothing more in this whole world. A daughter, Kayla, who started our family, and a son, Brandon, who completed it.

Kayla adored her younger brother, and Brandon thought Kayla was the most beautiful girl in the world. As the years passed and he grew into a teenager with maturity beyond his years, this never changed for either of them. I can remember watching out the back door of our home and seeing Kayla patiently teaching Brandon how to pedal his tricycle. I remember that pure love and profound pride that comes from total bliss as I watched our family learn to love and laugh together.

As the years passed, Brandon grew into a young man with maturity beyond his years. He loved and protected his older sister, still looking at her as the most beautiful girl in the world. Even though she was younger, she would call Brandon to fix anything from her broken heart to her truck, and he always could.

They had the same circle of friends and were always together. Kayla proudly asked Brandon if he would walk her down the aisle when the time came, if she ever found someone she decided to marry, and he proudly accepted. Kayla always said she knew Brandon was the one guy who would never leave her. Today, she says he didn't leave her; he was taken from her. Kayla had limitless patience and love for Brandon, even though he was very sick all the time. Countless times a week we went to the doctor, because Brandon was sick; crying, stomach pains, lethargic and weak. No one could ever tell us what was wrong, yet his spirit was so resilient that his infectious smile soon reappeared once the pain had passed. Finally, after years of sickness and suffering, Brandon was diagnosed with celiac disease at age ten.

I was so grateful to know finally what was causing him to suffer so much. We promptly changed his eating habits, and I saw a dramatic change in his physical appearance. He had color in his face; he was not stricken by such terrible stomach pains, but sadly the doctors said his learning disability was caused by the non-diagnosis for this disease. He struggled in school right from his first day of kindergarten, and finally we had an explanation. Brandon's effort and good nature in school encouraged his many teachers and mentors to help him with his education challenges, and he thrived with their help, although never overcoming his struggles in school. We, as a family, focused on the many amazing things he could do! I know he felt our pride in everything he could do and, in turn, was so secure in his life, where he was going, and himself.

Things started to change in the house, but never the love between Kayla and Brandon, or either parent and the children. But my husband and I were growing apart. We were changing, and although we never fought, I think we both knew that it was time to separate and go our different ways. With as much grace as we could, we separated when Brandon was six years old. For a while the children and I lived in the same town, but I was trying to work three part-time jobs and raise the children, I was getting tired and filled with sorrow for all the precious moments I was missing in the children's young lives. Eventually the children and I moved to Whitecourt, in northern Alberta, where I worked full-time during the day as a school/church secretary. Our life settled in, and we became, in a different way, a complete family again. The children wanted to stay close to their father, and we encouraged that, knowing how vital it was for Kayla and Brandon to spend time with both of us. How they loved those visits to their dad's house. They visited as often as his job allowed and he was able to see them.

Our stay in Whitecourt was short. After a year, the school was looking at closing, and I knew that the church would not be able to employ me full-time. I began preparing to move our family again. In 2003, we moved to Cochrane, Alberta, where we still make our home today. The move was one of the best decisions I had ever made for my family. I opened a day-home and was able to work from home. This turned out to be the perfect situation for our family. I was home when my children left for school and when they returned from school. There were so many friends for them to play with at home, but there was never anyone who took the place of one another. Brandon grew up with an ever-changing roster of day-home kids, all of whom he befriended regardless of their temperament or age. He could be found on the floor, even when older, playing cars with the boys or dolls with the girls. He was so kind and patient, never frustrated or angry, never raising his voice. He engaged and played with them in his typical caring and protective way. There was also a soft spot in Brandon's heart for the many family pets; he treated all with a loving hand. Even as he got older, Brandon wasn't one to worry about what others thought of him; he stayed true to himself. In fifth grade, he went through a lengthy pink phase. Just at the age when others are trying to fit in and be like everyone else, he wanted to be himself. Brandon had the most amazing long curly hair and long thick eyelashes. He never wanted his hair cut, and I never pushed him to do it.

We had a neighbor who was a police officer, as well as a backyard mechanic. Brandon was so curious about what was going on in the neighbor's garage, all the noise, tools and vehicles. I smile now, thinking of how he would ride his bike around on the sidewalk, stopping on the sidewalk with his bike to talk to our neighbor, Mike, until finally his bike would be in the garage and so would Brandon. He would race home and tell me about all the new things he had learned, like the names of tools and how to use them. I wondered then if Brandon's path in life was being set out for him. He also loved to BMX, anything with wheels. Twice a week I put his BMX bike in the back of my car with all his gear, and we would head to the track. He won some and lost some, but Brandon always tried his best, and he was never discouraged or disappointed in himself, and neither was I.

He never lost his love for Mike and the mechanics that was now his passion and would be his chosen career. He had found something he understood, something he loved. At thirteen, Brandon secured his first job at a small engine repair shop. He was determined to gain some experience and earn some money; he already wanted to buy his first vehicle. That same year, he was able to purchase a Toyota 4x4. An addiction had been created. A year later Brandon could take the transmission out of a vehicle, fix it, and replace it. He continued to work full-time in the summer and after school and weekends during the school year. When he was fourteen, he bought his second vehicle, a BMW. Now he had his learner's license and could drive. Once in high school, Brandon became involved in the Registered Apprenticeship Program. Mike gave him the gift of his dream, to graduate from SAIT and open his performance shop called Cross Piston Performance. He always knew what he wanted to be, and worked harder than anyone I knew to learn as much as he could about cars.

Brandon was always the first one to welcome a new student, or walk with anyone being bullied to their class to ensure their safety. To him, all people were created equal, and if someone was a good friend to Brandon he was a loyal friend forever and would always put those friends above himself. He had many friends and he kept them all, of all ages and all groups within our town. He made friends easy with his infectious smile, his kind, goofy and generous heart, and the true genuine caring that he felt for everyone. I remember the countless times Brandon came creeping up the stairs late at night and ask if he could go, because a friend needed him. He was always there for everyone. He had a way of making you just feel good, and important. Brandon was true to his friends and to himself, even if it wasn't always the easiest path.

After he was killed, one of his friends told me that when they thought of Brandon, they thought of unity and his ability to bring anyone and all groups together. Another friend told me he was one of the greats. I sobbed and said, "What did Brandon do that was so great? Die?" and they said, "No, Kim, it was the way he lived." This has stayed with me forever and let me know that Brandon truly was and is one of the most amazing young men ever. Every single day I learn things that make me more proud of him.

Brandon studied his core school courses in the morning and then in the afternoon traveled to a job in the field of mechanics where he worked for wages and school credits. His boss and the school monitored his success together. Brandon had a refreshing work ethic, and his evaluations reported on his strong abilities, complete dependability, and of course also his being fun to work with. His boss and I, knowing of Brandon's struggles in school, offered him a full-time position without the education if he ever decided he wanted to quit school and work full-time. The reply we received was, "No, thank you. I want to graduate, go to SAIT and become a trained mechanic." Again, my heart was filled with pride for the amazing young man he was becoming.

He traded his BMW for a Jeep when he was fifteen. I can still remember the uncountable times I would help him take off the roof and doors, see that amazing crooked smile with his hair flying in the wind driving off on another amazing adventure. Brandon could make anything an adventure. At the young age of sixteen, in September 2012, he purchased his dream car, s Subaru Impreza WRX STI, a beautiful blue sports car that Brandon had dreamed about since he was nine years old. The day I called him and told him he could buy the car he said to me, "Mom, I just fell on the floor." He was so happy. He soon mastered superb handling of his car and was drifting and driving with a cautious confidence. When time allowed, he was off with friends hitting the trails, off-roading at the racetrack, in Mike's garage, or camping and enjoying his youth with all the successes and struggles that come with being young.

Brandon's body finally grew to match the size of his heart, and people gravitated toward him. He had hundreds of friends of all ages, some younger, some much older. He had many girlfriends, each of whom say he treated them like princesses. Brandon stayed close to each and every friend and girlfriend over the years. I watched my little boy turn into an amazing young man. The pride I felt daily for him never wavered. I gave Brandon the tools he needed; he decided how to use them and who he wanted to become.

December 6, 2012, started out at as a normal day at our house. We were feeling happy, another day was starting, the holidays were getting closer, and this would allow me to spend more time with my children. The kids would both get some time off from school and work, and all our gifts were almost bought, the tree was up, and we were ready for the holidays with our family. That Thursday morning, I woke Brandon for school, as I did every morning. I called down and told him it was time to get up and shower. I waited a few minutes, listened for any movement from his room, and smiled. I knew I would be heading down the stairs to wake him up. That was always a special time of the morning for me, as I could watch him sleep and witness his peace. I rumpled his hair, told him it was time to wake up, and smiled at the groan and moan that came from him. I turned and left his room. Shortly after that he came stumbling up the stairs, heading for the shower. I knew he would shower until all the hot water was gone, as he did every morning. It never bothered Kayla or me; we would just plan around Brandon's shower. I breathed deeply, smelling his Axe shower gel. Soon the hot water was gone; I watched Brandon with a towel wrapped around him head back down the stairs to his room, back to bed for the precious twenty more minutes of sleep that he always needed.

I put on my boots and went out to the garage to start his car and back it out of the garage so it would be warm when he woke up. It was the only time he let me drive his car. Soon after that, I called down to tell him it was time to leave if he wanted to stop at Tim Horton's for his coffee before school without being late. I knew he would be late, though; he was every morning, and his teachers good-naturedly knew it as well. He came up the stairs, I gave him his lunch, kissed his warm cheek, told him I loved him and to have a good day. He opened the door after hugging me, stopped, then looked back at me and gently said before he closed the door, "I love you too, Mom." I watched as he backed his car out of the driveway and waved.

At 11:30, after Brandon finished his classes for the day, he called to tell me he had a good morning and was heading into work in Calgary, an hour commute one way. We talked for a few minutes and then he hung up. As the day went on, I kept looking at the clock, knowing he would call between 5 and 5:30 p.m. after he got off work to let me know he was on his way home. As 5 p.m. came and went, I wasn't too worried. At 5:10 p.m., the phone rang, and I was relieved to see it was Brandon. He was calling to say he had a great afternoon at work and was excited about his work Christmas party the next night. There was no snow, and the roads were good. We talked for a few minutes and I told him the same thing I did every night when he called. I said, "I love you, Brandon. Drive safe." He said the same thing he did every night, "I love you too, Mom. I always drive safe."

My daughter came home and had a quick supper as she was off to archery with her boyfriend. I looked at the clock, and it was 6:30. Brandon still wasn't home, I hadn't heard from him. This wasn't like him. He always called, because he knew how much I worried. I thought traffic might have been bad, but I still wasn't too worried.

At 6:55 p.m., I started to worry, I called Brandon a few times, never getting an answer. I called his friend, who said he was waiting to hear from Brandon too, but hadn't yet. They had plans to meet after Brandon had supper. I called our neighbor, Mike, the officer, and asked if he was working or had heard of any fender benders, because Brandon wasn't home yet. He told me he wasn't working, but not to worry, Brandon probably just got sidetracked. If anything were wrong the police would be at my door. I knew it wasn't like Brandon to get sidetracked. I called and called what felt like thousands of times, but still no answer. Real panic set in; my heart was pumping and I couldn't catch my breath.

I kept walking around the house, thinking I should do something, go somewhere, and then I would take a deep breath, tell myself to stop being silly, that nothing had happened. Brandon was safe, what could happen? At 7:50 p.m. there was a knock on the door. I raced down the stairs, thinking someone had some news or would know where Brandon was. It was two police officers. I didn't look at them; I looked beyond them for Brandon, but he wasn't there. I then looked up and saw our neighbor running over. I saw the tears in the officers' eyes. I started screaming, yelling, "Where is Brandon? Take me to Brandon!" Mike talked to the police officers, as he knew them. I remember hearing him ask, "It's bad, isn't it?"

The officer answered, "Yes, Brandon is dead."

Everything stopped; everything just stopped. A haze so deep, so heavy, covered my world with a disbelief so intense, a pain so raw, a gaping hole opened up and continued to grow.

I heard Mike say, "The driver was drunk, wasn't he?"

They replied, "Yes."

Mike fell to his knees sobbing as I stood there quietly, and then it hit. I was yelling, crying, running around the house screaming, "This isn't real! This isn't real, it's a dream! This can't be real. Brandon is coming home, he's coming home. Not my boy, Brandon is not dead, he's coming home. Go away, go away! Brandon is coming home!" I called Brandon's dad, Kayla, Brandon's grandparents, and his Uncle Jim, yelling, "Brandon's dead, Brandon's dead!" I can vividly remember Kayla running in the house screaming, "No, not Brandon, not my brother, I still need him here; not Brandon." Some of Brandon's friends came to the house wondering where he was because they didn't know, only to leave in disbelief and tears.

Parts of the night are still so vivid and painful that it seems like it was yesterday. There are still some parts I don't remember. I can remember vividly that they wouldn't let us see Brandon. They wouldn't let us go to the morgue. I thought it was a mistake, that it couldn't be Brandon, but then the officer handed me my son's wallet. Still I thought, No, no, this isn't real, Brandon's coming home. I stayed awake, not just for that night but for weeks, waiting for Brandon to come home. Three years and two months later, I still wait.

The next day we went to the morgue to see Brandon. They cautioned us; we could touch his face and kiss his face but couldn't hug him or move him in any way because his body was so broken. Finally we were allowed to see him. Cold, the room was so cold. I remember walking up to the glass, feeling the cold. I remember seeing the sheet lying over Brandon, and saying, "Please turn up the heat, Brandon must be so cold." I entered the room and looked at my baby, my boy, the reason my heart kept beating and the joy in my life. My son. Oh, God, my son, his eyes open, blank, void, yet just a day before twinkling and filled with laughter. I remember touching his face, as I memorized it even though the beautiful face I knew was now full of glass, cuts, scars and huge gashes all over.

I touched his face; there was no warmth there. I cried, I sobbed, I talked with Brandon, begged him to wake up and told him how beautiful he was. How beautiful he will always be, in life and death. I touched his chest; I put my head on his forehead, and swore I could feel his chest moving, taking a breath. The tears streamed down my face as my heart shattered and my knees buckled to see my child lying there, so still, so hurt, so empty of everything that made him who he was. So empty of the *life* he brought to everyone around him.

They made me leave him there, alone and cold. I would have stayed there with Brandon forever, never leaving his side until I could be reunited with him. I know that Kayla and my dad were with me, and there were many people there to see Brandon, but even now I don't remember who. I thought to myself, why do I have to leave? I don't want to leave. I want to stay here until Brandon wakes up.

The next place I remember being is the funeral home. I was in a fog, a haze, and I didn't know where we were. I can remember thinking, why are we doing this? I don't think I can do anymore.

Why are we here? The funeral director asked us a lot of questions: "Do you want Brandon to be buried or cremated?" Neither, we want him to come home, I thought. "What kind of verses would you like in his funeral cards?" "He's coming home; we don't need any." I replied. "Please come and pick an urn you would like." So many decisions and questions. Wait; stop. If we don't do this, if everyone leaves me alone, Brandon will come home. Can't you all see that if you keep talking like this, Brandon won't come home? Go away, everyone, so Brandon can come home to me, my mind screamed. We decided to cremate Brandon; it was the only way I could bring him home in some way. I had to pick out clothes for him. They wouldn't allow us an open viewing, as his body was too broken.

The trip back to our house was short, but endless; when we arrived there were millions of flowers and cards, and many people. "Where is Brandon, why isn't he here? When is he coming home? Where is he?"

It was two days before I got to see Brandon again. Those days were filled with hope that this was just a dream. They were also filled with horror; that this was a reality. I was in disbelief that this had happened, and the grief was so intense that it knocked me to my knees. Every single breath hurt until the pain was so bad I knew I couldn't endure the next one, but it kept coming and coming, and there was nothing I could do about it. Kayla, myself, my parents, and his special lady were the only people allowed to see Brandon two days later before they took him away again.

The haze and fog remained. It was, at least, warm, and Brandon was dressed. He wouldn't be cold anymore. I walked up to him lying in his casket, and looked at my beautiful baby. His eyes were closed, but the makeup was thick to cover the scars and cuts. His lips were sewn shut with black thread. My mind screamed in pain to see my son this way. His fingers were glued to the back of his hands, so they rested on his chest. The tears poured from my eyes, the wound in my heart flowed with the blood of a mother's love, and I whispered, "Stop, please just stop. Everyone go away, leave me alone." I wept; I sobbed quietly at some moments and screamed at others, as I sat with Brandon. I stayed for as long as they let me. The bright sun of the day turned into the blackness of the night; I stayed because I knew that when I left I would never see him again. I couldn't walk away, I could never leave my son, and I could never let him leave me. I said, "Please, please, let me come back tomorrow morning to say good morning to Brandon." They refused, saying Brandon would be cremated in the morning. I wondered how anyone expected me to walk away, knowing I would *never* see my child again. I thought if I don't, this won't be real.

I am ashamed to say I left; I left Brandon there alone again, as he was when he was killed, to die and suffer alone. I felt like a failure at every single part of being a parent. I wasn't there to save him, to trade places with him, to die for him; I wasn't there when he was suffering for that final hour he was trapped in his car, alive, breathing, blinking, alone. I made Brandon face it alone. I can never forgive myself for not being there for him when he needed me the most. I failed my son in every possible way.

I remember my brother, Jim, agreeing to do the eulogy for Brandon. I remember him staying up late at night to make it perfect. The church was full; I don't remember actually seeing anyone, or being aware of my surroundings. I do remember driving by the church and thinking how big it was, though. I chose to wear Brandon's suit. Somehow I thought it might be like he was wrapping his arms around me. It wasn't. The tears fell endlessly. I remember the songs being sung by Brandon's friends and the courage Kayla had to speak about her brother, but more important, *to* him. I remember my brother speaking and his voice so filled with love and sorrow. I remember Brandon's girlfriend talking about him and how much she was going to miss him, how well he had treated her, and how much she loved him. I remember a few small smiles when she said God probably needed Brandon in heaven to teach him how to drive. In a daze, I watched the slide show of

Brandon on the monitor in a daze and a fog. I heard the pastor talk. I cried and stared at the urn that held my son's body, and I fell to pieces inside. There were hours of hugs and tears and people giving us their condolences. There was a beautiful balloon release, then going home to an empty, void house, a home without Brandon. My parents and brother were constant companions to Kayla and me during this time.

A roadside memorial was erected shortly after Brandon was killed, a large white cross where Brandon was hit by the drunk driver. I visited once a week on Thursdays, as this is the day of the week he was killed. Many people often stopped; I could tell that from all the precious memories and gifts that started adorning Brandon's roadside memorial, all with remembrance of a young life taken too soon. There were so many expressions of love from those who loved him; an Xbox controller Brandon used at his friend's house, a key to another friend's car, stuffed animals, dream-catchers, stones and rocks of every color, plaques, hot wheel cars, a cigar in the same brand that Brandon use to smoke, necklaces with crosses, flowers, so many beautiful things to let Brandon know he was loved and missed.

My parents decided to sell their home and moved in with Kayla and me. I could not cope, could not function. I started lying in Brandon's bed, wrapped in his blankets, with his smell surrounding me, clutching his urn and a picture of him I always carry with me. Sometimes I didn't get out of bed for days; I just lay there crying. Sometimes I didn't lie in bed for days. I didn't ever sleep; I was consumed by horrific nightmares in which Brandon was trapped and suffering, in intense pain and screaming for me. These nightmares often consisted of the terror and pain I imagine Brandon must have experienced. These nightmares still consume me. When I wake I can't even tell myself it was just a dream, because it wasn't, it is a reality. I couldn't eat, food would choke me, and I started losing weight. I went weekly to the doctor who monitored my weight and gave me so many different pills to cope through the day. Nothing helped, no matter what I did or anyone else did, Brandon still didn't come home. I wanted to die; I begged and pleaded with God, Brandon, and everyone to please just let me die. I wanted to be with Brandon.

Just a few weeks after the crash it was Christmas. I saw Brandon's unwrapped gifts sitting in the corner, never to be used. I watched as my family opened the gifts Brandon had bought for them. No shared laughter, no thank-yous, no kisses and warm hugs for gifts appreciated and love. Only a river of tears and wracking sobs every time we acknowledged that Brandon was not there to share in this with us and the knowledge that he should have been. The knowledge that the selfish actions of one man took everything from Brandon and us, forever.

Kayla and I started fighting; we yelled and screamed at each other, not understanding each other's grief and having no room outside our own grief to try to understand. She began to drink, and I began to die. She clung to her friends, Brandon's friends, and I clung to death. She was terrified every time she left the house that when she returned, I would be dead. I could not reassure her that would not happen, because I didn't know if I would die, and I truly wanted to. She spent as much time away from the house as she could. For various reasons, she was scared to watch me die, and scared of the reality of an empty house that Brandon would never live in again.

Ryan, the twenty-two-year-old driver, had spent the day drinking and snowmobiling on the trails. Upon leaving the trails, he went to Cochrane to continue drinking at a friend's house. Sometime around 5:30 p.m. he decided to return home to Calgary. The highway Brandon was traveling is extremely busy at that time of night, as many people commute from Calgary to Cochrane after work. In his drunkenness, the driver attempted to pass two semi-trucks going up a hill on a solid line. The drunk driver was heading north in the southbound lane. The first vehicle heading south was able to see the oncoming drunk driver in his lane and swerved into the ditch to avoid contact. The second vehicle in line had less time to react and ended up being sideswiped and rolled into the ditch. The third vehicle in line was Brandon, who had no time to react (from reports) and was hit head on.

Later I would view the results from the black box and find that the drunk driver never once attempted to return to his lane after he had safely passed the semis and never once attempted to touch the brake pedal on his truck. In fact, the results showed one hundred percent acceleration before impact with Brandon. There were many witnesses there to see the crash. The drunk driver was detained by witnesses, partly due to his vehicle being unmovable. Brandon was alive, breathing and blinking when help got there. A wonderful man got into the passenger side of Brandon's mangled car and held him, talked to him and hugged him until he felt Brandon take his last breath. They were unable to free him from the wreckage before he passed away; he couldn't hold on any longer. Later we learned that the drunk driver was released by a justice of the peace over the phone the night he killed Brandon. He went home and Brandon went to the morgue.

The court process and all those involved were almost as unbelievable as the death of Brandon itself. We attended the first court date on December 16, 2012, not having any idea what this part of the journey would look like. The drunk driver did not have to attend, and he didn't. There was no plea entered, and we were left wondering what was next. The prosecutor briefly spoke to us but gave very little information, knowledge or insight as to what would happen. We were left stunned to realize that we were mere observers, that nowhere in the legal system would Brandon or our family be represented.

A few weeks later I was approached by a local newspaper to do an interview. In my interview, I stated that no one would talk to me, not the police and not the prosecutor. The day that paper came out and the story was released, I got a call from the prosecutor who asked to meet with Kayla and me. We attended along with my dad and someone from Victim Services. He went up one side of me and down the other side for that statement, because it made him look bad; he was very angry with me. I was devastated with grief and disbelief, but still had some hope in the justice system, because hope was so very hard to find and I needed something to hold onto. I met with him only two other times before the preliminary hearing in January 2014, thirteen months to the day from when Brandon was killed. Both meetings were granted after much persistence on my part, the first time only because I spoke with the prosecutor's superior after my phone calls were not returned. I knew at this point that there would be no justice with this prosecutor. I felt certain that he would not fight for an innocent young boy or his life.

He informed me that there were problems with the arrest, that there was not enough evidence at the scene to warrant an arrest. However, later I talked to the police about this statement and saw the evidence. The police assured me there was enough evidence, enough witnesses and enough reason to detain him and charge him with impaired driving causing death. The police were even baffled as to why the prosecutor would say what he did.

After the sentencing, when the driver appealed the sentence, even the three appeal judges saw no reason why this should not have gone to trial and resulted in a term of anywhere from five to eight years, as asked for by the prosecutor and granted by the court. In my opinion, and the opinion of many, this prosecutor didn't even try to seek justice or a fit sentence.

I begged and pleaded, I asked him not to take a plea bargain; to at least fight, at least try. I would not blame him if he lost, but I wanted him to at least try. He told me he would likely seek a two-year sentence. Again shock and disbelief hit me. When I asked why he wouldn't suggest a four-year sentence, he told me he would be laughed out of the courtroom for asking for that long a sentence. I looked at him, my eyes grew cold with hatred, and I stated that there was nothing funny about the death of my son. I spoke with the regional chief prosecutor's office in Calgary and Edmonton and got no further answers; they all stuck together, right or wrong. I spoke with the Alberta Justice Minister, who, believe it or not, had and has no political power over anything that goes on in the courtroom. I shouted from the rooftops, but not loudly enough, that this was wrong, that again our family and Brandon were being wronged in so many ways.

Sometime in October 2013, before the preliminary hearing scheduled for January 2014, I wanted and needed to speak with the prosecutor to know where things stood and what to expect. Time after time I called during October and November, but there was no answer, no calls ever returned. Finally, in December, I called Victim Services to request a new prosecutor. I received a call promptly from the prosecutor's office, and a meeting was set up. In this meeting, he was very rude and not willing to help in any way. He told me I was right; the driver would likely receive a two-year deal. However, at that point there was no talk of that between lawyers.

On January 6, 2014, we and many supporters attended court. I saw the driver for the first time, the man who killed my son, the man who took everything from Brandon, from Kayla and myself. The intense, fierce hatred that welled up inside me was overpowering. Along with the hatred was, as always, an intense suffering and pain somewhere so deep inside that I had never known existed. I clutched a picture of Brandon and vowed to do everything I could to seek justice in the eyes of the law for his life and his death.

The tears rolled down my face, I had to look away, I felt physically sick just being in the same room as the driver. I saw his family with him; even more painful was that I saw him with his family. I saw him able to hug his mom and dad, knowing I could never hug my son again. I saw a monster who would be going home with his family although he tore my family apart.

Court was scheduled for 9 a.m., but we were made to wait at least another hour, maybe more; it seemed like forever for the proceedings to start. However, before they began we were called into a room and told the defense and prosecution had decided on entering a two-year joint submission in exchange for a guilty plea of driving over .08 percent causing death, and driving over .08 percent causing bodily harm. The plea was accepted, with the sentencing date set for March. Court was adjourned. I never spoke to the prosecutor again. The driver again went home to be with his family, and we again went home to an empty house without Brandon.

We returned to court in March with our victim impact statements; I believe in my heart these are truly only to appease the victims, to make them feel they are being heard, when in fact everything is decided long before the court date. Again there were many supporters in court. We heard the prosecution go first. I was still hopeful, although I don't know why. I thought that finally we would hear some details of the crash, of the driver's accountability, of what he did. How foolish I was. We heard the prosecution rise and actually defend the sentence, the offender, and his actions. We heard him defend the driver's actions as being the first offense, how this was an accident; we heard him enter into evidence previous cases that had no relevance to our case. The entire courtroom was in disbelief at what we heard; anyone who attended with us that day agreed that there were in effect two defense lawyers in court.

The courtroom was anything but silent; there were mutters of disbelief, voices of outrage, people saying it was a farce. The judge never once reprimanded us in any way. In fact, one comment made was, "You know, Kim, there are two defense lawyers up there today." All these comments were made loudly enough for the lawyers and judge to hear. I sat in disbelief and wondered why I had expected anything different, because truly I always knew there would be no justice with this prosecutor or in this system. I knew the driver would get to walk away. He hadn't spent one night in jail since he killed Brandon, not one holiday without his family and friends, and not one night behind bars.

The judge then asked about the victim impact statements. There were over forty submitted. Finally, after hearing the argument from the prosecution about why we should not be allowed to read them, the judge ordered the prosecution to get the victim impact statements in order; that he would allow those who wanted to read and were present. During the reading of some of the statements I glanced over at the driver, and I and many others witnessed a stone-faced, emotionless man sitting there, showing not an ounce of remorse. During the reading of my statement, the prosecutor kept clicking the button on his pen, click, click, click, appearing to be very bored and disinterested. The driver then read his statement, saying how sorry he was and how he would honor Brandon, his life, speak to schools, and was ready to accept whatever punishment would be given to him by the court. However, some of the bigger words he didn't appear to be able to pronounce very well, so my only conclusion was that someone else wrote it for him, and he just read it. The judge then stated he was not accepting the joint submission of a two-year sentence and wanted to review the evidence and statements more thoroughly. The court adjourned until May. Again, the driver went home.

The following May, we returned to court for sentencing. The judge ruled that he was increasing the sentence from two years to two years and eight months, increasing the sentence by a mere eight months, which means it would be about two weeks more detention in jail or minimum security. Our legal system in Canada requires the offender to serve only one-sixth of his sentence before being eligible for parole. However, the judge stated that the driver could apply and be eligible for parole in six short months. The driver finally would not be going home with his family, even if only for a short six months. He went to a minimum security facility that day in May where he was evaluated in a reception-type place, not behind bars and not in jail. He was approved for minimum security, which was a small cabin in Drumheller, Alberta, with a normal front door and no fences, much like a dorm setting.

Two days after sentencing, the driver, who was obviously so full of remorse, if we are to believe his statement to the court, immediately appealed the extra eight months. We were now going to attend appeal court. We were assigned a new appeal prosecutor. I was filled with hope once again. Another chance! I met with the appeal prosecutor, and we talked about all the evidence. He seemed surprised by my knowledge of the police files, records, and the black box evidence. I begged and pleaded with him again to please ask for an increase, as it was my understanding that during the appeal we could ask for the sentence to be upheld or increased. My hope was soon crushed again, and he told me he wouldn't ask for an increase because if it wasn't granted, it was their reputation on the line. The knowledge that yet again their reputation was more important than an innocent life left me filled with confusion and disbelief. I felt defeated, hopeless, and sick to my stomach with all I had learned about how little an innocent life means and how much the guilty person is valued.

We attended appeal court, which was much more informative; the three appeal judges asked many questions of both lawyers. Sadly, I heard evidence of some of the injuries Brandon had sustained and some of the evidence that I knew should have been brought forward in the first court dates. The appeal justices were very thorough and seemed to be very impatient with the defense lawyer. I am hopeful, but I know that they will not increase the sentence, because the appeal prosecutor didn't request it. In my heart, I know they would have increased that sentence. At the end of the appeal court, the justices decide to withhold their decision to discuss the case. I am still hopeful.

While waiting for the appeal decision, the driver had now spent his six months in minimum security and has applied for day parole and full parole. In November 2014, his application for day parole and full parole was heard. We again were in a court-like setting to read another meaningless victim impact statement. The driver received day parole and was moved to a halfway house where he was free to come and go during the day but had to return to the halfway house at night to sleep. He can apply for weekend or overnight passes. I was informed by the parole office that if he were late for his curfew, there would be no repercussion for that. Another Christmas he spent with his family; he hasn't missed one yet. Finally a decision was reached by the appeal board, and the sentence given by the judge was upheld at 2.8 years. However, the appeal judge stated that the prosecution wrongly interpreted the law in this case. He said the sentence should have been no less than four years and as much as eight years. He went on to say that the reckless and dangerous way the driver drove that night put far more blame on him than in most cases.

The appeal justices would have granted an increase had the appeal prosecutor filed the paperwork asking for an increase. I am left knowing that if just one of them had listened to me, and had the principles and heart to fight for an innocent young man, the outcome for the drunk driver would have been different and possibly more fitting.

In August 2015, the driver applied for full parole, and we again attended a parole hearing with our statements in hand, our eyes full of tears and our hearts broken. We tried to explain the impact that the loss of Brandon has had on our lives; we tried to explain what coping is like for us. We fought to find words that could explain the depth of grief we have. The outcome of the driver's choice has truly destroyed us in every way. He was granted full parole, and his debt to Brandon and society was paid in full. Truly, if I had not experienced this joke of a justice system I never would have believed how wrong it is. He was free to walk away and move on with his life, to make right and wrong choices, to get married, have children and fulfill his dreams.

There is not a moment in any day or night that I don't grieve for Brandon, his life and how the right he had to make choices was so selfishly taken away from him. There is not a moment that I don't grieve for what he brought to my life. I never got to see Brandon graduate and continue to SAIT as he dreamed of. I never got to share his eighteenth birthday with him, and the happiness of celebrating his transition into adulthood. I will never get to share in all his successes or guide him through all the struggles that would have been. I will never get to watch him walk Kayla down the aisle when and if she decides to marry. I will never be the mother of the groom, and I will never have grandchildren with their father's twinkling green eyes and beautiful crooked smile.

Not only will I never do these things, but, more important, Brandon will never do them. There will never be a Christmas spent with a tree heaped with gifts; there will never be any time we will be together as a family. On family days, there is a huge hole and tears remind us that half our family is missing, not sharing in the special day with us. On Valentine's Day, instead of sharing a day of love with each other we crawl through a day of sorrow, no chocolates or hugs, only tears and emptiness. At Easter, no colored eggs to be decorated; no Easter egg hunt; no happy laughter and no turkey dinner. Since Brandon was killed, we don't acknowledge any of these days. These are only a few of the lifetime milestones and special days I will endure without Brandon, and that he will miss. Every day is filled with horror. Now we experience devastating days and extremely devastating days; there just is nothing else.

I love my daughter Kayla; she is the only thing keeping me here. Her life is important, and Brandon's life and memory are important. I struggle with choosing one child over the other. I struggle with staying in this world and leaving Brandon in the unknown alone, and I struggle with the thought of leaving Kayla here and being with Brandon. I struggle with how to feel any joy for Kayla in her life when I know Brandon will never have that. I don't know how to be an Earth mom anymore; I don't know how to be a Heaven mom. I don't know who I am or why I am here.

It has been just over three long years without my baby. Not much has changed for us since that day Brandon was killed. I still visit his roadside memorial twice a week. I sit with him there and talk to him. It is the place where I feel closest to him; the place where I would have died for him; the place where I still would die for him if I could only give him his life back.

Every single morning when I open my eyes to start another day, it's like Brandon dies all over again. The grief is crippling when I realize that today will not be the day Brandon comes home, nor will any day. Every night when I lie in Brandon's bed, I am consumed with emptiness for him and the realization that he missed another whole day of his life. Yet I am comforted by the knowledge that I am one day closer to seeing him again. I still have unimaginable night terrors and still sleep very little to not at all. I still ache and crave for the smell of him, the sound of his voice, his laughter, and the sight of him.

I still take pills to get through the day. A simple trip for groceries leaves me in tears for hours as I see his favorite foods. A census form in the mail asking how many people live in our home leaves me sobbing for hours in Brandon's bed. A smell or thought, someone who sounds like Brandon saying "Mom," all these things cause the most painful existence. I can't lock the door at night because both my children aren't home yet. I long to hear what every parent takes for granted — those amazing three words: "Mom, I'm home." I would give anything to hear those words again.

I carry so much guilt wondering why I was left here in this world and Brandon was taken. My life ended with my son's death. I am still here, I still breathe, but I am not alive. I am waiting until I can be with Brandon again. I think often of joining him, knowing that he can't come home to us but I go there to be with him.

Kayla is strong young lady, but not as strong as many think. I hear her cry often and I see the hurt just behind the fake smile or bright eyes. I know she loves and misses her best friend. I know she carries Brandon with her. She believes he is with her always, in everything she does. She is living her life not only for herself, but for her brother too. Grief for me has not changed. Time heals nothing; you don't even learn to live with it. You are left with this horrible grief, a heavy heart, a mix of emotions that crash all at the same moment, leaving you exhausted and broken. This is my world. I don't blame Brandon; I know he would have stayed with us if he could have. I know he never would have left us. I do blame the drunk driver, and I do blame God, and I do blame the legal system and the courts. Not everything happens for a reason.

Losing Brandon taught me that there are amazing people who will step forward and support a family whose innocent child was killed by a drunk driver. I have learned that those people are the ones you are least likely to think will do that, or even complete strangers. I have also learned that those you think will support and stand by an innocent young boy and his family sometimes don't. I have learned that people will get tired of your grief and walk away or be frustrated. Sometimes it's because they want to help you and then they realize the old you is never coming back, or they just get tired. As tired as they get, imagine living it every day. I don't know if this is because of fear that they might find themselves in my position one day, or see their child taken like Brandon. I don't know if it is easier to look away and therefore not have to be touched by grief and the death of a child. I have learned that nothing stays the same. I have learned to embrace those beautiful people who *are* there for Brandon. There are so many amazing people who are part of my daily world, and they mean so much to me.

There is no more common sense in this world, because nothing makes sense. There is nothing in this world that is the same as it once was. There are no beautiful colors, everything is gray, and there is no feeling of joy deep inside for anything that happens. Truly, I have not felt one spark of life since December 6, 2012. I cry when the sun shines, because it is not tanning Brandon's shoulders. I scream into the wind, because it can't ruffle his hair. I weep when it snows, because the snowflakes don't melt on his nose, and I am devastated when the raindrops don't kiss his cheeks.

We have in place so many things to honor Brandon and the way he lived his life and the things he loved in life. We also do many things to raise awareness, to fight against the way he was killed. Immediately after Brandon was killed a friend of his started a Facebook page, RIP Brandon Thomas; his story can be viewed there. In August 2014, we started a Show 'N Shine called Show Your Ride for Brandon, because he loved vehicles and wanted to become a mechanic. Over the past two years, this has become one of Alberta's biggest events. Last year we raised $16,489 toward a scholarship to the school Brandon would have attended to study mechanics.

Kayla, I, and many others also support a petition seeking mandatory minimum sentencing for anyone convicted of impaired driving causing death or bodily harm. I am so thankful for those who stepped forward to support Brandon and us in so many ways. With this support comes the overwhelming grief that it is because he was killed. There never seems to be gratitude without grief. Those two emotions crash together at the same moment with such intensity that it takes my breath away. Grief is exhausting; it is physically and emotionally tiring. It drains the body, the mind, and leaves me barely able to function through a whole day. What others consider a normal day, working, cleaning house, grocery shopping, taking care of the kids, now is something I could never consider doing in one day. The smallest of tasks is viewed as a mountain of defeat; no matter how hard I try to climb that mountain, the result it always the same. I never wanted or needed more than what I had with my children. We could do it all and had it all because we had each other. I always knew that my greatest gifts in life were my children. I cherished every moment with them, every second, and I never take it for granted. The day I leave this world behind and see my son's amazing crooked smile and the laughter in his eyes will be the next greatest gift in my life, and when my daughter joins Brandon and me it will be the final greatest gift of all.

KIM THOMAS
COCHRANE, ALBERTA, CANADA

BRANDON THOMAS

MEMORIAL TATTOO

KAYLA, BRANDON & KIM

BRANDON AS A BABY

BRANDON WITH SISTER KAYLA

CHAPTER TWENTY-THREE

MY LIFE CHANGED WITH
ONE PHONE CALL

BY CANDACE WEBB

God has a reason for allowing things to happen we may never understand his wisdom but we simple have to trust his will (Psalm 37:5).

I met my future husband, Todd, in 1992. You might say it was love at first sight, because after a short courtship we found out I was pregnant and we decided to get married. Todd had custody of his son, Christopher, from his first marriage, who was seven years old at the time. Because of Todd's work schedule, Christopher had been living with his grandmother next door. He did move in with us for a short time after we married, but preferred living with his grandmother because that was what he was familiar with. Within the first year of our marriage, we welcomed our healthy, beautiful bouncing baby boy on May 21, 1993. We were proud parents as we held Shane in our arms and looked at our little miracle. I was never supposed to have children, so I felt that Shane was a gift from God. I loved being his mother. Little moments like feeding, bathing, dressing him and showing him off made me happy.

When I had to return to work after maternity leave, I wasn't disappointed when they laid me off. It gave me the opportunity to stay home and spend the first year watching Shane grow. I got to be there for his first word, first roll over, when he first crawled, and when he took his first steps. It was such a blessing to be able to see those things firsthand. As Shane grew, his love for his brother was obvious. He lit up when Christopher walked into the room. Shane was always right on Christopher's heels, but couldn't do a lot of the things Christopher did because of the age difference. Christopher liked hanging with his friends, and Shane was just too young. Shane had a hard time understanding that. Christopher married and moved away when Shane was fifteen years old. Shane looked forward to the weekends because he could spend time with Christopher. He thoroughly enjoyed their time together.

The weekend of August 21, 2009, Shane left the house that Friday night in my Jeep, excited because Christopher was taking his four-year-old stepson and Shane out in the boat the next day. As he left, I told him to be careful and have a good time. He said they were going to meet his grandmother at Whataburger for breakfast the next morning before they headed for the river. I wasn't worried about him going because Christopher was a responsible boater. With his stepson being so young and being with them; I knew they would be even more cautious.

Todd and I had plans that Saturday with some friends. We were to meet at their house and ride with them to the restaurant for a birthday celebration. We left the house around 2:30 p.m. and got to the restaurant around 4. We were talking and enjoying ourselves and preparing to order when my phone rang. Something inside me told me that I needed to answer it. I picked up the phone and saw that it was my mother-in-law. I answered the call, and she said, "The boys have been in an accident. Shane is in surgery, and they can't find Christopher." I couldn't believe what she was saying, so I said "*What?*" She repeated herself and it finally sank in.

She told me Shane had been taken to Biloxi Regional Hospital in our home state of Mississippi. I got up and said, "Come on, we got to go!" I explained things as we went out the door.

We had driven to the restaurant with our friends, so they took us back to our car, and we raced to the hospital. It kept playing over and over in my mind what my mother-in-law had said: "Shane is in surgery, and they can't find Christopher." I could not comprehend what that meant. When we got to the hospital, I jumped out of the car and ran into the emergency room while Todd found a parking place. The lady behind the counter got the nurse, and she told me to follow her down the hall to a little room. I had been in that room before when they told us that my father-in-law, George, had died. I started backing up, saying, "No, I can't go in there." The nurse said, "It's not what you think." Todd and Cricket, my mother-in-law, came down the hall and we went into the room together. I asked her if she had heard anything, and she said she didn't know any more than what she had told me on the phone.

We waited for what seemed like forever. I couldn't sit down; I paced the floor. There was a knock at the door, and the coroner came in. If the nurse was right and it wasn't what I thought, then why was the coroner there? He started telling us that Christopher and Shane were fleeing from the law in their boat and crashed into another boat. My mother-in-law said, "No, Christopher wouldn't do that, he had the baby with him." The coroner told us that they still had not found who they believed to be Christopher and that they had called the dive team in.

The nurse kept coming into the room asking questions about Shane. She asked how old he was, and I said, "Sixteen. He was born in 1993." With a puzzled look on her face, she asked me, "Are you sure?" Between what the coroner said and the nurse, we didn't know whether it was Christopher or Shane they had at the hospital.

The coroner left the room and we sat there in complete confusion. We were left there by ourselves, not knowing what was going on or if our boys were dead or alive. Again there was a knock on the door, and it was the coroner. He said there had been a mix-up in the report. He said, "Christopher was not the one fleeing from the law; the other boater was." The other boater was running from law enforcement and appeared to be impaired when he collided with Christopher's boat. The coroner also said that the dive team found who they believed to be Christopher, and also that Christopher's stepson had a few bruises but was fine.

I said, "Who do they believe to be Christopher?! Which one of our boys is dead, and which one is fighting for his life?"

The nurse came in and said for us to follow her. She said that the reason she questioned me about Shane's age was because he was such a big boy for sixteen. We entered the room, and it was my Shane. He had so many tubes and IVs that it was almost impossible to recognize him, but I knew it was him. This meant Christopher was dead, but he was only twenty-four years old. How could this be possible? We were living a nightmare. The nurses and techs in the room were busy preparing Shane to airlift him to the University of South Alabama Medical Center. They were stabilizing him while they waited for the helicopter to get there. Since the USA Medical Center was an hour away, our friends who came to the hospital volunteered to drive us. I didn't want to leave Shane, but we needed to get to USA so we would be there when he arrived.

The staff at Biloxi didn't give us much hope of Shane making it through the helicopter ride. I feared that I was going to lose my son. It was the longest hour drive that I have ever taken. I didn't know what to do with myself, so I called everyone I could think of to ask them to pray for Shane. My heart was breaking for Todd. I loved Christopher, but I couldn't imagine what Todd had to be feeling. He had lost his son. How do you deal with that? And then he didn't know if his other son was going to make it or not. How much could a person take? I was so thankful for our friends. It was comforting to have them there with us. When we arrived at the hospital, the helicopter had not gotten there yet. It seemed like a lifetime before it arrived. To this day it is still hard to hear a helicopter; my heart just seems to skip a beat.

I had to know if Shane was okay. When they told me that he had made it, I can't explain the relief I felt. It was hours before he was stable enough for us to see him. He was in the ICU, and it was 2 in the morning as I walked into the room. I noticed a cut above his eye that had been stitched, and the silence in the room was deafening. He was in a coma, and the right side of his body bore the brunt of the trauma from the crash. His upper arm was broken along with all of his ribs, and he had a subdural hematoma, a brain injury. The next twenty-four hours were critical, and they gave us little hope that he would survive. After leaving Shane because we were limited by how much time we could spend with him, we went to the waiting room. I don't believe we comprehended the extent of what was happening. We were in shock. There was a lady in the waiting room who offered to let me lie down on her air mattress. Todd sat in the corner. As I was lying there, my mind was racing. I kept thinking about Christopher being dead and that we would never see him again. And what were we going to do if Shane didn't make it? Our lives had changed with that phone call from my mother-in-law.

The next few days we stayed in denial. We weren't making any arrangements for Christopher, because we just knew Shane was going to wake up and we would go home. We kept thinking that he only had a bump on his head, a broken arm, and broken ribs. He would be fine in a few days. And besides, he needed to be there for Christopher's funeral.

One week went by with no change. Two weeks passed, still no change. The funeral home kept calling Todd and telling him he needed to make the arrangements if Christopher was going to have an open casket because the bacteria from the water had begun to set in. Being pulled in two different directions Todd went ahead and made the arrangements to bury Christopher.

On the day of the wake, Todd left the hospital. My heart was broken in two. I had to stay with Shane, but I wanted to be there for Christopher also. A dear friend came and stayed with me so I wouldn't be alone. There were so many feelings of sadness that are still indescribable to this day. On the same day as Christopher's funeral, August 30, Shane was to have a procedure. They were putting in a feeding tube. I went to see him at the scheduled visitation. He was so swollen that he looked pregnant. His blood pressure was up and he was running a temperature. I knew something was wrong, but the nurse kept telling me that everything was fine. I just didn't have a good feeling! I left the room when visitation was over. I kissed him and told him I loved him. I went back in at the next scheduled visitation. He was even more swollen. I asked the nurse what was going on. She said they had to blow his stomach up with air to put the feeding tube in and that they also had given him medication that would help him to have a bowel movement. Shane was still in the coma and could not communicate with me, and Todd was in Mississippi, and I didn't want him to be any more stressed out than he already was, but I wanted to call him to tell him what was going on. I was beside myself.

During the last visitation that day, I didn't know what to think. Shane's fever and blood pressure were still up, something that he had not had issues with until they inserted the feeding tube. I knew he was going downhill and wasn't sure what to do. All I could do was pray. I called a friend who prayed by phone. I still couldn't call Todd. He was dealing with so much as it was. My friend and I went back to the hotel. I paced and paced. I couldn't eat or sleep. I knew something was wrong.

The phone rang at 11 p.m.; it was one of his doctors. He called to tell me that Shane was unresponsive and that they were going to be taking him down for a CT scan to see what was going on with his brain injury. I told him I was on my way, and he said to just stay where I was because it still could be a few hours before they could get the scan done. He said he would call me back.

We sat there at the hotel, not knowing what we should do. Should we go to the hospital and wait, or just stay put? I would not be able to see Shane because visitations were over for the day. I felt so helpless, a feeling I had never felt before as a mother. The phone rang again thirty minutes later. Instead of the CT scan, they were taking Shane to surgery because of his stomach problem, and needed my permission. I gave permission, and we left for the hospital. It was a ten-minute drive. When we arrived, they had already taken him to surgery. The surgery lasted two hours. They replaced the feeding tube and because of bacteria in his stomach they put in drain tubes. When I finally got to see Shane, there was a tube coming out of every orifice of his body.

Todd made it back that afternoon. I was so glad to see him. I filled him in on all that had happened. We went back for the scheduled visit and started asking questions. Why were Shane's temperature and blood pressure still up? Why did this happen? What was going on, and what should we expect? Whenever we would ask a question, we could never get any answers. He had a team of doctors, and they never came out to talk to us about how he was doing, what they found, or what was going on. It drove us crazy. It was like it was none of our business what they did. We never did get a straight answer on his condition. I found out months later when I read his medical report that when they placed the first feeding tube, his intestines had been punctured and were spilling out into his body. Gangrene was setting in. When I read that, it explained a lot of what had been going on.

A couple of days after Shane's surgery, the doctor came and said they were going to have to do a tracheotomy on him. We were told that he wasn't breathing on his own, so they needed to do the trach because the respirator could damage his vocal cords. I called every nurse or medical person I knew. I just had a gut feeling that he did not need this procedure. After talking to everyone, we still did not feel comfortable. We knew that once Shane had the trach, it would be weeks before they could remove it and he would not be able to talk to us when he woke up from the coma. But we went ahead and signed the papers giving them permission to do it. When we saw him the next morning, I was so mad. He was breathing on his own. In my opinion, the trach was not necessary.

For the next week, Shane battled fever and blood pressure issues. He did open his eyes at one point. I would sit and talk to him and tell him to wake up. We put pictures all over the room, so when he did, he would know that we were there. I was so afraid he would wake up and not know what was going on and be fearful because he didn't know who all these strange people were. And with him having the trach, he would not be able to ask any questions. My feeling of hopelessness was so overwhelming, along with the helplessness that I felt. He finally did wake up, but with all the drugs in his system, he was groggy and didn't know what was going on.

During the fifth week at USA Hospital, they told us that they were going to move Shane to the Methodist Rehabilitation Center in Jackson, Mississippi. We were so glad to be getting him away from USA Hospital. We had to hire an ambulance and nurse to ride with him to Jackson. Finally the day came. It was on a Thursday. We left mid-morning, followed the ambulance, and arrived around 4 p.m. We signed the paperwork, and Shane was admitted. We noticed that it was a shift change, and the doctors and therapist were leaving for the day.

What we didn't know was what a huge impact this was going to make on our night. Shane had not had any pain meds since we left USA Hospital. At 7 p.m. he was in unbearable pain and was like a crazy person. He would take his legs and push himself in the bed to the point where we thought he was going to hurt himself. Nothing we did helped him. The night nurse ordered him a bed cage, which was netting that went around the bed and zipped up so he couldn't fall out. It was like he was a caged animal. The nurses informed us that they could not give him any meds till the doctors evaluated him the next morning. I tried to talk and get him to calm down, but nothing worked. If looks could kill, I would not be here today. I begged the nurses to help him, but they said they couldn't do anything without a doctor's order. I sat all night watching my child suffer, and there was nothing I could do. He could not communicate with us because of the tracheotomy. I prayed the doctor would hurry and get there so Shane would have some relief. At 7 a.m. the next morning, the therapist came into the room to take Shane to start rehab. My reaction was "What? Are you kidding me?" I explained that he was in pain and that we needed to see the doctor as soon as possible. We were told that the doctor would be seeing him shortly, but that Shane needed to come with them. They put him in the wheelchair, and you could see the pain on his face. He was as white as a sheet and lifeless. Again I begged them to help him. We kept telling them that he was in pain. They ignored our pleas and asked us to leave the rehab area. I felt like we had jumped out of the frying pan into the fire.

At 10 a.m. the doctor sent him down for an x-ray to check his feeding tube and incision. The feeding tube wasn't in place, and his stomach incision had herniated, so by 1 p.m. he was in surgery to repair his stomach and replace the feeding tube. With his arm still broken, they were hoping to get the orthopedist to look at it while they were working on him. The bones were not in line, but had tried to heal which left his arm deformed. It looked like he had a softball on the inside and the outside of his arm. We knew that his right arm was drawn up, but we didn't understand why.

He was admitted to the University of Mississippi Medical Center which became our home for the next five weeks. The orthopedist who looked at Shane's arm told us that he would do surgery on Monday, September 28, to repair Shane's arm, but that there was a chance that he would never have full use of it. He said that when there is a brain injury along with broken bones, the body generates bone quickly, and that is what had happened. The arm had tried to heal itself but with the bone separated, all his nerves and tendons were now entangled. The surgery for this took six hours. They had to chisel the bone away and put the bones together with a plate.

On Thursday, Shane went back into surgery to insert a chest tube because a blood clot had clasped to the bottom of the right lung. My poor child had been through hell, and it wasn't over.

Because of all the surgeries and the chest tube, he was put on blood thinners. They had to start a new IV for them. He had only one arm for the IV, and they were having problems because with his veins blowing out. The blood kept leaking into the surrounding tissue, and they had to try again. It was so bad that they called the helicopter medics to come and do it, but before they had gotten down the hall after doing it, it blew again. At that point, we stepped in and refused to let them stick him again. We went to the head of the hospital to request a PICC line which is a soft, flexible tube placed in the vein that is used for a prolonged period. Life was easier for him from that point on as far as being stuck with needles.

We had a blow-up mattress in Shane's room which Todd and I took turns sleeping on, but most of the time I slept on the little couch that we pushed next to Shane's bed. He wanted us to hold his hand, which was tied down because he kept trying to pull his trach out, and if we let his hand go he would pat the bed until we held it again. He could be sound asleep, and I would get up to go to the restroom, and he would be awake, waiting for me to come back to hold his hand. He started trying to let us know that he was thirsty, but we could not give him anything to drink or even ice chips because of the trach, and they were not sure if he could swallow. They didn't want to take the chance of it going into his lungs. The nurse brought us some foam oral swabs that we could brush his teeth with, and we would wet them a little. The moment he learned they were moist, he started sucking the heck out of them. If we went anywhere toward the sink, his mouth would open, almost like a little bird ready to eat when his mother returned.

The day came to downsize his trach. We called it "giving him back his voice." Once someone has a trach, it's not a matter of taking it out; it has to be downsized, and they get it to a point where you can cap it and can make sounds which allow you to speak. That was a great day, but it came with questions that Shane asked. The first one was "Where is Christopher?" And then "Give me the phone, I need to call Christopher." We had to delete Christopher's number from our phones. We were afraid that the news of his death would be too much for Shane to bear. We were not sure how long we could put off telling him, but we didn't want to chance a relapse.

Two weeks into his stay at UMC, the physical therapist started working with him. It was like watching an infant. He had to learn to balance himself to sit on the side of the bed. I have to say it was funny at times, because he would just start falling to the right or the left and we would have to catch him. The therapist got him to where he could sit and stand with help. It was time for the hard work to start, so we transferred back to Methodist Rehab. We were excited but apprehensive, because we knew the pain he was going to have to endure. It broke my heart to think of it.

On the first morning back, the therapist came to get him. They would not let us go. We waited in his room, both of us pacing back and forth wondering how he was doing. They brought him back for lunch. He was so tired that he just slept. He went back to therapy after lunch, and that evening he was wiped out. He was a trouper, though, and never complained. We truly learned a lot from him.

Every day Shane went to therapy, and we made sure he had the best of the best. He had good days and bad days. He couldn't lift his arm because of the damage, and they said he would not have full use of that hand. But he was determined to get full use of his arm, so in the evenings he would lie on the bed and throw his hand back and lift it over and over again to exercise it. Through his determination, he did eventually get the use of his arm back.

The day came when they could remove the trach. We were so excited. He would be able to eat and drink again. Each day he got better with being able to keep food down. He still had the feeding tube to assure he was getting the nutrition he needed. He worked hard and progressed fast, even though it seemed like a lifetime. The funny thing is how much control the insurance companies have on our health care. They said that as soon as Shane was able to walk down the hall and back with a little help, they would release him to go home. Although we wanted him to go home, we knew he wasn't ready. He still wasn't holding food down as he should, and we still had to tell him about Christopher. We wanted him to be in the hospital when we told him, just in case he had a relapse. We talked to his doctors and set the date to tell him.

A week before his release his grandmother came up. We had pictures of the wake and funeral so we could show him that it was the truth. The doctors were on standby. We sat around him on the bed; we told him the whole story about the boat crash and that Christopher was killed. Of course he cried, but his eyes were unable to produce tears because of the brain trauma. But he took the news better than we thought. His neurologist met with him each day before they released him to talk about what had happened.

The day came for us to go home. It had been thirteen weeks since the boat crash. Thirteen weeks that never should have happened, but because someone made the choice to go boating after drinking, we lost Christopher. Shane would never be the same, and neither would Todd or I. We were both scared and excited. Scared to be home and also the possibility of Shane having a relapse, and excited that maybe we could get some normality back into our lives. We lived three hours south of the rehab center, and once we were home we would have to travel back twice a week for therapy. Shane handled the drive home fairly well. He was glad to be home, but we didn't have any time to relax. It seemed like as soon we got there we received a phone call from the district attorney; he wanted to meet with us.

During the whole time we were gone, the man who had killed Chris and injured Shane was still free and not in jail. His blood alcohol content was .08 percent four hours after the boating incident; he was also a repeat offender. A few years before our tragedy, he was involved in a DUI crash that killed his brother and left himself paralyzed from the waist down. It was still a few more months before we went to trial.

Justice is a process, and in my opinion it takes too long. I didn't think Shane remembered anything about that day, but to our surprise he remembered everything up to the point when the boat hit them.

On the day of the trial, we met with the district attorney at the courthouse. He presented us with a plea deal. We were told in the beginning that the crime carried a sentence of twenty-five years per incident, which is equal to fifty years. The plea deal was for him to serve twenty years. But then we found out that the sentencing laws are different for water crashes. Mississippi law states that since the crash happened on water, it would be only ten years per incident, not twenty-five. We were livid. What did it matter whether it was land or water? After talking with the district attorney, he explained things and said that if we didn't come to some agreement, the judge could give the offender less time. We wanted the full twenty years and nothing less. We were not going to take a plea deal.

We decided that whatever the judge handed down was what it would be. After going back and forth with the district attorney, it was time to go to the courtroom. The offender was late, he was high on marijuana, and had also taken a Xanax that wasn't prescribed to him. The judge was displeased, and gave the offender the full twenty-year sentence. Yay! Victory! It wasn't long enough, but at least he didn't get less.

At the end of the process, the judge asked if we had anything to say. We had prepared a letter that a friend of ours read. I was not sure if anything said that day would change this young man's way of thinking, but part of me felt sorry for him. His grandfather was the only family member who showed up to show him. Neither of his parents were there. Even if my child had done something this terrible, I would still be there for his support, not agreeing with what he had done but just letting him know that he still was loved.

I would love to be able to say that we lived happily ever after, but we didn't. This whole ordeal has caused mental and financial stress on all of us, especially Shane. He isn't the person he was, and now has issues that he has to deal with for the rest of his life. The major one is that his brother is gone.

Shane became obsessed with any and everything that had to do with Chris. For instance, I was cleaning his room and dusting his shelf and found a razor head, the kind that is removable, and I threw it away. I did not think anything of it, and a couple of days later Shane was mad as hell. "Where is the razor that was on my shelf?" I explained that I had cleaned his room and had thrown it away. He then informed me that it was the last razor that Chris had used. I didn't know; I thought I was helping.

Chris was twenty-four years old and living on his own. There were things he did that we didn't approve of. Shane, wanting to be like Chris, started smoking marijuana. We tried everything to stop him. Part of his outpatient rehab was meeting with a psychologist twice a week. We spoke with him about Shane's behavior, and he spoke with Shane, who said it was his way of being close to Chris. We fought with him so much about this that one night I thought he would take his own life. That night I slept outside his room, praying and listening to see if I heard him try to do something. How do I help? I keep asking what I can do for him. Where are the answers? We had never dealt with anything like this before.

While dealing with Shane, we were in the process of losing our home. It was for sale, but no one was buying. We were dying financially. Todd was searching for work, and I took a job that paid so much less than I used to make. We were going down like a sinking ship, and there was nothing we could do. I think part of it was that we didn't know what to do.

I heard an analogy one day while watching TV. A family who had lost a child said "It's like a family picture fell off the wall, and it's in millions of pieces. You are trying to put all those pieces back together, and some are missing." I thought oh, my God! That's it, that's how I feel. Our lives are in pieces, and the puzzle isn't going back together the same way it was!

We are all different; we are dealing with the hurt and loss in the best way we can. Even if it's not the best way, we are trying to figure what our new normal is.

It's amazing how time passes. On the first year anniversary we went to the site where the incident happened and placed a wreath in the water. That was a very emotional day. We cried and talked about Chris. We decided that Shane was going to make a cross, and we would put at the river's edge where we could hang a wreath. We went to the grave and visited. Shane goes there often, but I can't. I'll go with the family, but not by myself. I am not ready yet.

A year out, Shane is still in so much turmoil and pain; it breaks my heart. His shoulder is still causing him a lot of pain. We have seen so many doctors but they see nothing on the MRIs or the x-rays that would cause Shane such excruciating pain. They just kept saying that he was looking for pain meds. At first I would say no, not a chance, but after months of being told this, I started to wonder if that was the case.

One day Shane called me. "Mom, I need help!"

"Where are you?" I asked.

"I'm on my way home from the property. I was going to kill myself, but I couldn't find a place that would not remind you and Dad every time you went there."

I met him at his grandmother's, and we went to the hospital. He was admitted to the psychiatric ward for a week. He was placed on drugs for depression and anxiety. During this time, I was on the phone with the psychologist in Jackson. I was again feeling helpless, not knowing how to help Shane, not understanding why someone can't find out what is going on with his shoulder. Shane said that sometimes the pain is just unbearable. I asked, "If someone is willing to take his life, is he doing it just for pain pills?" I just kept praying and asking God to please help; if you want him here on this earth, please give us the answer and the help he needs.

A few months later I got another call from Shane. "Mom, there is an older guy who is dancing across the room. He will come through one wall and go out the other. He reminds me of the guy that did the commercials for Six Flags." Shane was staying at his grandmother's house because we didn't want him left alone. I called her to ask what was going on, but all she could do was cry and say that Shane was going crazy!

We decided to take him off the meds he was put on. I consulted with his psychologist about what should we do. He referred us to a special psychologist in Jackson who charged five hundred dollars an hour to help us get Shane on something that would help and not make him crazy.

We went to see him. He took Shane back first, and then sent for me about half an hour later. We were in this huge room. He was at his desk about ten feet away. I felt I needed to yell to speak to him. He said Shane wasn't talkative, and he was going to place him on another medication that he might have to tweak a couple of times before they got the dosage right. I thought, what just happened? Shane and I talked on the two-hour drive home. We decided that he was not going to take any of these drugs, and we were going to find a doctor to deal with the pure raw pain he was having.

A few months passed and we found a sports orthopedist. He said, "I know what's wrong with you, and I'm going to send you for an MRI and inject you with dye." Sure enough, he saw the problem, and the next week Shane was in surgery to repair a torn shoulder. The doctor said that when the boat hit him, it would have been better for it to have dislocated the shoulder. Instead, it had ripped it, and it has continued to rip over the past couple of years. The doctor said he didn't see how Shane dealt with the pain from such extensive damage. We explained what he had been through, and this great doctor never charged us a thing. He wrote it off! Thank you, Jesus.

We still deal with issues. We finally sold our home, but had to practically give it away just to get out from underneath it. We've had several things repossessed. The decision the offender made to drink and operate a boat that day not only killed Chris, but destroyed us financially. We learned that if you are not directly injured, you have no claim in the eyes of the law. Shane was a minor, so all the financial burden fell on us. And even though there's a lawsuit, it's only for all the pain and suffering Shane underwent. We are not part of the suit at all, because we were not directly injured. Therefore the only thing that will be paid in all of this is Shane's medical bills.

In the process of our journey, I am trying to change the law in Mississippi regarding sentencing for boating under the influence. The maximum sentence for a DUI in Mississippi is twenty-five years, but for boating under the influence the maximum is only ten years. This *has* to change. I started what I call Webb's Law, and we're in the first stages of lobbying for changes. The consequences of driving and boating impaired are the same, so the punishment needs to be the same. It's a difficult process to make this change, but in time it will happen.

CANDY WEBB
BILOXI, MISSISSIPPI
Co-Founder, AVIDD—Advocates for Victims of Impaired/Distracted Driving

CHRISTOPHER AND SHANE WEBB

SHANE WEBB'S 21st BIRTHDAY

CHRISTOPHER'S SON, CHANCE

CHAPTER TWENTY-FOUR

CRUEL IRONY:

THE JANAKAE SARGENT STORY

BY KANDI WILEY

If Irma Jean would have had a
Janakae in her life, then my Janakae
might still be here safe with me. -KANDI WILEY

All I had ever wanted to be my entire life was a mother. I dreamed of being a mom. I gave up a full ride to college to get married nine days after my eighteenth birthday. Very dumb, considering that I found myself going through a divorce at age twenty-six. However, what it gave me were two beautiful children, a daughter, Janakae, and a son, Matthew. I had my youngest daughter, Tygelia, when I was twenty-nine in what would ultimately be another failed marriage, but I would spend twenty years in that very abusive relationship.

In the early years, I gave birth to Janakae at age twenty-one. I had gone through what the doctors were unsure was either a miscarriage or a false pregnancy between eighteen months and two years earlier. I was beyond ecstatic when I was told I was pregnant again. My pregnancy was easy, no complications until my last trimester. I ended up being scheduled for an induction a day after my due date. I worked through my due date and left work for a doctor's appointment. I had quite a bit of bad news that day. My

413

dad had been rushed to the hospital by ambulance, my uncle had been admitted to the hospital, and my PawPaw was also in the hospital. I was also running late to my doctor's appointment due to a project my boss needed to be finished. It was not a big surprise when my blood pressure was high at the appointment, but they sent me to the hospital for a stress test and to check on the baby. They sent me home for the night, but I was scheduled for an induction early the next morning and told to rest and do nothing at all once I got home, but to lie on my left side.

Having taken childbirth classes, I had prepared for labor to hurt really badly. I never felt what I had prepared myself for. I was in labor for eighteen and a half hours, and she wasn't coming out. They put in a fetal scalp monitor, as they were worried about her being engaged into the birth canal for so much time toward the end. They came to speak to me about doing a cesarean, but I didn't want one, so they held off. They came back to me a little later and told me that she seemed to be really stuck and didn't give me a choice. I signed the consent and asked to be awake during the surgery, but they urged me to be out since it had been such a long labor and it was almost 1 a.m. I was extremely tired, so I conceded.

I awoke the next morning begging to see my baby. No one in our family was still there. I didn't even know if I had a boy or girl or if he or she was healthy. I didn't know the weight or length. I wanted to count fingers, toes, and to inspect her or him. I pushed the call button and demanded to see my baby. They brought her to me, an angelic baby girl. She was the most beautiful baby girl ever. She weighed eight pounds fifteen ounces, and twenty-two inches long. I unwrapped her and found that she was absolutely perfect from head to toe.

I learned that I had almost died during surgery. While they were trying to get her unstuck from the birth canal, they ripped a main artery, and while trying to stop the bleeding they sutured in a catheter. I spent seven days in the hospital waiting for the sutures to dissolve and was given IV antibiotics for the infection that set in.

Janakae could have gone home days before me, but they discharged her and left her there with me. She was the only baby in the nursery those last few days when she wasn't in my room with me.

Janakae proved to be the best baby and child. She was so smart. She talked in full sentences, knew her alphabet, and could count to one hundred before she was two. She had broken herself off the pacifier and the bottle, and pretty much potty-trained herself. She was such a joy. I didn't go anywhere without her except work.

Janakae started reading to me by the time she was four. Having grown tired of her Little Golden Books and her Dr. Seuss books, she was reading encyclopedias by age five. Her favorite volume was the letter "C." C for Canine. She loved animals and started bringing in all that she could find, wanting to keep them all. She would play with grasshoppers and crickets until their legs fell off, then bring them in for me to tape, glue, or staple them back on. Throughout the years we owned everything from hermit crabs, hamsters, guinea pigs, chickens, and pot-bellied pigs to cows, dogs, cats, birds, and fish. I am sure I am leaving out a creature or two. I always heard "Madre, can we keep it? It just followed me home from school." Or "Look what I found under the bushes." Everyone knew that there was a little coaxing on her part to get them home. Her passion for animals was evident her entire life, so it wasn't a big surprise when she said she wanted to be a veterinarian.

Janakae tested as gifted and talented as a kindergartner and stayed in that program throughout her school years and graduation. She also had been invited by Duke University to take her SATs as a seventh grader. She wrote poetry. She never ceased to amaze me. She was a graduate of Barbizon School of Modeling, yet didn't know she was beautiful. She had a heart of gold. She started out as a flute player in the seventh grade, made flag corps her freshman year of high school, then taught herself to play tuba over the summer before her sophomore year. She continued playing tuba throughout her years of high school and into college. She also learned to play saxophone in high school for the jazz band, clarinet for a woodwind ensemble, and had started learning trombone. She had set a goal to learn how to play every instrument in the marching band before she graduated college.

She graduated with honors from Mineral Wells High School in 2004. She was accepted to Texas Tech University. She didn't have a very good first year of college, having overloaded herself her first semester with sixteen credit hours, marching band, and a part-time job that would end up being full-time. Her great-grandmother died over Christmas break, and she started her second semester on academic probation. The first day of her finals that semester, her stepfather was injured and almost killed in a job-related oilfield accident. I made her stay at school and take her finals, all of which she must have bombed, because she then was academically suspended. Luckily, she had already registered for the summer session, so they counted that as her suspension. She started back in the fall of 2005. The week of Thanksgiving that semester, I brought her home, and she had surgery to remove a 4.9-centimeter lump from her breast and faced possibly having breast cancer at the age of nineteen. She went back to school but while awaiting the pathology results her grades suffered, and she was suspended again. Luckily, the pathology was benign and she took her suspension to regroup. She entered college again in the fall of 2006 as a freshman with her little brother, Matt, by her side.

Those two had been inseparable. The previous two years had been difficult, being both good and bad for each of them, but they were together again. They even had two classes together. I was happy as I didn't have to decide which child to see on the weekends. For years it had looked like I would have them at two opposite ends of Texas. Then came November 2006.

On the night of November 11, 2006, Janakae was serving as the designated driver for college friends. She and I had both worked that day, but when I got home I was channel-surfing, and the Red Raiders football game was on television. I texted both of my college children, saying, "Go, Red Raiders. Love, Mom." Janakae called me. We watched the game by phone. We both love sports, and she always credited me with her knowledge of the game, saying I was the mom on the sidelines of all of her brother's games, explaining them to the other moms and sometimes the dads who were there. She would tell people that we were big time sports chicks. She was also my concert buddy and would often come back home for us to attend a concert, or call to ask me to come to Lubbock to go clubbing or to a concert with her and her friends. Toward the end of the game, she told me she needed to finish getting ready and told me of her plans for the night. I told her to make good choices, be safe, and to call me the next day to let me know how her night went and that she was safe.

Janakae's being the designated driver that night didn't surprise me. This was something she had done since getting her license three months before turning seventeen. She had a passion to take care of her friends, to keep them from making an irresponsible choice that could forever change or damage their quality of life. I honestly never worried anymore about her when she was serving as the designated driver than I did any other time she was away from me. After all, she was being the good friend and keeping others safe. I never worried about other drunk drivers being on the roads either. I spoke to her one more time that night. About 10:21 p.m. I called to ask her a silly Texas country music question. After all, if I didn't know, she would. We both had a love for all music genres and eras. She was leaving the party from dropping the friends off and heading to a former coworker's house to hang out and wait until the friends were ready to be picked up from the party. I again told her I loved her and to make good choices and be careful. I had no idea that would be the last time I would talk to her.

I had met friends at the VFW to listen to their friend's band. Upon getting back home, I watched a movie, then went to bed about 2:05 a.m. The next thing I remember is being awakened by the phone ringing at 2:44 a.m. I jumped up out of bed, and the caller I.D. said University Medical Center and had Lubbock's area code of 806. I had not spoken to my son all day, and since he was more green to college life, my first thought was "What has Matthew done?" I answered the phone expecting to hear his voice, but neither what the man on the other end of the line said, nor the sound of his voice, are things I will ever forget, no matter how long I live.

I said "Hello?"

The man asked, "Who am I speaking to?"

I answered, "My name is Kandi Sargent-Lowe."

The man replied, "My name is James. I work in the surgical ICU here at University Medical Center in Lubbock. We have a Janakae Sargent here as a patient in our surgical ICU." I replied "Who?" No, not Janakae; she was fine. I had talked to her. Not that I wanted it to be Matt either, which would have destroyed my world just as severely.

The man on the phone repeated her name, and I demanded that he put her on the phone. He then told me he couldn't. I asked "Why? I'm her mom and I need to talk to her."

He told me that she was a patient at the hospital. He then started listing her injuries and said she had been involved in a fatality crash, she was the only victim their hospital had received, they had already done a few procedures on her, and she had come to their unit from surgery. She was on life support with a severe head injury, severe brain trauma, a cracked sternum, a bruised heart, a lacerated liver, and several broken ribs, and they thought her arm and leg were broken. They were about to repeat x-rays of those. I asked if he knew who the fatality was or how many vehicles were involved, and he said he did not have that information. I told him I was four hours away and asked him to tell my baby girl that I loved her and was on my way. He said he would and told me to be careful, but hurry. I had started packing while I was on the phone with him and getting dressed to leave.

I woke Janakae's stepfather and told him she had been in a wreck and I was heading to Lubbock. I told him not to wake our youngest daughter, and that I would call when I got there and learned the severity of things. He suggested I call my parents; I said I would call from the road when it was a little later, because they would be sleeping. He told me I had better call them before I left. I knew he was right. I called my parents and then waited half an hour for them to pick me up so we could make the long drive together.

I chose not to call my son yet. Honestly, I feared he might have been with her and had been the fatality or was lying in another hospital. One of the last things Janakae had said to me was that she was going to call him to see if he wanted to hang out and help her pass the time. I had no idea if he had done so or not, but part of me didn't want to know, and the other part wanted to protect him from going to the hospital and sitting alone until we could get there. Once we reached Lubbock's city limits, we tried to reach him. It took two of us calling over a dozen times for him to answer. I was relieved when he did.

Along our drive, I called the hospital many times to get updates on Janakae. Each time I spoke to the same nurse, and she would ask our location. The last time she said we would be arriving during shift change, but that if I knocked on the unit door and asked for her, she would take me to see my baby girl. In between calls, I prayed that God would not take Janakae before I got there, and that if there couldn't be improvements in her condition, to please just let there be no change at all.

I don't even think I let my dad throw the truck into park before I was unbuckled and out the door, running up to enter the hospital. I couldn't get to Janakae fast enough. I did as the nurse asked me to, and she led us to bed seven. Janakae was lying there as if she was sleeping, just as beautiful as ever until you noticed all the machines around the room with the wires, tubing, and lines running in and out of every part of her body, the tube running down her throat, and the big bolt-like thing with a tube in the center of it that was drilled into her head. She had been unresponsive and had only moaned as the paramedics and hospital staff moved her from truck to gurney, and then gurney to a hospital bed, etc. I touched her right arm and told her, "Mommy's here, Baby Girl. I love you, and it's going to be all right." She postured and leaned toward my voice. In that moment, at least I knew my baby girl was with us. The man who called hadn't mentioned that even though Janakae was on life support, she was breathing on her own fifty percent of the time, alternating breaths with the respirator. He also didn't mention that she had a seatbelt fracture. Her back was broken, and it was more probable than not that she would be paralyzed from the waist down. I had no idea just how important that piece of information would be until ten months later when I found a poem Janakae had written seven years before. Because touching Janakae stimulated her and caused her brain to swell more, they asked us to leave, and closed the glass doors behind us. It would be hours before we could do more than look at her through the glass again. During the wait, the police who were investigating the crash came to speak to us. Also, word of the crash got out, and the crowd of her college and hometown friends continued to grow. The police filled us in on details about the crash, and answered questions that came to mind since receiving that call.

I had already asked the nursing staff if Janakae had anything in her system. I had to know that information. I knew that she would never drive under the influence knowingly. I asked the police if she had been the cause of the crash. They said no, and that according to many witnesses Janakae had done everything right. They then explained that the other driver, a forty-eight-year-old female, was at fault. They also said that the woman was the fatality.

They confirmed that both drivers were alone in their vehicles. They also told me that Janakae had hesitated when her light turned green, allowing approaching motorists time to stop before Janakae eased into her turn. I know that she was on the phone with a friend at the time of the crash, and he simply said he heard her say "Oh, sss. . . ," before the phone went dead. Janakae had a habit of saying "Oh, snap," and I can only assume that she saw the headlights coming toward her and that was her reaction.

I have prayed that it happened so fast that she never had time to feel afraid or alone. The police said there were multiple calls to 911 alerting them to the other woman's erratic driving and that there was actually someone on the phone with the 911 operator at the time of the crash. There was also a report of the woman leaving the roadway approximately a mile before this intersection and correcting back to the roadway within three feet of hitting one of those big utility poles that line highways. There were no skid marks, so the woman never hit her brakes as she approached the red light and made the choice to run it by switching to the left turn lane. She was avoiding the two cars that were stopped, occupying the two lanes that continued eastbound.

At over one hundred miles an hour, there was no time for her to hit her brakes before striking the front right passenger side of Janakae's pickup either. Janakae's truck was thrown down the eastbound side of the divided highway. She had been on the westbound side turning south. There was no way to tell how many times it spun before coming to a stop head first into the guardrail. The crash happened at 1:11 a.m., with my phone call coming at 2:44 a.m. My baby girl was going through so much for an hour and a half, and I had no knowledge of it. She needed me, and I failed her. These were all feelings and emotions that went through my head for years.

We spent four and a half days at the hospital. During this time, the doctors said that with head trauma patients the first three to five days are critical. If she could make it three to five days, she might have a chance. They also said her days started at midnight. I told more than one doctor that she was tough, stubborn, and opinionated and that before they gave up on her, asking me to do the same, they should make sure that they had exhausted every means to save her. With her being in the surgical ICU, we had to abide by the hospital's visiting hours. They were courteous enough to allow us to let anyone visit her during each two-hour session as long as we were courteous to other patients and families. I allowed anyone to see her as long as they left me enough time to be the last one at each session. I always looked through the glass at all the monitors before entering her room. Upon entering I would get down to eye level at the foot of her bed, touch her piggies, and say, "Madre's here, Baby Girl." With her eyes being slightly open, I could see her. She was in there. I needed her to know I was there.

On Wednesday morning, November 15, the neurologist came out to speak to me. He grabbed my hands and said, "You're right, she's a fighter. Today's a better day." He continued, "We would like to do a couple of procedures on her, since she's more stable now. The nurses will be out to explain them to you and ask you to sign the consent forms." I asked him what type of procedures. He reminded me that she had tested positive for thrombocytopenia and needed her heparin tubing exchanged for non-heparin tubing and that they wanted to insert a feeding tube. Her being stable, a feeding tube; it all sounded like we had made it through the worst and turned a corner for the better. I eagerly signed the consent forms, knowing that we would lose all of that day's visiting hours and opportunities to see her. They allowed me to go back to see her before they started the procedures, as it would be 8 p.m. visiting hours before we could see her again. I spent the day hyped, excited, visiting with her friends who came to help us pass the time. We all sat and shared Janakae stories. We laughed so hard we cried, but they were tears of laughter. Bonds were made during those days that comfort me now. Janakae was a wise old soul, more than she should have been for a twenty-year-old.

We had just started to cycle through to see her at 8 p.m. I'm not sure exactly what time it was, but one of Janakae's aunts came to get me. She said the doctors were with Janakae and that I needed to go now. I rounded the corner and stared at the monitors. Janakae's intracranial pressure had climbed and was continuing to climb higher. That morning when the physician spoke to me, it had been at its lowest since before the crash, and now it was at its highest and still climbing. I knew that I needed to pray and ask God for a sign. I am not sure who was in the room with me, but I remember my parents being there. I remember praying, asking God for my sign. I remember that my mom and I began singing hymns. I remember that Janakae's intracranial pressure decreased if we were praying or singing and rose when we would stop. I took that as my sign and knew that I needed to talk with Janakae. I needed to know if she felt it was her time to go with God and had only been fighting because I had begged her to all week. I needed to give her permission if that was the case. Remember, she had not been conscious at all since before the impact of the crash. However, I knew the bond we shared.

This was my child who told her friends "Oh, yeah. My Madre has the look that can penetrate through doors, walls, and ceilings." True, I only needed to look toward her room upstairs with a certain look until she opened the door, asking if I was giving her *the look* and whether I needed her. I also could simply speak her name and she would call within five minutes, asking, "Madre, did you need me?" At this moment, I knew that if she could feel me from four hours away so many times, then her heart could hear me and communicate with me now.

I started our conversation like this: "Baby Girl, if God is pulling you His way and I'm pulling you mine, you have to go with God." I clearly heard her ask, "But will you be mad at me?" I answered, "No, Baby Girl, not mad. Heartbroken, but not mad." She then apologized for disappointing me. I told her, "Baby Girl, I've been frustrated with your procrastination at times, but I have never been anything but proud to say that I am Janakae Toinette Sargent's Madre. You have made me who I am, and I will forever love you and be grateful for that."

I can't tell you what time it was, but I watched as my baby girl took her very last breath, leaving only the respirator causing her chest to rise and fall. I watched as her eyes glazed over and suddenly were empty. Her tongue came to the front of her mouth by the tube and turned the ugliest shade of gray I had ever seen. I watched my baby let go of me to go with God. I asked the others in the room if they saw what I saw, and I remember my mother saying, "I did, Kandi. But you'll need to explain it to the others." I screamed out "My baby girl has left me to be with our Lord and Savior." I ran out to tell the nurses what I had witnessed. They told me they would call the doctor. I reminded them that Janakae was an organ donor, something she had made me pinky promise when she was merely eleven years old. As I said, she was wise beyond her years. The nurses told me that the doctor would come and check on her, and they were scheduling a brain scan, but that it would probably not take place until the next morning, as it was too late that night.

At 10 a.m. on Thursday, November 16, they took Janakae for a brain scan. A volunteer took all of us to a hospitality room filled with food, snacks, and beverages. Around noon there was a phone call and the volunteer told me that we were wanted back in Janakae's room. She escorted me along with Janakae's biological father and her stepfather back to await the report of the brain scan. I already knew what they were going to say, but I prayed that I was wrong. With her stepfather on her left side and me and her biological father, or as she called him, the sperm donor, on her right, the doctor said the words I feared more than any in the world. He told us that she was clinically brain dead. He said that the only thing keeping her alive was the machine and that we could turn that off if we chose to do so. He started listing our options, and I told him, "No. She's an organ donor." He said she could remain on life support while they located recipients for viable organs and scheduled the organ harvest. He also asked if I had already spoken to LifeGift. I said yes, earlier in the week. He said he would notify them of her test results.

Everyone started leaving the hospital, but I had made a promise to Janakae. I would leave when she did and not a moment sooner. Promises mean something to us, and pinky promises meant even more. I was seeing this through and not leaving until she did. I continued to sit with her, except that now visiting hours didn't matter. They allowed me to stay. The cool thing had been that all week when I wasn't sleeping at night, which was most of the time, they left the back doors to the unit propped open, and I was allowed to walk in and sit with her for as long as I wanted to every night. I was with her most of the day and into the night. I started to look underneath her hospital gown. I saw a bruise that resembled the entire lap and shoulder seatbelt. I saw bruises on her hips where she must have hit the console and the driver's door. I examined her from head to toe, something I had wanted to do all week, but was afraid to. I also had wanted to climb into the bed and hold her, but it seemed pointless now. I apologized to her again for not being able to kiss her and make her better.

I had gone back into the family room where we had set up early on that Sunday morning upon arriving around 1:30 a.m. on Friday. They wheeled her to surgery around 2:30 a.m. They stopped and allowed me to kiss her and whisper that I loved her before heading off to the operating room. They were breathing for her with an Ambu bag. Five hours later they wheeled her back, covered completely by a white sheet. Suddenly it was all too real.

They got her settled back into her room and allowed me to sit with her until the medical examiner came to pick her up. The very first thing I did was uncover her. I felt her, and she didn't feel like a real person. We had allowed them to harvest anything that was viable. This included her four heart valves, two kidneys, her liver, her eyes, upper and lower arm and leg bones, other bones, tissue, and skin. They had wrapped her depleted body like a mummy. I gathered her belongings from the room and stayed with her until around 10 a.m. when they asked me to step out so that they could package her for the medical examiner. I found some of the terminology cold and without consideration that she was *my* daughter.

I gathered my things, and we left the hospital at the exact same time that the medical examiner was going through the back door with her. We met family and friends at Chili's by Texas Tech campus for lunch and then learned that there was a news reporter who wanted to interview me. One of Janakae's friends offered to let us use her house for the interview. We also received an invitation to a memorial service that was being held on the Texas Tech University campus by some of the students at Memorial Circle. We attended that along with many of her friends, professors, and university staff members. Everyone gathered and took turns sharing Janakae moments. It was comforting hearing how well liked she was by her peers and those there to guide her.

We went to stay the night at my cousin's house with plans to leave for Mineral Wells the next morning. Little did I know that would change too. We received calls that the TTU Goin' Band from Raiderland would be dedicating their pre-game and halftime performances to Janakae. We were being asked to attend the final home football game and that there were enough tickets at the south gate for all of us. A college football game was not really where I wanted to be, but truthfully, I didn't care to be anywhere. My world as I knew it was spinning out of control and I was completely numb and at a loss. We attended the game. I remember most of it well, but parts are a blur. I had attended several games over her three football seasons there; I've attended a few more in the nine years since her death. It will never again be the same as attending while she was a student there.

We left the game, went by her apartment to pick up a few things, and I looked in her closet for something to bury her in. We then left Lubbock for Mineral Wells. I had a 9 a.m. appointment at the funeral home on Sunday morning to plan a funeral, something I had never done before and wasn't prepared to do for the first time for my daughter. This isn't the way it's supposed to be; it's not the natural circle of life to bury your child.

I arrived at Baum-Carlock-Bumgardner Funeral Home just before 9 a.m. on Sunday morning, November 19. Before leaving my house, I had called my parents to see if they would be meeting me there. My father, who is a very smart man, asked if I had called my ex-husband to ask him also to meet me there. I said, "No. Why should I?" My dad answered, "Well, all of Janakae's life you have done the right thing by including him and his family. Why wouldn't you do the same at this last moment?" He was right. I had always notified them of band concerts, awards assemblies, sports schedules, modeling graduation, high school graduation, etc. It was always their choice to attend or not to attend, but Janakae, as well as my son, Matt, knew I always extended the invitation and that their attendance or lack of it, never had anything to do with their not knowing, so I made that call.

Honestly, it was uncomfortable sitting in that room with members of the funeral home staff, one who happened to be a family friend, my parents, Janakae's stepfather, her biological father, and his mother. I was asked to write an obituary, pick out a casket, and pick a date and time for her funeral. The next week was Thanksgiving. When do you plan a funeral for Thanksgiving week without totally messing up everyone's holiday?! I knew that the college kids had classes on Monday and Tuesday. We planned a Tuesday evening family visitation with a funeral at 10 a.m. Wednesday. There was one catch—would we have her body back by then? Texas state law says that an autopsy is mandatory when death is the result of a car crash.

I received a phone call on Monday evening saying that Janakae's body was on its way to Mineral Wells. One of her high school friends, Ryan, was a paramedic in Lubbock. I had feared that Ryan had been on the ambulance that responded to the crash, but thankfully he wasn't. However, he researched all the legalities and paperwork needed for him to ask his ambulance service to allow him the use of an ambulance to bring her home. He was special to my heart before then, but even more special after because he cared so much and wanted to ensure that she was brought home with care. He even came by the house to see me before heading back to Lubbock.

I received a call later that night from the funeral home that Janakae was ready to view. We all loaded up and headed to the funeral home. This was real. I couldn't wake up from this horrible nightmare. She still looked beautiful to me. It would be months later while looking at pictures when I would realize that she didn't even look like her.

Her funeral was huge. There were more people than there was seating for. I remember being led from where we gathered up the aisle through the crowd to where we would all be seated for the service. There were so many people. I can remember thinking how Janakae must be in total awe that so many people came. We had had the conversation many times about how when we died no one would come but the other one.

Her funeral procession was also huge. It went on for miles. Then we got to the cemetery, and there were people already there waiting, so I realized that not everyone wanted to be part of the procession. After the graveside service, I sat and just stared at her casket until they came over to tell me it was time to leave. I watched from the car as they started to work and lowered her casket into the ground. Since we had all been together that day, no one wanted to gather for Thanksgiving. My mom and I had always gone shopping on Black Friday, but we didn't that year, nor have we since. I sat and stared at the television for days. I can't tell you anything that I watched or did. Everything was a complete daze.

On Black Friday I remembered that one of Janakae's credit cards had not been with her belongings the hospital had given me. It hadn't been in her truck, purse, or backpack once we had gained entrance to her pickup. It hadn't been anywhere in her apartment either. I found the previous month's statement and made a phone call to the company to report it lost or stolen. My instinct told me to press the option for the most recent transactions. I knew that she had paid a campus parking ticket with it on November 5, a week before the crash. I wasn't expecting any other charges, but then starting with November 12, and continuing to that very morning, which was November 24, there were charges or pending charges that put the card over its credit limit and totaled over five thousand dollars. I was in a panic. I pushed the option to speak to a representative and waited my turn while growing more impatient and panicked by the minute. I explained the past two weeks to the company's customer service rep and then found myself saying, "No, my daughter was on life support fighting for her life or lying in the morgue or funeral home at the time of all of these charges, except for the fifty-five dollars on November 5." Then I said, "No. While my daughter was fighting for her life nor in the week since, I was not out shopping either." I asked to speak to her supervisor, quickly going through everything again and choking back the tears, and told them that I was reporting the card lost or stolen, but would be paying the only charge that I knew was my daughter's. The rest of the charges they could handle in whatever manner they needed to. My thought was, how dare someone stoop so low! Then I thought about how many times Janakae was on the news the week I was in Lubbock, and asked myself how any store clerk could be handed that card and not know that name and question the person using the card.

The weeks went on, and we all returned to work or school. Everyone went back to their normal lives but me. Oh, I returned to work, but what was normal now? My family didn't gather for Christmas, and we had a small Christmas at home. We didn't do anything for New Year's either, but I had taken January 5 off, as that's my youngest daughter's birthday. She was turning thirteen. I was letting her sleep in and was just piddling around on the computer and about the house. My cellphone rang. I checked it and saw that it was one of the detectives from the Lubbock Police Department. I answered it, and he told me he had the toxicology reports on both drivers. I had asked about alcohol when the police came to talk to me at the hospital that Sunday. They had told me they didn't smell alcohol at the scene, so I hadn't been prepared for anything else. I reminded him of that, and he said, "Well, first, I want to tell you that you must be very proud of your daughter." I said that of course I always was, and he said that she had nothing in her system, not even an aspirin. I told him thank you, but I knew that because I had asked the hospital staff. I also knew she would never drive impaired, much less be the designated driver for friends if she had anything in her system. I kept asking him about the other driver. He kept saying he wanted to talk about Janakae. I finally told him I needed to know about the other driver's results. He asked me to sit down. I told him I was sitting, but I wasn't. I was pacing. He started by telling me that he was present for both autopsies. He told me that the smell of alcohol when they opened the driver's stomach almost knocked him over. He said that even though they hadn't smelled it at the crash scene, it was simply because she wasn't breathing. He then told me that her blood alcohol content was .25 percent.

How in the world was someone older than me less responsible than my twenty-year-old daughter and her friends? Didn't that woman know the dangers of drinking and driving? Didn't she care? Didn't she have anyone she could have called to pick her up? Why didn't someone stop her? Why couldn't the police have gotten to her before she crashed into my daughter? All of these questions. I felt like someone had kicked me in the gut and I suddenly couldn't breathe. I had had seven weeks to start the grieving process, to come to grips with our reality. Now I was learning about all those times when Janakae was the designated driver for others, and I was proud, but not worried more than any other time she drove. I should have been, because there were other irresponsible drunk drivers out on our roads.

I felt just as I had the day they told me Janakae was clinically brain dead, except I was filled with so much anger. I realized that it was a good thing that I hadn't known this information earlier, as I had brought home the driver's obituary and researched to find addresses for all her survivors and mailed them sympathy cards. I don't believe I would have done that had I known she was intoxicated.

Wow. What do I do with this information? I contacted MADD and learned that I could share about my daughter at victim impact panels. I did my first one the very next month.

Ten months after the crash, I found one of Janakae's binders that contained her poetry writings. I had been looking for the perfect thing to share, as I had been invited to come back for an annual memorial service at Texas Tech University for all students, faculty, and staff who had passed away during the past year. In this binder of poetry, I found a poem that was dated November 27, 1999, that describes the crash almost perfectly. In her poem, it was a male drunk driver, and they both lived. Our reality was a female drunk driver, and they both died. The thing that got me about the poem was that Janakae had written that she was paralyzed from the waist down. How did she know? She was only thirteen when she wrote the poem. She had never driven, much less for drunken friends. Why hadn't she shown me this poem? I knew that she had her reasons for writing it and that she never showed it to me because it was meant for me to find in the right time and to use in what would become my new normal.

That first year was extremely hard, but there haven't been any that were easy either. Within that first year, my youngest daughter would almost drown in the bathtub twice. I would later find out that it wasn't an accident and that she was trying to take her life. My son would distance himself from all of us for that first two years, and it felt more like I had lost two children than one. My marriage, which wasn't much of a marriage to begin with, continued to spiral until we finally separated and divorced.

It's been nine years now, and I have shared Janakae's story more times than I can even remember. I have shared at VIPs, schools, universities, churches, civic organizations, candlelight vigils, angel tree ceremonies, basically anywhere and everywhere that I have the opportunity to do so. You see, I had asked God to guide me on how to live without Janakae physically present in my world. He has opened so many doors and helped me cope and hopefully turn our negative event into a positive while educating others to the dangers and ripple effect caused by such poor and irresponsible choices. I have also moved from our hometown, starting over, and remarried. It's hard, but true when I say I'm happier than I've ever been, but it still hurts to breathe, and I miss Janakae every single day.

With my move, it was no longer convenient or easy to take flowers to her grave on special occasions or to do balloon releases with family and friends. I moved two and a half hours away to a town where no one knew her. I also moved just before the seventh anniversary of the crash and her death. That was rough. The seventh anniversary of her death fell on a weekend, and we were able to travel back home, but her birthday in January was during the week. I had to find a new way to honor her, so my son had seen something on Facebook and shared it with me. I decided to do it. We went to dinner at a local restaurant. We picked a table and paid for that table's dinner. In lieu of their check, they received a letter telling them about Janakae and that we were celebrating her birthday and in honor of her we had paid for their dinner. We have now done that for two birthdays and two angelversaries. Her thirtieth birthday was in January 2016.

I wouldn't be who I am had I not become Janakae's Madre when I was merely twenty-one years old. Even though burying her two months shy of her twenty-first birthday was not my plan, I can't thank God enough for loaning her to me, even if only for the brief twenty years, nine months and twenty-five days that she was physically on this earth.

My mother's heart sometimes battles my belief and faith system. I believe that our birth and death dates are decided and known long before we are ever placed on this earth. I also believe that maybe her dying in the manner in which she did was better than what might have faced her at a later date from her illness or some other horrific and painful death.

KANDI WILEY
TEMPLE, TEXAS
FORMERLY FROM MINERAL WELLS, TEXAS

KANDI WILEY & JANAKAE SARGENT

JANAKAE, MATT & TYGELIA

LIFE
Written by Janakae Sargent at age 13
Date written: 11/27/99

I went to a party where they were serving beer
I didn't drink once that night because the results I fear.
I know the effects of drunk driving now more so than ever
the choices some people make just aren't very clever.
I was leaving the party so I would be home by curfew
I saw headlights on the wrong side of the road the other driver didn't have a clue.
That he was about to hit me; there wasn't anything I could do
to avoid being hit by him, now I'm in a hospital where everything is new.
The other driver sent a card, I hear he'll be all right.
The doctors told me he didn't need to stay the night.
They also said I'm paralyzed from the waist down.
That's the thing about doctors, they don't mess around.
I'm lying in a bed that isn't mine, and I have a few questions to ask.
My future's uncertain, my present dark, and I don't wish to speak of the past.
I didn't drink and drive, and I wouldn't let my friends.
So why am I to be the one who will never walk again?

KANDI WILEY AT CRASH SITE   **TOMMY & KANDI WILEY**

CHAPTER TWENTY-FIVE

WHAT HAPPENED TO MY DADDY?

BY RACHAEL WILLIAMS

The pleasure of remembering had been
taken from me because there was no longer
anyone to remember with. It felt like losing
your co-rememberer meant losing the
memory itself as if the things we'd done
were less real and important than they had
been hours before. -JOHN GREEN

I met my soulmate in 2007, his name was Matthew Thompson. He was my everything. We were engaged in 2008 and had a beautiful daughter in September 2009. Our daughter, Kaylynn, was the best thing that could happen to him. On June 16, 2010, we got married in front of close family. We came home and decided that we no longer wanted to live in an apartment, so we began looking for homes. In 2011, we decided that we were going to expand our little family. On December 23, 2011, we found out that we were expecting another baby. It was exciting to us; we were growing our family, and we were hoping for a little boy. In April 2012, we found out that our second little bundle of joy was a girl! Little did I know that she would never know her daddy or what a hardworking man he was. He was only thirty when he was suddenly taken from us, although he had so much more to give in life.

It was May 9, 2012. Matt called and said he was going to get a ride home from work, so I didn't need to get him. He said, "I'll see you about 11:30." I said, "Okay, I'll see you later," and we hung up.

It was close to 1 a.m. and I still had not heard from him. So I began calling his cellphone and his best friend, who I thought was driving him home. I got no response, so I laid down with our daughter, Kaylynn, and went to sleep.

At about 2:30 a.m. I woke from a deep sleep and started calling Matt repeatedly because there were police with search dogs combing the area where we lived, but Matt still wasn't answering. At that time our car was broken down. Usually if he wasn't home, it meant that he had someone drop him off on our road and he walked the rest of the way. I couldn't even look for him, and I'm glad that I wasn't able to. I went back to sleep.

I was up with Kaylynn at 7 a.m. I immediately called the restaurant Matt worked at, and they said he left last night at 11:30 p.m. with someone they didn't know. I got dressed and then got Kaylynn ready when two unremarked black cars pulled into my driveway. I was little confused as to why they were unmarked, and at the same time scared. My life changed forever at that moment.

I opened the door to find two detectives. They began to ask me a series of questions. "Do you know a Matt Thompson?"

"Yes, that's my husband," I answered.

They asked me when I last saw Matt. I told them yesterday, but he never came home last night. They asked if they could come into my home. I was getting anxious, and wanted to know why these men were standing at my door.

I asked, "What's going on? Why are you here?"

They said my husband had been involved in a serious car accident. I asked, "Is he okay? Where is he?"

They asked me to take my daughter into the next room so they could speak with me privately. I tried, but she wouldn't leave my side. I sat down and they told me that a drunk driver hit my husband, and he didn't make it.

I sat there thinking "Is this happening? Is this some sick joke?" I thought they were there because Matt had a warrant for unpaid tickets, not to tell me that my husband was killed. I called my mom; she didn't answer, so her answering machine kicked on. The second I said, "Matt's been killed," my mom picked up the phone and said, "I'm on my way." I was in tears, but trying to be calm as I called my sister-in-law, who was coming to take him to work because he had no other ride. I told her she needed to pull over to a place where she could talk, because I had something very upsetting to tell her. I then had to tell her that Matt was killed while walking home last night. She didn't believe me, and I told her that there were two detectives sitting in my home. I then completely and utterly lost it. She immediately went to her mom's, because she couldn't break it to her over the phone.

They asked me if I could identify Matt. I couldn't pull myself together to do that, and asked if my mom could, because she was almost to our home. She walked in the door, and they asked if she could step outside and identify him. She was upset about having to do it, but I just couldn't do it. I sat and just sobbed for hours.

My mom confirmed that it was indeed my husband, Matthew Thompson. They began giving us information about what was going to happen. They told me that the driver hit my husband and then drove into a culvert. He climbed out of the car and walked up to the witness, asking if he could use his phone. The witness said no, as he was on the phone with 911. He asked the driver what he had hit. The driver replied, "Whatever I hit, I hit good," and walked away. He was found underneath a car two streets down, hiding from the search dogs. He kept saying, "You have the wrong guy. I saw him at the front of the park a few minutes ago." The police officer drove the witness over, and the driver was identified as the man who had hit and killed Matthew.

I was told that I needed to wait until after 12 p.m. because an autopsy was being performed, and then they would release Matt's body to a funeral home. I was contacted by Gift of Life asking if I would be willing to donate any of my husband's organs. My first response was that he had been hit by a car, and I hadn't seen his body, and I didn't even know if any of his organs could be used. They told me that if I felt there were any, to please call them back. I was upset and snapped at the lady, because I felt like this was too soon. I went home with my mom, because I couldn't stay by myself; I was heartbroken. I still had to call all my family and some of Matt's friends and people at his workplace to let them know what had happened.

My daughter Kaylynn didn't understand at this point, and it was very hard to make a decision on whether she should be taken to the funeral or left at home with a sitter. It broke my heart knowing that she would be screaming for her daddy to wake up. She used to call him and scream *"Daddy"* until he would wake up saying, "What's the matter, baby?" This couldn't have happened; I couldn't allow her to feel my heartbreak.

Later that day I met with my mother-in-law and sister-in-law to discuss funeral arrangements. My mom was so good to me during this time. She had already called a funeral home and set an appointment for us to come in and make arrangements. Walking into that funeral home hurt more than anything I had ever known. I was such a mess; I just couldn't hold it together no matter how hard I tried. I kept saying this is just a dream, wake up, Rachael, wake up.

Sitting at the funeral director's desk filling out all the paperwork and discussing what was going to be done and how it was going to be paid for was so stressful. My sister-in-law mentioned that Matt had a life insurance policy that I did know about but wasn't sure how much it was for. We looked at prayer cards, and I chose one that fit him best. Then his mom and I fought over him being buried. He didn't want to be buried in the ground; he wanted to be cremated. She didn't want me to have any of his ashes; she wanted all of him, because when she died she wanted to take him with her. Because I was Matt's wife, I got it my way.

We settled on a one-day viewing and a service that night and cremation the day after his funeral. After we decided all this we then had to choose which casket to use for his service. I couldn't do it; I walked in and lost it, so hurt that it was like reality hitting me in the face. I had to sit down; I told my mom I could not and would not do this. I let his mom and sister pick out the casket. I kept thinking, I'm pregnant, and now I'm alone. I have two children, and I'm alone. Half of my heart had been ripped out.

We set it so his funeral wouldn't fall on a weekend, because it was Mother's Day on Sunday. We then left the funeral home, all of us going our separate ways. Matt's sister was so heartbroken, and his mom was not showing any emotions. It hadn't yet hit that her son was gone.

I had to get Matt an outfit so he would look nice, and to be cremated in. Everything I looked at wasn't him. He never wore things like this; he would have been happy wearing the pants that drove me nuts, the pants that most wear as warmups to cover their shorts. He wore them every day, because he said it kept the grease from burning his leg at work. He was a cook at a restaurant called The Aspen. But I couldn't let him go like that. I chose a nice dress shirt and dress pants that he had at home.

On May 14, 2012, we showed up at the funeral home. I was scared to see him, scared to say goodbye, scared to know that this would be the last time I would see the love of my life. It took me a little longer to walk in, because I wasn't ready. His mom went in first, and I finally saw her cry. She just kept saying "Matthew, Matthew, Matthew." When I was finally able to walk up to the casket, I held my mom's hand. She walked with me and so did the funeral director. They told me that the police came and took a sample of Matthew's hair, and that was why he was missing some hair in the front. He had to have a net over his body because of all the bruising. I looked at him like I had never seen him before; he didn't look like himself. He wasn't his happy, smiley, joke-telling self. He was gone; no life left. I kept telling the funeral director,

"That's not him, it's not." I grabbed one of the cards we had printed. It said: "Matthew Thompson. February 10, 1982 - May 10, 2012. Married to wife Rachael and father of Kaylynn Thompson. He was preceded by his cousin and grandparents." He always said that no one loved him, but over one hundred and fifty people attended his service, mostly from work and close friends.

When the family visitation was over, his friends began to enter the room to say their goodbyes. I felt so hurt and upset because Matthew's family didn't introduce me to none of the family I hadn't yet met. They just ignored me and were upset because I had made the decision not to bring my two-year-old daughter to her daddy's funeral. I felt that would have broken her heart. I felt that she would have been screaming at his casket telling her daddy to wake up, talk to her, love her like he did when he was home from work. This time he wouldn't wake up; he wouldn't kiss her or tell her how much he loved her. I didn't care that they were upset. I was her mother, and I made that decision. I asked my family how they would feel about it, and they all agreed with me. It was my daughter, and I understood they wanted to see her, but this was not the time or place.

All of Matthew's coworkers walked up to me and gave me hugs. They told me how much Matthew loved Kaylynn and me, how much they were going to miss him, miss his jokes, his pranks at work and even his sense of humor. His best friend, Nick, was there the whole time standing next to me. I even had him sit in the front row with me.

We had a viewing all day and then the same night at 7 p.m. a priest from our local Catholic church said a few words and also prayed the rosary with Matthew's close family. His family was upset because our daughter wasn't there at the funeral. At that point I didn't care who liked me or who didn't. I had my family there, and that was all I needed.

I had picked out a poem to read from Kaylynn, but I just couldn't get up and say it. I was a mess, so I tucked it into Matt's casket with pictures of Kaylynn and me. We had beautiful red roses for all his friends to place in his casket, and his mom and sister and I all had white roses. We were the last to say goodbyes. I couldn't bear to get back up and walk to him one last time. I let all his family say their final goodbyes. When they were done and everyone but my mom was gone, I walked up and told Matthew that I was sorry, and this wasn't goodbye. I kissed the top of his forehead and walked away, falling apart.

Later that day I received a phone call from a victims rights advocate for Macomb County. Her name was Johanna Delp. She was able to give me the drunk driver's name, John, and his age, thirty-nine. She also was able to list the charges he was facing: one count of operating under the influence causing death or serious impairment, for which he faced a fifteen-year incarceration and ten thousand dollar fine; one count of failure to stop at the scene of an accident resulting in serious impairment or death, with a five-year minimum incarceration and five thousand dollar fine; one count of operating while impaired or with the presence of a controlled substance, third offense, with a minimum one-year incarceration; and one count of driving with a suspended license, which is only a misdemeanor, with ninety-three days in jail and a five hundred dollar fine. She asked if I would like to be present for all court dates or just receive notification from the prosecutor. I asked to be included in everything, and said I would like to be present at the court dates. My sister and mother-in-law also wanted to be involved. At this time our two families were not getting along, and we couldn't communicate with one another.

May 23, 2012, was the first court date to schedule a preliminary exam, at which the driver made eye contact with me for the first time. He winked at me; maybe he didn't know that he murdered my husband or maybe he was just trying to make himself look good while in court for killing a man. I was so angry; I wanted to get up and call him a murderer and tell him how I truly felt about his winking or comments he was whispering to his attorney. He was laughing and joking, and I just sat there thinking, you are a real

441

piece of work; how can you laugh and joke when you killed someone? The driver never showed one bit of remorse. The attorney said they needed to get more information, so court was rescheduled for the following month.

On June 13, 2012, I once again showed up to court only to find out that because the driver was on probation in adjacent Wayne County, Michigan, for his second drunk driving offense, he was transferred to the Wayne County jail, and there was a hold until he was arraigned on his violation. His attorney didn't even know the driver had been transferred. So it was rescheduled again.I was getting so angry, because I was pregnant and getting close to my due date. I was very emotional.

On July 10, 2012, the driver was again in court, but the toxicology reports on both my husband and the driver were needed. I got very upset and asked to speak with not only the prosecutor, but also Judge Hackle. I had expressed how upset I was that this kept getting rescheduled. I said that I would like to be present for the remainder of the court dates but was scheduled for a Cesarean on August 10. The judge gave me his promise that I would be at the next court date, and that the preliminary exam would happen.

On August 9, 2012, the preliminary exam was held. My whole family was there, MADD was there, and so were most of Matthew's best friends. Court lasted three hours. We first heard from witness one who drove up and saw my husband lying in the road in blood. She explained how my husband was found, where his shoes were, and if he was alive or deceased when she arrived. She called 911, as did witness two, who had passed my husband five minutes before he was killed. She said that the drunk driver exited the vehicle, staggering and smelling like alcohol. He asked if he could use witness two's phone. The witness said no, and asked the driver what he hit. The driver replied "I don't know, but whatever I hit, I hit it good." The witness then asked the driver where he was going.

He said he was going to his buddy's house down the street, and he proceeded to walk toward Americana Community.

Next, we heard from the officer who assisted in the arrest with a police dog. The dog traced the driver into the park and found him underneath a parked car. The driver said they had the wrong guy, that he'd seen a guy who fit their description about fifteen minutes ago. The witness was taken to where they found the driver, and he was identified as the man who hit and killed Matthew Thompson.

Next up was the medical examiner who did Matthew's autopsy. He went into great detail about the damages to Matthew's body from the car that hit him. Both of his legs were broken, and one femur was destroyed. Matthew had head trauma, and one finger was missing. He had multiple blunt trauma over his body, and the severity of his injuries prevented organ donation.

The driver's attorney asked questions, and kept bringing up my husband's drinking, saying he wasn't behind the wheel because he had lost his license. They tried the suicide defense, but concluded that Matthew was not suicidal and that he never would do that because he loved life too much. That day the judge made the decision that there was enough evidence to push for trial.

At 5:30 a.m. on August 10, 2012, I was on my way to the hospital to give birth to our daughter Addison. While getting ready for the C-section, my doctor said the sweetest thing to me: "Don't worry. He is here, he is watching. And he will see his beautiful daughter born." My doctor was so supportive. He held my hand while the spinal epidural was administered, and told me everything would be all right.

Once my mom was able to come into the room, I felt at ease. Addison was born at 9:04 a.m., and she was so beautiful, yet I was so sad. She looked so much like our oldest daughter, Kaylynn. When we were finally heading back to my room, my doctor came and checked on me. He requested that I keep the room I was in instead of moving to the other side of the hospital. He told me that

Addison did excellent on all her testing, and that he was okay with my going home on Sunday but that I could stay until Tuesday if needed. I just felt so lonely in a huge hospital room by myself. My family worked so they couldn't stay with me at night, so I stayed alone. I had the C-section on Sunday so I could be close to my family.

On September 12, 2012, there was a pretrial for the driver. He tried to say that the police didn't read him his rights. He also said that he was forced to make a statement at the hospital when his rights were first read to him and then again when he was being questioned. There were so many pretrials, it was upsetting. I thought this was never going to end.

Fast forward to August 13, 2013, when the judge finally set a trial date of December 13, 2013. I was looking forward to this and beginning to finally get past all this upsetting stuff. But there was an emergency pretrial in September that I wasn't aware of. I got a call after the court hearing that the driver had fired his attorney, and they were pushing the trial date to January 3, 2014. I was so upset hearing this, because it had already been a year, and now it was going to be pushed to another year.

On October 4, 2013, I went to court and found out that the judge was going to give the driver a COBB agreement, meaning he would plead guilty to the charges but would not serve more time in jail. He faced twenty-five to thirty years in prison but would only receive time served. I asked to speak with the prosecutor handling the case and my victim advocate. They told me they didn't have the evidence to prove that my husband had been hit by the vehicle the offender was driving. They had him behind the wheel driving, but there was no evidence regarding the vehicle. Mind you, they didn't bother to test the vehicle until August 2013. I found this out and was very upset and angry. I just sat there crying, telling them that they were going to let a killer get out and allow him to kill someone else. My husband wouldn't get the justice he deserved. They just kept saying they were sorry, and I just kept saying, "You're not.

Otherwise this wouldn't be happening." I had so many questions that they couldn't answer. They told me they were giving the driver and his attorney time to discuss the situation, and if they agreed, they would set a sentencing date.

The following week on Tuesday, I received a phone call saying that the driver had agreed to plead guilty, and the sentencing date was set for December 13, 2013. They told me to prepare my victim's impact statement and bring pictures of my daughters. They told me that I wouldn't be able to speak to the driver or look at him and that I needed to make contact only with the judge. It took me some time to decide that I would go up to the podium but wouldn't speak unless I was spoken to. I asked his sister to speak, and I took pictures and wanted my daughters to be there, but I felt that might have been too much for them and me.

On December 13, 2013, there we were at the sentencing. I was so upset and had so many mixed emotions. I walked into court with my sister-in-law and her close friends. When it came time to walk up to the judge and speak, he asked us who we were. I told him I was Matthew Thompson's wife, and Matt's sister introduced herself. We handed the judge pictures of my girls. The judge looked at them while Matt's sister spoke. She was strong at first, saying "My brother was a loving man and loved life. He loved his family, and most of all loved his daughter and daughter who wasn't born yet. He has a daughter he will never meet because of a careless, heartless man who chose to drive while drunk. He took a soul who so many will miss; he took something from us that we can never get back. He still has a chance at life and a chance at having a family. Matt was only thirty years old and lost his life so tragically, and it has taken a toll on our family. My mother-in-law was admitted to a nursing home at the age of fifty-eight because she had the beginning stages of dementia, but this tragedy made it worse."

After we were finished the judge asked us to take our seats and said he was very sorry that things had happened the way they did. He began to speak to the driver and read him his sentencing report in detail. The driver was given eighteen months of time served. He was responsible for all attorney fees, five thousand three hundred dollars; had to wear a monitoring device for one year, that there was zero tolerance, and he would receive five years of probation. The driver was to abstain from alcohol and drugs, and would undergo testing every week. The judge was very strict on zero tolerance. The driver was to get into no trouble and if he did, he would receive the full term of twenty-five years. The driver agreed, and he was released from jail that night.

After everyone had left the courtroom, I just sat there and cried. It wasn't enough punishment for a driver who had taken a man's life, taken a daddy away from two little girls, and taken my happiness. I'll never get that kind of love again. The driver's sister and friends were very upset and were saying things to his attorney when he walked out of the courtroom. I just needed to leave. I needed to go home to my daughters and find a way to tell a four-month-old about how amazing her daddy was and to tell a three-year-old daddy's girl that she would never have him to take her to a daddy-daughter dance, walk her down the aisle, or to be her protector. How do you tell children that?

In September 2014, the driver had a probation violation. I wasn't informed or even thought of when I should have been notified. I didn't find out until I went to the court website and saw that the driver had been brought in for a probation violation. In February 2015 he tried to cut off his monitor. From my understanding, if the driver violated probation he would be sent to prison for the original term of twenty-five years. Instead, they extended his probation another year with a monitor for another year, and that was it. I was very upset, because that meant he was again getting away with illegal criminal activity. Why was he getting away with so much? Why did he get to walk yet again? None of my questions were answered. The prosecutors didn't return phone calls or show up in court to find out what was going on. It's like they didn't care, and neither did the judge.

By September 2015, no justice had been done for my husband — his killer is free. The driver enjoys family outings, and just welcomed a daughter into the world. He even got to see his daughter born. He gets to spend nights with his family. He gets to support his family. He gets to be there to take his daughter to her first daddy-daughter dance. He will watch her get married, and he will there for her first heartbreak. My children were robbed of such an amazing experience. I was robbed of a happy ending. I hold John accountable, but no one else does.

I currently work a full-time job and go to school full time so I can provide for my children. It's hard to do when you're a widow; so many responsibilities fall on my shoulders. The questions are always being asked by schools or the doctor's office, and even my daughters, when they wonder where Daddy is or why he isn't around to help. Currently my daughter is in counseling. She has grown an interest in knowing how her daddy died, who killed him, and how come that person isn't in prison.

My family is supportive, except for my mom. She thinks I just can't speak to my children or have enough courage to do so. To be honest, that's true. I have my own problems with being able to speak about Matt. I sometimes can't talk about him. I often find myself crying at night. The pain never goes away; this is the reality. You lose what you never thought you would. You lose part of your heart because some individuals choose to make wrong choices. They choose to be selfish to make themselves feel good. They never take into account what could happen or whom their poor judgment will affect. Don't ever take love for granted, because you never know when they will take their last breath.

RACHAEL WILLIAMS
ALGONAC, MICHIGAN

MATTHEW THOMPSON

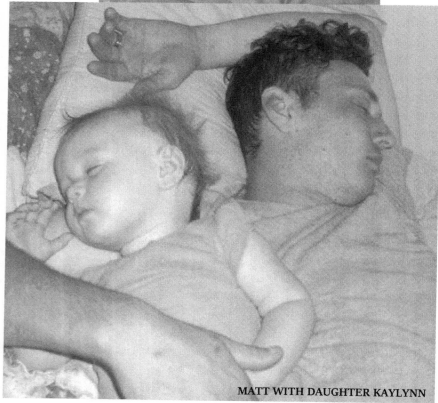

MATT WITH DAUGHTER KAYLYNN

SHATTERED

MEET THE WRITERS

*
PAT BLUTH
patbluth@brainerd.net
facebook.com/PatBluthAuthorFromPaintoPeace

Pat Bluth is the author of *From Pain to Peace — A Journey from Rage to Forgiveness*, a bereaved parent, licensed family therapist, grief facilitator, and speaker.

Pat holds a Master's Degree in Community Counseling and is a certified chemical dependency counselor. She has served as a Christian family therapist, facilitated hospice grief groups, and is a frequent speaker for Mothers Against Drunk Driving and other groups.

Following the death of her seventeen-year old daughter Tammy by a drunk driver, Pat co-founded a chapter of MADD in her county. She is a trained victim advocate.

Pat's passion has been spending her time educating and changing attitudes about drinking and driving. As a certified Toastmaster, she has spoken to thousands, sharing her story of hope and healing. Pat speaks from her heart and has brought hope to many who thought life was hopeless after a tragedy. Her message of hope and healing has been an inspiration to thousands.

Her book is Pat's compelling story tracing her journey from rage to forgiveness and healing. If you read it, you'll discover how love and forgiveness can conquer and win over bitterness and rage.

*

AMY CARTER

Amy Carter was born in El Paso, Texas. Her father, David, was stationed there while in the Army. A couple of years later her parents moved back to Independence, Missouri, and divorced. Amy had visitation with her dad every other weekend and one month in the summer. She and her mother, Annette, lived in Independence until Amy was in the third grade. They then moved to Blue Springs, Missouri. Amy continued with her education all the way through high school. She then met the love of her life in 2005. They married in 2006, and have been together ever since.

*

NANCY CLAY

Nancy Clay is the mother of eight and grandmother of nine, and lives in Mesa, Arizona. She regards her family as her greatest ambition and accomplishment. She attributes her ability to handle the many challenges of life to her faith in God. "With Him, I can bear all things." She believes there is great power in our pain, and trying to use that for the greatest good is what she strives to do. The motto she tries to live by is "Be the change you wish to see in the world." She is a speaker with MADD, helping to educate others on the consequences of driving impaired.

*

BILL DOWNS
www.advocatesforvictimsofimpaireddriving.org
avid4duivictims@cableone.net

Bill was born and raised in southern Mississippi, where he met and married his wife Julie in 1982. God blessed them with two children, Cynthia and Brad. Bill is twice retired, first from the Air National Guard in 2006 and then from the Gulfport City School District in 2015. His wife Julie is self-employed, and also cares for their handicapped daughter, Cynthia.

In 2007 when their son Brad, his wife, Samantha, and Chris, a young man they loved as a son, were killed by a drunk driver, their focus turned to advocating for and supporting victims of impaired driving. Bill is president and co-founder of AVIDD—Advocates for Victims of Impaired/Distracted Driving, a nonprofit organization. He is also an administrator of four online support groups for victims, and hosts an educational class called AVIDD Voices, where victims share stories with offenders who are court-ordered to attend. Bill recently coauthored *Grief Diaries: Loss by Impaired Driving* with his wife Julie and renowned author and publisher Lynda Cheldelin Fell. Bill is dedicated to the fight against impaired driving, and hopes one day to see an end to this preventable crime that is the only socially acceptable form of homicide.

*

JULIE DOWNS
www.advocatesforvictimsofimpaireddriving.org
avid4duivictims@cableone.net

Julie Downs was born and raised in Gulfport, Mississippi. She graduated from high school in 1978, and completed two years of college before she married her soulmate, Bill Downs, in 1982. She is self-employed part time, along with being a housewife and mother of two. Her oldest daughter, Cynthia, is mentally challenged and still lives at home. Her second-born son, Brad, is asleep in Jesus.

In 2007, a drunk driver killed Julie's son, his wife, and a young man Julie loved as a son. Julie joined and volunteered with MADD until 2014, when she and her husband Bill co-founded AVIDD-Advocates for Victims of Impaired/Distracted Driving. Julie is board secretary, and devotes her time to operating four online Facebook support groups where she lends a listening ear and makes graphics for the members to help comfort and bring awareness to the devastation of impaired driving. Julie is coauthor of *Grief Diaries: Loss by Impaired Driving*.

*

NANCY EDWARDS

Nancy Edwards, one of five children, was born in Illinois and raised in North Carolina. While remaining active in Girl Scouts, horseback riding, and babysitting, she has volunteered with children since she was thirteen. She was also a nanny for three young boys. After earning her Masters in Social Work at the University of South Carolina, she was employed with Behavioral Health. A coworker introduced Nancy to her soulmate, Randy, and in 1984, they moved to Charlotte,  North Carolina, and were married. Nancy's focus has always been on children, and she knew her life would not be complete until having her own. Nancy and Randy were eager to begin their family right away and in May 1985, their first daughter, Jennifer, was born. Blessed again, their second daughter, Kathryn, was born in 1988. Although Nancy continued volunteering at schools, hospitals, agencies for troubled teens, and Girl Scouts, her own children were her primary focus. Nancy quit her job and started an in-home daycare center when she couldn't find daycare meeting her standards. Three years later she found her ideal job as a licensed clinical social worker for women with high-risk pregnancies, and has now been with the HealthCare System for twenty-seven years.

*

ROSE HELLER

Rose Heller was born and raised in Sunbury, Pennsylvania. She is the mother of three children, and has four stepchildren and eleven grandchildren. They are not all biological, but are family. Rose works as a purchasing agent in a state facility with individuals with intellectual disabilities. Her family and two dogs, Harley and Tucker, are the joys of her life.

*

DIERDRA ROSE

Dierdra Rose was born in Lincoln, Nebraska, the second of five children. She traveled abroad with her father, an airman first class in the Air Force, until age seven. At that point Dierdra's family settled down, making Minnesota their home. After high school, Dierdra went on to earn two college degrees in accounting technology and a certificate in computer information systems. Three times married,  widowed once, Dierdra's world was her eight children. She suffered her first devastating loss when her husband, Donnie, was killed by a drunk snowmobiler one early Sunday morning in January 1993. She pieced her life back together one piece at a time. She became employed as a supervisor at Goodwill Industries, and went back to school for a third year to earn a certificate as a computer support specialist. As a member of Phi Theta Kappa, she maintained a 3.85 GPA. Her passions included her eight children, her grandson, bowling, photography, computers, and antique collecting. Just when things were looking up she suffered a second devastating loss in April 1998 when her oldest child, Travis, was killed by yet another DRUNK driver. Two devastating losses in five years shattered Dierdra's world completely, leaving her FOREVER "Twice Broken."

*
GINA LANCE
Facebook.com/ginalance

Gina Lance has lived in McMinnville, Tennessee, her whole life. She was the third youngest in a family of eight children, all boys except one older sister. The greatest joy of Gina's life is her children. She is the mother of three. Travis, now twenty-two, is an angel baby, and Ashlyn died at seventeen. The height of Gina's life was when her children were little. After the devastating death of Ashlyn, Gina was unable to work for over a year.

She is currently a customer relations manager in Antioch, Tennessee. She also is an advocate for victims of impaired driving, organizing, supporting, and attending walks. In the future, she hopes to bring more awareness and help with legislative change.

Gain says, "Impaired driving is no accident and ten months in jail for murder is ridiculous. Ashlyn's right to live is worth fighting for. Some days I don't feel like fighting, as all I can muster is survival. However, watch out for those other days, because my child was murdered!"

LAURA G. HERRON-SMITH

Laura Herron-Smith was born and raised in Texas. She has three children, two sons and a daughter, whom she raised as a single mother. She has five grandsons and one granddaughter whom she loves and adores!

Laura is trained and has worked in health care. She was a certified habilitation training specialist, working with developmentally disabled children and adults. Her training includes First Responder and Basic EMT. She went on to become a certified nurse's aide and a certified medical assistant in a long-term residential nursing home where she provided care and medication to the residents. Laura has been an advocate and a speaker for victims impact panel. Traveling around southwestern Oklahoma, she has spoken to offenders and high school students about drinking and driving. She currently lives on a farm with her friends and pets. Laura enjoys writing, gardening, painting, drawing, and has many other talents. Laura is of the Christian faith and gladly shares her love of Jesus with anyone who will listen.

*

MICHELLE LAWSON

Michelle L. Lawson was born at Camp Lejeune Naval Air Base, North Carolina, on June 26, 1982, to Sgt. Clifford and Peggy Eckert. She was four weeks early and came into this world weighing only four pounds, four ounces. She had to stay in a hospital incubator for two weeks, but her mother never gave up on her, and she prayed every day. From day one Michelle has always had ambition. In December 1984, Michelle and her mother took a bus to Kokomo, Indiana, to stay with Michelle's grandparents.

Michelle has always striven to do the best she can, to be better than what she believes she can do, no matter the circumstances. She has passed this quality on to both of her kids.

In school she was involved in an array of clubs including chess, sign language, volleyball, and the Kokomo Police Cadets, where she became a lieutenant. She is now a Cub Scoutmaster, PTA member, football mom, and Sunday school teacher, and helps tutor students at her kids' school. She is currently in college, working to get her associate's degree.

Michelle currently resides in Indiana with her husband and two children.

*

BRIDGET MCWHORTER
bridgetmcwho@hotmail.com

Bridget McWhorter was born and raised in Monticello, Iowa, where she was involved in choir and cheerleading. She went on to get her BBA at Mount Mercy University. She decided to further her education and get a MBA at Capella University. Bridget married her husband Tim in October 2005. They have two beautiful daughters, currently sixteen and ten years old. They are active in basketball for both AAU and school. Bridget is a cheerleading coach at Benton Community High School. She is also a substitute teacher for the Benton Community School District. Bridget enjoys spending time with her family (especially watching her girls play basketball), crafts, camping, and spending time with her friends.

*

DUSTIN POINDEXTER

Dustin was born and raised in North Carolina, and lives in Greensboro. He has six brothers and one sister, and currently works for a roofing company. Dustin was at his brother's accident site and had to identify his brother in the car.

*

JEFFERY POINDEXTER

Jeffrey Poindexter was born and raised in North Carolina. He has six brothers and one sister. Jeffrey is the father of a three-year-old daughter, Rhyleah, and has another baby on the way. Jeffrey lives in Randleman, North Carolina, and works in Asheboro as a code enforcement agent for the state.

*

SONYA POINDEXTER

Sonya Poindexter was born in Fairbanks, Alaska, and raised in Randleman, North Carolina. She is the mother of five boys: Jeffrey, Nicholas, Dustin, Zachary, and Jacob, and stepmother to Jarrod, Stephen, and Felicia. Sonya loves to read, do crafts and help others.

She and her husband, Stephen, help out with MADD and go to the DUI checkpoints and help feed the police officers, hoping to spare families from suffering the heartache they have suffered.

*

NICOLE RAMOS

Nicole Ramos was born in Riverside, California, and moved to Texas for college. She earned her B.S. In Child and Family Studies from the University of Texas of the Permian Basin. Nicole coached softball at junior college, high school, and competitive level. Her time in the classroom and on the field brought her joy for many years. She also taught four-year-old children at church every Sunday. Her job, volunteering, and coaching came to a standstill one brisk October night when someone chose to drink and drive. She has undergone over nine surgeries and several rounds of physical therapy to try to put her life back together. Her family has been her biggest support system through many difficult times. MADD and AVIDD have been able to relate to the emotional baggage, chronic pain, and day to day struggle that comes with being a victim of drunk driving. Nicole is married to Tommy Ramos and has two children, Audrey and Elijah, and three stepchildren, Thomas, Breanna and Sarah.

*

SANDRA RAWLINGS
www.lockedinmemories19.org

Sandra Rawlings was born and raised in Cleveland, Ohio. She has three children, one of whom was killed by a drunk driver. Sandra then started speaking for MADD at high schools, court appointed meetings, victim awareness programs, and The Justice Center. Sandra believes that is what her daughter Tiffany would want, to help others and save lives.

She now lives in Lagrange, Ohio, and recently retired from United Airlines. She now spends her free time traveling the world and spending time with her children and eight grandchildren.

*

NICOLE RIBALKIN

Nicole was born in Kelowna, British Columbia, Canada. She is the youngest of two. She loves to spend time with her friends and family, travel, go to the gym, study, and much more. Her motto is to stay strong and to never give up on life. She cherishes every moment, and lives her life to the fullest.

*

SUSAN RILEY

Susan White Riley was born and raised in the small Texas town of Brady. She earned a B.S. degree in education and dance from North Texas State University and a Master's of Education degree from Southwest Texas State University. She worked in education for thirty-five years, mostly in the area of special education.

In 2010 she took up writing for therapy after the loss of several family members, and has had several stories published in the Sisters in Sorrow series. She now spends her time writing, mystery shopping, reading, and spending time with family and friends. She resides in central Texas with Ceryl, her husband of almost forty-five years, and her adult children, Erin and Benjamin.

Since her loss of adopted son, Randy, in 2010 at the hands of a drunk driver, a passion to educate people on the impact of drunk driving on both the drivers and the victims has become very important to her. Another passion is her role as a "crazy cat lady" and mama and grandma to eight cats, five of whom were bottle-fed and range in age from seven to seventeen, and three rescue dogs.

*

LEANNE SALTAR

Leanne Saltar is a Colorado native. In her early years she lived in Englewood, Colorado, until her parents bought a house in Lakewood, Colorado, so they could have their horses in the backyard. After high school she married Steve Saltar in 1988 and attended Bel Rea Institute of Technology to become a veterinary technician. She and Steve have two children, Ruby Jo who was born in 1991, and Ethan Cody Bleu who was born in 1993 and passed away in 2010.

Leanne has worked in a veterinary diagnostic laboratory since 1990. When her son Ethan was killed, the family was raising Ruby Jo's two sons, Zane who was born in 2007, and Elijah who was born in 2009. Since Ethan's passing his family has welcomed Ruby's youngest child, Amiyah Bleu.

*

JONI SMITHHART

Joni Smithhart was born in Flowood, Mississippi. She has four amazing children and currently resides in Columbia, Mississippi.

*

KIM THOMAS
www.showyourrideforbrandon.com

Kim Thomas was born in New Westminster, British Columbia, and grew up in a loving home with her parents and a younger brother. Most of her youth was spent in northern Alberta in Swan Hills. When older she moved to Peace River and met the man she would marry. After her marriage she moved to her husband's hometown of Fort MacLeod, Alberta, and they started their amazing family. Kim became someone new, she became a mother to two amazing children, and that was all she ever wanted.

*
CANDY WEBB

Candy Webb was born in Tampa, Florida, on March 21, 1965. She's the oldest of three sisters and three brothers.

On September 26, 1992, Candy married a wonderful man, Todd, the father of Christopher. Candy welcomed a baby boy, Shane, on May 21, 1993, to complete her little family.

Candy attended Catholic school until tenth grade, when she entered Gulfport High School. After graduation she continued her education and received an Associate's Degree. Later in life she went back to college and obtained a Bachelor's Degree in Business. She currently owns and operates Webb's Bookkeeping, as well as LifeVantage.

Candy She is also a co-founder of AVIDD—Advocates for Victim of Impaired/Distractive Driving. She and AVIDD are working toward changing the sentencing laws for boating under the influence offenses.

*

KANDI WILEY
Kandi.Lowe64@yahoo.com
https://youtu.be/E1n2nbivaqQ

Kandi is a fifty-one-year-old who was born and raised in a small Texas town. She married her childhood sweetheart at age eighteen, and had two children, a girl, Janakae, and a boy, Matthew. She and her husband later separated and divorced when Kandi was twenty-seven. She married a second time and had a daughter, Tygelia, but then later separated and divorced when Tygelia was eighteen, shortly after her high school graduation. Kandi is currently married and has relocated to central Texas, where she is working as a hospice biller. She also helps to raise two of her three stepchildren. Kandi also has a foster daughter, Adrian, who came to live with them during the early 2000s when Adrian and Janakae were in high school. Kandi now has six grandsons and one granddaughter.

"Some days just aren't as hard as others,
but none are ever easy."

*

RACHAEL WILLIAMS

Rachael Williams was born in Georgia and raised in Algonac, Michigan. She has two daughters, ages four and seven. Rachael graduated from the University of Phoenix—Detroit campus with her Bachelor's in Science and Health Administration with a focus on long-term care. She lost her husband in 2012 to a drunk driver.

Shared joy is doubled joy;
shared sorrow is half a sorrow.
SWEDISH PROVERB

*

ABOUT

LYNDA CHELDELIN FELL

Considered a pioneer in the field of inspirational hope in the aftermath of loss, Lynda Cheldelin Fell has a passion for groundbreaking projects that create a legacy of help, healing, and hope. She is an award-winning author and creator of the book series *Grief Diaries*, board president of the National Grief & Hope Coalition, and CEO of AlyBlue Media. She has interviewed Dr. Martin Luther King's daughter, Trayvon Martin's mother, sisters of the late Nicole Brown Simpson; Pastor Todd Burpo of Heaven is For Real, CNN commentator Dr. Ken Druck, and other societal newsmakers on finding healing and hope in the aftermath of life's harshest challenges.

Lynda's own story began in 2007, when she had an alarming dream about her young teenage daughter, Aly. In the dream, Aly was a backseat passenger in a car that veered off the road and sailed into a lake. Aly sank with the car, leaving behind an open book floating face down on the water. Two years later, Lynda's dream became reality when Aly was tragically killed as a backseat passenger in a car accident while coming home from a swim meet. Overcome with grief, Lynda's 46-year-old husband suffered a major stroke that left him with severe disabilities, traumatically changing the family dynamics yet again.

The following year, Lynda was invited to share her remarkable story about finding hope after loss, and she accepted. That cathartic experience inspired her to create groundbreaking projects spanning national events, radio, film and books to help others who share the same journey feel less alone. The Grief Diaries series was born and built on this belief.

Because of that floating book her daughter left behind, Lynda now understands that the dream in 2007 was actually a glimpse into a divine plan destined to bring comfort, healing and hope to people around the world.

lynda@lyndafell.com | www.lyndafell.com | www.griefdiaries.com

ABOUT THE SERIES

It's important that we share our
experiences with other people. Your story
will heal you, and your story will heal
somebody else. -IYANLA VANZANT

Grief Diaries is a series of anthology books exploring true stories about the life's challenges and losses. Created by international bestselling author and bereaved mother Lynda Cheldelin Fell, the series began with eight titles exploring unique losses shared by people around the world. Over a hundred people in six countries registered for those first eight titles, and the books were launched in December 2015. Following their release, organizations and individuals began asking Lynda to create additional titles to help raise awareness about their plights. To date, more than 450 writers are sharing their courageous stories in more than thirty anthology titles now in the works.

Now a 5-star series, a portion of profits from every book in the series goes to national organizations serving those in need.

Humanity's legacy of stories and storytelling is the most
precious we have. All wisdom is in our stories and songs.
DORIS LESSING

*

ALYBLUE MEDIA TITLES

PUBLISHED
Grief Diaries: Surviving Loss of a Spouse
Grief Diaries: Surviving Loss of a Child
Grief Diaries: Surviving Loss of a Sibling
Grief Diaries: Surviving Loss of a Parent
Grief Diaries: Surviving Loss of an Infant
Grief Diaries: Surviving Loss of a Loved One
Grief Diaries: Surviving Loss by Suicide
Grief Diaries: Surviving Loss of Health
Grief Diaries: How to Help the Newly Bereaved
Grief Diaries: Loss by Impaired Driving
Grief Diaries: Through the Eyes of an Eating Disorder
Grief Diaries: Surviving Loss by Homicide
Grief Diaries: Loss of a Pregnancy
Grief Diaries: Living with a Brain Injury
Grief Diaries: Hello from Heaven
Grief Diaries: Shattered
Grammy Visits From Heaven
Faith, Grief & Pass the Chocolate Pudding

FORTHCOMING TITLES (PARTIAL LIST):
Heaven Talks to Children
Color My Soul Whole
Grief Reiki
Grief Diaries: Through the Eyes of a Funeral Director
Grief Diaries: A Guide for the Newly Bereaved
Grief Diaries: Life After Organ Transplant
Grief Diaries: Raising a Disabled Child
Grief Diaries: Living with Rheumatic Disease
Grief Diaries: Through the Eyes of Cancer
Grief Diaries: Loss of a Client
Grief Diaries: Poetry & Prose and More
Grief Diaries Life After Rape
Grief Diaries: Living with Mental Illness
Grief Diaries: Through the Eyes of D.I.D.
Grief Diaries: Living with PTSD
Where Have All The Children Gone: A Mother's Journey Through Complicated
Grief

There's a bright future for you at every turn,
even if you miss one.

*

To share your story in a Grief Diaries book,
visit www.griefdiaries.com

PUBLISHED BY ALYBLUE MEDIA
Inside every human is a story worth sharing.
www.AlyBlueMedia.com

Made in the USA
Charleston, SC
13 November 2016